OCTOBER 1917

By the same author

The Russian Revolution of 1917: the Fall of Tsarism and the Origins of Bolshevik Power (1972)

The Great War 1914–1918 (1973)

OCTOBER
—1917—

A social history of the Russian Revolution

Marc Ferro

translated by Norman Stone

Routledge & Kegan Paul

London, Boston and Henley

First published in French as La Révolution de 1917:
Octobre, naissance d'une société *by Aubier-Montaignes*
Paris, 1976

This translation first
published in 1980
by Routledge & Kegan Paul Ltd
39 Store Street,
London WC1E 7DD,
Broadway House,
Newtown Road,
Henley-on-Thames,
Oxon RG9 1EN and
9 Park Street,
Boston, Mass, 02108, USA

Set in 11pt Plantin by
Oxprint Ltd, Oxford
and printed in Great Britain by
Unwin Brothers Ltd
The Gresham Press
Old Woking, Surrey
A member of the Staples Printing Group

British Library Cataloguing in Publication Data

Ferro, Marc
October 1917.
1. Russia – Politics and government – 1917–1936
2. Russia – History – Revolution, 1917–1921
I. Title
947.084'1   DK265   79-41592

ISBN 0 7100 0534 2

Contents

v

Preface

The October Revolution is still almost a contemporary event. Since 1917 we have had to face the questions posed by its meaning and outcome: the Bolshevik seizure of power, the 'building of socialism', the origins of the Stalinist terror, the vast contrast between the strict centralization of the Soviet state and the extraordinary heady atmosphere of 1917 itself.

As we look into the origins of all this, and contemplate a new society emerging, we can see that some changes came more rapidly or more completely than others: things did not happen in the same way in the north and the east, nor were all aspects of life equally affected. The October Rising and the crises that marked the history of the Revolution did not have everywhere, and for all of the people, the same significance or outcome.

A study concerned purely with these crises and with the Bolshevik seizure of power, can show only one aspect of the upheaval of 1917, and reveals only one viewpoint — that of the leaders of the Revolution, the politicians and the militants. This is certainly essential, because they determined what was to come, but it is only part of the story. We must also consider the various groups, ethnic or otherwise — peasantry, factory workers — for each of them had its own history and chronology, its periods of sterility or energy, its crises; and that history did not necessarily proceed at the same pace as the historical process that occupied the headlines, the seizure of power, the end of great nations, or the rise of socialism — the kind of history which the leading figures and their opponents composed, in their writings, their speeches or the principles on which they based their activities and their right to govern, and which historians, for all the critical spirit they apply, treat in a privileged way, and with a sense of piety.

The accounts of such historians have to be complemented by others; and for this, the forefront of the historical stage has to be abandoned so that we can use sources of a more modest kind than the classic ones – not sources dealing with leading personalities or institutions, but sometimes just simple scrawls, fleeting images, often not intended for reproduction, use or preservation. This enables us to penetrate the body of society, to witness its change and decay from within. Using different vantage-points – a factory in Petrograd, a village in the area of troubles, a military unit, a university or a district committee – it is possible to detect how the movements inspiring various social groups converged or clashed, changing, or being changed by, the actions of the parties and political organizations. In fitting such records together, it is important not to take them too literally: with the written sources, as with the visual ones, the statistics and the films, though they are vital records for any alternative analysis of the traditional sources, the intention behind them as well as the contents have to be taken into account. What is left out is frequently more important than what is put in; the implicit may be more important than the explicit, and what is imagined more than what is real.

This being so, the Revolution of 1917 becomes, in this second volume, a many-faceted picture, and the chronology has been differentiated, so that the dates of beginning and end vary according to the particular aspect of the Revolution. Following the pattern of the first volume, the story of the struggle for power is taken up to its outcome, the Bolshevik victory on 25 October 1917; however, my study of the forces that supported Bolshevik power and the birth of the bureaucratic system of the new people's state (the origins of which I have traced to pre-October days) has been continued up to the point where the elements of this state had all been fitted together, at a much later date. The problems of the Revolution in the factories, the villages and the family have led me to go much further back into the past, and to extend my account further into the future.

For obvious reasons, these considerations govern the principle of the book rather than the ordering of chapters. In the first two, I examine the forefront of the stage, the political crisis and the struggle for power. As the régime of February collapsed and the Kornilov Putsch failed it became evident that the helplessness of the state was not simply a consequence of defects in the system of dual power, but equally a reflection of the decay of all kinds of traditional authority: government, church and army were unable to discharge their traditional functions of repression.

'The state is like a jug,' runs a Russian proverb. 'When it cracks, water flows.' After February 1917 society itself began to move. In chapter 4 and thereafter, I have investigated how, both before and after October, first the nationalities – on the far periphery, and only weakly linked with the body of the Russian state – and then the peasants, the factories, the organizations of the young, the women, the soviets and similar committees freed themselves and started to bring in changes in social, political, economic life, and even in the family. I have gone on to show, again both before and after October, how the central forces and the institutions that were born during the Revolution affected the schemes of one or other of these groups. This process was associated, in a twofold way, with the emergence of a parallel state: the bureaucratization of it, even before October, and its Bolshevization or the evolution of its social structure account both for the October insurrection and the subsequent development of the régime (chapters 7 and 8).

Translator's note: A common-sense system of transliteration from the Russian has been used throughout. In the notes, a bracketed figure refers to the bibliography — those from (1) to (500) refer to the bibliography of volume I, and those from (501) to (750) to that of volume II. Throughout, 'volume (or vol.) I' refers to Marc Ferro, *The Russian Revolution of February 1917*, translated by J. L. Richards and Nicole Stone, Routledge & Kegan Paul, London, 1972; 'volume II' refers to the present work.

Acknowledgments

To those friends mentioned in volume I and who have accepted over several years the task of being involved with me even more closely in the preparation of this second volume, notably Georges Haupt, Pierre Souyri, and Lucette Valensi, I should like to add the following new members of the *Cinéma et Histoire* seminar group, friends also, who have encouraged me just as much to persevere and continue in the work: Alfredo Margarido and Claudine Eyzicman, Guy Fihman, Annie Goldmann, Lena Grigoriadou, Robert Paris, Beatrice Rolland, Pierre Sorlin − this book owes a great deal to them all. My thanks are also due to those who generously commented on individual ideas and chapters: S. Coben, C. Duchet, R. Daniels, S. Grosskopf, G. Lasfargues, L. Manigat, S. Rozenker, F. Starr, N. Stone, M. Rebeyrioux, and to the team at *Annales* who helped me learn my trade: Fernand Braudel in the first place, then A. Burguière, and J. Le Goff, E. Le Roy Ladurie, C. Morazé and J. Revel.

If I respect tradition in thanking again, with the deepest gratitude, the archivists of Leningrad and Moscow whose help has been invaluable, as has been that of my librarian friends at the BDIC, the most efficient library in the world, I shall break with those traditions, not only in expressing my gratitude to the members of my board of examiners, whose advice has been most valuable to me − J. B. Duroselle, R. Giraud, B. Kerblay, E. Labrousse, R. Portal − but also in thanking the general editor of the series in which the French edition first appeared, Paul Lemerle, and the editor of the French edition, Mme Gabail, who bore with endless patience the ten years that this volume has taken me.

M. F.

Chronology

All dates are Old Style for 1917

1917

23 February	The insurrection begins in Petrograd
27 February	The Duma forms a committee for the re-establishment of order. Petrograd Soviet formed
1 March	Order Number 1 issued to the army
2 March	Formation of the Provisional Government, abdication of Nicholas II
3 March	Michael renounces the throne
14 March	Call from the Petrograd Soviet to the peoples of the world
25 March	First fraternization with German troops
31 March	Allied socialist mission (Cachin/Sanders) to Petrograd
4 April	Lenin returns to Russia
18 April	The Milyukov Note; the beginning of the 'April Crisis'
25 April	The soviet calls for a socialist peace conference. Conference held at Stockholm
5 May	First coalition government with socialist participation; Milyukov resigns
May	The wave of large-scale strikes begins
30 May	The moderate socialists win the municipal elections
3 June	First Congress of Soviets opens: 105 Bolsheviks out of 822 delegates
10 June	First Universal of the Kiev Rada
16 June	Kerensky orders an offensive in Galicia
18 June	Demonstration against the war
1–3 July	The July Days

5 July	Kerensky becomes prime minister; in Finland, the Seim proclaims its sovereignty
11 July	The Germans occupy Tarnopol
12 August	Conference of State at Moscow
21 August	The Germans occupy Riga
28 August	The Kornilov Putsch
30 August	The Putsch defeated, Kerensky becomes commander-in-chief. Formation of the second Kerensky government
8 September	Trotsky elected president of the Petrograd Soviet
14 September	The Democratic Conference opens
25 September	Kerensky's third administration
7 October	The Council of the Republic opens: the Bolsheviks walk out
8–9 October	Lenin lays down insurrection as the objective: Trotsky constructs a Provisional Revolutionary Committee out of the Petrograd Soviet
24–25 October	The October Days
25 October	The second Congress of Soviets opens: 382 Bolsheviks out of 562 delegates present. Lenin becomes president of the Council of People's Commissars
November	The Kaledin Rising and the beginning of the Civil War
7 December	The Brest-Litovsk negotiations open; Finland's independence recognized

1918

| 18 January | The Constituent Assembly dissolved |
| July | The first constitution of the Soviet state promulgated |

Introduction:
the illusions and
delusions of revolution

'Russia varies her propaganda infinitely, according to the people or country towards which it is directed. Yesterday she said, "I am Christianity"; to-morrow she will say, "I am Socialism" '.

Jules Michelet, *Légendes démocratiques du Nord*, quoted in
M. Rubel,

'Marx, Engels: Ecrits sur le tsarisme' in *Cahiers de l'Institut de science économique appliquée* (Geneva) (July 1969), p. 1288

'The Warder: "Why are you here?"
The Prisoner: "I wanted to stop you from being beaten and insulted." '

A. Ivanovsky, *The Castle and the Fortress*, 1926

'The people have never known of constitutions; they have no idea what the division of powers is.'

Herzen, *Letters from France and Italy*, as quoted in Yuri Gurvich,
'All Power to the Soviets', *Proletarskaya revolyutsiya i pravo*,
(Moscow) I, 1918.

The February Revolution had been the greatest in all history. In the space of a few weeks, Russia got rid of all of her former leaders — the Tsar and his law-makers, the police, the priests, the landowners, the civil servants, the officers and the employers. Not one citizen could fail to feel quite free — free to determine at any time what he would do, in the present or the future. Within a short time, virtually everyone had his own notion of what should be done to achieve national regeneration. It was, as the poets of Revolution wrote, a new era in the history of Man.

From the very depths of Russia came a great cry of hope, in which were mingled the voices of the poor and down-trodden, expressing their

1

sufferings, hopes and dreams. Dream-like, they experienced unique events: in Moscow, workmen would compel their employer to learn the bases of the workers' rights in the future; in Odessa, students would dictate a new way of teaching universal history to their professor; in Petrograd, actors would take over from the theatre manager and select the next play; in the army, soldiers would summon the chaplain to attend their meetings so that he could 'get some real meaning in his life'. Even 'children under the age of fourteen' demanded the right to learn boxing, 'to make the older children have some respect'. It was a world turned upside-down: hence the apprehensions of men who derived their authority from ability, knowledge or public service, let alone the old Divine Right of Kings. They had never imagined that such a revolution could ever occur. Up to, and including, the high priests of the most extreme religion, Bolshevism, they were at one in their belief that they need only be patient, and that the people would in the end come to their senses. In March, Stalin, like all the revolutionaries, called for discipline, a sentiment repeated in June by Kropotkin. Maxim Gorky, too, was irked by men's failure to go back to work, and told them repeatedly, 'enough of this chattering'.

Much to their surprise, Lenin took a different view from these stalwarts when he returned to Russia. He rejoiced in the wreckage, and wanted the old world to disintegrate utterly. In his *April Theses* he was among the very few who demanded 'Abolition of the army, the police and the civil service; instant revocability of any election to office; immediate peace; transference of all power to the Soviets.' His first task was to persuade his own party that moderation was imbecility, for it could not be the Bolsheviks' work to act as intermediary between society and the government, but rather to lead the masses, to set up new institutions. He had to preach this doctrine, which was Marx's, for eight months for his comrades to agree with it, for the party to lead rather than trail behind the masses, and for October to pick up the challenge of February.

'Between February and October, the tide of Revolution became a flood, and we could not halt or direct it', said Kerensky, and it applied to the leaders and the militants of all of the parties. They had expected to lead the movement, to hasten or to retard it; unless they could at least follow it, they would be swept away. They were aware of their own powerlessness, but they did not understand it. They had worked for the Revolution but, now that it had broken out, the masses behaved in ways they had not foreseen or planned. The Revolution took forms and had effects that every time took them by surprise, 'like the proverbial foolish virgins'.

The revolution they had foreseen before 1917 was an imaginary one, but at least it had happened, and so they did not have doubts as to their own analyses and expectations. They believed, for instance, in progress, and thought that history moved in clear stages and phases; the leaders of February, whether in the government or the Petrograd Soviet, had not yet got over the unique upheaval of the Tsar's collapse, and quite sincerely believed that, since they were now installed in power, history had entered a new phase and must settle down. They were sure that the epoch of 'bourgeois revolution' would be a long one, and that 'Russia has not yet developed an objective basis for social revolution'.[1] 'Russia', said Plekhanov, 'is not ready for Bolshevism'; Struve added that 'it would be mad or foolish to think otherwise'. Middle-class personalities, in these circumstances, urged people to study Marxist works; like the leaders of the Soviet, they thought the future was safely theirs, and they were in no hurry to carry out reforms. The socialists in the soviet supported the middle-class figures in the government, acted similarly and wished to avoid 'precipitate behaviour'.[2] Both sets expected things to go in success-ive phases: first, 'democracy' was to be consolidated – in other words, their own power should be strengthened – and then they would regener-ate the economy, win the war and restore the state. They remained deaf to the aspirations of the masses, even though these were shouted from the roof-tops. They failed to appreciate that their strategy and objectives had no relevance to the aims of the men and women of the country. These aims amounted to immediate demands – peasants wanted land, workers wanted improvement in their lot, non-Russian peoples wanted to be recognized, and all of them wanted justice and dignity.[3] The leaders of the Revolution also did not understand that, once they themselves had invited the people to take over local affairs, the people, who had had enough of being led and regimented, would eagerly respond to the idea of self-government through soviets, of ending the fighting; they would dream of a new life.[4]

There was another aspect to this. The February leaders supposed that, although the citizens of the new Republic had freed themselves from the Tsar and their old masters, they would easily accept the leadership of new masters. But this did not happen: not one of the new leaders' decisions could be carried out if it encountered the slightest opposition. Contem-poraries were especially struck by the fact that the members of the Pro-visional Government, like the members of the old Duma, had only the authority that the soviet let them have. Similarly – as was shown in the first volume of this work – the deputies of this alternative to the govern-ment could only be heard in so far as they went along with the masses' desires. After February, no order or appeal could make the workers go back to work, or the peasants hand back the land, or the soldiers obey their officers again. They would do so only if they had themselves decided to do so. The revolutionaries of both February and October appreciated this well enough, as their memoirs show, but they never really discussed it, even among themselves, for it meant having to recognize the weakness of their supposed right to govern. They supposed that it was based on elections, majorities, delegation, and in June 1917, when Lenin, at the Congress of Soviets, demanded power for his own party although it was very much a minority one, the deputies heard him not with fury but considerable ridicule.[5] However, the ideas and political practices of the people at large were not necessarily those of representative democracy. Quite often, they were in ignorance, or even contemptuous of it, experimenting instead with a wide range of political systems, representative or direct, democratic or otherwise; and they aimed to institutionalize the new methods in the ways that would create parties or trade unions, or would even set up entirely new institutions.

The Revolution, though often made out to be a conflict between political parties, socialists, or even anarchists and Marxists, was equally a conflict between institutions that were not politically identified. There was, for instance, rivalry between trade unions and factory committees, district committees and soviets of deputies; between soviets of deputies and national organizations, political parties and the separate organizations such as those of the young or of women.[6]

There was a further factor in the February leaders' inability to govern, foresee or lead. They did not relate the past and the present in the same way as the masses. To them, the Revolution had been the inevitable outcome of a process, an inheritance from the past, but to the masses it was a rebirth or resurrection – providing a clean slate for the reconstruction of society;[7] the old world had gone for ever, only the present mattered, and no one could therefore claim rights stemming from the world of before 1917, because this past, these rights blessed by the popes or the Tsar had been infected with gangrene and had gone for ever. The past was dead, and it was no good trying to revive it. Even the most famous militants discovered this – for instance, when Khrustalev-Nosar, the former president of the Petrograd Soviet of 1905, claimed as of right a seat on the executive committee of the new soviet, his name was acclaimed as that of a martyr, but his demand was rejected, with booing.[8] The Menshevik Yermansky met the same fate at Kronstadt in July, when he claimed the right to speak for a longer time than other speakers 'who have not had the same revolutionary experience and have not, like me, spent twenty years in Tsarist prisons'. He too was booed, and was forced to stop speaking.[9]

Such episodes, which symbolized a society where men were adapting to the novelty of free speech, had a more general importance that only the most clear-sighted militant appreciated. Any reference to the past was a challenge to the latent egalitarianism that was the dream of February. Film shows how this feeling was expressed: in public speaking, coachman succeeds dandy, officer follows private soldier.[10] A rich man has the right to speak, as does a poor man, but only on condition that he will not justify it in terms of his pre-revolutionary status or rely on the rights he gained through privilege. At last at this stage there was no discrimination, which was another way of denying the past.

Lenin appreciated this better than anyone else, and jettisoned one after another the points of the party's former programme; he nicknamed 'Old Bolsheviks' those of his comrades who wanted to continue applying to the new conditions the anticipations of them that they had had in the past. He always adapted to the changing world,[11] and his greater adaptation to the social realities of 1917 had much to do with his success in October. Even so, the main contradiction continued, for the past was still present, and it made trouble for every demonstration of the revolutionaries' will − the inadequacy of the productive capacity of the country, social and cultural inequalities, hostile social claims, racial and religious prejudice, political rivalries, the existence of an outside world, a foreign war and an enemy invasion.

This heritage was a cause of February's success, but it also governed the course of the Revolution − the nature and shaping of its régime, the political crises, the victory of October. It also shaped the difficulties to come: after 1917, the Bolsheviks in their turn tried to apply to the new conditions the vision of the future that they had had in the past.

PART ONE

The disintegration of the February system

CHAPTER 1

The Political Crisis

In the system established by February 1917, power was shared between the Provisional Government and the Petrograd Soviet, the former stemmed from the old Duma, the latter represented the workers and soldiers. If the workers and soldiers did not obey the soviet, its leaders would blame the Bolsheviks, who had voted against the agreement of 2 March by which the dual power had been set up. In reality, the workers' and soldiers' behaviour was not determined by the soviet's leaders or their Bolshevik challengers, but by the workers and soldiers alone. In March, when the soviets were set up, they had followed Mensheviks, Trudoviks or Socialist Revolutionaries; in October they followed the Bolsheviks and overthrew the Provisional Government. In the interim, they obeyed neither authority. In the days of upheaval during the Revolution, when they demonstrated against the policy of dual power, they destroyed the fiction on which the system rested, that the Revolution's leaders were representative and united against the bourgeois threat. Later on, a further fiction was ruined by the Kornilov Putsch, the *Kornilovshchina*, namely that 'force' − or what was thought to be force − could end the process of revolution.

1 The theory and practice of dual power

The duality of power set up in February reflected a principle derived from Marxism, that society was divided into hostile classes. There was a fundamental contradiction in the way it worked, for each of the two institutions talked in the name of society as a whole, although representing only part of it. There was, on the one hand, a Provisional Government that, in the eyes of the soviet, represented property and capital, and on the other there was the soviet, 'Democracy', which, to the government, represented labour and the masses.

The government included politicians and members of the middle-class parties, with no socialists.[1] In the executive committee of the soviets, the *TsIK*, all of the proletarian organizations were represented, including anarchists and Bolsheviks, but not the middle-class parties. There was a clear, universally-recognized, political boundary, running exactly between the left wing of the Constitutional Democratic Party (Kadets), the most radical of the middle-class parties, and the Trudoviks, the most moderate of the socialist groups (Table 1). This line governed political behaviour and popular representation. On the one hand stood the organizations and the institutions of property: *zemstva*, municipal councils, middle-class political parties; on the other hand were the forces of 'democracy', the socialist or anarchist parties, the trade unions and the like. Only the co-operative movement, which tried to be 'neither capitalist nor socialist' (as Chayanov said) offered a general theoretical alternative method of representation. But, although it was active and energetic as an organization, it did not have much political influence.

From the very first, the workers and soldiers were open in their suspicion of the Provisional Government, which was composed of 'bourgeois' and 'corruptly elected' members of the Duma. The members of the Petrograd Soviet's executive committee (most of them Menshevik-Internationalists) sympathized with this and refused to sit in the government of Prince L'vov. The Marxists gave a further reason: 'As long as Russia lacks the means to make a proper proletarian revolution, the presence of socialists in the government could only weaken the self-consciousness of the labour movement, give it illusions and discredit its leaders.' None the less, since Nicholas II's intentions were not yet clear and there was a chance of military action, the executive committee of the Petrograd Soviet decided to recognize and support the Provisional Government so as to stop the Duma from swinging over to the side of counter-revolution. This recognition was made on a condition that formed the basis of the agreement setting up the new system: it would continue only in as much as the government's policies were in accordance with democratic principles – such as universal suffrage, a constituent assembly to be convoked in due course and given the task of determining the new régime, and rapid convocation of this assembly. Their support was expressed in the well-known formula 'poskol'ku postol'ko' – roughly, 'quid pro quo'. The bourgeois government was threatened with the alternative of a popular régime, a government of the masses, if it failed to secure the achievements of the Revolution. Apart from the Bolsheviks and anarchists, all the proletarian organizations approved the agreement.

Table 1   *Parties, organizations and newspapers during the Revolution*[1]

Organizations and parties of 'democracy'					Parties of the 'propertied classes'	
Bolshevik Social Democrats	**Menshevik Social Democrats**	**Populists, Socialist Revolutionaries**	**Anarchists**	**Trade unions**	**Constitutional Democrats**	**Octobrists**
Unitarists — Internationalists	Right — Defensists	Left[2] / Centre-left / Centre-right			Kadets	
Lenin*, Kamenev — Trotsky*, Lunacharsky	Chkeidze, Dan*, Tsereteli — Plekhanov*, V. Zasulich, G. E. Breido	Kamkov, M. Spiridonova* / V. Chernov / Gots, Avksentiev, Breshko-Breshkovskaya	Bleikhman, Volin* — Kropotkin*	Grohman — Tugan-Baranovsky, Kuskova	Left — Right	Guchkov, Savich
Pravda / *Vpered* / (*Novaya Zhizn'*) *Letuchy Listok*	*Rabochaya Gazeta* / *Yedinstvo Den*	*Znamya Truda* / *Delo Naroda* / *Volya Naroda*	*Burevestnik, Anarkhiya*	Co-operative movement	Nekrasov — Milyukov, Kokoshkin	Extreme right
Lettish, Ukrainian, etc. Social Democrats		*Golos Truda*			Konovalov	Shulgin, Purishkevich
Bund		Socialist Populists (Trudoviks)[3]			*Rech*	*Malen'kaya Gazeta, Groza*
		Peshekhonov, Kerensky			(*Novoye Vremya*)	
		Narodnoye Slovo			Zemstva Organization (Prince L'vov)	
		Finnish, Ukrainian, etc. Socialist Revolutionaries				

1 For the importance of the parties' tendencies and programmes, see vol.I *passim*
2 The formal split occurred only after October
3 The fusion occurred in May
* Arrived in Petrograd only in April–May

The Petrograd Soviet immediately instructed the provincial soviets that had been formed in the meantime that, while legitimacy remained with the Provisional Government, local soviets should supervise its activity and help solve problems by conciliation.[2]

This compromise implied the mutual recognition of two separate and conflicting bodies, the subordination of the propertied classes to the government, and of the workers and soldiers to the soviets of deputies. It sketched out the rules of a political game, the stake of which was in principle a victory in the constituent assembly elections. From now on each side had its formal aims and watchwords, and the Bolsheviks proposed a complete alternative to the system of shared power, namely that all power should be taken over by the soviets (see Table 2). Thus, the men of February, while saying they would not prejudge the nature of the new régime before a constituent assembly had met, none the less prescribed the procedure by which it would be established; and this implied, not only that there would be a representative system, but also that the empire would remain united — which provoked considerable objection, particularly on the part of the nationalities.

Table 2   *Concepts and slogans during the Revolution*

	Kadets	Bolsheviks	Mensheviks and Socialist Revolutionaries
Principle	Unity	Class-struggle	Conciliation and mediation
Foreign policy	War to final victory	Immediate peace	Peace without contributions or annexations; defensive war
The historical stage	Revolution over	Revolution beginning	First phase of Revolution not over
Economic system	Liberalism	Nationalization	State control
Government and society	Trust	Mistrust	Persuasion
Political slogan	'Parliamentary republic'	'All power to the soviets'	'Constituent assembly'
Future	Democracy	Socialism	Democratic socialism

In the weeks that followed, 'democracy' seldom let up in its attacks on the government for being dilatory about calling elections; and the government responded by saying that these were difficult to organize in wartime. On both sides this was mere manoeuvring. The fact was that the socialists who had only just ceased to be outlaws, did not feel ready for an electoral campaign; and when they eventually came to share power with the 'bourgeois', they themselves were in no hurry for one.[3] The middle classes for their part understood what risks they would be running in an election, and, although nothing was publicly said, their more aggressive elements expected to be able to manoeuvre in such a way that no such risks would have to be taken.[4]

Other implications of the agreement of 2 March were evaded in similar fashion. The entry of Kerensky into the government was an early offence against the principle of dual power, because, as a Trudovik leader, he had already been elected as vice-president of the Petrograd Soviet. He ignored the protests of other committee-members and − unlike the Menshevik Chkeidze, who had also been invited, but who refused − he accepted the cabinet post and successfully appealed to the soviet's general assembly for approval.[5] A few weeks later, after the 'April Crisis', the entry of a number of socialists into the government challenged the principle of dual power. This crisis broke out because the Kadet Milyukov, who was minister of foreign affairs, tried to force the soviet's hand by unilaterally laying down the government's war aims. His fall was a success for the 'democratic' side as a whole, but it caused the soviet's leaders to deal once more with the question as to whether they could participate in a 'bourgeois' government. Opposition to this lost some of its steam because the Kadets, a 'bourgeois' party, themselves disavowed Milyukov on the vital question of war-aims, and adopted the soviet's own programme of 'peace without annexations or contributions'. Most of the Social Revolutionaries and the Mensheviks accepted this, and agreed with Kerensky's attitude; 'democratic' opinion acclaimed the entry of the soviet's leaders into the 'coalition' government as a second revolution.

Opposition to duality of power, mark two, nevertheless increased, and now included, on the left, not only the Bolsheviks and anarchists but also the left wing of the Socialist Revolutionaries and the Menshevik Internationalists; on the right it was swollen by many Kadets and the Octobrists.[6] Thereafter, soviet and Provisional Government were not separate, but associated bodies; and there were strict limits to the hostility that remained. Even in March and April Kerensky, far from being a hostage of 'democracy' in the 'bourgeois' government, as men had feared, had been completely at his ease. In the April Crisis, the split within the government had not been one between Kerensky, as soviet member, and the other ministers; it had been between Guchkov and Milyukov, the 'party of resistance', and the other ministers, 'the party of movement'.[7]

This pattern continued after April. The splits in the coalition governments were not between socialist and 'bourgeois' ministers. The first, over state control of industry, put Konovalov, another Kadet minister, against all his colleagues. The next, which went on until September, was between Chernov, who would not disavow the actions of the agrarian committees, and all of the other ministers, who formally condemned illegal seizures of land by peasant committees. The political frontier between the two sides was not, as duality of power implied, between the representatives of soviet and government; it lay in the margin, and still more on the frontiers of the system as a whole. The logical outcome of this evolution was arrived at after the great convulsions of the summer, the July Days and the *Kornilovshchina*. The members of the government who called themselves socialist represented only a small fraction of the socialist organizations present in the soviet, whereas those representing the propertied classes were mandated only by the Kadets. The political basis of the last Kerensky government lay at the point of equilibrium between the two bodies set up in February, the geometric centre of political representation; but, reduced to this, it no longer represented anything.[8]

In any case there was little difference between the delegates of the two allegedly separate bodies. As the Kadet Prince Trubetskoy wrote, 'There was apparently a wall between ourselves and the left, but it fell down.'[9] Whether 'bourgeois' or 'socialist', the 'conciliatory' ministers were equally anxious for their system to be respectable. They were fascinated by the example of western democracy, carefully imitating the gestures and styles of its leaders. Their initial reaction was thus to refuse the claims of the masses – whether for an eight-hour day, reduction of land-rent, peace, the weakening of military discipline, for, in so doing, they imagined they were showing the firmness of true statesmen. They did not see that, if they remained deaf to the masses' pressing wishes, they, although ministers of the Provisional Government, would change, in the masses' view, into figures similar to those of the old order they had themselves overthrown.

The 'conciliatory' socialists stated that it was too soon to meet all these demands – the war, the economic crisis, the situation of Russia ruled it out, and no one could manage the impossible. Besides, they said, the employers, the priests, the industrialists, the statisticians, the Cossacks, the French, all opposed the demands made by the workers and soldiers; and to make peace now would require the consent of the enemy and of Russia's allies, which could not be forced from them. In saying these things, the men of February were not necessarily behaving in bad faith: they admitted that none of the aims was wrong, and merely said that, taken all together, they could not be realized at once, and it was up to the constituent assembly to set the priorities. In February, these attitudes did not strike the masses as offensive, since they were concerned for justice, and would not have wanted decisions over the country's future to be taken without its defenders' having had some say. Nevertheless, it was soon appreciated that the legalism of the revolutionary ministers was having the effect of prolonging a social order that the people had risen to abolish. The people of Russia, in these circumstances, might be patient for another few weeks; but the weeks had to be added to the months and years of suffering and waiting. The demands that were made in March were quite modest, and appeared to be reasonable; they expressed great hopes. The people did not quite suppose they were being deceived, but they suspected a trick somewhere, because with all their commissions and subcommissions set up to bury the old order, the new guides of the people might in fact be burying the revolution instead. 'Their hands trembled', said Trotsky; as soon as real progress was involved, they feared that history might accuse them of acting illegitimately, and so they would not advance unless pushed on by a majority of the people. Even then, they said 'no' when people tried to force their hands because these elected or co-opted democrats would have felt done out of the rights of the competence they associated with their offices – the judgment and decisions as to the future of the Revolution, of which they had been the prophets.

The impatient masses, disliking the endless compromising and waiting, began to move themselves.[10] Strikes increased; then the workers had to face a wave of lock-outs; they started occupying factories, and managing them themselves. Peasants started confiscating land; and, with the help of the soldiers, they all carried out a social change that was to result in a total transformation of society.

The depth and the multifariousness of this change was not appreciated at the start, because politics, in the form of the various 'Days' of upheaval, held the centre of the stage. These upheavals were naturally linked with the social background, though there seemed to be a more direct link with the question of the war: some people could see a correlation, in that the leaders, sham democrats, who were most opposed to reform were also those who said peace was impossible and that the war would have to go on. This might be trickery, fraud. At the time, it was certainly clear that the problem of the war was at the heart of all the conflicts and crises. With hindsight, we can now see that here, as in other matters, the chief conflict did not reflect the duality of power; it was rather between the dual system and the forces on its periphery.

2 The war and political crisis

'For the bourgeoisie, keeping the war going means stopping the Revolution, and for the working class stopping the war means keeping the Revolution going', wrote Bukharin.[11] Milyukov had seen this from the first, although his opponents were longer in doing so. Prolongation of the war let the army commanders shift the mutinous troops to the front and keep the army in line, which preserved the military hierarchy. It also enabled the bourgeoisie to reinforce its connections with the west, and the ruling classes could also use the patriotic emergency as a way of getting the peasants and workers to carry on working and 'Supply our brothers at the front with bread and shoes'.

When Milyukov drew up his Note for the Powers, he believed that it would rapidly win over the democratic side and pin the new Russia to the 'imperialist war'. But there was a crisis. Guchkov and Milyukov were expelled from office; Russia's war aims were changed; and the soviet· leaders, particularly the Menshevik Tseretelli, imagined that their programme of 'peace without annexations or contributions' would prevail throughout Europe. It was not an illusion shared by Lenin, who demanded an immediate peace, or by Milyukov, who did not want any peace at all. However, at the time their listeners were few, and the rulers of Russia were confident of success.

As ministers of the coalition government, they officially asked the Allied governments to re-define their war aims; equally, as socialists, they organized a pacifist conference at Stockholm to co-ordinate the pressures that the various socialist parties would put on their own governments. In order to keep the Allies' confidence, and to limit the misgivings of the Russian military commanders, these 'conciliatory' socialists agreed that it might be necessary to resume 'active operations', as an essential prelude to one final offensive.[12] They were also at a loss as to how to force the Allies or the Germans to conclude a general peace. Some of them thought that a separate peace would be shameful; others regarded it as a blunder, and even Lenin felt that in the long run such a peace would mean helping German imperialism to victory. The Germans, once freed on the eastern front, would defeat France and England, and would then turn against Russia. Their victory would give the Kaiser great prestige and would be a body-blow to the German labour movement, which socialists regarded as essential to the ultimate victory of revolution.[13]

The 'conciliatory' ministers had taken on a war they had condemned, and had to fight it while looking for ways to end it. Their consciences were clear; and besides, there were some advantages in the situation: the army command, too busy fighting the national enemy, would have no chance to promote a military reaction; and the ordinary soldiers would also be kept out of politics for, with their great numbers, these 'peasants in uniform' — who were politically unaffiliated — could 'falsify the workings of the soviets and of democracy'. But these ideas were deceptive. Abroad, the socialists were unable to weaken the war aims of even a single one of the warring states, and the socialist conference at Stockholm was abortive. In Russia, too, prolongation of the war did not have the expected results.

This scheme also failed at the diplomatic and financial levels: it brought not a single inter-Allied conference, not a franc, a pound sterling — merely a few yen and the promise of American help.[14] On the home front especially these policies provoked lively reaction. Despite the claims of 'national defence', they still did little to alter the lives of workers and soldiers. Soldiers still had to go on risking death; workers had to go on with their jobs — all of it in the name of patriotic necessity, which would cover the military authorities' regaining their authority and the civil government's resuming its privileges. A process similar to that some months before was going on, for, in the eyes of workers and soldiers, the socialist ministers were beginning to look bourgeois. Kerensky, as minister of war, required the soldiers to maintain discipline, whereas they wanted to transform the system; the minister of justice prohibited the peasants from illegally seizing land, whereas that had been their first thought; Skobelev, as minister of labour, did nothing to compel the employers to improve factory conditions, but censured factory committees for forcing management to do so. It became difficult to see any difference between the old rulers and the new. The Menshevik Tseretelli, summoning the soldiers to get back to the front on 23 June 1917, unwittingly used the same words as general Polovtsev, who was soon to be in charge of the repression.

There were universal signs of discontent — strike after strike, mutinies, collective disobedience. From early June there were daily signs, too, that the rulers meant to end the process of disintegration. This delighted the army leaders, and counter-revolutionaries openly expressed their pleasure, though both felt that the government, having chosen the right path, should show greater firmness of purpose. There were incidents at Kronstadt and the Villa Durnovo, the two citadels of anarchism, which provoked a violent press campaign: *Malen'kaya Gazeta* and *Novoye Vremya* attacked the Bolsheviks and anarchists for causing disorders — and apostrophized all of them, as 'Jews'. The chorus was swollen by members of the government who declared: 'We cannot govern with all these strikes and troubles.' The employers locked their own workers out; landowners, similarly, stopped their sowings. The bourgeois ministers warned their socialist colleagues that they would follow the example of

Konovalov and leave the government in disagreement with its policy. It amounted to the threat of a political lock-out.

In this climate of reaction, Kerensky's campaign for resumption of military operations and the announcement that an offensive was being planned – which the Allies continually demanded, but which had been postponed from April onward – had an unmistakable significance. The Bolsheviks spelled it out, and the soldiers reacted, demonstrating as they had done in the days of April.[15] At the same time the army command saluted the beginning of the offensive with noisy patriotism, and several regiments demonstrated in favour of war 'until final victory'. On 19 June the Union of Army and Navy Officers, the Military League and the Cossacks responded to the demonstration of 18 June with a counter-demonstration to celebrate the initial successes of the offensive. General Polovtsev, commander of the capital's garrison, was present, and, in front of Kerensky, the Tsarist anthem *Spasi Gospodi* was sung. At Peterhof participants in this event attacked pickets of soldiers who were hostile to the counter-demonstrators. That evening, Polovtsev, thus encouraged, packed off 500 machine-gunners of the 1st machine-gun regiment, which was known for its pacifist convictions, to the front, and later went ahead with other transfers, arranging to send off from the capital sixteen of the seventeen armoured cars normally stationed there.[16] The measures were meant, as at the time of the Stokhod skirmish in March, to test the extent of the troops' nervousness and enable the commanders to find out what might be achieved. This would also allow them to push the Petrograd Soviet into a corner, for it had promised that the troops who had freed Russia from the Tsar would not be sent off to the front. This promise was not kept. On 23 June *Izvestiya*, the soviet's newspaper, gave prominent place to a resolution that summoned the units of the capital's garrison to obey the appeal immediately: 'the reserve forces have their duty to do, like the other soldiers.' Some days later, news came that measures had been taken on the northern front against recalcitrant soldiers: the commissioner Makurenko, although himself a Socialist Revolutionary, prohibited meetings. 8,000 arrests were made by the army commanders: traditional and ostensibly 'revolutionary' authority was thus acting in concert.[17]

'Up till now, we have been able to decide whatever we wanted, but from now on it won't be possible', said a worker, Skalov, to his district committee. He told his comrades to keep on the watch, and 'not let the workers' militia be disbanded'.[18] Though only an obscure militant, he was right in seeing that there was a connection, for that same day general Brusilov urged Rodzyanko, president of the Duma, 'May 18 June be a turning-point in the history of our country'.[19] Grass-roots militant and commander-in-chief had arrived at the same conclusion: the offensive was in fact an assault on the Revolution.

From the Milyukov Note to the launching of an offensive, and subsequently to the loss of Riga and the threat to Petrograd, the question of the war acted as a catalyst for the political crisis. Unlike the social struggle, it was not a matter that the Russians alone could determine, as the failure of the first attempts at fraternization had shown.[20] Only the government could make peace, so the problem of peace became a problem of political power. The new factor was that workers and soldiers now appreciated that there was a connection between the carrying out of reforms, the conclusion of peace and the change of government. Thereafter, each action by the political rulers was judged in this triple light; and the new awareness became clear just before the July Days. As the American Dennis Garstin observed, 'The Bolsheviks have taught the people to think.'

3 The July Days and the failure of the system of dual power

There were crises in April, June and July. On each occasion, the crisis was started and developed in the same way. Each came from the inability of the men of February to listen to the people's wants, and each was detonated by the problem of the war, which was also, later, to be the catalyst of the Kornilov Putsch and the October Insurrection. The days of crisis of 1917 had each, as during the French Revolution, its leading personality; and there were other common features.

(a) Chronological patterns. After meetings and agitation, delegations would go to the headquarters of the Bolshevik party, the military and proletarian sections of the Petrograd Soviet and the soviets of Kronstadt and Oranienbaum, which were regarded as activist, to enlist help. Then the leading speakers of the *TsIK* (the executive committee of the Congress of Soviets, which was dominated by Mensheviks and Socialist Revolutionaries, and where Stalin, Kamenev and Zinoviev figured among the Bolshevik delegates) would appear. Their moderate addresses had little effect at the grass-roots level, though they were more successful in some factories or regiments that could not participate in the movement or even, as in the July Days, opposed it.

(b) Route taken. When the demonstration got under way, the people collected on the northern bank of the Neva and took the same itinerary as in February, towards the Tauride Palace along the Liteyny Prospekt. At the same time the government would assemble troops reckoned to be loyalist behind the Kazan and Nicholas Cathedrals.

(c) Participation and slogans. In February, the participants and by-standers became mingled, and the people of the capital marched, singing and shouting slogans such as 'Down with the Tsar', 'Liberty and Equality', 'No distinction of sex, race or religion' and the like. After March, citizens living in the centre would not join in the demonstrations, but did accompany them in a friendly spirit. Slogans on equality and liberty were still prominent, but there were also demands for 'a peace without annexations'. When these predominated, the citizenry of the city centre no longer paid attention to the demonstration, and got on with their own affairs. By May and June, the films show that the demonstrators were becoming nervous: orderlies were in action, and soon there were two different sets of them, one to keep order and one to resist any possible counter-demonstration. Among the marchers who demonstrated for a peace without annexations, no civil servants, students or women's hats can be seen: the ranks are made up only of the soldiers in the capital.

As these cinema films show, the vanguard of the anti-war movement in these street demonstrations was composed of those most directly affected by the war, soldiers rather than workers. The workers were making revolution in the factories, while the soldiers mastered the streets – parallel, but not necessarily co-ordinated activities.[21] In the three crises of April, June and July the leaders – never the same ones, but always accompanied by soldiers – tried to involve the chief elements of the Bolshevik party in their action. In April they were successful, though not in June. In July they ignored the Bolsheviks' own objections, and the Bolsheviks lost control of the vanguard. Nevertheless, though divided by each of the crises, the Bolsheviks ended up by displaying solidarity with the demonstrators. The soviets of deputies and the majority of socialist members remained opposed to them. Relations between the Bolsheviks and their allies on the one hand and the 'conciliatory' leaders on the other deteriorated after each crisis and each of the turbulent Days. It came to confrontation on 4 July, which marked the end of the unity of 'demo-cracy', one of the bases of the system of dual power.

The Bolshevik party swamped and divided[22]

Pravda was constant in its denunciation of the government and the soviet leaders collaborating with it. The soldiers demonstrated, logically enough, against them both, simultaneously, but since the soviet for them was revolutionary authority, it was towards it that they marched. They were keeping going an old quarrel, which had begun in February, and which Lenin, returning from exile, had revived.

Even in February a few, mainly Bolshevik, militant workers had attacked the agreement struck between government and Petrograd Soviet. There had been talk, in the Petrograd committee of the Bolshevik party, of starting up a demonstration against the agreement, on 2 or 3 March. The scheme was rejected at the time, for the masses were still putting their trust in the soviet and would not have sympathized with a hostile attitude; and besides, the February events had shown how weak the party was, especially among the soldiers. It had therefore to organize, gain a majority in the soviets, and spread its influence among the politically unaffiliated and even potentially hostile mass of soldiery. It seemed sufficient for the Bolsheviks to attack the Menshevik and Socialist Revolutionary leaders' policies, and to demand greater radicalism of attitude towards the bourgeoisie, and this line was adopted when Kamenev and Stalin had charge of the party's management. Lenin denounced this when he returned to Russia, attacking the 'parliamentarism' of the Bolshevik leaders, whom he nicknamed 'Old Bolsheviks' because of their persistent application of the old pattern of 'bourgeois revolution', soviet democracy, etc. He wanted an end to the imperialist war, and a total break with the social democrats who worked with the bourgeoisie and had concluded a 'separate peace' with it. Lenin appreciated that the masses were becoming radical, and thought that Bolshevik policy should go in parallel. *Pravda* published his *April Theses*, and they had immediate effect for, when the Milyukov Note revealed the aggressiveness of the Provisional Government's war aims, demonstrators of the anarcho-Bolshevik vanguard were much more numerous than their opponents. Soldiers, not workers, were at their head, and they grew in numbers and determination when the coalition government, while ostensibly promoting a policy of 'peace without annexations or contributions' (the soviet's own formula), wanted to see active military operations resumed. They looked to the Bolshevik party, as in April, for support. The central committee was paralysed by the conflict between Kamenev's and Lenin's arguments, and vacillated, but it inclined towards demonstrations, for it had become sensitive to the radical mood of the Petersburg committee and the then emerging Bolshevik military committee. The leaders were, once again, soldiers rather than workers.[23]

The party's decision provoked such disapproval among the soviets that Zinoviev swung round, which lent a majority to the 'democratic' arguments against the demonstration because the new coalition policy had been adopted by the majority. Although they did go ahead and demonstrated on 18 June, the Bolshevik soldiers were angry at the central committee's switch: in *Pravda* the party attacked the leaders but yet when the masses decided to act it had vacillated and held them back – was this illogicality or treason?[24] A split began between the party leadership and the vanguard, where Bolsheviks co-operated with anarchists, and in July there was conflict.

Since the offensive had been announced, the Bolshevik soldiery of the 1st machine-gun regiment had suspected that the military authorities would take advantage of the situation and send them to the northern front. The trick was obvious, and a test of strength approached. The regimental committee had been elected in March, and inclined towards 'conciliation'; ensign Golovin, a Bolshevik, therefore wanted to constitute the regiment as a general assembly, given that a question as serious as this transfer to the front could not be determined in authoritarian fashion by the regimental committee alone. He won a majority. Zinoviev arrived to agitate, saying, 'Now you have the choice of death in the trenches for interests that are not yours, or death on the barricades in your own cause.' The military authorities heard of this, and regarded armed rebellion as inevitable — a view also taken by activists of the most revolutionary regiments. The Bolshevik military organization and the anarchists alike saw it coming:[25] as Fedorov said, 'Since the affair of the Villa Durnovo, we have been told to surrender our machine-guns, and we are obviously not going to.' He went on, 'For us there can be no way out except taking to the streets in arms to destroy the Provisional Government.' The Bolshevik soldiers agreed: the all-Russian conference of Bolshevik military organizations could be changed into a body to take power, while, at the same time, the central committee, with its pointless vacillation, would be swept aside since 'the idea of containing the masses is no good . . . the party must be ready to fight even if it does not want to'. The leaders of the Bolshevik military organization knew that these were the activists' feelings; as Podvoysky said, 'We spent most of our time calming them down.'[26]

But the party's leaders, far from guessing the extent of the militants' rage, had taken a rest, it being a Sunday. Lenin was in the country, Nogin and Milyutin had also left the capital. Ilin-Zhenevksy and Semashko declared, 'We have enough machine-guns to overthrow the government and no one can stop us.' The anarchists told the soldiers that they were in disagreement with the Bolsheviks' formula of 'All power to the soviets' — as Bleikhman said, 'We want to overthrow the government, not to hand power to the bourgeois soviet but to take it ourselves.' Nevertheless the actual watchwords remained 'Down with the capitalist ministers' and 'All power to the soviets'.[27]

One witness said that Bleikhman was spoiling for a fight, being in an excited condition, and telling the soldiers that they could count on the workers and sailors, for they would join in if there were a rising.

The soldiers who were there said, 'Yes, go ahead, we're ready for it.' The machine-gunners were nervous, for they had to strike the first blow. . . . Then a plan was drawn up, if it can be called a plan: (1) men were to go at once and throughout the night (of 2 – 3 July) to the districts and prepare for revolt at eleven o'clock; (2) Kolobuch-kin, Bleikhman, Pavlov and Fedorov were to lead the 1st regiment, arrest the Provisional Government – especially Kerensky – and occupy the telephone buildings and the station; (3) the workers would then be led towards Kronstadt, to meet up with the sailors and occupy the press of *Novoye Vremya*.[28]

Bolsheviks and anarchists also set up a provisional revolutionary committee – *VRK* – which elected Semashko as leader. Golovin signed the orders to agitators in the factories and barracks. The *VRK* summoned the people to take to the streets, armed, on 3 July, but only at five o'clock. Throughout the evening, a vast meeting was prepared, and it occurred late at night, assembling twenty-six military units that refused to go to the front. The actual document was more moderate than the speeches of the people who drew it up: there was no talk of overthrowing the government, merely of expelling the 'capitalist' ministers; and at the fourth point, the demonstrators announced that they wanted 'not a separate peace, only an end to the war'.[29] The delegates of the Kronstadt sailors explained, like Golovin, that the offensive was launched against the will of the people, which was universally agreed, as was the need for a demonstration.

The Kadet ministers' resignation, news of which came through in the small hours of 3 July, increased the rage of the demonstrators: it added fuel to the fire, although – contrary to what the politicians thought and said for some time – it was irrelevant to its origins, as was the failure of the offensive (news of which came through in the afternoon). The resignation only convinced the most activist groups that 'something is up'. As the demonstration began, there was serious disagreement between the vanguard and the Bolshevik party leaders, and also, as Alexander Rabinowitch has admirably demonstrated, within the Bolshevik party.

Many regiments had arrived, some of them vacillating or even hostile; their great problem was not whether to join in, but whether to load their arms. The workers of the proletarian suburbs were ready for anything, and, as soon as the machine-gunners' lorries appeared, they fetched their own weapons and joined the troops, though they were only a minority.[30]

At this stage, while the demonstration was building up, the Bolshevik leaders were all against it and the party's representatives in the *TsIK* still more so. In the proletarian section of the Petrograd Soviet 'the Bolsheviks worked to calm down the machine-gun regiments' and, according to

Ashkenazi, who took part in the discussions, 'they expected to manage to avoid armed revolt . . . but, realizing that they could not, they decided (early on 3 July) to elect a decemvirate to lead the movement. Zinoviev, Trotsky, Yenukidze, Kornev, I and others whose names I have forgotten were involved'.[31] At Kronstadt, in the meantime, the most popular of the Bolshevik leaders, Roshal, sought to show that the time was not ripe for this demonstration, but he was booed by the sailors and had to give up speaking.[32] The Petersburg committee of the Boshevik party was then in session. It regarded *Pravda* as too moderate, and by 53 votes to 19, with 16 abstentions, won the right to tell its newspaper what to do, and to lay down its own line. This question was so serious for the party members, and so far challenged the very nature of Bolshevism, that they would talk about nothing else — they ignored the mood of the barracks and did not even mention the demonstration that was going on. They were discussing the grievances of the Petersburg committee against *Pravda* when I. N. Ilinsky rushed in to say that the 1st machine-gun regiment was marching against the government. Volodarsky immediately spoke out against it. Stalin telephoned to the *TsIK* to say what was happening — a way of denouncing the event. Everyone was angry. They would not, of course, join in, but, on Slutskaya's advice, there were proposals that the party should at least take over the movement's leadership so as to remain 'in close contact with the masses'. 'However, no decision was taken, and, like the Paris Commune, they debated while the enemy acted.'[33]

The demonstrators had begun, going towards the bridges of the Neva, with Semashko, Golovin and Bleikhman mounted on lorries, giving orders. The 1st regiment would not give over its artillery, but this was confiscated, and the demonstrators, led by bands, moved over the bridges. They went towards the centre of the city, irresistibly advancing and snowballing as they collected workers. There was no stopping them — 'Is this happening without the central committee's authorization?' 'Yes, without it.'[34]

A delegation moved past the headquarters of the Bolshevik party, at the Xeshinskaya House, the Sverdlov, Nevsky and Podvoysky tried in vain to get the demonstrators to go home. The Bolshevik military organization, however, was told to join the movement 'to take the leadership of it, stop it from getting any larger and prevent any premature action against institutions or the state'. At the Tauride Palace, however, Kamenev regarded the whole thing as an anarchist provocation, though he still tried to get the proletarian section to support it, so as to 'sovietize' it. This section, which was Bolshevik in majority, announced that 'the demonstration is pacific and organized'.[35] When the head of the demonstration reached the soviets' headquarters Chkeidze and Voytinsky went out to tell the people to go home, saying that their demands would be investigated. They were greeted with booing. Zinoviev, Steklov and Trotsky, on the other hand, were cheered, and said 'the time has come to take power, arrest the soviet's executive committee and transfer all power to the soviets'.[36] This heartened the demonstrators, whose own mood it matched, and they cheered frantically. Then, content but ineffectual, they went home.

The anarchist Bleikhman had thought that 'once we are in the streets, we'll get organized'. But the street organized nothing.[37] By the evening of 3 July the demonstrators had gone home again. As Podvoysky noted, 'the morale of several regiments was falling, while that of the workers and non-participants was high'. The *VRK* had actually allowed Kerensky to escape — it had arrived at the Warsaw Station to arrest him, but a quarter of an hour too late, for his train had already gone. There was a similar failure by the detachment sent to arrest the cabinet: it had met at Prince L'vov's house and the detachment did not feel strong enough for a mass arrest. Nothing was decided for the next stage — the Pavlovtsy and Finlyandtsy regiments refused to carry on, while the 171st and 176th, and the Kronstadt sailors, wanted to do so. No one knew what the government intended; and, as the fever rose in the factories, the Bolsheviks became increasingly divided.[38]

The central committee still regarded the demonstration as inopportune. This was certainly what Lenin felt when he arrived in Petrograd in the small hours of 4 July. He did not know, however, that, under pressure from the Bolshevik military organization and the Petersburg committee, the central committee had had to withdraw from *Pravda*'s typesetting an appeal against the demonstration, signed by Kamenev, Zinoviev and Nogin, and also did not know that the Petersburg committee had, on the preceding day at 11.40 p.m., issued an appeal in favour of the demonstration 'to give all power to the soviet', though without saying whether the demonstrators were to take up arms. The signatories, not trusting the central committee, had handed their document to the press of *Soldatskaya Pravda*: it appeared on the morning of 4 July, while *Pravda* came out with a great blank space on its front page — Stalin had arrived too late to have another appeal printed, though it did come out as a pamphlet, summoning people to join the demonstration peacefully, i.e. unarmed, and ending with the words 'there must be a new power to consolidate the Revolution, and it can only be the soviets'.[39] Thus, as Raskol'nikov, one of the Bolshevik leaders of Kronstadt, put it,

this document tried, without explicitly talking of taking power, to reconcile all of the tendencies that divided the party. The ambiguity showed how hesitant the leaders were, for they could not come to a decision at all – they summoned their men to take to the streets, and knew they would arm themselves if they were summoned to revolt.[40]

When the Kronstadt sailors and Oranienbaum gunners arrived in Petrograd on the morning of 4 July, they were welcomed by the workers, and Bleikhman again urged militants to overthrow the government. A long column set off for the Tauride Palace. At its head was the most famous revolutionary woman of Russia, 'the little peasants' general', Maria Spiridonova, tiny, and Quaker-like in her blue serge dress; this old Socialist Revolutionary militant told Raskol'nikov to make a detour via the Bolshevik headquarters. Lenin was there, but would not appear on the balcony because people might then think he opposed the demonstration. In the end he gave way, and received a lengthy ovation. He said he was convinced that the slogan 'All power to the soviets' would soon become a reality, and insisted on discipline, determination, vigilance. The accent was on the demonstration's peaceful character, and this took the sailors aback, because they were all armed.[41]

A few hours later there was fighting between demonstrators and troops loyal to the government and the soviet. The government's revelations as to Lenin's 'treachery' and 'being a German agent' had convinced some of the garrison, and reinforced their loyalty to the system of dual power.[42] Troops from the front arrived to execute repressive action, and in less than twenty-four hours the situation in the capital was reversed; the witch-hunt of Bolsheviks began.[43]

July: the end of the united Revolution

There are obvious parallels between Petrograd in July 1917 and Berlin in January 1919 – the irreversible split among the social democrats, the moderates' appeal to the army, and the initiation, by socialists, before Noske and Ebert, of a terror in the name of democracy. There was a further similarity in the policy of disengagement adopted by the traditional authorities hoping to regain power. There the analogy stops, and it needs correction because, at bottom, the unity of the Russian social democrats had for some time been mythical, although some appearance of unity had been created by risks incurred in common, the victory of February and the pressures of the masses, who disliked factional splits. Unity had also been needed in presenting the system of dual power, but it could not survive for long in view of the disputes, the rivalry of organizations and the spectacular failure of the men of February.

Since February, Bolsheviks and Mensheviks had obviously been involved in a dialogue of the deaf, though of deaf who talked each other's language.[44] The Bolsheviks accused the Mensheviks of betraying the hopes of the masses, and of cheating as regards representative system and method of election. The Mensheviks attacked the Bolsheviks for departing from the party programme and for demagoguery; especially, they attacked the Bolsheviks for flouting the rules of democracy, for taking part in demonstrations that a soviet majority had failed to approve. In fact the Bolsheviks' hand had been forced, but they could hardly admit it, because doing so would have amounted to questioning their own legitimacy and their position in the vanguard. It was true that the Mensheviks cheated over the electoral system to their own advantage; it was equally true that the Bolsheviks had not opposed the demonstrations for going ahead against the 'democratic' majority of the soviets but rather for being launched at a time when the conditions for success were not ripe. It was a question of timing. Some of the Bolsheviks admitted as much − as Bukharin said, in June, 'hitherto we have been too democratic and insufficiently socialist; now it must be the other way about'.[45] In this he was in full agreement with Lenin, who had demanded power for his party despite its mere 10 per cent of the seats in the soviet. Lenin also wanted the Bolshevik party's name to be changed, abandoning 'social democrat' for 'communist'.[46]

As long as Kamenev's view prevailed among the Bolsheviks, the two sections had left the myth of unity intact, even if they quarrelled; and, under pressure from the working-class base, discussions over reunification of the party continued. This situation was not profoundly altered either by the radicalization of the Bolsheviks under Lenin's guidance, or by his attitude to the taking of power, or even by the Mensheviks' participation in the government, which, on the contrary, deepened the gap between the Mensheviks and the Socialist Revolutionaries. Martov and Kamkov condemned such participation, and it led to the grafting of a small group of unitarists (Trotsky, Lunacharsky and others) on to Bolshevism.[47]

The turning-point came with the affair of 10−18 June. Dan and Tseretelli accused the Bolsheviks of 'stabbing democracy in the back' by demonstrating just when democracy had to contend with military reactionaries. Tseretelli said the Bolsheviks' ideas were 'criminal'; they must be 'disarmed'. Lenin answered in *Pravda* on 18 June, 'the working class must respond with the utmost calm, prudence and firmness to the attacks on us, and remember that the time for peaceful demonstrations has gone.' After that, when Kamenev talked of 'anarchist provocation', and declared his party's 'innocence', he would find few believers, even if he did do what he could to stop the demonstration and even tell Roshal and

Raskol'nikov not to bring in Kronstadt; similarly, few people would give credence to Zinoviev and Trotsky, who were on the one hand calling for the overthrow of the régime and on the other setting up a 'provisional revolutionary committee' to make sure that the demonstration went peacefully.

The fact was that the leaders kept two irons in the fire. They tried to keep in close contact with the masses; but they also wanted to work a manoeuvre within the soviets, to form a government without bourgeois members. The demonstration put this manoeuvre at risk, and this was why Kamenev and Sukhanov, who favoured the idea, saw the demonstration as an anarchist provocation.

That evening, the Kadet ministers had indeed resigned − officially because the agreement with the Kiev Rada had been struck without their consent[48] but in fact, as with Guchkov's resignation in April and Konovalov's in May, to put pressure on the socialists. It was a political lock-out, along the lines of those in the factories. In the leadership of the soviet, where the masses' true mood was ignored, the demonstration of 3 July was linked with this Kadet tactic, and the talk was only of this challenge. The Mensheviks and Socialist Revolutionaries wished to meet it by setting up a purely soviet government. The 'minority' Mensheviks, led by Martov, were in favour of this solution, and they expected Dan to join them so that the Mensheviks' attitude to power would be wholly changed. Gots and the Socialist Revolutionaries would, they expected, be concerned for unity and so would follow them.[49]

However, when Dan heard suddenly that there was an anarcho-Bolshevik-led demonstration demanding 'All power to the soviets' he changed his mind, for it would look as if the new government had been formed under a threat of force. Dan and his friends therefore voluntarily went into the 'bourgeois' trap of taking power in a coalition with the bourgeoisie, whereas when workers and soldiers demanded it, it was alleged to be intolerable pressure. In order to stop the demonstration, Dan and Tseretelli did as before, and had the soviets adopt a resolution by which the inhabitants of Petrograd were summoned not to follow the regiments of a single city which claimed to speak for the whole country and was in fact treacherously letting down the soldiers who defended the Revolution by fighting at the front. Throughout the morning of 4 July the factories and the barracks were divided by this and the *Soldatskaya Pravda* appeal.[50] A demonstration which was designed originally to expel the bourgeois ministers was thus changing into a confrontation between the extreme left and the soviet executive committee. The demonstrators, heading on 4 July, as on the previous day, for the soviet rather than the government buildings, were not misled. The soviet committee, with its electoral majority, appealed to public opinion, summoning representatives of fifteen of the capital's military units and explaining to them that 'any demonstration, armed or not, which begins without the soviets' consent or without that of the central committee of the Socialist Revolutionaries and Social Democrats is inopportune'. They would appoint a commission to find out who was responsible.[51]

The new factor in this was that, in view of the scale of the preparations made by the organizations responsible for the demonstrations of 4 July, the government took two decisions. The first was taken independently of the *TsIK*. Perevertzev, the minister of justice, announced that 'grave news' had reached the ministry of foreign affairs that Lenin and the Bolsheviks were German spies. The second decision, which was taken with the *TsIK*'s agreement, was that front-line troops were summoned to defend the soviet against 'Bolshevik' rebels. The action would be led not by the military authorities but by political commissioners, to avoid provocation. The idea emanated, apparently, from the Menshevik Vilenkin, who suggested it to Chkeidze and Tseretelli, and it was accepted because, as Tseretelli said, everyone thought that 'the Bolshevik soldiery will not dare confront the great mass of soldiers drawn up to defend the soviet'.[52]

The demonstration of 3 July had not been foreseen, and all passed quietly; but on 4 July it was different; and the scene — in the form of a snapshot subsequently expanded by Eisenstein for his film — has been immortalized. The sailors shot up towards the windows, in virtually all directions, and there were several dozen dead. By this time, the head of the demonstration was reaching the Tauride Palace. The sailors were ready 'to smash it all' but they had no precise objectives, and the Bolshevik leaders of Kronstadt were paralysed because they had had no directives from the central committee, just as the military organization had been unable to make up its mind. Sukhanov's account states:

Once they had arrived at the soviets' palace, the sailors demanded the minister of justice, asking why he would not release one of the sailors arrested in the Villa Durnovo raid. Perevertsev was not there, and the soviet leaders asked Viktor Chernov to go and calm the demonstrators down. He started explaining the soviet's attitude to power, and attacked the Kadets. One of the workers shouted at him, 'Take power, you stupid bastard, it's being handed to you on a plate', and another demonstrator asked why they were doing nothing about the peasants' problems. Chernov said they were being looked into. Then he tried to stop speaking, but the most agitated of the demonstrators would not let him. They grabbed the Socialist Revolutionary leader; and all the while, the members of the executive committee of the Socialist Revolutionaries tried to ignore the demonstration going on outside, and disapproved of it; they went on discussing their agenda, and stopped only when they heard that Chernov had been grabbed. Meanwhile Trotsky had already arrived. Chernov had been seized by powerful hands, and he was forced into a car . . . thrown on his back, and then obviously lost consciousness. Trotsky was well-known and trusted throughout Kronstadt, but when he started talking, the crowd went on heckling, and if a shot had sounded, there would have been a massacre – all of us, including Trotsky, would have been torn to pieces. He was listened to with hostility, and when he tried to get through to Chernov, the people drew up round him angrily. He said, 'You have come here to show what you want, and to tell the soviet that the working class wants to put the bourgeoisie out of power. But you don't have to attack individuals. They aren't worth it. You have shown how devoted you are to the Revolution, you're all ready to die for it, I know; let me shake your hand, comrade – your hand, brother.' He seized a sailor by the hand, and the sailor shook him off. He pulled away his hand – maybe these were men to whom the Revolution meant nothing, or provocateurs, but for them Trotsky was worse than Chernov – they would deal with him in turn . . . but the men of Kronstadt finally released Chernov and Trotsky hurried him back into the Palace.[53]

In the city, fighting went on, and the government let it continue while it waited for the soviet to request intervention. By the evening, general Polovtsev had received the appeal for help: 'I was finally able to play the role of liberator for the soviet.'

The Tauride Palace was now surrounded by hostile sailors and soldiers, with thousands of workers as well; no defence was possible, and the regiments that guarded the building said they were 'neutral'. 'Suddenly', says Sukhanov, 'there was a loud noise coming from the distance, and it came closer and closer. Soon, the tramp of ranks of marching soldiers became audible. They were arriving at last. The worried faces of the deputies looked out in all directions to see what was happening, whether it was another threat.' By a strange twist of fate, the deputies of the Congress of Soviets wondered just as the Duma members had done in February, whether soldiers were coming to attack or preserve them. Dan suddenly rushed on to the podium, unable to conceal his joy. 'Comrades, be calm', he shouted, 'there's no danger, it's the loyal regiments that have arrived, and they've come to defend our central executive committee.'[54] There was general hubbub, and the *Marseillaise* was struck up. The Izmailovsky, Preobrazhensky and Semenovsky troops had arrived to help the soviets.

Terror in the minor key: the democrats set a pattern

There were many reasons for the change of fortunes in the July Days, but two stood out. In the first place came the patriotic reaction of the garrison of the capital which, on the strength of a report personally made by the minister of justice, Perevertsev, accepted a terrible charge against the Bolsheviks and Lenin, that of taking German money through an agent in Stockholm. It had been proven, allegedly, that Lenin had started the revolt in the capital in co-ordination with the German counter-offensive on the south-western front. These revelations by the ministry of justice were so effective among the regiments which had been active in the February Revolution – the Preobrazhensky and Pavlovsky – that Perevertsev took the news round other regiments. Very late that night the news was going round the whole city that Lenin had been proved to be a German spy. The accusation was made public in the *Malen'kaya Gazeta* and the *Zhivoye Slovo*, supported by statements from leading politicians such as Alexinsky. Lenin's party was heavily discredited by them, and the wavering regiments came round to the soviet and government side (see Note A).

The second reason for the change of fortune was probably more decisive still: the information that front-line units were marching on the capital, decent servicemen who were willing to give their lives for their country, and now answered the soviet's appeal to cleanse the capital of traitors and agitators. The leaders, though social-democrats, were thus prepared to use the language and imagery of patriotism; and the alteration in psychology and politics was immediate.[55]

By 5 July, loyalist forces were in control of the capital, and general Polovtsev had his hands free to rid the city of the last rebels. He began by cutting off the telephones of organizations that had taken part in the demonstrations; then, expecting still more help with the arrival of new regiments from the front, he contented himself with raiding the Xeshin-skaya House and the *Pravda* printing presses.[56] The Bolsheviks had actually underestimated what was happening, and their military organization even tried to assemble the activists and demonstrate again. But most of the regiments that had marched on the previous evening and in the morning refused the leave barracks again; many workers went back to work, and the anarchists had quite disappeared. In ignorance of the activists' mood, Kamenev and Mekhonoshin struck an agreement, in their party's name, with the *TsIK*, represented by Lieber, of the *Bund*. There was a final display of social-democratic solidarity to limit the workings of repression: it was agreed that no imprisonments would be made, and that activists already imprisoned would be released unless they were held on criminal charges, while the Bolshevik-held bridges would be surrendered and the sailors would go away to Kronstadt. There was to be no armed resistance to the loyalists' patrols.[57]

However, although Lenin, Zinoviev and Kamenev ordered the Peter-Paul Fortress to give up without a fight, there was still some firing, and Illin-Zhenevsky in the fortress even prepared for full-scale siege. Raskol'nikov's sailors in any case rejected the choices they were offered, of going away or being disarmed. Thereafter the *TsIK* did not feel bound by the Lieber-Kamenev agreement. General Polovtsev had not even been told of it, and he attacked the working-class quarters. As Skobelev put it, 'bayonets and machine-guns have always been the best arguments' − the Menshevik minister not apparently realizing that the soviet was from now on powerless, and that, in the military authorities' eyes it was useless. The repression went ahead, Polovtsev setting up punitive expeditions into the headquarters of the insurrection, the working-class suburbs of Vyborg and Vasilevsky Island, followed by ransacking, house-searches and arrests without warrant. Witch-hunts for Bolsheviks began, fully supported by those who had been frightened since February and those who bore a grudge against Lenin's men. Eisenstein, in *October*, brilliantly recaptured the climate of White Terror that came after the July demonstrations.[58]

On 6 July, Kerensky decided that all who had organized or led the armed demonstrations, as well as those who had issued appeals or fomented and encouraged the demonstrations, should be arrested and put on trial as 'traitors to the Revolution'. The soviets' executive committee agreed, and the decree was followed by an order to arrest Lenin, Zinoviev, Kamenev and Lunacharsky.[59] On 7 July, again at Kerensky's prompting, a decision was made to disarm all of the units that had taken part in the July Days, to send those most heavily compromised off to the front, and to appoint a special mixed soviet-government commission to investigate responsibility. Kamenev, Trotsky, Lunacharsky and Rakhia were arrested and imprisoned, the Bolshevik military organization was completely disbanded, and its leaders were arrested. Podvoysky, Nevsky and Lenin managed to get away. The offices and printing press of *Pravda*, *Soldatskaya Pravda* and *Golos Pravdy* were closed, and, since the wind was now towards reaction, no printer could be found to take on any document with a Bolshevik signature. Lenin and his friends could put their case only in leaflets printed in the provinces, especially Helsinki and Moscow. They asked *Novaya Zhizn'* to publish, on 11 July, an open letter in which Zinoviev and Lenin rebutted the slanders against them; but since, having resolved collectively on 5 July not to let themselves be tried by a tribunal clearly stacked against them, their rebuttal was not taken up in political circles even though it might well have been taken seriously, given that the *TsIK* itself had protested, on the 4th, before its great fright in the demonstration, against the assertions made by Perevertzev. Thereafter, party grievances counted, and the democrats treated Lenin's refusal to appear for trial as an admission of guilt. They also failed to protest when the mixed commission was swept aside from the enquiry to make way for 'regular' justice.

'100,000 Bolshevik workers of Petrograd are not German spies', ran a resolution of the Vyborg workers. Their anger and astonishment at being described as traitors by both the government and the soviet aptly symbolized the ambiguity of the July Days.[60] The leaders of the government and the soviet felt that any weakening of the dual power system would strengthen the enemy within and without the country; the representatives of democracy did not appreciate that the whole rising had been caused by their own failure to realize the aspirations of the workers and soldiers, and they blamed it all, as blind governments have always done, on 'agitators'. Obviously the Bolshevik leaders had not caused the July Days, but, once they had come in to identify themselves with the vanguard, they immediately saw that the demonstrators, calling themselves Bolshevik, were very much further to the left than the party leadership. Lenin had proclaimed as much in April, and it was once more verified, though neither Lenin nor the party had seriously measured the extent to which it was the case. With the reaction, they did so. No collaboration between Bolshevik and Menshevik or Socialist Revolutionary leaders was now possible, such that the slogan of 'All power to the soviets' became meaningless so long as it was not Bolsheviks who dominated them. Lenin, drawing the lessons of events in *Three Crises*, calculated that the new Bolshevik watchword must be 'All power to the working class, led by its revolutionary party, the Communist-Bolsheviks'.[61]

A breach had thus come with the majority bloc, and Volin attacked it, saying,

> In the name of the Revolution, death penalty and military courts have been brought back into an army broken, tortured and exhausted after three years of war. In the name of the Revolution, the vote for the constituent assembly will be removed from soldiers whom their officers suspect. In the name of the Revolution, the best revolutionaries, the heads of revolutionary social democracy, the party of the revolutionary working class, are being arrested, while Gurko, Vyrubova and other Tsarist servants are being released. In

the name of the Revolution, the working-class newspapers, the working-class printing presses lovingly built up by so many small subscriptions collected by the poor from the poor, are being closed down. In the name of the Revolution, the calling of the constituent assembly is being postponed, and instead an assembly of dead souls has been summoned to Moscow, there to be revived by ministerial appeals for sacrifice. In the name of the Revolution, the secret police has come to life again, the individual's liberties have been suppressed, and the old atrocities of the police-chiefs will be started again. In the name of the Revolution, the Imperial laws are to come back into force, and the gains of the great Russian Revolution are to be abolished; in the name of the Revolution, the gates have been opened to the most hideous counter-revolution.[62]

The majority Mensheviks and Socialist Revolutionaries were hostile, and even vindictive: Tseretelli and Dan set the tone, ceaselessly flailing 'the traitors who stabbed democracy in the back, and played into the hands of counter-revolution'. The left wing of the Socialist Revolutionaries now broke with the majority.[63]

Plekhanov declared that there could be no compromise with anarchy; Lieber, of the *Bund*, compared the Bolsheviks with scavengers at the front; Berg, a Socialist Revolutionary, wanted them to be given no quarter; the Menshevik Lebedev, as secretary of state for the navy, confirmed to the loyalist naval forces an order 'to sink any ship from Helsinki'; and Chernov, though on the left of the Socialist Revolutionary majority, had still not recovered from the adventures of 4 July and reacted by writing eight editorials that very evening against Bolshevism. *Delo Naroda* thought that four would do, at which Chernov recovered and 'recalled the rights and liberties of the New Russia'. Kerensky regarded the violence of the troops as 'excessive', but remarked that he had to cover them with his authority; on 6 July there were ninety-one arrests for 'violence and mayhem', 'drunkenness' or simply 'Bolshevik agitation'.

The signal had sounded, and repression got under way. The old right, which had peeped out just before July, was much encouraged and made a triumphant return. *Narodnaya Gazeta* announced, 'We are winning.' In the Kazan district of Petrograd, pamphlets circulated with the names of fifteen members of the soviets' executive committee bearing the remark, 'they are all Jews'.[64] Only Kerensky tried to stop this.[65]

Repression then shifted from the Bolsheviks to their neighbours, friends and even rivals. The leaders were in prison or in hiding, and the government muzzled their press: on 6 July Burtsev complained to Gorky, editor of the Internationalists' newspaper *Novaya Zhizn'*, that he was being 'defeatist'. Tseretelli discovered the joys of a progressive slide into terror, and signed a warrant for the eviction of *Rabochaya Gazeta* from the printing press it had illegally taken over, and where it had been installed since March. The newspaper of the left Socialist Revolutionaries, *Zemlya i Volya*, was similarly persecuted. In thus attacking the newspapers of the opposition, and even a daily newspaper belonging to his own party though to a different wing of it, this Menshevik leader was setting an example that the right fully supported.[66] It was not one that the Bolsheviks, after October, were to forget.

CHAPTER 2

The failure of counter-revolution

1 A model: Russian resistance to the Revolution

Since the fall of the Tsar and the establishment of the system of dual power, the Revolution had not diminished at all: it had grown immensely. In the towns, demonstrations, strikes, factory occupations and lock-outs came in unremitting succession, and industrial output began to collapse. In the countryside, the greatest anarchy prevailed, at least according to the estate-owners who fled to the towns; and in the army the situation was worse still, since supreme command and officers had lost their authority. The offensive of late June had failed, and there were tales of whole regiments fleeing before the enemy at Tarnopol. Military disaster seemed inevitable: Russia was heading for the abyss.

'Our Revolution has created a country of shame and treachery, not a great and free Russia', said Maslennikov in the Duma. 'We are ruled by a handful of madmen, fanatics, barrack-room lawyers who called themselves the soviet executive committee; if these filthy traitors, profiteers and German spies are in charge, making whatever mess they want to, it is because they have liberty [the speaker is called to order]; we have to punish not just desertion in the field, but also men who corrupt the field army. Shooting and punishment are carried out at the front, but it's here at home that we should hang them, for the source of the trouble is here.' The Duma made no response: 'Its benches are empty, emptied because of deserters.'[1] To the upper middle class, the military leaders and the Allies, there had already been far too long a delay in dealing with the general disintegration. Dual power would have to be stopped, the soviet dispersed and a strong government set up.

But the ruling classes, not quite understanding the rules of a political game that was not their own, did not have much idea how to set about this. They naturally thought of calling in a military dictator, but, as the army stood, such a plan was hardly realistic. When, in their disarray, Kornilov turned up, they welcomed him, with pitiful results in the adventure of improvisation that then emerged.

A model of anti-Bolshevism was being assembled, and it was reconstituted in the Civil War. It was shaped between February and October, and there was some similarity between it and the Fascist model that came later in Italy and then Germany: it began with resistance to social revolution, the primary role of leading financiers and industrialists, with action by the army and the church, denial of the class struggle, and an appeal to servicemen's masculine solidarity; it was followed by the use of 'special action groups', the denunciation of governmental weakness, the emergence of new men (often former revolutionaries who had supported the war), with a leadership cult, anti-semitism, attacks on democratic organizations, and, finally, the sympathy and armed intervention by allied governments.

The bourgeoisie await their moment

The Menshevik and Socialist Revolutionary leadership of the soviet would not take power alone. In July, they had called in loyalist regiments to escape from popular pressure, restore order in the working-class districts and bring back the Bolshevik regiments to discipline; then they began a witch-hunt of their enemies. Such methods were traditionally used by the ruling classes who naturally felt that, if such was to be the nature of government in Russia, they might as well take it over themselves. As Milyukov said, 'It is not yet time to set up a purely middle-class government, but it may well come, and quite soon at that.'[2]

The socialists would not govern without the liberals, so the latter controlled political life. Four months after the February Revolution they had apparently managed to turn the situation about to their own advantage; the time had come when the bourgeoisie could start laying down conditions to the soviet deputies and to 'democracy'. Neither the Kadets nor the other 'moderates' wanted, however, to ask too much of 'democracy's leaders', because they could lose their credit in the masses' eyes and become 'useless'. They must remain worthy of government. As Prince L'vov said, when he resigned as prime minister just after the July Days, 'To save the situation we could have broken with the soviets and shot at the crowds: I could not do it, but Kerensky could.'[3]

The liberal leaders knew, of course, that Kerensky was no tyrant. Using a Man on a White Horse, a true military dictator, seemed to them to be too dangerous and unsure, however: it was what the left feared, and the right prepared for. It might provoke a return of the flame, which was still smouldering under the cinders, and the middle classes wanted above all 'a return to normal conditions'. The Allies, on whom they relied, wanted the same; for both the ideal would have been a general restoring order under 'the red flag of democracy', with 'socialist' ministers neutralizing the soviets and general Kornilov neutralizing Kerensky.

While waiting for their 'Napoleon-figure', the leaders of the economy and finance began organizing to resist the progress of the Revolution. The first step was taken by the great industrialist, A. I. Putilov, who by March had established a kind of secret committee composed of representatives of the banks and insurance companies, including Guchkov, minister of war, and prominent figures such as Vyshnegradsky, chairman of the International Bank and president of the boards of a dozen large companies. This group speedily decided to become publicly known, under the title 'Society for the Economic Recovery of Russia', with the aim of collecting funds and of financing the bourgeois electoral campaign for the constituent assembly, acquiring newspapers and combating Bolshevism.[4]

Putilov's initiative met a ready welcome in high finance and heavy industry, which had the strongest connections with foreign capital. N. N. Kutler, a member of the Kadets and president of the Urals Mining Company which also controlled several metal companies in the Donbass region, joined in, as did representatives of the Russian-Asiatic and Azov-Don banks and of other large companies, subscribing 4,000,000 roubles. However it rapidly became obvious that a campaign of this type would be ineffective: there would have to be a military dictatorship. Kornilov was the obvious choice, and, as it happened, there sat in his cabinet one of the directors of the Russian-Asiatic Bank, V. S. Zavoyko, who was a member of the 'Society for the Economic Recovery of Russia'. He was to be the Cossack general's political adviser.

Another group, associated with the Bank of Siberia and the businessmen of Moscow, aimed at similar results. It was led by textile manufacturers and owners of light industry like Ryabushinsky and Tretyakov, and was less straightforwardly reactionary than the Putilov group because it was directly interested in an extension of the market for consumption, and could see advantages in a more flexible arrangement of society. To begin with, it had links with men close to Rodzyanko, who wanted to strengthen the Duma's political role, and they established the 'Republican Centre', which took as its motto the programme 'Order, Discipline, Victory'.

The Centre sought to become a movement rather than a party and, although industrialists financed it, it was intended to assemble 'patriots' of all descriptions, and even had a moderate socialist, K. V. Nikolayevsky, as chairman. It intended to bring the military organizations into the task of consolidation, and invited generals Alexeyev, Brusilov and Kornilov, with representatives of the 'Military League' and the 'Union of Officers', to join its military section. The prime choice seems to have been Admiral Kolchak, who was associated with Milyukov and was thought to be more flexible in his attitude to the Revolution than the other military men. Kerensky judged it prudent to send him away on a special mission to the USA, and the centre, thus caught short, chose instead general Kornilov who, it was alleged, would have known how to stop the soldiers retreating at Tarnopol.[5]

The bourgeoisie were organizing, collecting money, appealing to the military; soon the two groups were conjoined. Monarchist and anti-semitic groups started up at Petrograd and Kiev; whether or not associated with the bourgeois groups, the Kadet leaders seemed to be secretly pulling the strings.[6] The Kadets seemed to be the greatest political force in the country, at this time when the Bolshevik organization had been dismantled, and when the populists, despite the Trudoviks' fusion with the Peshekhonov socialists, had not been brought together to form a great Socialist Revolutionary party, and were now as divided as the Mensheviks. The Kadets had some twenty newspapers which re-peated the ideas of *Rech*, and there were more than a hundred sympathetic newspapers or journals such as *Russkiye Vedomosti* in Petrograd; the party also had guaranteed circulation via its adherents in the Moscow railway-network. At the seventh Party Congress in June L. A. Krol' had pre-sented a report on the need to increase provincial organization, especially in the countryside, if the party wanted a majority in the assembly elections. Agronomists (particularly numerous in Russia since the start of the century), doctors and co-operative members helped set up a plan of action, which resulted in a great increase in the number of Kadet sections, from 183 on 25 May to 269 on 22 July and 370 in October. The party was represented in 268 localities and, according to Astrakhan, totalled 70,000 and 80,000 members.[7]

This democratization scheme failed, however, despite the energy with which it was promoted, because the whole right joined the Kadets as the only organized political opposition to the Bolsheviks. It was not just the Octobrists − whom Savich officially invited to join the Kadets − but also monarchists and Black Hundreds; this changed the party's character and caused many people who had joined it, especially in the countryside, to leave it again. Milyukov's party, led by prominent men possessed of scientific and technical skills, associated in the countryside with the Landowners' League and in the towns with the industrialists, also got support from the military. On 12 August Milyukov wrote a draft speech advocating this policy: 'In the government [Kerensky's] conflict against the healthy elements of the army, our place is with the army.[8]

The generals organize

The military had also begun to stir. The supreme command had supported the Revolution but, at the time, no one had imagined that the Revolution would actually undermine discipline in the army as well as changing the government. The generals blamed the Soviet for Order No. 1 and urged the government to abolish this declaration of soldiers' rights. It was agreed that new military regulations would be introduced, but only in conformity with the military tradition. There could, however, be no agreement between men who wanted discipline to be more flexible and men who, with the general staff and the commander-in-chief, Alexeyev, regarded any concession in this domain as a prelude to disintegration and the collapse of the army.

In the meantime, 'disorder had increased'. The soldiers had set up committees and soviets where they challenged the officers' behaviour, the conduct of operations and the government's policy in general. If matters proceeded in this way, it seemed, the army would soon be useless. General Denikin shows how the officers of general headquarters felt impelled, from early April, to set up a 'Union of Army and Navy Officers' as against the soldiers; the officers felt victimized, and wished to coordinate their activities to restore discipline and recover their rights. Brusilov approved of the end, though not the means, saying, 'In the first place, it is dangerous to legitimize the principles of collective self-government that have been driven into the soldiery, and have ended in the formation of committees, soviets and congresses – these principles have done enough damage to the army. Moreover, the existence of an independent officers' organization would simply widen the gulf between officer and man'. He was completely against the scheme, but 'reality was destroying the framework of authority, and made mock of arguments and reasoning'. Since a draft law had already allowed the soldiers full liberty to organize committees, 'it would be unfair to deprive only the officers and stop them from using the means to secure themselves'.[9] A 'Union of Army and Navy Officers' was then constituted, under generals Alexeyev (former commander-in-chief) and Denikin, in the presence of Rodzyanko, president of the Duma, and the monarchist deputy Purishkevich. It stressed the rights of officers and demanded their restoration, and set up branches in Petrograd, Moscow, Kiev, Odessa, Sebastopol, Saratov and elsewhere. Military dictatorship seemed to be the only way of restoring order in Russia. Krymov's 3rd corps of IX Army was to be the spearhead, and the Ukraine and Don area would be the operational base.[10]

Brusilov, who had succeeded Alexeyev as commander-in-chief, was against these organizations, and he was considered by his colleagues to be a demagogue. Most officers felt that 'for centuries the officer has been the loyal and unstinting sentry guarding the Russian state, and only death can deprive him of his function. There could never be the slightest compromise with Revolution from those who saw the officer as something other than an acolyte of the tyrant.'[11] There were two possible ways of restoring the army's strength: either to set up, via the officers, a kind of army-within-the-army, or to install key elements in each regiment, via shock battalions composed of volunteers, to act as a fermenting agent of patriotism. The second idea, put forward by general Lukomsky, was preferred, and these *udarniye* were given better food, good equipment and, in the event of death, a pension for their families. They were energetically organized by the generals, as were the Battalions of Death, which were usually composed of officers who had been dismissed by the committees, and of soldiers who had remained loyal to them. However, some of these battalions were set up in a hurry and they refused, as others did, to attack. Their counter-revolutionary function was at once obvious, and on 26 June at Minsk, the soldiers' committees demanded that the *udarniye* should be dissolved, along with the other special units.[12] Brusilov, unlike his colleagues, had never been very enthusiastic about this kind of activity, because 'it divides the army'; and, at the conference of commanders-in-chief organized at general headquarters just after the failure of the offensive on 16 July his rivals managed to have him removed.[13]

Clearly he had lost his grip. He was followed by Kornilov who had been appointed as commander-in-chief of the south-western front some time before, and had sent a telegram to the Provisional Government on his own initiative, with only a copy to the supreme command, saying: 'This army of crazed fools is running away . . . we are going to ruin. . . . My duty is to say, though I have not been asked for my opinion, that the offensive must be stopped on all fronts so that we can salvage the army and re-organize it on the lines of the strictest discipline'; he thereby dared to say aloud what the generals did not dare even whisper, with Brusilov and Kerensky supporting the principles of democratization. It was also said that Kornilov had acted in consequence − dissolving units that refused to fight, disarming over 7,000 soldiers, shooting deserters and looters (marking their bodies with placards to explain why), forbidding meetings at the front, and dispersing them by force. The officers saw him as a way out of the imbroglio.

He did not attend the conference of ministers and commanders-in-chief on 16 July at general headquarters. Denikin wanted draconian measures; Kerensky and Savinkov, the commissioner, opposed them, but it was well known that the generals were deserting their commander – 'the atmosphere was dreadful'. Kornilov, who had been detained at his own headquarters, sent his suggestions by telegraph and was clearly behaving like a commander-in-chief; and the officers at the conference were quite ready to support him. He wanted the death penalty to be restored at the front, the officers' corps to be purged, the government commissioners' authority to be strengthened through the right to confirm death sentences, the competence of soldiers' committees to be limited, meetings, assemblies and Bolshevik propaganda to be prohibited, and delegations from the interior to be given the right to address servicemen only with the military authorities' permission.

These demands were universally accepted because Kornilov, unlike Denikin, Klembovsky and Markov, the commanders of the northern and western fronts and their chiefs of staff, sought only a restriction of the committees' competence, and not their abolition or that of the government commissioner system, the two 'gains of the Revolution'. He thereby bore out his reputation as 'plebeian general', and displayed his republicanism and hostility to any restoration of the old order. This was guaranteed by Savinkov, a former Socialist Revolutionary who had become commissioner on the south-western front – Kornilov would not restore the Romanovs. He was the son of Cossack peasants, and now he gained the confidence of his colleagues where Brusilov had lost it. His appointment as commander-in-chief was held to be the way to save the army and the Revolution. 'Kornilov, whose views are similar to those of the Provisional Government, is the man to save the situation.' Kerensky later said[14] that 'In a similar situation, forty years later, de Gaulle had to appoint general Salan. Like me, he promised him his confidence, but, like me, he had to be on the look-out.' The military had been won over to Kornilov, and so had the leaders of the economy; both believed that the future government would have to come round to their opinions, and pressure from the Allied governments was added to the internal urgings.

The prehistory of intervention[15]

When Tsarism collapsed, the Allies had one chief interest, to make sure that the Russian offensive planned for the spring would actually take place despite the upheavals caused by the change of government. However, despite initial satisfaction, the governments of Paris and London were soon wondering, not merely as to the effectiveness of the Russian alliance, but as to its very existence. To head off a disaster, they sent a twofold mission to Petrograd to revive the enthusiasm for war of the new

Republic. The Henderson-Thomas mission discussed what relations between the governments should be, while the Moutet-Cachin-Sanders deputation forged links between socialist parties. But it proved impossible to strike a bargain, whether on war aims or on methods of assembling a peace conference. As the Polish social democrat Kozlowski said, 'It has to be recognized that the working class of the western countries has developed excellent relations with the imperialist governments.'[16]

The mission was not altogether fruitless; when it came back, it neutralized to some extent the mood of open hostility that prevailed in official circles towards the new Russia, and it counter-balanced the effects of the ambassadors' and military missions' reports. Thomas and Henderson spoke warmly of the coalition government, and ordered a halt to the blackmailing of Russia in matters of supply which the economic and military missions had wished to exert 'as long as the Russians don't fight'. The Western Powers allowed Prince L'vov a respite until the offensive, which had been promised and constantly postponed. France and Great Britain had attacked in the west, and their generals were impatient for the Russian offensive, the delay of which was put down to 'events'. That comedy, they thought, ought to be ended at once.[17]

The Allies, while waiting for the Russian offensive, staged all kinds of delaying tactics against an international socialist conference at Stockholm. In fact 'disagreements between the socialist parties had been enough to block the assembling of this conference', but passports were refused to the socialist delegates by Allied governments none the less. There was much discontent in Russia at such 'sabotage', at least in circles where there had been faith in the efficacy of the conference.[18] When the offensive failed, the Western Powers' hostility became more open, and the Russians were held to be 'letting down' their Allies who would thus have to take on all the forces of the Central Powers. In reality the Central Powers − in the belief, shared by the Americans, that free Russia would fight better and further than Tsarist Russia − instead took troops from the west (the Nivelle offensive having just failed) and sent them to the east, where, in both absolute and relative terms, there had never been such strength before the summer of 1917. It was a fact not given prominence by the Allies or, later, by the Soviets.[19]

By the middle of July, it was the Russians' turn to ask their Allies to relieve them with an offensive: if it did not happen, then Russia's granaries would be within enemy reach and the remnant of the Romanian army would be threatened with extinction. But in the west, Pétain did not want to resume the offensive, after the failure of the Chemin des Dames attack and the ensuing mutinies; the British made promises they could only redeem later.[20] The French would preach to the Provisional Government and even think up sanctions against it, but on their own front all was quiet, whereas in the east there were large-scale operations – in Galicia, at Riga and later at Oesel.

There were other motives behind the Allies' hostility, which reflected older disputes between Russia and the Allies since 1914, and partly also the nature of the change inside Russia, for it could not fail to be harmful to the interests of capitalist states. The Allied governments, referring to the now ineffective Milyukov Note, pretended not to have heard of the coalition government's programme of 'peace without annexations or contributions'. They did not even answer these notes, except in Wilson's case, and even he, though apparently the least hostile to the new régime, let it be understood that he would not take account of the new policy. Lloyd George, Ribot and later Painlevé demonstrated their mistrust of the Provisional Government by not even informing it when they intervened in Greece and by successively postponing the inter-allied conference on the Balkans that the Russians expected to attend; when it met, in London and then Paris, the Russians were not invited, on the excuse that it did not concern them militarily. The Allies handled the question of Turkey and the Straits without reference to the chief interested party.[21]

The Americans had been similarly excluded, and since they had shown signs of good will towards the Provisional Government since March, it attempted to link up with the USA in both Near Eastern and Far Eastern affairs. At the same time, to forestall any 'trickery' by the British, French and Italians in Asia Minor, the Provisional Government planned an expedition to the Dobrudja for March 1918. In the Turkish rear, this expedition was to be paralleled by recognition of the rights of the Kurds and by military assistance to Kurdish guerrillas through Persia. The British accelerated their own advance on Mosul.[22]

Russia, though not represented at the London or Paris conferences that followed, none the less took the centre of the debate. At a time when the idea that Russia could be revived by dictatorship was still prevalent, the Allies wanted to 'help' the Provisional Government 'by a campaign of propaganda against the extremists' as well as military and economic assistance. Again in the Russians' absence, and even without informing the Russian chargé in Paris, Sebastopulo, they examined ways of reacting to a Russian withdrawal from the war. Each of the Allies had its function laid down, and the forms of intervention were thus emerging even if, as yet, the spirit was wanting.[23] In so doing, the Allies were not only ignoring the needs of Russian democracy, and asserting their own expansionism and predominance; they were also discrediting the régime in the eyes of its own public opinion by refusing it the kind of prestige satisfactions they would never have dared refuse to His Imperial Majesty the Tsar. Like the blackmailing over supply, it was a further means of indirect intervention in Russia's internal affairs.

After the turmoil of the July Days was ended, the Allies would not respect or spare the feelings of the Provisional Government. At a meeting of the Commission on Arms and Munitions Supply for Russia, on 11 July, they claimed that supply was delayed by the U-Boat war, then, of course, at its height: of the 195,000 metric tons promised in January, barely 65,000 were delivered. They also told the Russians that 'the revolutionary upheavals must be halted, order re-established and the army restored to its function, otherwise it would be pointless to go on with supply'.[24] The only answer could be a strong government; the Bolsheviks were the chief enemy. The Allies had already announced and spread the legend of the 'sealed carriage', and the discovery of documents that allegedly proved Lenin to be a German spy was guaranteed wide publicity. The diplomats were not slow to add some features to the documents: a Japanese attaché in Berne sent the information round the chancelleries that Lenin, after the July Days, had taken refuge in Berlin, whereas he had in fact hidden in Vyborg; the Italian minister at Oslo sent word, in his turn, that the Bolsheviks meant to open the way to Petrograd to the Germans. He never offered any evidence, but the British and American embassies at once demanded the arrest, trial and execution of the Bolsheviks.[25] Just after the financial and military leaders had put their faith in Kornilov, Buchanan began his own campaign, and, in government circles, acted the part of 'minister from abroad'. There was little scruple about interference in the internal affairs of an allied, sovereign state: 'he was "disappointed" at the softness of the repression after July. . . . The chance had not been taken for a complete break with the Bolsheviks. . . . There was cause for alarm. . . . Kornilov was the only man able to restore order',[26] were the British ambassador's words to Kerensky, and he added that Petrograd 'should be classed as coming within the front area'. In fact it depended directly on the prime minister, and Kerensky replied, 'You might as well tell me to pack up and go.'

As far as the Allied missions were concerned, it was just this that they wanted. General Knox reported that Kerensky relied too far on his gifts as a speaker, whereas action was now needed. He suggested sending a note to Kerensky where the British government, referring to the need for order, 'might drop Kornilov's name'. Later, he asked for a further note explaining that in the interest of the Anglo-Russian alliance, an understanding with Kornilov could be recommended to the prime minister.[27] The British secret service, of which at the time Somerset Maugham was a member, maintained links with the republican centre and the general staff. It counted on the commissioner Savinkov, a former terrorist who was now 'a sworn enemy of the Bolsheviks'; he had some influence with Kerensky and persuaded him to name Kornilov as commander-in-chief. Later still, when the Kornilov tactics turned into a Putsch, Locker-Lampson of the British military mission put his armoured cars at Kornilov's disposal. British soldiers, dressed in Russian uniforms for the occasion, were engaged in training certain units close to general head-quarters. However, Buchanan was against such direct complicity, and believed, like the Kadets, that the answer lay in closer collaboration between Kerensky and Kornilov. His sympathies were of course with Kornilov, and were obvious enough. But the scheme was not a test of strength, which no one, at least to start with, really imagined possible. The *Kornilovshchina* was to begin, under the *Kerenshchina*'s cover.[28]

2 Kerensky and Kerenskyism

Kerensky's popularity was enormous, and had grown continuously since February. He had persuaded the Duma to join the Revolution, had opened the prisons, proclaimed the rights of citizens, talked of equal rights for women and been first to mention peace; he remained the darling of the nation. He was the incarnation of the Russian people's generosity of spirit as they nourished the illusion of the bloodless revolution. It was well known that Kerensky had helped the men who had formerly imprisoned him to flee abroad, and he protected the Tsar's life as well. Men were grateful for this. Though Lenin mocked at him as 'the balalaika of the régime', he, better than anyone else, could sing the virtues of collaboration between the classes; he expressed with such fervour the mis-fortunes of the country and the need for sacrifice that even the Bolshevik Krylenko, though an opponent of the offensive and meaning to rebut his arguments, burst into tears when he listened to Kerensky in June, and swore he would attack, 'if necessary, alone'; in August, in the Bolshoi Theatre in Moscow, where a flag had been spread out to take gifts for the needy, Kerensky appealed to the generosity of bourgeois women and they threw him their jewels.[29] He was adored, and there are thousands of proofs of it in the archives – among them a poem of thirty-five stanzas, each with forty-four verses. The archives also show how people sent their love to all who were close to him: when his old babushka, or grandmother, took the train one day in August 1917, the word spread all around by telegraph and she was handed flowers at Smolensk, Oryol and Khar'kov.[30]

There were increasing numbers of servicemen, reservists and workers as well who agreed with the Bolsheviks that Kerensky, by virtue of this very popularity, was a dangerous man, the incarnation of policies that prevented the social revolution. He also failed to gain the sympathies of those who otherwise approved of the policy of class collaboration, and they were even frankly hostile. The Menshevik and Socialist Revolutionary leaders were especially irked at Kerensky's popularity, since they found it scandalous that such public acclaim should go to the very one of their number who had never written a word about socialism. This annoyance is expressed in their memoirs after the event: they stress Kerensky's histrionic talents, and thus show his lack of consistency. He was received in icy silence when he went to the *TsIK* on 4 August. The generals were also contemptuous or hostile. Alexeyev called him a 'chatterbox'; they might admire his eloquence when he toured the armies, but they could not help blaming him for all their troubles. At bottom they hated him and accused him of demagoguery because his strength lay in his oratory, because he regained his courage through them, and talked in private of the need for a strong government. They felt he was playing a double game, and did not realize that, as a democrat and liberal, he was essentially against party quarrelling and even soviets. Nor did they understand that Kerensky, son of a Jewess and hiding his shame, identifying himself with liberty and with Russia, was never so proud and content as when he did something he had always imagined impossible for him – taking the salute at a military ceremony.[31]

Kerensky, though attacked by the generals and despised by the party leaders who begrudged his popularity, could still impose himself as the indispensable man because he stood at the exact geometric centre of politics. To the right, the Kadets wanted 'all power, not just its shadow'; the same demand came from the Bolsheviks, to the left. His position as arbiter was a constant, as it were, and, like all politicians, he equated the centre with the point of equilibrium. He was entrusted by Prince L'vov with solving the ministerial crisis that had begun with the Kadet ministers' resignation and he behaved as if the July Days were merely an episode.[32] The crisis was solved in the classic manner of response to ministerial resignation – responsibility was thrown back. The Kadets imposed their conditions, identical with those of the Industrialists' Association or the Moscow Stock Exchange – war to final victory, postponement of social questions until the constituent assembly had met, war against anarchy and extremism, restoration of military discipline. To these was added a demand for the expulsion of Chernov, who was held responsible for disorders in the countryside. This suited Kerensky quite well but, although he bore Chernov a grudge for barring his way to the leadership of the Socialist Revolutionary party, he declared solidarity with 'the ministers of the *muzhiks*'. As his part of the 'bargain', Kerensky said he would not be responsible to the soviets, which again suited him perfectly. The Mensheviks gave way over this essential point, but Tseretelli, the champion of such responsibility, would not take a post.

The new cabinet, in which the strong man was Savinkov,[33] stemmed neither from the Duma committee, like the first Provisional Government, nor from agreement between it and the soviets' executive committee, like the coalition cabinet; it needed some sort of legitimation; for this purpose, Kerensky decided to assemble a conference of state in Moscow. Later on, after the Kornilov Putsch, he took up the scheme once more, with the Democratic Convention and the Council of State: it became the régime's only ideological offering. It was meant to terminate quality of power by depriving the soviets of their representative authority, and to restore the state by reinforcing central power. Because of the way in which the body was assembled, the first idea was achieved, and the debates were designed to make achievement of the second possible. 'The soviets' representatives must be given the physical sensation of not representing the whole nation' for, swamped in the midst of *zemstva*, municipalities, Duma, co-operatives, employers' organizations, officers' unions, these representatives of the soviets, as a new Third Estate dressed in smocks or uniforms, would inevitably be abashed by the prestige, the ability, the glamour of the élites, the 'vital forces' behind commerce, industry, technology and science. Power must be theirs as of right. One of the old order's crimes had been to prefer courtiers, incompetents; and it would be equally insane to hand any power to the soviets on the grounds that they represented the suffering people. The soviets must be given their due place, but no more.[34]

The opposition, which greatly disliked the method of representation chosen by the government, felt that 'they are setting up a cross on the tomb of the soviets, who are to be quietly buried'. The soviets, the real people, found themselves drowned by the 'political nation' for they were reduced to 229 deputies as against 488 from the four Dumas, who had been brought in for the occasion, and the soviets had only one-ninth of the seats. There were increasing numbers of protests and demonstrations. By 5 August the political committee of the peasant soviets of Ufa province put the question: why, if a convention is able to be assembled, is it not the constituent assembly on the basis of universal suffrage?[35] The resolution of the Bolshevik central committee supplied an answer:

The counter-revolutionaries are trying to consolidate. ,. . . They need popular approval and 'the nation's sanction'; and with this success, they will try for new ones. How will they do it? If they hurry the convocation of the constituent assembly . . . most peasants will disapprove of the war policy and the ruin it brings, with the arrests, massacres, executions; and they will not endorse this counter-revolutionary policy. So what is the way out? It is to convoke the Moscow conference of merchants, industrialists, landowners and bankers, members of the Tsar's Duma and tame Mensheviks and Socialist Revolutionaries so as to obtain, with the proclaiming of a conference, some kind of national assembly to approve the imperialist and counter-revolutionary policies. That is the solution they have dreamt up. Counter-revolution needs its parliament, its centre, and that is what they are doing. They need public 'opinion's' confidence, and they will get it. . . . This conference is just a conspiracy against the workers and soldiers, disguised in socialist phraseology.[36]

The political parties were hesitant in deciding how to react. The Mensheviks and Socialist Revolutionaries finally decided to take part 'so as not to run away' and to oppose reaction.[37] The Bolsheviks had been kept out of the soviets' delegation by the Menshevik-Socialist Revolutionary administration, but they did have a right to be represented, as a party. They decided to attend, but only to read a proclamation and walk out, as spectacularly as possible. They suggested to the Moscow soviet that a general strike should be organized for the day of the conference, but this was voted down by 364 to 277. They went ahead with instructions to strike, against their own soviet; and the order was followed by train and taxi drivers, electrical workers, some of the factories and office workers, for the people wanted to demonstrate in their own way. The same occurred with the booing that greeted the speakers from the propertied classes in the Bolshoi Theatre.[38] as to the democratic delegates, it scarcely needed the spectacular setting, the triple cordon of soldiers and subalterns in the bronze precincts of the Bolshoi, to make them feel ill at ease. They were not much affected by the eloquence of the military and the right, and they applauded only their own men. Conversely, only the well-dressed speakers received applause from the bedizened officers and the elegant feminine toilettes in the audience.[39]

In effect, there were two simultaneous debates at the conference of Moscow. In the first, orators of the 'hostile' classes spoke against each other. Chkeidze and Tseretelli, for the workers, stressed the legitimacy of soviets and said that it was not possible 'to act independently of the social forces sustaining the government . . . and the Cossacks cannot keep order without the democratic organizations'. Maklakov and Milyukov replied in the name of the propertied classes that the interest of the state must prevail over sectional interests.

A second debate went on among those who, while identifying themselves with the state, did not have the same ideas about the relationship between government and society. Kerensky and the right wing of the 'democratic' forces relied on representative institutions (not exclusively the soviets) and wished the government to act in their name; the right and the military, on the other hand, wanted to put direct pressure on the executive, and to force it along the right lines. General Kornilov, who was madly acclaimed, incarnated this idea.

Proletarii asked:[40]

> Who was the victor in Moscow? The capitalists won, the government having agreed 'not to let the workers be involved in business management'. The landowners won, because the government promised 'not to undertake any radical reform in the agrarian question'. The counter-revolutionary generals won, because 'revolutionary democracy', so-called, has been used as a tool, as a screen against popular anger. Now the counter-revolutionaries are not alone; the whole of revolutionary democracy is collaborating with them, and the result of the Moscow conference has been the coronation of counter-revolution.

There was more to it: the political exploitation of the cult of the glorious dead, spectacular ceremonials, draft laws on conscription of labour and the restriction of profits, continual reference to the state and the supreme interests of state, all amounted to a Russian variant of the para-Fascist model being assembled in 1917. One characteristic was to be the militarization of society, which Kerensky would not accept.

3 The Kornilov Putsch[41]

Kornilov had said on 30 July that 'We need three armies – one in the trenches, one in the factories or the rear, and one in the railways to link them . . . all three must be as disciplined as the front-line one.' The country was to be militarized, and the death penalty introduced on the home front as in the front-line zone. In the area he controlled directly, Kornilov used his authority to settle agrarian conflicts and telegraphed Kerensky 'not to interfere with my orders'.[42] The Kornilovites of course meant to pursue the war, but with a purified army. The authorities would demobilize four million men, and give them eight *desyatins* (about 2½ acres) of land each; the liberated officers would then undertake to regiment the home front, relying, in the countryside, on the peasant clientele that had been satisfied by the distributions of land. In industry and commerce, the government would close down the state monopolies and state intervention in the economy, which was an essential requirement of the bourgeoisie. A constituent assembly might then be summoned, but it would be immediately dissolved. Kornilov thought, to start with, that 'Kerensky and Co. will make way for me', and so did Buchanan, Lukomsky and many others. Men close to Kornilov imagined that he could come to an understanding with Kerensky. To him and the Kadets, it would be a stage on the way to the essential solution, military dictatorship. The Putsch would be a last resort.[43] However, Kerensky, who now felt trapped, had the sole intention of getting rid of Kornilov. He refused tc sign a draft of the general's regarding militarization of the factories, although, under pressure from a Kadet ultimatum, he did promise to take measures 'which might, in a concrete instance, empower use of the death penalty'.[44]

Kornilov was encouraged by the success of the Moscow conference and knew that a breach was unavoidable; he intended to push home his advantage. He prepared to transfer loyal troops – the 'Savage Division', composed of Tatars, Ossetes and Chechens – to compel Kerensky to purge the capital of Bolsheviks. An incident would be staged on 27 August, six months to the day from the beginning of the Revolution.[45] General Krymov was to be placed at the head of the expedition because Kornilov knew 'he would not hesitate to hang all the soviet members if need be'. In the large cities, the counter-revolutionaries could rely on the Volunteer Battalions, the Knights of St George and the dozen counterrevolutionary organizations existing in Petrograd and containing about 4,000 men centred around the 'Union of Army and Navy Officers'.[46]

The soviets and the Bolsheviks were rightly suspicious of Kornilov's real intentions, and denied that there was any kind of demonstration planned for 27 August. To provoke a fight therefore became more difficult. Kornilov substituted a variant: if the front at Riga fell back, then the Petrograd area would come into the front-line zone, and that would allow him to arrest the Bolsheviks, disband the soviets and control the government. 'Loss of Tarnopol turned Kornilov into commander-in-chief, and the loss of Riga will make him a dictator', prophesied the Bolshevik press. When Riga did fall, it may well have been arranged in advance for, by the end of July, Kornilov had had withdrawn from Ikskjuli the guns that protected the town so that when the German attack began on 19 August, despite the Russian resistance with inferior artillery, Kornilov ordered a retreat although his lion-heartedness in other similar circumstances had made him famous. The Lettish units that wished to 'fight for their capital' were brusquely rejected. A remark made in confidence by Kornilov to general Verkhovsky gives some indication of events: 'These chatterboxes can hardly stand up', he said with reference to the Provisional Government. 'We'll frighten them with a new break-through at the front. I didn't hesitate to retreat at Riga and that fairly put the wind up them.'

As had been foreseen, Kornilov required the capital area to be included in the military zone. Plan B was put into effect, with Savinkov acting as intermediary. To head off the coming conflict, he asked Kerensky to sign two decrees, extending the competence of courts martial and introducing the death penalty in the rear areas. Kerensky refused to sign.[47] He was warned by L'vov, Procurator of the Holy Synod, as to what Kornilov really intended, and he pretended to enter negotiations with him and to accept his conditions. In this, he used a ploy: he got Kornilov to repeat his demands in writing to L'vov, as if L'vov were the questioner. Kornilov fell into the trap and confirmed what he had said to L'vov orally. These demands were for transfer to the military authorities of all civil and military responsibility; resignation of the government; martial law in Petrograd.[48] Kerensky at once called a cabinet meeting, showed the tele-gram, then issued a proclamation announcing what Kornilov intended, and dismissed him.[49]

Savinkov intervened, and the four Kadet ministers, as if they were reacting to an order, resigned. Pressure was increased to make Kerensky hand over, but he would not.[50] The 'bourgeois' politicians failed to under-stand that, since 27 August, the initiative had lain with Kerensky, contrary to what they had imagined would happen. He, in excellent humour, and constantly breaking into airs from opera, drafted a *prikaz* (order) outlawing Kornilov and prepared an appeal to the country. In the general headquarters, where, a few hours before, the new government had been constituted around a bottle of champagne, the *prikaz* burst like a shell. The friends of Kornilov had never imagined that he would have to act militarily against the government, and the troops were intended to force Kerensky's hand, not to fight him. Kerensky's *prikaz* turned coup into Putsch. The Man on a White Horse could not turn back,[51] but his plans were collapsing. The lion-hearted general imagined entering Petrograd 'without a shot being fired'; but when he received the telegram dismissing him, the Redeemer's nerves of steel failed him: 'I fell ill, blew my nose a great deal and did not have the usual energy.'

Kerensky issued a second appeal which was more revolutionary in tone than the earlier one. At the same time, the administration of the military section of the soviet addressed the country: 'General Kornilov has betrayed the country and the Revolution.' Kerensky opened negotiations with the soviets' executive committee for the formation of a National Council; an appeal to the railwaymen was sent out; Chernov attacked 'the criminal plot against the liberty of peasants in uniform and against their right to land'. Postal workers and telegraph operators had been the first to react, by refusing to transmit on the telegrams and telephone calls from the general staff, and the railwaymen continued this by re-routing trains and putting the network into confusion. The Kornilovite forces 'looked on without understanding or doing anything': it was the Ivanov affair, repeated after six months (see vol. I, ch. 2). The printers in Mogiliev refused to handle Kornilov's pamphlets, and the town soviet clandestinely organized a meeting for the soldiers to react against the 'criminal general' and his orders. Even at general headquarters a battalion of the Knights of St George would not shout 'hurrah' to one of his harangues. The Petrograd press might give a prominent place to news of support for the rebels, but the adventure was obviously beginning badly.[52]

It was in fact coming to an end before it even started. At Luga, a place ill-fated for counter-revolution, loyalist militants and sailors from the capital told the Cossacks and the Russian soldiers with the Savage Division what was happening: they were won round, Krymov was arrested by the town soviet and sent to Petrograd. He was abandoned by the generals. Kerensky spared his life, but he put a bullet through his own brain forthwith. Kornilov, now a commander-in-chief without troops, was soon arrested in turn. Kerensky congratulated the armies on the 'bloodless failure of the mutiny'. In Petrograd, opinion had been alerted for the past few days, with soviet, district committees, trade unions and parties – especially the Bolsheviks – appealing again and again for vigilance.[53]

Organizing the defence against Kornilov had brought about a rapprochement among the leaders of the 'democratic' parties. They had fixed their line in the night of 27–28 August during the extraordinary meeting of the soviet. The Bolsheviks, who were speedily released from prison so as to take up the fight, had one constant and one variable: the former, 'that the conflict between the coalition and Kornilov is not that of revolution against counter-revolution, but simply that of two different methods of counter-revolution. Both Kerensky and Kornilov have to be fought by us, though in different ways.' The variable was that the theory held up to now, that 'association with the Mensheviks and Socialist Revolutionaries will bring us out of isolation', could no longer automatically be rejected, for, as the social basis of the combat broadened, the soviets' role could again become what it had been before July, and the Bolsheviks could consider collaborating again with the soviet leadership. Once more the Bolshevik organizations took up the cry 'All power to the soviets'. Lenin approved and supported this change of line, though it happened in his absence, because 'if we reject association with the

Socialist Revolutionary Mensheviks we will only weaken the fight against Kornilov'. In the 'Committee for Popular Defence', however, the Bolsheviks maintained their stance: no 'bloc' was set up. At the demand of a Bolshevik, Bubnov, a Committee for the Defence of the Revolution had been formed, under soviet patronage, and it took the name 'Committee for Popular Defence against the Counter-Revolution' (*KNBPK*). Its executive committee included five members of the soviets' central executive committee, two representatives of the trade unions, two of the Petrograd Soviet, three each of the Bolshevik, Menshevik and Socialist Revolutionary Populist parties, among them Bogdanov, Dan and Chernov. The committee called on Kerensky to express opposition to any military government. 'I'll stay on,' said Kerensky. For the first time, a Bolshevik (Nevsky) took a leading position at the heart of revolutionary democracy.[54]

4 The outcome of the Putsch: Bolshevism surfaces

We do not know what happened to the lion-hearted Kornilov's cold in the head; but we do know that, by the second day of the Putsch, Kerensky was no longer singing airs from opera, and this is not as illogical as it might seem, since Kornilov, once defeated, was of no interest. 'The importance of the episode was exaggerated'; it was a 'misunderstanding', said the Kadets, the bourgeois newspapers and the government's men. Kerensky was, however, still present; and if he no longer sang, it was because he knew his days were numbered. As he later said, 'If the Kornilov Putsch had not happened, neither would Lenin.' At the time he was more discouraged by the resignation of the Kadets in the middle of the crisis than by the Putsch, for he saw it as a sign not that they were in collusion with Kornilov but that they were abandoning Kerensky. Losing the confidence of the 'political élite' of the country discouraged him, for he could no longer count on it and the authority that it had over the military to counter-balance the soviets and the Bolsheviks' influence there.

At the political level, the Kornilov affair permitted the revival of the soviets, as well as the release and return in force of the Bolsheviks. Once more, the soviet could act as the 'proletarian fortress' of the social-democratic tradition, and all the popular forces rallied round it to defend it against the 'military-bourgeois element'. The Bolsheviks had taken a prominent part. They had been mobilized, after spending the weeks since July in proscription, to organize the action against repression. In their newspapers, they repeated that, ambition and character apart, this fight between 'two would-be Bonapartes' was occurring within exactly the same ideological framework – hence their utter surprise when the Putsch exploded – this 'completely unexpected insurrection' as Lenin called it. The slogan 'Down with Kornilov, and no support for Kerensky' allowed them both to fight the reactionaries, which popular opinion wanted, and to ignore Kerensky's own action, thus depriving the head of the government in advance of any credit he might have got for his own part in the victory. 'You must not think that, in adopting this slogan, we have departed from our real goal, the conquest of power by the working class,' wrote Lenin, 'No, we have got much closer to it, but diagonally rather than directly, and we now have to carry out indirect rather than direct agitation against Kerensky while fostering energetic action in the best revolutionary way against Kornilov. Only with such action can agitation bring us to power, but we must be discreet in our talk, even though we know that we may be carried to power by events, even tomorrow. Once there, we will never let it go.'[55]

Kerensky understood all of this. But he released the Bolsheviks, and accepted soviet help, thereby showing that he did not mean to abolish them or restore the death penalty. He was a democrat, and he felt only hatred for the reactionaries and anti-semites who clustered round Kornilov. After the July Days, in mid-reaction, he had been one of the few leaders to resist that tide. But he was fascinated by the liberal and reformist bourgeoisie, and identified with it; he failed to appreciate that it was prepared to sacrifice democracy to order, if need be at the price of military dictatorship. For it and for him, the main enemy from now on was Bolshevism, and it is significant that, just after the Putsch, Kerensky used the units trained by Kornilov to stop popular demonstrations from overwhelming the government's forces. Fifty years later, when he surveyed his own behaviour at the time, he remarked that 'During the Salan Putsch, de Gaulle was in the same position as I was – his quarrel with the generals had gone so far that he had to show them he was not the Communists' prisoner. He managed to persuade them, and I failed.' But there was much more to it than that.[56]

In previous crises, in April, June and July, the spontaneous initiatives of Bolshevik and anarchist soldiers had caused street demonstrations. The leading elements of the Bolshevik party had been forced, in the end, to assume responsibility for a movement launched by the young men of the military organization. As the cinema films show, there were considerably fewer workers than soldiers and sailors.

In the Kornilov affair, when the action was defensive, the reverse happened. The proletarian districts were first to mobilize, recruiting 40,000 men and arming 25,000 from the factories, through their committees, or from weapons left by the Kronstadt sailors during the July Days.[57] At Kronstadt and in Finland, these sailors were still the vanguard, but at Petrograd the soldiers had been affected by 'the July complex' and were relatively few, at most about 12,000. A further difference was that since the disappearance of the anarchists as a motive force, the militant grass roots and the higher echelons of the Bolshevik party came closer together. They remembered the effects of the lack of discipline in July, and were prudent with agitation that might provoke hostile action; the authority of the party leadership, which had been perspicacious in July, was greater. As the party requested, no demonstrations took place on 27 August. However, the grass-roots militants were ready for action; they responded instantly to the organizations' appeal against the Putsch because, unlike Lenin, who was pre-occupied with questions of overall strategy, they were not 'taken aback' at what had happened, because they had analysed things differently. Thus it was even possible for the Petrogradsky district committee to organize defence by 23 August, four days before the appeals issued by Kerensky, Chernov, the soviet and the Bolshevik party. Under the leadership of the Bolshevik Skorokhodov, this committee co-ordinated its actions with the other committees of the capital, planning for cars to go round to maintain communication, guarding factories, arranging information briefings at set times and the like. The inter-district meeting in Petrograd, the Red Guard (which revived owing to the *Kornilovshchina*) and the trade unions organized in the same way; and it was almost always at the Bolsheviks' urging that this happened, though sometimes the Internationalists or left Socialist Revolutionaries were involved. It was in August that the Red Guards and the soldiers first linked up. The people were mentally prepared, and the means for defence were made available, such that, when the organizations appealed, every citizen, tree, house and stone was set to oppose the advance of Kornilov, whose telegrams failed to arrive and whose locomotives got no water. The ground crumbled under his feet.[58]

There was no apparent necessity for the great mobilization of the populace that occurred in the next few days: not many people, either in Petrograd or in the seven other towns where a *KNBPK* was established, suspected that it was a dress-rehearsal for October. Six months earlier, in the evening of the shooting on 26 February, when the government side had won, no one foresaw the utter change that was to occur the next night; no one imagined that 'Revolution had gone three-quarters of the road'. At the end of August, just after the Kornilov affair, the changeover was just as complete. Before Kornilov's appeal to the country, reaction appeared to be winning at Petrograd, in the army, and the countryside, among the nationalities: the military, the notables, Duma deputies, bankers and traditional leaders seemed to be riding high. Milyukov observed, 'the Revolution is finished.' The church, seemingly effortlessly restating its traditional attitude, required sinners to submit, and there were prayers that the executioner would show mercy. The men of February had never been so submissive, recommending further post- ponement of the constituent assembly, and voting, in Tseretelli's case, against a motion recommending abolition of the death penalty. Political opposition appeared to be broken. The anarchists had vanished since July, the Bolsheviks had fled, or were in hiding. Lenin was concealed, under a disguise, in Finland; Trotsky and his friends, imprisoned since July, feared they would be murdered. Reaction had succeeded so well for two months that Lenin was sure that a Putsch would be quite pointless, dismissing rumours of it as 'absurd'. Kornilov equally felt he needed only to stretch out his arms for power to be his.[59] The appearances were deceptive, for, two days later, and without any serious trial of strength, the situation was reversed, Kornilov's authority disintegrating and Bolshevism being at the gates.

The military coup had of course stimulated the democratic side, and the logic of the resistance movement played in favour of the Bolsheviks, who had been the most consequential and determined.[60] But their strengthening, which was apparently so abrupt, was also the symptom of a much deeper, latent phenomenon – the radicalization of the masses, which the crisis so suddenly showed. The politicians and the militants had been unaware of it because, as usual, they had been measuring the discontent on the scale of their own organizations' activities, and from one pole to the other they made the same mistaken analysis. 'Bolshevism is dead: it died a sudden death', said *Rech*, the Kadet newspaper, just after the July Days. Lenin's companions thought the same.[61] Question- naires sent out to the delegates of the Sixth Party Congress in August showed, the investigators concluded, that the party had reached a new low in popularity. The militants were disheartened: as S. N. Ravich told the third Crogress of Towns,

We have been hard-hit by the July Days, so much so that for the next three weeks we could not even mention action, . . . By and large only the Menshevik-Internationalists have been able to carry on agitation . . . and the defensists had little success compared with them; at this time, only between 200 and 1,000 would appear at political assemblies, and at most 2,000 at meetings. Three of us were always, and everywhere, ready to volunteer – Slutsky, Yevdokimov and Volodarsky, who had to make only about forty speeches. By August, this had changed: the hundred efforts they made were not nearly enough, and suddenly, in September, our organization became swamped. . . . It was a tragedy for us, because we could feel our influence growing everywhere, but we had fewer and fewer resources, in proportion to needs.[62]

If this was true in Petrograd, it was still more so in the provinces, where the repression had not proceeded with the same energy as in the capital, or the army. The latent radicalization there had been shown in ways other than the strikes, factory occupations, arson of landed property or acts of collective disobedience in the army before it came out into the open: it had been translated to the representative level but in ways, or at strata that did not affect higher forms of political life. In the municipal elections which took place in the provinces later in July, for instance, the 'conciliators' had greatly predominated, winning over 70 per cent of the seats as against 40 per cent for the Bolsheviks and 15 per cent for the Kadets; and the Mensheviks' and Socialist Revolutionaries' success was greater still in the small towns. But there were 52 per cent abstentions in these elections, because no one bothered about them. In the very next set, however, which the Bolsheviks prepared for carefully, and where their opposition to the 'conciliators' was clearer than before, they won 23 seats to the Socialist Revolutionaries' 25, the Kadets' 2 and the Mensheviks' 4. In the municipal elections of the Petrograd district, on 22 August, the Socialist Revolutionary-Menshevik coalition took 72 seats, the Kadets 44, the Bolsheviks 69 and their Internationalist allies 8. A month later, in Moscow, 51 per cent of the votes went to the Bolsheviks, 20 per cent to the Kadets, 4 per cent to the Mensheviks; the Bolsheviks won an absolute majority in eleven out of seventeen district *dumy*. In the municipal *duma* their numbers rose from 11 to 475. Their progress was greater still, and began earlier, in the grass-roots of the proletariat: by 3 August, in the sickness co-operative elections held in some large factories of the capital, they took 190 seats out of 230.[63] But who bothered with elections to sickness co-operative boards? Yet, the Bolshevization of grass-roots institutions was the evidence of a very large-scale movement which came from the depths of society.

CHAPTER 3

The failure of the traditional institutions and authorities

The failure of authority was not solely a matter of the Provisional Government and the men of February. It also affected the kind of organizations and individuals that, despite the great crises of the past, generally maintained continuity, permanence and domination by a small number. In 1917, the upholders of order and morality, the officers, the judges, the civil servants, the priests and the professors were all challenged in their authority and rights. All kinds of authority were contested, as were all restrictions: orders, contracts, the law itself all came under fire.

An anarchist newspaper wrote,

Some of the leading social democrats believe that our time is characterized by a failure of authority, the want of government as a power organizing the country's life. The Revolution has rejected such authority altogether. It is a mass movement to smash all the old forms of life. Rousseau was right when he said that when peoples trust deputies, they lose their liberty. The people will no longer obey them. It is not just a crisis of government and authority: it is a Revolution.

The guardians of the various institutions said that all of this amounted to a rejection of country, family, morality, knowledge, culture, religion – the very basis of civilization. The institutions of society were identified with these virtues, and it was this civilization that the men of 1917 challenged, not necessarily the principles that the institutions claimed to represent.

In 1917, state and institutions collapsed, all of a sudden, once Tsarism had gone. The first to fall were those most closely identified with the old order, and then the priests and bureaucrats.[1] Then came others, particularly the military, whose old work had been not only to defend the country but also to maintain the social order that the Revolution sought

to overthrow. This chapter examines the disintegration of these institutions, and the collapse of the old authorities, especially in the army,
which was the object of the power-struggle and the keystone of social
order. In 1917 there came a dichotomy of social and patriotic functions,
an experience not met elsewhere in modern times.

1 The destruction of civil authority

'If no one will obey the laws of a revolutionary government, then it is utter
disorder,' wrote the chairman of an agricultural society to the ministry.[2]
An estate-owner said, 'The peasantry have totally ignored the instructions
contained in Volume X, Part I of the Code.' This was far from unique.
The marshal of the Yekaterinoslav nobility announced that 'here the land
committees have taken the right to interfere in the landowners' affairs,
and have replaced the courts in all matters of dispute. They begin by
stating that all written or oral agreements regarding the renting and use of
land are null and void, and, more rarely, they have even arrested landowners who protest.'[3]

Elsewhere the peasants were more aggressive, despite appeals for
order. They had absorbed the lesson of 1905, that the town authorities
would readily assist the landowners; therefore, they would disarm the
landowners and, in their turn, would arrest men whom they described as
'agitators'. On 20 July the Provisional Government forbade arbitrary
sequestrations, under pain of criminal law. It did not matter. 'Confidence
in the law has gone', wrote the Landowners' League of the Saratov area,
'the commissioners are supine, and when the peasants stole 300 stooks
from an *otrubnik* [a peasant who had detached his land from the rural
commune] one of the commissioners said "I can do nothing, it's a matter
for the people", while another explained that he could not summon up a
militia and a third that his militiamen had no arms.'[4] At Kazan in May, a
peasant assembly decided to take over certain estates. At the second
session of this assembly, in September, 'counter-revolutionary activities'
were noted, for twenty activists who had attended the session in May had
been imprisoned, and the assembly demanded an explanation from
Karasev, the public prosecutor. He would not give it, whereat the
prisoners were liberated by force. Similarly, at Saratov in September
demonstrators set free Bolsheviks who had been imprisoned there. At
Kiev, according to the press, the public in a court-room became enraged
at a priest serving the oath on a witness, made mock of the jury and
enforced an acquittal. The minister, to save his life, had to flee to the roof-
top of the court.[5] Law was no longer law, and, as with the old ways of
justice, the administration itself had collapsed.

Its upholders had known this for several months. In March, a commissioner of the Provisional Government at Penza telegraphed to his ministers that 'the election had gone smoothly. The civil servants have been expelled, but all is calm and there have been no excesses.' Later on a local newspaper announced that 'the peasant assemblies have disposed of the commissioners sent by the Provisional Government, in orderly fashion.' Commissioner Kuguchev then sent a corrective telegram to the minister, 'Not all have been expelled, and some have even been re-elected by the committees; it is the committees that have the authority.'[6]

It was the Kadets who were largely responsible for the administrative void, even though they, later, were loudest in complaint at it. By 5 March, without even a request from the Petrograd Soviet, the Kadet ministers had dismissed the governors and their assistants, a whole section of the administration. At the time, they imagined that they would be in government for a long time, and they allowed power to be transferred to locally-organized committees (*KOO*) that they controlled. When, as against these committees, and the municipal *dumy*, the power of soviets and other popular committees constantly grew, the Kadet ministers appreciated their error for, as the 'bourgeois' committees weakened before their rivals and the soviets, no administraion could provide for the continuity of institutions or the permanence of the law. To fill the gap, they increased the appointments of commissioners, who travelled quickly from the capital to the provinces. However, in Shingarev's words, 'journeys cannot replace a working administration'.[7]

Besides, as an administrative report of May showed, the appointment of a civil servant or commissioner appeared as an attack on fundamental liberties. What happened in Samara was not an isolated instance: at Novgorod and elsewhere the commissioner named by the Provisional Government had to submit to the test of election.[8] The next stage of the process occurred when the government gave the local committees the task of choosing candidates for the commissioner's post; and soon it was only these committees that had authority. In August the second conference of commissioners recognized the failure: power came, not from the central government but from the local bodies, the soviets, which had already constituted the elements of an alternative government, independent of the state.[9] To gain obedience, the state could no longer add to its own power that of the priest or the professor; above all, it could not rely on the armed forces, for the army no longer filled its traditional repressive role.

2 The Revolution in church and university

'Nowadays we feel quite useless', wrote the vicar of Kostroma to his bishop, and a priest in Barnaul said the same: 'My parishioners will nowadays only go to meetings of the soviet, and when I remind them about the church, they tell me they have no time.' A chaplain observed the same thing in the army: 'Earlier on, you could not count the worshippers – 200, 400 would come. But now there's only a handful of them, and most are officers.' Observance dropped away, but religion had marked the Russian people too deeply for religious needs, sentiments and habits not to revive in some form; and after February aspirations for a new life led to disaffection from the church: 'Prayers don't liberate; your praying is futile.'[10] There were long roots to this disaffection. Although, in Alain Besançon's words, 'Christianity was a point of warmth in a cold world, and one of beauty in a harsh age; it created an equilibrium which, until the Revolution, allowed men to put up with impersonal relationships and the hard realities of service',[11] once the Revolution had come, the old church, having failed to regenerate itself, could only lose yet more credit. The Russian clergy were 'greedy, drunken and corrupt' – abjectly servile towards the state, contemptuous of the misfortunes of the poor. It had not participated in revolt as the western churches had done; in 1671 it had excommunicated Stenka Razin, and in 1905 had accused the rebellious workers of being in Japanese pay.

The history of the Orthodox Church was a very selfish one, with endless demands and forgetfulness of its mission. The clergy had some 'social work' to its credit, particularly as regards schools, but even then the children of the poor deserted them, early in the century, for the *zemstva* establishments, whilst the religious revival that converted part of the Marxist intelligentsia to Christianity was of too recent date to affect relations between church and faithful significantly. Besides, Struve, Berdyayev and Bulgakov challenged the mystique of revolution, saying that 'the love of egalitarian justice and of the public good . . . merely paralyzes the love of Truth', so that they were hardly likely to get a hearing.[12] The First World War brought the faithful back, and the bishop of Vladivostock gleefully recorded that 'this war has revived religious sentiment, creating a great change among the people, for the churches have never been so punctiliously attended. The war is a punishment from God for the people's lack of faith.' There were many miracles accompanying this revival. In the Kozlov area in 1916, for instance, a female fanatic set light to a village where she had seen the Anti-Christ. When a woman teacher said it was not possible, she had to take refuge in the school from villagers trying to murder her.[13]

By the early weeks of 1917, the bishops noted a relapse. The war was lasting too long, and 'people came to confession less than they did last year' while 'front soldiers no longer come to church'. The village priests saw this as 'youthful folly', but many of them had an idea that the end of the war would be the end of religion. When the Revolution came, they noted that, 'Where people used to hide their feelings, now they proclaim them openly; they insult us, and say they do not believe in God or the Devil any more.' The clergy were naturally opposed to the Revolution from the beginning. They told the faithful to support the L'vov government – as a way of combating the soviets – but refused any role in the funerals of victims of the Revolution so that even the Kadets regarded the church's attitude as excessively conservative. The higher clergy rapidly became a simple reactionary chorus, preaching restoration of the Tsar. After the July Days they anathematized the Bolsheviks and they publicly supported Kornilov, sending ikons and gifts to him 'for the military to restore religious principles'. There were several appeals to the soldiers: 'The spirit of the army can revive only through that faith in Christ that alone can accomplish miracles.' The church also wanted to see 'the power of the military authorities restored to the full'.[14]

The Revolution even brought about a return to a measure of community of faith among the churches. The Old Believers, for instance, who traditionally and for centuries had been in the vanguard of the social struggle (Lenin and Bonch-Bruyevich stressed their revolutionary mission) declared solidarity with Milyukov and Kornilov at their national congress, held in August in Nizhny Novgorod, and demanded Constantinople as 'ancient centre of ecclesiastical culture, the hope of the Russian clergy as a whole; the government must be deaf to the Germanophiles and traitors, and . . . do all it can to bring these ancient sanctuaries under the guardianship of the Russian people'.[15] The Baptists were liberals, and they tried to be more democratic. They set up a party, *Voskreseniye* ('Resurrection') in March, the programme of which allowed freedom to strike, women's rights, the eight-hour day, etc. In the July Days there was a reversal of attitude; in *Slovo Istiny* they attacked all social democrats and said their ideas were 'against the spirit and teachings of Our Lord'. At the democratic conference, I. S. Profanov demanded in their name a 'revival of the army'. But they were not Kornilovites, and they did not go so far as the counter-revolutionaries. Nevertheless they, with other democratic organizations, condemned the October Revolution, and public opinion lumped them together with the priests of other churches.[16]

In these conditions, the reforming priests in the council did not have much effect, and in any case they were mainly concerned with the status of the church and its relationship with the state; while the demands of the more radical priests really concerned the clergy themselves – they wanted to use the church lands themselves, but said not a word of the *muzhiks* who wanted the lands of the great estates. In so far as the Orthodox Church recognized the Revolution, it was purely an internal affair: the liberals trying to win power in the clergy assemblies, and the radical lesser clergy deposing bishops who were recalcitrant or reactionary. No one bothered with peasants, workers or soldiers save at the great assembly in August which 'exhorts the people to return to order and the authorities to show mercy', and then returned to its favourite theme, relations between the bishops and the council.[17]

Thus, while the masses dreamed of a new world, their spiritual guides took advantage of the liberty they had been accorded to resume a quarrel of an earlier epoch, and such behaviour could only further discredit the church. A chaplain, Dmitry Polyansky, told his bishop:

> I should like to relate to you some details that reveal the moral and religious attitude of the troops. . . . In the 170th regiment, in which I was chaplain until I left in June, the soldiers said they disapproved of my priestly function, and at a meeting on 21 May they said why: it was because I fought tirelessly against Bolshevik slogans such as 'Down with the war', 'Fraternize with the Austro-Germans', 'Distrust your officers' and 'Elected officers'. They did not like my distributing ikons and religious leaflets. I was also told at the soldiers' assembly that no one believed in me, because I was an acolyte of the old order; they said I had better go, or violence would be done. This is not simply a matter of mistrust of individual priests, it is a rejection of God, and the same attitude as is taken to the priests is also shown to those who listen to their 'fables', which is why, with only from ten to fifty men turning up to my services, I requested a transfer.[18]

Resentment of the priests was much greater in the countryside than in the towns where, in October, the queues 'standing before the church porches to pray for the delivery of Russia from her internal and external enemies were as long as the ones for bread'. In the countryside the priests were often allies of the landowners, and peasants 'look at us with hatred'. Another priest in the Voronezh region reported that 'the *muzhiks* are taking over our land'; in the Romanovo-Borisoglebsky district, the deacons and psalm-singers got together in arms to defend themselves; in the Moscow area, a bishop wanted government intervention to help the priest at Ulitin, for 'the peasants have taken over all of his arable land and most of his harvest . . . they threaten to take the timber he has felled. . . . They are united, and do as they please. The church is powerless, and from now on the parish may do without its priest, because no one comes to mass.' It was the same in the Ukraine, in Volhynia, where peasant attacks on priests were many. Here the movement also seems to have affected the towns: priests at Khar'kov and Zhitomir were expelled from their churches because of their politics.[19] One priest said that a peasant had told him: 'We are bound hand and foot, and delivered over to the evils of Tsarism. . . . You went along, and confused us so much that we could not even see who the executioner was';[20] another remarked that 'for centuries a few nobles and landowners subjected millions of poor people, bled and sweated them − and you priests said it was right, chanting in chorus "Long Life to the Tsar and our Leaders"; yet, now that the people has power and is trying to establish equality, you, the "Holy Men", will not recognize us. We have seen how futile are your precious mitres, your golden crosses and your rich vestments.'[21]

It did not need Bolshevism for the Russian church to be persecuted. That movement came up from the depths, for the masses had associated priest with Tsarism, officer and gentleman. Pierre Pascal said that 'the established church, deprived of its most religious elements, and forced by the authorities to betray its mission and serve political ends, lost both the ability to satisfy its parishioners' needs and its character as independent, religious society'. The people's hatred of the church was not a matter of anti-clericalism or atheism or irreligion; it went much deeper.[22] Moreover, the Russian Marxists, who had learned Robespierre's lesson, never laid the accent on the war with religion, where they would have risked unpopularity. Like all the Marxists of the time, Lenin believed that 'we should destroy the social roots of religion rather than attack the clergy and the faith with anarchist phraseology',[23] and after October the Bolsheviks did not take any discriminatory measures against orthodoxy. They did take over the church lands, but only as part of a general campaign against large estates, not as an action against the church as such. Similarly, although there were measures against the counter-revolutionary activities of the clergy, the exercise of worship was left alone, while civil marriage and separation of church and state were measures that all of the socialist parties, and even the Kadets, had proposed. These measures were none the less resented as discriminatory − for many centuries the church had regarded itself as persecuted if it were deprived of its position as the established religion, or even if it were prevented from persecuting in its own way. The first real discrimination against it, according to Kolarz, occurred during the great famine in 1922: it was stipulated in the decree of 23 February that the churches (and they alone) should give up objects of value.

It was the new patriarch, Tikhon, who in 1917 opened fire, pronouncing the Bolshevik régime anathema. Attacks on individuals did in fact occur before 1922, though they affected the hierarchy rather than the lesser clergy or the faithful; moreover – a pattern reproduced elsewhere – the persecution did not stem from the Bolshevik party, at least to begin with, but from the masses, with the various committees acting spontaneously though never disavowed by the party.[24] The real persecution came later, during the second revolution of the Stalin period, when the nature of government changed and freshly-urbanized rural elements took over from the Old Guard of the Revolution. Persecution was not merely covered by the government: it came from the state[25] and affected not only counter-revolutionary activity but religious observance in general.

The universities followed the church into shipwreck. The professor had, within a few weeks, become as discredited as the priest, the bureaucrat and the judge. One instance was the university of Odessa, the minutes of whose council meetings have, fortunately, survived to give a daily record of the revolutionary events as the professors saw them.[26] Since the reform era there had been some democratization of student intake. There were no sons of working men among the students, but there were, at Odessa, 147 sons of better-off peasants among 2,267 matriculations (6 per cent – one of the lowest such figures in Russia). This university counted as the most reactionary in Russia.[27] Sons of civil servants, nobles and clergymen formed a large majority of the students, but there were no legal obstacles to stop entry into the university of men who had the necessary paper qualifications and could pay their way, and the non-privileged categories, benefiting from the democratization of education since the turn of the century, were beginning to enter in larger numbers. The only restriction was the *numerus clausus* affecting the Odessa Jews – they were unable to take up scholarships, and if they taught they could not rise above an assistant post.[28]

After 1905, in fear of the violence that had accompanied the revolutionary events at Odessa, the professors of the university abandoned their feeble liberalism, and there were no limits to their docility as regards the government. In 1916 the rector ordered them not to admit to their number a professor, Shchepkin, and they obeyed, although they themselves had adopted him as candidate for the the electoral college. Again in 1916 they did not dare to change the lectures in oriental art history from Fridays at ten o'clock a.m. to Mondays at the same time without authorization from the ministry, which they solicited through the proper channels. The request was sent off with the correct amount of notice, and the ministry's agreement had still not arrived by February 1917. In fear of sanctions, the subject was not taught at the university at all. The same had been true since 1897 of western literature, since 1910 of art history, and since 1907 for history in general. The municipal council's reaction to the university's request for funds was 'Go to the Devil' – 'If we could just close the place down, what a good thing it would be.' There was a strike, 89 per cent of the students joining in, but most of the professors would not follow: 'We are not politically active.'[29]

It was this that annoyed the students, whose view was that 'study should train us for life, and not be an end in itself', and who wanted the university to help them understand the world — not to shut itself off. But, as the students discussed such things, and held meetings, the college of the professors of the faculty of history and philosophy busied themselves with an altogether different matter, the election of a rector. The first procedural skirmishes were fought, before the voting could take place, and the atmosphere was tense, when a noisy crowd entered the university — the students had come to tell their professors of an event that was not on the agenda, the final success of the Revolution, and the abdication of the Tsar.

A meeting was held in the university, and students of the teachers-training institute joined in, much to the annoyance of the council, the minutes of which complained at the attendance at this meeting of 'students not of the university'. The Odessa students sent greetings to Rodzyanko, to their proletarian brothers, and to the commander-in-chief: with a people's army, they said, victory would be secure. A few days later, another student resolution declared that 'the war must be fought until the people's will is expressed through the constituent assembly', and they requested the people of Odessa to remain orderly, 'so that reactionaries cannot exploit the situation'.[30] The professors drafted and signed, for their part, a declaration of their own on 'the need for victory'. The students wished to know how they reacted to this extraordinary event, the collapse of Tsarism, and students of various faculties went to the first lecture to take place after the announcement of the great event. It was given by the professor of the faculty of medicine, Batuyev. He barely touched on the events, although reminding the students of 'his brothers at the front'; then he came to the political crisis with the remark that one of the main problems in Russia was that of the nationalities — which enabled him to talk at length about his own interest, which had to do with the Cheremis. Then came the professor, Orlov, who told the students that now the Revolution was over, and they should get on 'with hard work'. The students were disappointed and kept their applause for the old professor, Lyasenkov, who said, 'I envy you, because you'll have a new life; and I'm glad to have lived to see the day.' A few days later, the university council assembled and suggested bringing in the professors who had been kept out in Tsarist times: Shchepkin's case was mentioned, but a majority of the votes went against him 'because he does not belong to the university'.

The students met, and re-started the criticism of the teaching that had begun just before the Revolution. Students of history and philosophy demanded: (a) that the type of examination should be changed, because the term had been shorter, (b) that the marking system should be different, (c) that certain compulsory subjects should be dropped, such as, classics, theology and the second modern language, as well as Sanskrit, Byzantine literature and the history of the Ancient East. There were other demands, rejected out of hand by the professors. The lectures were not attended, and classrooms filled only for political meetings. Work stopped, the government did nothing, and the conflict between students and professors grew in violence. On 27 March the rector resigned.[31]

Some weeks later, the nature of the battle changed. The students had set up committees and demanded a share in the running of the university; they also demanded the dismissal of professors who opposed the Revolution. The council had elected a new rector, one of the eight liberal professors. He sought government intervention against the 'troublemakers' who were supported by the town's soviet. There was in fact not one extremist on the student committee: there were 22 Mensheviks or Socialist Revolutionaries, 16 from various nationality organizations, such as the Jewish socialist labour party, Zionists, Bundists, Ukrainian Socialist Revolutionaries and 12 Kadets, but not a single Bolshevik. None the less, the students attacked the content of curricula, and the university tradition; the old programme, accepted only by a minority, was rejected by the young, and especially by the new elements that had entered the university since the explosion in February – the Jews, Romanians, Ukrainians, and, especially, the women, who had risen from 20 to 50 per cent of the intake between February and October. The rector had refused to let these newly-registered students attend classes, but his authority was constantly challenged, and he resigned, in his turn, in September. Professor Shchepkin was finally elected as rector, and the university then agreed to establish a set of lectures on politics, 'so as to train students for the constituent assembly elections' (8 October).[32]

It was obvious that the professors greatly disapproved of what had happened in 1917. The students' activities were regarded as an intolerable intrusion. Most of the students were in fact anti-Bolshevik, but, after October, *Narkompros* (the People's Commissariat of Education) decreed reforms that they had proposed or introduced – political and polytechnic courses, as well as a much wider intake of students.[33] What happened to the university at this time is unknown, for the city of Odessa was taken over first by the Germans and then by the Allies, but it is clear that the professors were very hostile to these reforms. It was still more hostile to the political supervision which Lenin, in the face of such ill-will, imposed on the universities and the schools.[34] From 1917 onwards, this resistance to change discredited the professors in the eyes of their students, and, for committees and soviets, the professors become identified with the old régime, except for a minority of scientists and physicists whom the future could only benefit, given the Marxists' keenness to conquer Nature.[35] In 1917 the professors, like the priests and the bureaucrats, could no longer play their self-set role as guides: and the officers' corps turned out, in this respect, to be even more wanting.

3 The dichotomy between the army's patriotic and repressive functions

'What was to happen to the army was a vital matter for every party,' said the Bolshevik Podvoysky. It was also a vital matter for the Provisional Government and Russia as a whole, because the army was the keystone of the social order, and the upholder of national independence. How would it be affected by Revolution, in the middle of a war? In February, the great question had not been what the army was supposed to do, but whether the Revolution would regenerate it, or weaken its capacity for offence and defence. The answer, a few weeks later, was unanimous: the country's ability to fight was being undermined, and the Revolution was destroying the army.[36]

This certainty has remained. Just the same, the German advance between February and October 1917, looked at on a map, was modest – even tiny. The losses of the Central Powers in the actions fought in the east were heavy; and the statistics also show that there were more Austrian and German divisions in the east in October 1917 than in March, and fewer in the west.[37] The certainty is thus a legend, and the legend a false riddle, quite failing to explain why the Russian generals regarded 1917 as marking 'the end of the army' whereas the German generals and soldiers found it unmistakably still there. The Russian military authorities felt that, since the army was not blindly obeying them, it could not be 'still there', but the soldier, guarding his country, was still present for the Germans. There had been a dichotomy in the two traditional military functions, repressive and patriotic. The patriotic function held up; the repressive one did not. This owed much to Bolshevik doctrines, which resulted in a change of consciousness, the effects of which were to make October possible. In this chapter, the processes and the results of this change of consciousness will be shown.

The change in consciousness

The army had been delighted at the fall of the Tsar. Soldiers at the front

and in the rear sent letters or telegrams to the Petrograd Soviet, expressing their sufferings, their hopes and their dreams. They behaved much as
did other parts of the population, but with a difference. The workers were
sometimes grouped in trade unions, or political parties that spoke in their
name. No one talked for the ordinary soldiers, except the ordinary
soldiers. For most of them, the Petrograd Soviet was the only power
whose legitimacy they recognized, and it was also their only means of
expression.[38] In obedience to its appeal, they set up company or battalion
committees (soon to become 'soviets') and their representatives participated in debate at the Petrograd Soviet, where they felt at ease.

The soldiers discover the social function of discipline

In March and April, soldiers of the front and rear had both expressed
desires which to some extent linked up with, and developed, various
aspects of Order (*Prikaz*) No. I. They complained, as the *Potyomkin*
sailors had done, at the abuse to which they had been subjected by their
officers – excessive punishments, violence, arbitrary behaviour. They
wanted to be treated as human beings, and did not want to be insulted
by being addressed in the familiar form (used with children or animals),
or with degrading formulae; they did not want to salute and present arms
in the old way. As citizens, they wished to keep their civil and political
rights of information, assembly and petition. Order No. I had stipulated
that the soldiers would adhere to strict discipline on active service and in
their units, but, in political and private matters, they were not to be
deprived of the rights the Revolution had brought, and these wishes were
repeated again and again, with many resolutions to demand total alteration of military regulations. To these grievances were added the
complaints of servicemen everywhere, who had undergone a nightmare
for the past three years, and who resented the incomprehension of people
at home of the extent of their sacrifice. They wanted improvements in
their conditions, and thought that the authorities should think about this,
and improve 'the awful food we have to gulp down'. Their wives often
had too little money, and they wanted pay increases, a raising of family
allowances and guarantees against loss of their ability to work 'because
many of us will come back invalids, unable to meet our families' needs'.
In these demands, the twofold character of the Russian soldier emerged,
as both citizen and soldier. Matters of class did not appear here, although
most of the soldiers were peasants.[39]

That there were so many documents demanding changes in military
regulations, or rights for a nationality to have its own military units, is
evidence that most of the soldiers did not expect to return home very

soon. They hoped, of course, that establishment of a new régime would hasten peace, but this did not mean they would demonstrate, or not do their duty. On the contrary, they said that 'the spirit of free Russia can only flourish from the granting of the soldiers' wishes' and that 'changes in regulations will not damage units or active operations'. They were always concerned to stress their sense of patriotic duty.[40] In their view, Order No. I and the resolutions accompanying it did not in any way mean 'the end of the army'. During the Stokhod alert on 10 March there was no desertion, and discipline was reinforced by the operation. It was only the end of a particular kind of discipline that they wanted, and, though they might accuse some officers of abuses of it, they ascribed the regulations as a whole to the autocracy, and assumed that a new régime would auto-matically alter them radically. As Wettig has properly demonstrated, the soldiers, apart from attacking opponents of the Revolution, 'had no consciousness of attacking their officers as such; they wanted to take part in the revolutionary movement, and intended not to change the military system but to participate [in all decisions] and where the officers announced their loyalty to the Revolution, they were recognized as legitimate superiors, the soldiers immediately returned to discipline'.[41] However, most officers behaved in such a way that the soldiers concluded that the military institution itself, and not simply regulations, belonged to the old order. The *Prikaz* had offended the officers, affecting their rights to command and decide: it had reversed roles, since the soldier's decision had been imposed on the officers, whose rights had been restricted by it. The officers were now anxious to legitimize the army's function, and to make an absolute right to command the principle, and reason, in their own commissions. In the soldiers' eyes they therefore became identified with the old discipline and hence also the old order.

Traditions of obedience to hierarchy did of course inhibit a large part of the officers' corps. General Alexeyev had told Guchkov that 'as commander-in-chief I refuse to consider ways of destroying the army'. This set the tone: and many officers, despite the commissions and the draft declarations of soldiers' rights, felt that any alteration of regulations was an affront to their dignity and honour, and a 'blow against Russia'. It was the same as regards recognizing soldiers' rights and the legitimacy of political discussion in the army.

They were affronted by this challenge to the military order. It was intolerable to them that ordinary soldiers should be regarded as citizens in the same way as themselves or that matters should be discussed on equal terms in a committee. They held the soldiers to be incapable of considering questions that were the officers' affair. Then they realized, anxiously, that they had themselves never thought about the matters raised in these committees, whether of politics or of discipline. They had never seriously analysed the ancient institution that protected them, or considered its relationship with the social and political order; they had always been very neglectful of public affairs and ignorant of political problems.[42] The Russian officers' corps had been more separate from civil society than in other countries and the first meetings in March brutally showed their want of political culture and their inability to deal with problems that were often easily within the capacity of some subalterns, NCOs and soldiers. In the first weeks of the Revolution, many officers had taken a part in political meetings, but after that they stood aside, because their inability to discuss matters of war and peace could discredit them as leaders: the soldiers might doubt their right to command.

Once the wind changed, by August, one of the first aims of the military authorities was to regulate the debates and compel the soldiers to tell their officers in advance what they were going to say in their contribution; the next stage was of course to forbid all political debates in the army. This was interrupted, and stopped, as an effect of the Kornilov affair.

There was a large minority among the officers who took a different attitude. It seems to have been composed essentially of adjutants and lieutenants who were living in the trenches, sharing the soldiers' lives and incurring the same dangers. Men who in civilian life would have been completely different could be united by the 'front-line spirit', and these officers and men frequently felt great resentment towards the staff, and towards all of those who ignored their sacrifice, whether shirking workers or war profiteers.

For most of the officers, however, Revolution or not, relations with the men remained primitive: the man was judged by how he obeyed, saluted or presented arms. Saluting was the true sign of submission. Since the *Prikaz*, the soldiers did not salute as before, nor did they obey as before. They would not take the oath to the new régime. The officers reacted, because they were convinced that without oaths and salutes there would be no discipline, and that without discipline there would be no army. Indiscipline in the face of the enemy became treason, and from treason to execution was a short step. This summary syllogism constituted the mental furniture of many of the officers − and without even very much animosity, for they even felt some pity for men they regarded as savage, drunk on liberty, and to be saved despite themselves from the effects of propaganda that might lead them to execution. 'This can't go on', they thought: but it did, despite the *prikazy* and the plans for reform.[43] After the July Days there was a common illusion that disintegration was over; and, as the soldiers and NCOs of the Kiev garrison wrote, it had been clear for some time 'that the officers have not really understood what the

Revolution is about'. For instance, general Ostrzhansky, still, six months after the fall of Tsarism, could send a report to the high command which proposed measures to restore the army: 'There must be preventive measures [sic] to give the soldier the habit of discipline; that will save him from the death penalty. We must in particular restore saluting, though in a different way – it could for instance be done away with at stations or in the front, and the distance could be reduced to 40 paces, even five paces in certain circumstances.' That summer, a general in the Caucasus army imagined that the virtues of obedience could be revived by substituting physical jerks for gambling and card-games in periods of rest, for the soldiers, tired out, would not have the strength to disobey. The men involved were Georgians, Armenians and Azeris; they mutinied, and this wretched officer was killed by them for his lack of psychology.[44]

Patriotic feeling and class struggle

The background to all of this was of course the question of peace, but its link with matters of discipline and officers' behaviour was not clear, and had to emerge from events. Oddly enough, the soldiers found it difficult to express their hopes for peace just after the Revolution, although before the fall of Tsarism peace had been the *leitmotiv* of their letters and claims. For the first two or three weeks, the soldiers, though hoping for peace, talked only of their patriotic duty – which is easy to understand.[45] Just after the fall of the Tsar the soldiers like everyone else wanted a constituent assembly, a democratic republic, and measures in the social and political fields that were not yet specific and did not yet have clear significance. They also insisted on those of their claims that affected them as combatants, rather than as citizens, which implied that they could not see an immediate ending to the war. They did want peace, of course, but said they would still do their patriotic duty. 'For the soldiers', they declared, 'the change of régime will mean the end of the war.'[46] Even so, the men of the 6th artillery park, who were still influenced by the propaganda of the old régime, asked the soviet whether pacifist speakers and people who supported the striking workers should not be regarded as provocateurs;[47] and they were not alone, because Bolshevik records reveal how much difficulty the militant workers had in discussing peace with the soldiers. In Russia as elsewhere there was an almost unspoken animosity, which had nothing to do with class, between the combatants and the home front. The fighting soldiers regarded the rear as being made up of shirking workers and profiteers, especially the bourgeoisie and the *kulaks*, 'who fill their bellies while we go hungry', but also the workers, who annoyed the soldiers by the demands they made, even though their lives were not in danger. Many soldiers' and sailors' letters stated that 'while the workers complain of having to work over eight hours a day they ought to remember that soldiers have to be in the cold of the trenches for all twenty-four in the day'.

After three years of war, many servicemen felt like veterans: priests, Tsar and officers were not alone in identifying themselves with Russia, for ordinary soldiers did the same. They hated people who talked of the war without joining in it, and thought they were wrong to criticize it if they had not experienced it — that was the soldiers' right, and theirs alone. To describe the war as imperialist was to question the rightness of the soldiers' sacrifice — hateful and intolerable to the soldiers, as the April demonstration by the war-wounded showed in animosity towards Lenin, whose victory would mean that, for three years, these unfortunates had been deceived.[48] Government propaganda for war until final victory was therefore favourably received, an agreeable surprise to military authorities and bourgeois politicians. In Petrograd, armed soldiers supervised the factories to make sure that the workers were at least working; and everywhere there were soldiers with notices 'Get the soldiers to the trenches and the workers to the factories'. There were incidents in Moscow. The intellectuals leading the soviet mistrusted the soldiers because, true to the Marxist pattern, they saw them only as peasants and hence 'the most counter-revolutionary element of the Revolution'. They did not understand that these soldiers were also soldiers who therefore conceived it as a patriotic duty to supervise the workers and stop them from striking.[49]

The militants of the proletarian parties found this very hard to combat, but the authorities gave them some — involuntary — assistance by making change, democratization or liberalization of the armed forces so difficult. Thereafter, the question was whether the soldiers would resent their authorities or the shirkers and protesters in the rear the more. It was the soviet representatives' activities in the military field that tipped the balance for, after April, many soldiers began expressing their solidarity with the working class. There was always an element of ambiguity, which appeared every time the soldiers and subalterns made a joint resolution: for instance, the soldiers and citizens of the 13th Hussars of Irkutsk stated their solidarity with the working class and added, 'Make arms for us to defend your liberty.'[50]

The soviet appeal for peace without annexations or contributions lifted a heavy mortgage: the problems of war and peace were now being raised, not by extremists, but by the official bodies of the Revolution. Resolutions for peace, given this legitimation, suddenly became more frequent, repeating, word for word, passages from the appeal of 14 March.

How this policy should be applied was a matter for the congress of soviets, which had the legitimate power: its word was Revolutionary Truth. It was also the word of Russia, and, with the soldiers' help, it could become Government Truth as well. It swept away obstacles, including Guchkov and Milyukov, like a torrent, in the April Crisis.

The class enemy and the national enemy

The soviet's authority was such that it not only was able to group the forces of democracy and defeat the bourgeoisie, but also to end the fraternization, although it had been popular. The episode of fraternization, in the spring, showed how far the soldiers sought peace, but it also showed them trying to reconcile this with their patriotic duty; understandably, it posed yet again the question of their relationship with their officers.[51]

In both front and rear, that relationship constantly worsened. The obvious reasons were complemented by another, the officers' attitude to peace. They wanted 'war until final victory', and based their opinions on the Kadets and government majority, in other words that continuation of the war should mean the stifling of Revolution. In effect they realized that the old structure of state and society was collapsing, and that only the army could survive by having a reason to do so, i.e. to fight the enemy. Any operation that the Germans started would thus be a service to the enemies of the soviets, who would then be able to take the troops in hand out of alleged necessity. Authority would once more play its part, recover prestige, require reinforcement from the interior, dominate the civil authorities, push the soviets into the corner and attack the pacifists. Socialist militants fully saw that offensive operations could be demanded for allegedly defensive purposes, so that a process might begin whereby the army would become a pliable instrument for the first stage of a counter-revolution. For this reason, any operational order, or any decision designed to restore fighting capacity, made by the discredited officers was automatically suspect.

Wettig has shown how, for many soldiers ignorant of Bolshevism, the officers might become a more fearful enemy than the Germans; it was feared that the officers would conceal 'their true orders' as had already happened in order to stop the soldiers from knowing fully what had taken place in February. There was also apprehension that the officers would consciously abandon positions to the Germans so as to work up a return to the offensive and thus 'regenerate the army'. If the artillery collaborated, the High Command might even spark off some incident at the front, whereas the calm there could have been a prelude to peace.[52] Thus the soldiers, in their April fraternization, showed not only their will to peace but their patriotism, for 'treason' by the officers could open the way to the enemy, whereas if there were no active operations then the double danger of invasion and counter-revolution could be averted. The coincidence appeared again in September, when Riga fell, and in October as well, when the direct origin of the revolt was fear of a relapse.

The Germans opposite were, after all, men like themselves, who had had to take part in the same tragedy: perhaps, the Russian soldiers thought, some understanding would be possible to paralyse any effort, from whatever source, to resume active operations, and convince the Germans that they were tools in the hands of Wilhelmine imperialism and militarism. In these simple demonstrations biscuits would be cordially exchanged, with 'souvenirs' (there were other instances of fraternization before the Revolution, but only on holidays, especially at Easter – though even in 1917 the fraternization occurred in the Easter period).[53] There was certainly no concerted obedience to an order: the idea was to rule out active operations by prolonging the cessation of hostilities through fraternization. The soldiers preferred to overlook the fact that the initiative often came from the German commanders opposite, because they could not understand what advantages these commanders could see in it, and because, mishandled by their own officers, they had no faith in them; and their confidence collapsed altogether when the officers told the artillery to fire on fraternizing groups.

Bolshevik propaganda later favoured fraternization, but had not started it. Lenin had even thought there was something anarchistic about the first wave of it, although he encouraged it when it began and wanted to use it in his fight with the régime. Militants sent to the army, such as Frunze (Mikhailov), were obliged none the less to abandon fraternization once the Petrograd Soviet formally condemned it. Yet again, the soldiers obeyed the legitimate revolutionary authority alone, and the Bolsheviks were caught short. They got some profit out of the situation because they could attack the methods used by the officers to end fraternization.[54]

In the rear, anarchist and Bolshevik arguments and propaganda helped soldiers, better-informed than they were at the front, to see the link between the Milyukov Note, discussion of the need for an offensive, their own transfer to the front, and their replacement by politically less active troops. All of this accounted for the soldiers' attacking role in the April Days, but in May, when Kerensky, vice-president of the Petrograd Soviet, was appointed minister of war, the soldiers calmed down. To many of them it would even be right to stage an offensive because the supreme revolutionary authority was in favour of it. 'Defensist' ideas gained currency in May, and Kerensky's 'tour' stimulated some recovery of fighting spirit.[55] Liberal officers noted that 'soldiers who are really ready to do their duty are few and far between, even if a great many say they are ready', but many units did in fact petition the soviet in favour of an offensive, some of them even approving a temporary cessation of leave, while others thought highly of the 'continual relief' system that Kerensky wanted applied for men who had not yet seen front service − as it was a measure that, at the time, could have set front soldiers against reserve ones. Similarly, it was in this period that there were the most petitions against deserters.[56]

The offensive took place on 16 June, and the troops did indeed fight. Already, however, many soldiers automatically mistrusted any order tending to restore the officers' authority as counter-revolutionary, whatever the aims intended by it, or allegedly intended. Some units refused to attack, while others in the rear refused to be transferred and demonstrated against Kerensky and the government.[57] In both the front line and the rear, it would be wrong to see the failure of the offensive as a cause of the July Days: the cause lay in the very principle of the offensive. Whether or not it succeeded, it was launching a process to regain the army, and then society, and stop any deepening of the Revolution. The decision to attack had also to be seen in a wider context, which revealed its real significance: it was a campaign against 'anarchy', laced with anti-semitism and national revivalism. This campaign was based on the Cossacks, the congress of *Stavka* officers and the Kadet party, which the troops regarded as the officers' party.[58]

From indiscipline to organized mutiny

The deterioration and collapse of authority can be well shown through the individual instance of a regiment in the 2nd Guard Division, the history of which is known in detail because of its refusal to attack on 20 June and to leave the village of Krosno. Sixty-seven of the men were court martialled just after the July Days. The following indictment reveals how soldiers and officers experienced the first months of the Revolution and how commanders lost their authority.[59]

In March, regimental and company committees were elected, as in other regiments. They included representatives of the soldiers and the officers. Lieutenant Dzevaltovsky was elected as president. To start with the committee was only concerned with routine matters and did not involve itself in operational questions.

At the end of March, lieutenant Dzevaltovsky was appointed regimental delegate to Petrograd. He returned about 20 April. After this journey he, until then a good officer and a man of honour, suddenly changed. He began by saying that the method of election to the committee had not been democratic: there ought to have been no separate representation for the officers in the committee, and there ought to be a new election in which common lists would be put up for soldiers and officers. On 13 May a committee was elected in this way, with one captain, two lieutenants, an ensign and thirty-two soldiers. Dzevaltovsky was re-elected president, and at his request the committee re-named itself a soviet.

From then on, the committee took part not only in the regiment's daily life but also in military matters, even operational decisions. This situation was arrived at because no decision could be made in the regiment without the agreement of the soviet. Lieutenant Dzevaltovsky had such ascendancy over the soviet that he became the real leader of the regiment, whose commander could no longer give the slightest order without first consulting him.

At sessions of the soviet and at regimental meetings . . . the bewitched soldiers listened only to Dzevaltovsky's remarks and trusted only him. To achieve this, he had used methods that are not habitual among officers. When, for instance, men asked him if he were rich, he answered that he himself had nothing but that his parents had money, which was certainly ill-gotten though he could not say how. Thus he ruined the confidence the men might have had in their officers. . . . On his return from Petrograd he brought back a draft declaration of soldiers' rights, and authorized it to take effect even before it was officially promulgated, expressing surprise [that this had not already happened], so that the soldiers suspected it had been hidden from them by the officers. It was now that lieutenant Dzevaltovsky started saying he belonged to the Bolshevik party, of Leninist tendency. . . . He began to organize this party in the regiment and held many meetings for its members alone, excluding others, especially officers. At these meetings he would say that the war was a bourgeois and capitalist one, useless to the proletariat, and deserving to be ended by negotiation.

Until then there had been no fraternization with the Germans, but it started after Dzevaltovsky returned from Petrograd. He believed that, through fraternization, there could be discussion with the enemy, who could be influenced towards a speedy ending of the war. To commanders' questions as to the prohibition of fraternization, he gave evasive answers, and when it stopped in other regiments lieutenant Dzevaltovsky announced that the matter was very complicated and had to be prudently handled. 'You might find it dangerous, but I think it is useful', he said. When he considered soldiers' grievances, Dzevaltovsky would express the idea — which found a sympathetic audience in the uneducated mass — that the government took no interest in the true needs of the people. On the agrarian question, he said land should be taken at once; in any case the district committees had already taken it, and should be imitated because no one ought to have confidence in the government. . . . He went on that the soldiers should have no part in the offensive because if they died, liberty would not help them, and he said that in any case they were under no obligation to obey orders since, from then on, all decisions had to be made by the soldiers themselves.

Lieutenant Dzevaltovsky also interfered in the private lives of members of the regiment, censoring correspondence received such that all newspapers to which officers subscribed had to go through the soviet, and many were confiscated, such as *Kievskaya Mysl*, *Kievlyanin*, or were handed on to soldiers instead of officers. Letters were also censored, and one witness even had a letter stamped by the censor of 9th company. . . . At a soviet session, it was decided that company soviets should know through a liaison what information the regimental commander received by telegraph. The decision was executed, and appears in the minutes for 18 June.

At meetings, it was lieutenant Dzevaltovsky's proposals that were adopted. They could not be ignored or countered, because at once . . . the soldiers would boo the speaker and force him to stop. It soon became impossible for speakers not approved by him to speak, such that when lieutenant Itkin of the delegation from the Black Sea Fleet came to our regiment 'to raise the morale of the grenadiers' and inform them of decisions taken [at Sebastopol] about the war, lieutenant Dzevaltovsky told him in so many words that it was of no importance, that he would not be allowed to speak and in any case it would be futile for him to do so. In the same way, when the commissioner of II Army wanted to give information to the troops . . . lieutenant Dzevaltovsky told him that the soldiers knew their duties quite well — through the press — and that any meeting or speech-making on the subject would be pointless.

In mid-May lieutenant Dzevaltovsky left for the congress of XI Army, as a delegate. At that time, 1 Corps was sent an order to go from the Lutsk sector to the Tarnopol area in Galicia . . . the regiment left the village of Korytnitsa on 19 May and marched towards the transfer area. A timetable had been fixed, but the soldiers, influenced by the regimental committee, did not wish to move more than two stages at a time or cover more than fifteen *versts* [sixteen kilometres] in a day. Although the destination was not officially announced, the men were soon persuaded that the regiment was intended for offensive operations. During the march, on 27 May, lieutenant Dzevaltovsky appeared at a village seven kilometres from Galicia. He called a meeting, said that there should be no more fighting, that peace could be won without further bloodshed and that only the capitalists and bourgeoisie were really in favour of the war.

The failure of the attempt to restore discipline and social order

This regiment, like others, had refused to go up the line.[60] The offensive was a failure, and the authorities publicly accused the Bolsheviks for this, without even waiting for the offensive to fail before officially producing this interpretation. A communiqué of 7 July stated that 'Our defeat was explicitly caused by soldiers who, under Bolshevik influence, ignored the order to attack and went to meetings instead'. The soldiers who had taken part in the attack were appalled, for they were having to take the blame for a failure that has many causes. Soldiers of 506th regiment, which had been explicitly mentioned, protested that they had lost 2,513 casualties in killed and wounded (out of 3,000); and appendix III of the report by generals Gavrilov and Gost'ev stated that 'the defeat was owing to the enemy's overwhelming superiority in artillery, with 200 guns to sixteen'. The authorities ignored this and refused to alter the communiqué.[61]

The soldiers knew in what conditions the offensive had been launched, and were angry because they knew that this failure was quite similar to other failures, before the Revolution, to which their comrades had fallen victim. Participants in the affair knew that the real responsibility lay with the leaders who had ill-advisedly launched the offensive – a coincidence of factors quite like the events that led to the French mutinies of 1917, though in Russia the mistrust and animosity towards the supreme command was greater, because men suspected it had started the attack in order to get rid of revolutionary soldiers, or with some other Machiavellian notion.[62]

The authorities did indeed have concealed reservations of a political nature, but many officers who were close to the men knew nothing of them or did not share them. They suffered profoundly from the moral degradation and the false position they were in. There is a letter in the archives from a captain Gilbich, wounded in the attack, who wrote to his wife,[63] 'My darling: to-day for the first time in many months I have been happy, and even overjoyed. There I am again, in the Germans' wire, with someone next to me that I can call "brother" without anyone calling me "bourgeois" or provocateur.' Yet, in his report, the military assistant to the commissioner on the south-western front stated that 'the talk is only of hanging and shooting'. The soldiers' mistrust and suspicion were directed not only to their officers, now, but to all politicians, even socialist ones, except for the Bolsheviks: 'Spokesmen for the parties are received with great animosity. They are prevented from speaking, while Bolshevik propaganda is gaining ground, being diffused not so much by the party's accredited militants as by the simple spreading of ideas. . . . Officers' horses and equipment have been removed.' Other officers lost their orderlies, and, in an implacable reversal of things, 'officers have been deprived of food for days because they spoke in favour of the offensive.'[64]

When, in July and August, the civil and military authorities tried to regain control of the army and the country, they had thus chosen the very moment when soldiers' mistrust and dislike of officers, commanders and leaders had reached the point of no return.[65] A report to the supreme command stated that 'restoration of the death penalty at once produced a very powerful impression. Those who call themselves Bolshevik were quite stupefied.' The officers were, in the main, happy: they were optimistic, talked of the 'sobering' effect of the courts martial. One general remarked that 'democratization of the army is not natural, it is ill-suited to the army's function, and has no technical foundation.'[66] *Stavka*, imagining that the tide of Revolution could be dictated by decree, stated that '*Prikazy* 51, 213 and 271 are self-contradictory; there must be a new *prikaz* to settle matters . . . committees should be appointed by commanders, and not merely emerge spontaneously . . . the delegates should remain on active service.'[67] In practice, the officers rapidly and without effort resumed their high-handed ways. This is clear in a report from the soldiers' committee of X Army:

On 28 July the soldier Dmitriev asked Adjutant Bereshchak why the 8th section was leaving with its equipment, and the 7th without it. There was no reply, and the adjutant went off to the mess. Other officers were approached, whereat the adjutant returned and said that filth like Dmitriev would sow treason. Dmitriev was arrested.

The soldier Altukhov stated that his captain had struck him on an unhealed wound, and threatened him with death or imprisonment; the soldier Usatsev said that he 'asked if we could still complain to the committee about an order, for instance on compulsory saluting, and the officers replied that committees had been abolished'. Another soldier asked why he had been arrested: 'it's because you talk.' 'Can't we talk any more?' 'No, all that's over.' Another complaining soldier was told by an officer 'Hold your tongue, don't answer back, the liberty business is finished, so just get back to work.' In fact most of the sixty-two imprisoned soldiers were released shortly afterwards.[68] General Bayov's essential measures to be taken included 'Abolition of the soldiers'-and-officers' committees, suppressing all but the company committees dealing with routine, restoration of officers' prestige and of compulsory saluting.' All was directed towards restoration of authority.

The soldiers felt that any compromise was pointless, for the officers still went on identifying themselves with the state, and claiming a monopoly of patriotism with 'rights' over 'their' regiment. That summer, the most frequently-expressed wishes and viewpoints were for democratization of the officers' corps, expulsion of defaulting officers, the removal of aristocrats from the army, the placing of officers in the reserve or under supervision, and purging of the army. It was the make-up of the army, and not simply its proper function, that was challenged from now on.[69] In this apparently reactionary period, moreover, the soldiers no longer demanded only the dismissal of the bourgeois ministers, the dissolution of the Duma, the transfer of power to the soviets, the end of the war through peace without annexations, the freeing of the Bolsheviks; they also refused to carry out counter-revolutionary orders and often protested against the arbitrariness of courts martial and against the death penalty. For the first time, they began to defend deserters, and increasingly adopted very radical social demands — the abolition of private property, the transfer of land to land committees, workers' control, compulsory labour for the middle class, establishment of a workers' militia and the like. It was an enormous step beyond the petitions made in March.[70] The generals who knew of this were very pessimistic. All soldiers who challenged the generals' attitudes were described as Bolsheviks; they were often court martialled ('which is virtually a return to the old order'), so that the government and the general involuntarily gave Lenin's party a popularity that it owed only partly to his activities. 'Who are these Bolsheviks? What party do they belong to? The government attacks them, but we can't see what's wrong. We used to be against them, because that's what the revolutionary government wanted, but with all those broken promises, we are gradually going Bolshevik ourselves. Send us some information.'[71] The line was crossed, and after July there was a Bolshevization of slogans, watchwords and arguments. In both front and rear, the popularity of Lenin's party went up, since he was thought to want an immediate peace, all power for the soviets, and a social revolution.[72]

Revolution and patriotism

'It is clear from the press that the Provisional Government acted rather gingerly over Kornilov', wrote two commissioners after the Putsch had failed,[73] 'and, not knowing whether these rumours are true, we believe it is our duty to state that such hesitation weakens the authority of the revolutionary régime in the soldiers' eyes . . . any hesitation would provoke a powerful response.' They wrote again two days later that 'the mass of soldiers expects exemplary punishments to occur . . . and assumes that courts martial are not just for deserting soldiers but also for traitors to the Revolution, regardless of their office and rank.' A torrent of letters and telegrams expressed the anger of the soldiers, who demanded 'exemplary punishments' and 'sanctions against Kornilov and his accomplices'. The soviet of soldiers of XII Army wanted not only courts martial for Kornilov and Kaledin, but also 'dissolution of the Union of Officers', a change in command, the reinforcement of commissioners' powers, and representation of the committees at *Stavka* and in the ministry; all senior officers were to be supervised.[74] 'The soldiers will defend nothing except their political committees',[75] 'We trust no one, we've been tricked, we had to take part in an offensive that was hopeless from the beginning, and now the government is doing nothing to stop the rise of counter-revolution.' As the Bolsheviks said, Kerensky and the 'conciliators' had proved to be 'traitors to the Revolution'. The soldiers and officers of the 2nd regiment in the fortress of Vyborg wondered why 'there has been no resistance to the bourgeoisie from the socialist ministers − with the crisis growing daily, no satisfaction for the people over anything, and Kerensky still goes on negotiating with the bourgeoisie. What is the meaning of it all − is it just supineness, or is it treachery?'[76]

The 'Bolshevization of the army' had reached its final phase.[77] Regarding the two southern fronts, Tkachuk has drawn up the figures shown in Table 3.[78]

Table 3 *Number of Bolshevik groups*

Front	July	September	November
South-western	44	108	135
Romanian	30	65	145
Total	74	173	280

Many investigations revealed how, after September, the army disintegrated: the differences that had existed in March − between the northern front, where the influence of the centre of the Revolution was felt, and sectors further off from the capital – was now barely noticeable. One of these investigations, concerning several battalions of the Caucasus army, gave the following results – the questions being more revealing than the answers (here summarized):

1 What is the overall situation? (tendency towards Bolshevism, but there are no disorders)
2 Fighting capacity? (reasonable)
3 Cases of refusal to obey orders? (varies)
4 Cases of disobedience? (frequent, but no explicit refusals)
5 Relations with civilians? (often difficult)
6 Role of political committees? (often thought by the commanders to be 'good')
7 Role of reinforcements from the rear? (often 'bad')
8 Role of political parties? (often 'weak')
9 Efficacy of military justice? (rare)
10 Desertions? (few)[79]

The problem of desertion

Many investigations showed, as this one had done, that there were 'few deserters',[80] which contradicts a very solidly-rooted tradition. Can the mass desertions have been a legend?[81]

There is no overall information, such that only isolated pieces of evidence can be used. There were, unquestionably, desertions among the Finns, for instance. On 4 August general Demidov calculated that these amounted to 35 per cent of the effectives; on 20 October the soviet of Helsinki sent a circular to all regimental and battalion committees to say that 'there will be draconian measures against the buying and sealing of military equipment'.[82] Again, in the Ukraine, and especially in Kiev, there were frequent complaints at the 'troubles brought about by bands of deserters' after the failure of the offensive. The same, later on, happened in the countryside. However, overall, desertions seem from the limited information we have to have been remarkably few – which is quite contrary to the assertions of the military authorities (who did not in fact state their statistical evidence). It may well be that the authorities were confusing things. General Golovin describes as deserters those delegates from the front who participated in meetings (of whom he counted nearly 800,000 and Verkhovsky 2,000,000) as well as malingerers and men absent without leave (which amounted 'after the Revolution, to 12 per cent'). If the calculation is made in this way, desertion can easily be made out to amount to millions of men, though even then it is questionable whether 'deserter' is the right term to apply for those men who wanted the war to stop and went back 'to take power and arrange an armistice' as seems to have happened on the northern front.[83] What occurred was a movement of collective disobedience, mutiny, refusal to enter the line, and commanders preferred to describe it all with the insulting term 'desertion'. In fact such 'statistics' merely lumped together all previous occurrences with all men who, after October and on the signing of the armistice, went home without leave. For most of the men, group solidarity counted until that moment, and, with a kind of consensus, they undertook to defend the country.[84]

Yet, as the authorities saw things, 'the army has ceased to be an army', the soldiers no longer accepting orders or blindly carrying them out. The army had lost its second, political and repressive, function; since there was complete disorganization and virtual operational impotence, the authorities confused German gold and Bolshevism just as, in France, general Franchet d'Esperey grandly lumped socialists and Germans together when the French mutinies occurred. In Russia, however, the soldiers knew enough to throw back the responsibility for defeat on to the ruling classes. In the Moonsund battle of 3–6 October they suspected their officers, as they had done earlier in Riga, of fomenting treason.[85] The strength of their patriotism was also shown in their mistrust of the non-Russian nationalists, those *aliens* who were often loyal to the traditional forces of authority. In the appeal of the people, and the Bolsheviks, to save Moscow from capture in October was an echo of the age-old Russian terror of the 'foreigner' – of the Tatar or the Pole, or the German; and an alien aristocracy.

4 The resistance: institutional structure and national identity

The Revolution destroyed the unity of the army, as had happened with the bureaucracy and the universities. It revealed conflicts that the seeming solidarity of these bodies usually concealed. In the army the conflict between revolution and counter-revolution was not only, or necessarily, that between soldiers and officers to which it is sometimes reduced; there were many variables to account for the mutiny of this regiment and not that – the character of the officers, the social and racial origin of various units, their function in the army; it was not merely a matter of rank. All of these must be taken into account to explain attitudes.

There were, for intance, many officers who dissociated patriotism from institutional structure, and who later joined the soviets to fight the Poles or the Germans: Tukhachevsky was only one instance of these men, the 'specialists' of the later Red Army, which, after October, became identified as the national force. Brusilov, former commander-in-chief, was another.[86] By contrast, many soldiers confused the national idea and patriotic duty with loyalty to the institutional structure. Later, they formed the framework of the White Army. They can be found in the special units, set up for counter-revolutionary purposes early in the summer (see Chapter 2); many were also in the army's specialist corps, such as the artillery or cavalry.[87]

The Cossacks were professional soldiers with the outlook of veterans, and they felt that the people owed them things, for they had defended the country and the Revolution. They were more democratic in organization than other corps, and did not have the same grievances towards their commanders; and they would have been content at the modest victory had not revolutionaries bothered them on the grounds that they, too, were privileged people in their way. Socialist theoreticians looked at the details of agrarian reform and challenged some of the benefits the Cossacks enjoyed; moreover, peasants seized Cossack lands. The Cossacks could well find the Revolution ungrateful, and in June their congress declared readiness to defend their interests 'with armed force'. It adopted powerful resolutions in favour of the offensive, and openly threatened the Bolsheviks with the *nagayka* (Cossack whip). They participated in the repression in July, and at the Moscow conference they entrusted their *ataman*, Kaledin, with speaking on behalf of reaction.[88]

Early in August, at their conference at Novocherkassk, with encouragement from Guchkov and Kadet deputies (Voronkov, Rodichev and others), the Circle of Don Cossacks appealed to the provincials against the 'excesses' of the capital, and wished them to rise in Russia's defence. Most − though not all − Cossacks followed Kornilov in the Putsch; in September, the 'Southern Russian Union of Cossack and other Free Peoples' Forces' was formed, and at the Yekaterinodar conference a large majority of the Cossacks remained loyal to the supreme command − they accused the government of being 'only a tool in the hands of irresponsible elements' and refused to think that there had been a 'plot' on Kornilov's part. The Caucasus Cossacks refused to use the electoral law laid down by the government for the constituent assembly elections, and instead drafted one of their own, the better to serve their interests. The Kuban Cossacks declared to Kerensky that they would not send troops to help the government restore order because it had failed in July to repress the opposition as it should have done. They would also not go on expeditions to control the mountain peoples, for fear that while they were away the peasants would seize their lands. By 21 September, at the Yekaterinodar conference, Makarenko, who in June had offered to whip down the

Bolsheviks, attacked the government, blamed it for the general disintegration, and demanded a 'territorial structure' that would guarantee at least the Cossack lands some security, in view of the central government's weakness. There was to be a territory for the Cossacks within the Russian Federal Republic, at least until the constituent assembly had passed its laws. It would 'keep order, defend the rights of each nationality, and support the central government; it will be governed by a legislative assembly and a political committee, and commissioners will be exchanged between it and the Provisional Government, although the decisions of the government commissioner in Yekaterinodar may be countermanded if opposed by a majority of the committee. No troops other than Cossack may penetrate this Territory.'[89]

On 24 September the first Cossack Rada was formed, of members of the military government of the Kuban, the conference of Cossack forces, representatives of the mountain peoples and the like. Its elected head was the *ataman*, A. M. Kaledin. He speedily protested against the Provisional Government's silence — it had failed to recognize the Union. The Cossack Territory, established before October, and a nucleus for civil war, was a paradoxical instance of secession 'to save the country from disintegration, disorder and anarchy'.[90]

The case of some units made of the nationalities was different. One instance was a communiqué that 'the executive committee of the union of Polish soldiers denies the insinuation that it had the slightest part in the Kornilov affair.'[91] Other such declarations came from Ukrainian, Moslem and Circassian units as well. Lettish riflemen had fought Kornilov at the soviets' side and again in the October revolt they fought for the soviets, along with other units made up of non-Russian peoples. Yet, if rumour was to be believed, the nationalities were supposed to be unfavourable to the soviets and the Bolsheviks; commanders would use them — apart from the Baltic peoples — for repressive purposes, where necessary.[92]

The assemblies of Russian soldiers had, under the influence of social democrats, frequently been against the demands of their non-Russian comrades. These demands had been rejected as 'reactionary' since, at the time, soldiers supposed that the new régime would start a new epoch in relations between peoples. To set up separate non-Russian units therefore seemed anachronistic and reactionary. Moreover, the small concessions made by the Provisional Government to a few of the non-Russian peoples provisionally associated them with the régime, even if secret, separatist aspirations continued[93] — as happened with the Finns and Ukrainians. Chauvinism came into it, and there was frequent fighting at Kiev between Russian and Ukrainian units. This was not the intention of the supreme command when it agreed to constitute such separate non-Russian units. It wanted a less equivocal counter-revolutionary instrument, and would rely on those peoples for whom the establishment of separate units did not threaten the unity of the empire. Thus, Circassian or Ossete units could be set up, and Polish ones as well, for Polish independence seemed unavoidable.[94] Armed Czech (or Slovak) units might also be set up from prisoners of war to the Austrian army; these would fight against the Habsburgs to gain independence. Later on, they formed a nucleus of the White Army.[95]

In order to show themselves equal to the Russians, the non-Russian peoples and foreigners had often fought very hard against the Turks and the Germans. On the battlefield they would show their equality with their 'protectors', and now they identified themselves with their military chiefs, Russians who, outside the armed forces, would have despised them. Overjoyed at this promotion, they had discovered that the status of combatant gave a satisfaction that no Revolution could equal; hence their loyalty to their military leaders, and hence, too, the fact that, when the counter-revolution began, the military authorities knew that they could rely on absolute loyalty from 'native' or other foreign troops. Kornilov and his Cheremiss units in 1917 were equivalent to Franco with his Moorish regiments in 1936, or Salan with his Foreign Legionaries in 1961.

PART TWO

The birth of a society

CHAPTER 4

The nationalities: disintegration, reunion and fusion

The failure of the Provisional Government, and even more that of the traditional authorities promoted the emancipation of those nationalities which had been forcibly grafted onto the Russian state. Most of them had not even waited for the state to disintegrate to express their hopes and prepare for autonomy and independence. To achieve this, some of them relied on the situation created by the war, and had a foot in each camp. There were many variables in the model of their relationship with Russia.

Not all had the same consciousness of separateness and some might not even want independence, in view of the forces involved or their relations with their neighbours – for instance, independence might mean genocide for the Armenians whose whole territory was threatened by the hereditary Turkish enemy. Another variable was that the nationalities, like the dominating power, did not constitute homogeneous societies. Nationalism did of course predominate in most cases, but there was a confused intertwining of social and political struggles on the one side with national aspirations on the other.[1]

The relationship between nationalities and Russians changed according to the general orientation of the Russian revolutionary movement and the changes this transformation led to among the peoples of the empire; 1917 both revealed and transformed the relationships between individuals, institutions and races in Russia; it displayed the different identities of the individuals and social bodies. Thus, some minority troops underwent a veritable de-nationalizing in the army, because of their identification with the values of the state and the traditional institutions; and in the Cossack case, there was secession. In other places, the resistance to October and its effects caused a second emigration.[2] This chapter will examine how the failure of the February Revolution sundered the structure of the empire, altering the relationship between Russians and non-Russians; then it considers the impact of October, which altered the terms of the nationality problem, and even the nature of international relations, because new boundaries were created between the internal and external policies of states.

1 February–October: the breach between the nationalities and the February régime

After February, attitudes among the nationalities towards the Petrograd government varied according to the depth of their national feeling, the political tendencies that appeared within each one, and the changes making for a radicalization of attitudes towards government. This affected both the nature of their relations with the government and their implicit or explicit objectives.[3] A number of approaches were possible.

1 There could be acceptance of the framework created by the Russian Revolution, with an intention only to quicken the pace or alter the methods of change. In the Ukraine, by March, the Kiev Rada had issued a manifesto in favour of the constituent assembly, and was supported by the Progressive Union, but both bodies wished the assembly merely to ratify their demands, whereas the Petrograd leaders thought that the constituent, sovereign, assembly would have to lay down the framework into which these demands could be fitted. A similar claim was made by the congress of Moslem soldiers at Kazan, where there was talk of proportional representation for Moslems in the constituent assembly. It was the same with the Lettish democratic party and with the Estonian national assembly.[4]

2 There could also be a rejection of the Russian constituent assembly as sovereign body, because it would be called by the Russians and they would obviously have the majority; instead, separate negotiations were wanted between the nationality's representatives and the Russian state. This was the attitude of the Ukrainian Socialist Revolutionaries, and it was repeated at the congress of Ukrainian soldiers on 31 May 1917 which stated that 'the fate of the Ukraine may not depend on a Russian constituent assembly'. The same standpoint was adopted, for Finland, in the Seim of Helsinki which was dominated by social democrats; and similarly with the Crimean provisional constituent assembly, which met in May, and the Georgian national committee, which met abroad. The Lettish democratic party and the Lithuanian provisional committee introduced a variation by wanting international mediation (in the shape of the future League of Nations) to underwrite the agreement between national Russian and non-Russian bodies in the future.[5]

3 Negotiations with the representatives of the New Russia could be

undertaken only provided there were guarantees regarding the war and Revolution. This was the attitude of some of the 'maximalist' social democrats in the Baltic lands and the Ukraine, who wished to set up a new relationship with the Revolution only after all power had passed to the soviets. Such socialists in any event militated more in the framework of the Russian Revolution than in that of the national struggle. S. Gonner, writing on behalf of the Yekaterinoslav social democrats, said 'We forgot that we were fighting in the Ukraine, and regarded Yekaterinoslav as an industrial town and no more.'[6] At the other extreme, 'Cossack nationalism' assisted the counter-revolution and threatened secession if 'anarchy' were not ended.

4 The government, which ignored nationalities, could also be simply ignored in turn, through a *de facto* separation regardless of the consequences. The Chagatay of Turkestan apparently acted in this way, after they had three times demanded satisfaction of their grievances – land reform, autonomy, etc. – without receiving an answer.[7]

There were points of resemblance among the demands of the non-Russian peoples. Essentially, they wanted a new political status: internal autonomy, territorial or extra-territorial cultural autonomy,[8] the establishment of a federal Russia, or a federation in which Russia would be a unit along with the others, and sometimes also independence with or without a link with Russia. Such independence was demanded by the majority of the innumerable Polish political organizations, the Luxemburgist social democrats being the only one to pronounce for proletarian internationalism – and they were a very small minority, even within social democracy. Independence was also the aim of Finns, Lithuanians, many Lettish parties, and several groups of Georgians, Chagatay, etc. In the meantime, the nationalities sought social and religious measures (especially the Moslems and Ukrainians) and in particular political guarantees – the grant of some autonomy, recognition of the right to self-determination, fostering of education in the native language and permission to set up separate military units.

This question of separate military units was very important to part of nationalist opinion, because they were the only real guarantee against a possible 'relapse' on the Revolution's part. The government could be judged by its attitude to the matter, as appeared at the congress of the Polish military administration in Petrograd on 29 May 1917, and also at the All-Moslem Caucasus conference, where a resolution was taken to establish a Moslem military force even without authorization from the government. At Samara, in May, soldiers of Ukrainian origin set up their own regiment, and late in May the Byelorussians at Minsk did the same. But the pressure on the government for this purpose came most strongly from the Ukraine.

The 'maximalists' of Latvia and Poland, often Luxemburgist, were alone in opposing the constitution of separate national military units, for, in their view, the army could only oppose 'revolutionary' collaboration with the Bolshevik sister party.[9] During the six months preceding October, the outstanding phenomenon was the rise of nationalism. In some areas it overflowed and absorbed other political and social conflicts; it became radical, and affected communities that the revolutionaries had never imagined capable of developing a collective identity.

The absorption of other conflicts was particularly obvious in the Ukraine, especially in Kiev where the Rada set up in March as a straight-forward body to promote the cultural expression of the Little-Russian intelligentsia managed to overtake the soviet of deputies, which was the expression of class-struggle. Soon, the Rada spoke for all Ukrainians. The same phenomenon occurred, to a lesser degree, in the Jewish communities, where *Poale Zion* took over from the *Bund*,[10] and also in Estonia where the soviet of Reval justified its representative character by being elected by all of the capital's citizens, including the bourgeoisie; it also agreed to send delegates to the Seim which was recognized as represent-ative of the Estonian people. At least until October there was also no conflict in Finland, for national identity proved stronger than class, and was expressed wholly in the Seim which wanted independence. More-over, in non-Russian regions, the class-struggle itself could appear as anti-national, because, in the soviets which represented it, non-Russians were kept out, and any demand of a cultural or nationalistic nature was taken as 'reactionary'.[11]

The phenomenon was more complex in Islamic regions. The first con-gresses had met in the name of the common religious identity of the various Moslem peoples of Russia. Early on in the Revolution there occurred a phenomenon unique in history: the women's delegations succeeded in making female emancipation a principle of the Russian Moslems' struggle, with, as a sign of their achievement, the first votes being taken on this subject. However, the strife between progressives and conservatives was speedily overtaken by conflicts between religious associations and political parties, and then, in the political field, by hostility between various nationality-movements, Tatar and non-Tatar, all of which adopted the platform of nationalism and struggle against the oppressor. This 'secondary' conflict soon superseded the others, that with the Russians, that between Moslem bourgeoisie and proletariat, and that between nationalist reformers and revolutionaries who advocated an all-Islamic socialism.[12]

There was a parallel radicalization of attitudes and extension of nationalism. In February, the Russian revolutionaries had supposed that independence would be necessary only for Poland, and possibly also for Finland. But it soon emerged that Lithuania and Latvia also wanted it; moreover, the demands of the Rada in Kiev became more outspoken, such that even internal autonomy was not apparently enough to satisfy it − in June 1917 its first *Universal* proclaimed its mission to achieve full sovereignty. The Provisional Government reacted strongly, and the aim was put off, but it had been a precursory sign of the rise of nationalism even among Slav peoples: thus, the Byelorussian Hramada though scarcely representative, still had its demands to make.

Among the Moslems, the centralist position of the Tatars was broken by an alliance of all who feared the supremacy of the Kazan Moslems and wanted a federative republic with a national territorial basis. Among the Kirghiz, Bashkirs, at Baku and elsewhere, the centrifugal forces won locally, and the Tatars, supported by the assembly of Moslem clergy, were virtually alone in wishing to develop institutions that would act for the Moslem people as a whole. In order to make possible the triumph of their own side, they took the preventive step of proclaiming cultural autonomy for all the Moslem Turks of Russia and so, without waiting for the constituent assembly, they took the vanguard of the Moslem movement. The Tatar Bolsheviks behaved quite logically in voting for this final resolution even though it stemmed from the bourgeois and the mullahs of Kazan.[13]

The radicalization and growth of nationalism took a spectacular shape at the end of the summer when, at Ukrainian initiative, a congress of the nationalities of Russia were held in Kiev. Delegates from 13 peoples took part: 6 Byelorussians, 2 Georgians, 4 Estonians, 10 Jews, 11 Kazakhs, 10 Letts, 9 Lithuanians, 10 Tatars, 6 Poles, 6 Bessarabian Romanians, 5 Turks, 9 Ukrainians and representatives of the government in Petrograd. As well, fifteen socialist parties representing these peoples, together with the Armenian *Dashnaksutyun*, the Ossete nationalist party, *Poale Zion* and the Moslem socialist party joined in, to establish the norms for nationality policy in the territory of the former Russian empire. The right to self-determination was recognized as fundamental, and the final resolution at Kiev was for the election, not only of a single constituent assembly for Russia as a whole, but of others, equal in number to the peoples. Each one was to determine the links that might unite it, whether to a state or a federation of states, if it did not decide for independence. The last point was not quite explicit; the section of the P.P.S. that attended the Kiev congress laid down, for Poland, that political independence would be an essential prelude to any later federation of Poland with the Ukraine or socialist Russia.[14]

From Mongol Buryats to Byelorussians, all the non-Russian peoples were effecting a disruption of the old state. What would become of the state, of Russia, of socialism, if at Kiev, at Kazan, at Dorpat the Double Eagle and the Red Flag were replaced by national emblems? The men of February, who had been warm advocates of national rights when they were in opposition, showed, in government, that they would allow such rights only on one condition: that they still had control. They, alone, would decide when and how the constituent assembly would meet, and the Great Russians would of course have a majority there. They saw that this meant that nationalities' rights would not really be respected in this procedure, but they still had a clear conscience because they would themselves take over the government of the New Russia; and there could be no serious divergence between them and the nationalities, because, as heirs of the great revolutionaries of 1789, 1848 and 1905, they conceived themselves as having a universalist mission.

This conviction was reinforced when, after the equality of all Russian citizens had been proclaimed, many Jews, Georgians, Letts and others fought not as members of a nationality but as part of a single social entity; even a large national organization like the *Bund* lost some of its adherents after a few months of Revolution, and this, like the instance of the Georgian socialists who joined the new régime, confirmed the notion that nationalist organizations could only be transitory in their legitimacy, until the memory of oppression had faded. In any case they were most often led – as in the Baltic lands – by landowners and notables or, in the Moslem case, by bourgeois and mullahs, and could be imagined to be defending interests hostile to the working class. If, among the nationalities, the socialist parties rallied to the nationalist cause, it was out of tactical necessity, or so the Russian socialists supposed, and this could even lead Lettish and Finnish social democrats to outdo the bourgeois or agrarian parties in nationalism, which could be deleterious to the Russian socialists.

Conversely, the nationality movement could not fail to see that, in their territory, the Russian minorities, whether or not organized in soviets, were against them. Some months after the Revolution, the Petrograd leaders themselves became suspect, for their 'concessions' to the nationalities looked like fraudulent promises, which had been got up as 'compromises' – thus the 'independence' promised to a Poland occupied by the Germans, or the promise to recognize Finnish 'rights', but only on the basis of the unequal treaty of 1809. Besides, although the soviets had voted for the extra-territorial cultural autonomy wanted by the nationalists, they had also stated that it would have to depend on what the constituent assembly decided.[15]

The Ukraine was a case in point. The agreement of 3 July with the

Rada was the archetypical compromise, by which the Rada, in return for government recognition, submitted to its jurisdiction. There was to be a secretariat-general, set up by agreement between Rada and the capital, to carry out government in the Provisional Government's name. The Rada was to decide the status of the Ukraine, and submit proposals to the constituent assembly.

This was only an agreement in principle; concrete proposals had as yet to be arrived at. When Kiev and Petrograd submitted drafts, there was a great difference between them. The Kadet jurists, who were once more in charge after the failure of the July revolt, 'limited the evil' by proposing an arrangement that was less than the Ukrainians had hoped for, and turned the secretariat-general into a mere administrative body at Petrograd's command (5 August).[16] This Instruction was heatedly debated in the Rada, and although the Rada discussed and accepted it, this happened only because, first, the non-Ukrainian minorities (Russians and Jews) were attached to the principle of autonomy which struck them as the lesser evil, and second, the Kornilov affair strengthened Ukrainian links with Russian democracy, i.e. the government of Kerensky.

Narrowly, and for the second time, agreement was struck between Kiev and Petrograd. But it was based on a misunderstanding, which soon became apparent. The Ukrainians were only barely satisfied by recognition of their 'identity', and wanted to forestall a possible 'relapse' on the Revolution's part; they therefore wanted a constituent assembly which, although the Russian minorities managed to prevent it from being described as sovereign, could not be subject to a Russian one. Petrograd was anxious, the more so as the Kiev conference of non-Russian nationalities was then taking place, and in this affair the Ukraine, which was closest to Russia by blood and culture, was acting as a force that might break up the entire old state.[17]

It was too much for Petrograd, the more so as blackmail in the form of the Central Powers – which had hitherto been latent – was now openly expressed, as Vinnichenko, chairman of the secretariat, declared in an interview with L'Intransigeant (it was censored) that 'the more the government resists Ukrainian demands, the more the Ukrainians will look to Germany and Austria-Hungary'. The Russian press noted that, among the ostensibly wounded prisoners sent back from Germany, half were quite healthy, and also came from the Ukraine. Troubles increasingly broke out between Russians and Ukrainians. In Kiev, the 'Bogdan Khmelnitsky regiment' remained to protect the Rada against a possible dissolution manu militari such as the government had executed against the Helsinki Seim. The authorities attacked this regiment for 'playing Bolshevik and defeatist, and refusing to go to the front'. The regiment responded to the patriotic blackmail and did go to the border, but on the way there was a clash between Russian and Ukrainian soldiers, with sixteen men killed. In the Black Sea, sailors hoisted the Ukrainian flag, and by the time the October revolt happened, a breach between the government and the Rada was at hand. In Kiev, there was an alliance between the Rada nationalists and the Russian and Ukrainian Bolsheviks against the February régime – an 'unnatural' alliance that provoked much objection, and later splitting, among the Bolsheviks. There was a similar pattern in the Moslem lands.[18]

Until July 1917, the government and public opinion paid no attention to the nationalist and revolutionary movement developing in the Moslem world. This happened because, in its first phase, it was canalized by the Tatar bourgeoisie which had the ear either of the Kadets or of the Mensheviks and Socialist Revolutionaries. There were no Bolsheviks at all at the Kazan congress: they regarded it as 'demagogy'; and even in July their newspaper *Qyzyl Barraq* ('The Red Flag') stressed the irrelevance of the concept of 'national unity' that the Moslem bourgeoisie upheld. A further reason for not recognizing it was that the political or social claims of the Moslems were intended to be held over until the constituent assembly, the framework planned by the government, had met.[19]

In May the all-Russian congress of Moslems, at Moscow, gave a tepid welcome to the government's representative and then condemned its foreign policy; but there was no great anxiety over this in Petrograd. When the Moslems asked for authorization to hold a 'military congress' they were turned down.[20] The May congress showed how fragile was the unity of the Moslems, and had also shown that there was willingness for change. The Tatars had taken the leading position, to which the Bolsheviks finally became attached; and, to palliate the radicalization of the nationalist movement, a delegation went to the government to propose, in exchange for cabinet places, Moslem help in July against the Bolsheviks, and later against Kornilov. The Provisional Government did not refuse this help, and permission to establish Moslem regiments was given. Chkeidze and Tseretelli none the less opposed Moslem entry into the government 'on the grounds that it was parties and not nationalities that should form the government'.[21]

The government and the newspapers were more concerned with the Caucasus, since it involved the sentiments of peoples near the Turkish front. There were several editorials between July and October in *Novoye Vremya* on 'The Danger of the Caucasus', no distinction being drawn between 'the Turkish peril' and 'the danger of the Mountain Peoples'. Conflict occurred, as in other cases, over land-use or the non-involvement of Moslems in the administration; and there was also a fight over separate military units. According to the American consul F. W. Smith, German agents were active here, at least in Tiflis.[22] The repression was aimed as before at peoples suspected of secessionism; it went ahead most spectacularly, not so much in the Caucasus (where Georgians and Armenians could be counted on to control their Azeri enemies) as in the Crimea, where the Mufti was arrested for appealing against the use of Moslem troops against the Turks, and in the Kirghiz region, where Russian colonists took the initiative in repression, and increasing called for help from the Petrograd Soviet. It issued an 'appeal to the Kirghiz' summoning them 'to live at peace with the colonists at least until the constituent assembly has met'.[23]

The Revolution also adhered to the 'colonial' tradition in Turkestan. Kerensky had spoken of 'the loyalty of the Moslems which is so well-known to me' − he had lived in Tashkent, although he knew nothing of the national problem within Russian Islam. General Kuropatkin had had arms distributed to the Russian colonists, and Kerensky saw nothing 'reprehensible' about this. The government did, in the end, recognize the 'individuality' of Bokhara and Khiva, and excluded these two emirates' inhabitants from any part in the constituent assembly elections. Government representatives carried out routine administrative changes, and dressed them up as reforms without consulting the reformist movement (*Jadid*), merely with the emirs' agreement; and when the soviets took power in Tashkent in September 1917, it was purely as a Russian force, though it soon became allied with the Moslem reformists to fight the emir and soon afterwards the Whites − not of course with a view to satisfying the national aspirations of the Russian Moslems.[24]

When the Moscow conference began, there had been failure everywhere − in Finland, where the Provisional Government dissolved the Diet, which met against its will; in the Ukraine and the Moslem world as well; and there was dissatisfaction too among the Poles and Baltic peoples. Yet at that conference, Jews, Armenians and Georgians, who were all Mensheviks or Socialist Revolutionaries, were alone in making themselves heard. There was, indeed, scarcely a false note, apart from Divilegov, for the Armenians, who criticized the government for pursuing Tsarist policies of conquering Turkish Armenia. To my knowledge, the organizations most hostile to the government − the socialist committee of Kazan or the *Milli Firka* of the Crimea − were not even represented. However, pressure from the nationalities grew so strong that, on 28 September, the government issued a declaration that went parallel, though not so far as, the soviet congress's resolution in June: 'recognition of the right to self-determination of peoples will be established on bases to be chosen by the constituent assembly', and, seven

months after the fall of the Tsar, the government would propose only to
establish commissions for each of the nationalities.[25]

The moment of truth came in October, when, in view of the inter-
Allied conference in Paris, the administrative bureau of the congress of
soviets instructed Skobelev (Menshevik) that Russia would grant complete self-determination to Poland, Lithuania and Latvia – i.e. the three
countries occupied largely by the Germans. That was the limit. Tereshchenko, who had succeeded Milyukov as foreign minister, even then
warned that 'if these three countries became sovereign, Russia would lose
access to a free sea'. Milyukov, at the Provisional Council of the Republic,
expressed his surprise at the government's adoption of soviet policies; and
he received unexpected support from the resolution of the peasant soviets
(controlled by right-wing Socialist Revolutionaries) which was also called
'an instruction to Skobelev'. It, as with the soviets and government,
approved the formula 'peace without annexations or contributions, on the
basis of the right of self-determination'. Point 2 laid down that the
formula would also apply to the Russian nationalities but added 'the
territory of Russia must remain intact'. Chernov (centre Socialist
Revolutionary) and Dan (Menshevik) developed the theory of this
nationality policy in the Council of the Republic: in Dan's words, 'The
programme of the Revolution is to give all nationalities the right of self-
determination. But it does not mean independence. We believe that this
right must be used to preserve close links with Russia . . . having received
their rights, the nationalities must remain part of free Russia.'[26] Much of
this was Leninism re-hashed, but there was a difference for, although the
Bolsheviks took much the same view, they were prepared to support
secessionist movements in order to weaken the 'bourgeois' state, which
the nationalist movements would hardly want to sustain; whereas the
Mensheviks and Socialist Revolutionaries who were in power fought
against the nationalists such that, in the event, they collapsed at Kiev, at
Bokhara and Tashkent, and among the Letts before the tactical alliance
of nationalism and Bolshevism.

2 October: peace, revolutionary strategy and the nationalities

After October, nationality policy was, for the Bolsheviks, only part of a
wider strategy aimed at world revolution. The soviet régime strengthened
within, its first aim was to turn the European war into a vast civil war.
Thus the decree on peace, stressing the right of self-determination of
peoples, applied as much to nationalities outside Russia as to those within
her borders. The immediate goal was to meet popular aspirations; but it

was also to sow the seeds of European revolution. By appealing to all warring states, the Soviet government was trying, not so much to keep up links with former allies, but to foster revolutionary propaganda everywhere: Russia, opening negotiations at Brest-Litovsk, was setting the example of a revolutionary peace, and it could be contagious.[27] An appeal of the Zimmerwaldian left from Stockholm, drawn up by Radek and signed by the foreign Bolsheviks and the International Socialist Committee, called on soldiers everywhere to lay down their arms and on proletarians to show solidarity with the Russian Revolution. A second proclamation, meant to forestall any anti-Bolshevik crusade, set out the significance of the negotiations at Brest-Litovsk – they took place with the Central Powers alone only because the Allies had not responded to the appeal of 26 October, and were meant to achieve, not only the self-determination of peoples that had just been decreed valid in Russia, but also the right of the people, the 'proletarian' and the individual everywhere to govern himself.[28]

These principles received a threefold application, as did the pursuit of the Bolsheviks' goals in general – the new Soviet state's diplomacy, the Bolshevik party's links with revolutionary parties elsewhere, and Soviet policy towards the nationalities. That such matters should be specifically linked in their treatment was one of the greatest changes that the October Revolution introduced in international affairs. In October 1917, Lenin's action was seen as part of a European pattern of successful revolutions, such that the very notion of international relations would become suspicious: diplomacy would simply come to an end. A precursory sign of this was publication of the Secret Treaties: 'I'll publish a few revolutionary proclamations and then I'll shut up shop', said Trotsky as People's Commissar for Foreign Affairs, and he added, 'I took on this job only because it leaves me time to get on with party matters.'

Things worked out otherwise. What Rosa Luxemburg called 'the corpse-like immobility of the German working-class' completely altered the perspectives of October. There was no revolution in Europe, and the negotiations at Brest-Litovsk merely turned into the peace of Brest-Litovsk: as E. H. Carr put it, Lenin had to reckon with the improbability of a German revolution in the event of its being given a last chance, and the certainty of the Germans' marching on Petrograd; he preferred a calamitous peace. The choice showed that the preservation of the Soviet state was now a first priority, and the approach was confirmed in August 1918, when the Soviet Republic, dangerously threatened by the Whites and foreign intervention, concluded another treaty with Germany by which, in exchange for military assistance, it undertook to stop revolutionary propaganda in central Europe. Long before Stalin, Lenin and

Trotsky found it necessary to sacrifice the European revolution to the preservation of their own régime, Soviet diplomacy was born, as Bukharin said, 'on a pile of dung'[29] in March 1918.

Revolutionary activity on the part of the socialist parties' left was a further lever in Bolshevik policy. Since the abortion of the Stockholm conference, the only organization able to stimulate such activity in each nation was the International Socialist Committee, associated with the Zimmerwald movement. In reality, participants in the third Zimmerwaldian conference, which was held at Stockholm in September 1917, had done much to cause the failure of the discussions leading to the intersocialist peace conference. Moreover, the Zimmerwaldian 'left' – inspired by Russian Bolsheviks, with Balabanova, Sirola and others – had already, in effect, split off from the other Zimmerwaldians, who later went back to the old Second International. The October Revolution, far from reinvigorating the Zimmerwaldians, who were already divided as to the question of participating in the stillborn Stockholm conference, led to their disintegration. By making public the appeal drafted by Radek, the left acted against general wishes, for the appeal assisted the Russian Bolsheviks alone; its publication exposed the Zimmerwaldians of other countries to attack from their own governments, and even part of the Zimmerwaldian left was against Radek's appeal, since they felt it amounted to giving priority to the new Soviet leaders over the western European proletariat.[30]

For some time Lenin had been considering leaving the Zimmerwald movement to set up a Third International with the left. The plan had been aired several times between April and October, and was even popularized. In September 1917 Lenin wanted an 'immediate' breach with Zimmerwald, but hardly had the time in the upheavals of October, so that the Zimmerwaldian movement died a natural death, without a death-certificate. At the initiative of the *TsIK*, the Soviet government prepared to resuscitate the movement with Russian (Bolshevik or left Socialist Revolutionary), Scandinavian, English and American delegates; and after some vacillation this developed into the *Komintern*, or Third International. There had been confusion as regards its competence and function from the start, because the policy did not emanate from parties, even from the Bolsheviks but from a government, that of Soviet Russia.[31]

In Russia, the third lever of the revolutionary strategy was policy towards the nationalities, and it required an immediate solution given that it affected the whole country. The Bolsheviks, who had had to consider the nationality problem for twenty years and regarded it as a purely temporary phenomenon, were caught in an insoluble contradiction: they could recognize the right of self-determination, and the old state would disintegrate; or they could subordinate this right to the accomplishment of Revolution, and the revolutionary movement would be split, even in Russia — this much had been shown in the crisis that had occurred in relations between the Russian social democrats and the *Bund*, and between the Russian Social Democratic Party and the Armenian social democrats.[32]

Lenin set about surmounting this contradiction. He was at bottom — as Georges Haupt has excellently demonstrated — close to Marxist orthodoxy, whether Kautskyist or Luxemburgist, in refusing to see the nation as a homogeneous entity; he analysed constitution, formation, and future in terms of class and culture. However, he had both to use the solvent of nationalism, and to safeguard the future of the great state, which he saw as alone able to solve modern problems of economic development; and he wholly reserved the tactics of his party by laying down the right of self-determination in his theses. The aim was to abolish constraint between nations — though right to divorce was not to mean necessity for divorce. Lenin thought that such an attitude alone would be able to stop the mistrust between Russians and non-Russians and to permit a later reunification under the aegis of the vanguard organizations on both sides. The nation 'remains a provisional category, which we should apply only with a view to hurrying its disappearance'.[33]

These theses might prevail (not without difficulty) in a party whose members felt hostility towards claims of a nationalist nature, but they had also to be applied with due account taken of the citizens and militants in each of the cases concerned. The Bolsheviks had first to deal with the case of Finland, in February and October alike. This case will be examined in detail, because it constituted a model for the relationship established between Bolshevism and nationalism, and its connections with the external and internal policies of the USSR.

3 Independence and internationalism

The case of Finland, February 1917–75

In 1917 the Finns, like the Poles, demanded independence. In the heady days of February, the Finnish social democrats, who had a majority in the Seim and were still united, proposed an indissoluble association with the Russian Republic. The Provisional Government, however, wished to regard the statute of 1809 as the basis for negotiations, and the Finnish social democrats wanted absolute independence. They were supported by the Russian Bolsheviks who, in the Finnish case, spoke of 'an agreement between two countries'. However, the Finnish agrarian and 'united bourgeois' parties were perturbed at an association that might lead to the triumph of soviets in Finland, and therefore drew closer to the Provisional Government, agreeing to temporize.[34]

The Provisional Government, given this reassurance, came back to the idea of compromise, and stated that the future of Finland would be decided by the constituent assembly. At once, the Finnish socialists broke with Petrograd, and the Seim refused to pay taxes ' to a government that fails to stop the war'. It proposed a law on separation, in March, much to the embarrassment of the Russian socialists; although, under pressure from the Mensheviks and Socialist Revolutionaries implicated in the Provisional Government's decisions, it declared that it only wanted the principle of Finnish sovereignty to be recognized. Among the Finnish Internationalists like Sirola, there was an idea of pushing ahead with Revolution – as was already happening in Latvia, although without dissociation from Russia.[35] This was connected with the July crisis, for, when it broke out, the Seim passed a new draft law which proclaimed the country sovereign; an amendment by the Young Finn, Valas, requiring the law to be submitted to the Petrograd government, was rejected by 104 votes to 86. The Provisional Government saw it as a *de facto* declaration of independence. Anti-Russian feeling ran so high in Helsinki that some of the agrarians joined the social democrats in the vote, which acquired a properly national dimension in July 1917.[36]

Just after the July Days, the Provisional Government was full of its apparent victory over the Bolshevizing extreme left, and engaged in reactionary policies that affected the Finns as well as others. They were obliged to fall back, producing on 12 July an Address, in the form of a confused apologia, in which they explained that the Act of 5 July had only been intended as a preparation for the future. The government, in Milyukov's words, 'for the first time acted firmly, and it made a strong impression'. There were more arrests in Helsinki, with the social democrats and fifteen members of the Socialist Revolutionary section imprisoned. The Diet was dissolved on 18/31 July, and new elections were ordered for 1 October.[37]

The energy of its activity was owing to the Mensheviks' and Socialist Revolutionaries' condemnation of the Finns' doings, because like Milyukov they detected connivance between Helsinki and the events in Petrograd. Chernov and Tseretelli joined with Kerensky to sign the decree of dissolution. When, a few days later, the Finnish social democrats approached the Petrograd Soviet to explain their attitude, the administrative bureau took the government's line and drily answered that 'the decrees [*sic*] concerning the supreme rights of Finland are a matter for the Provisional Government and mutual relationships are to be decided by the constituent assembly'. After the repression, *Rabochaya Gazeta* and *Novaya Zhizn'*, which were more to the left, were timidly critical, suggesting, essentially, that the government had been 'clumsy'. Only the Bolsheviks supported the Finns, though they did not use the term independence and talked only of Finland's 'rights'.[38]

The food crisis worsened things, and great strikes broke out at Helsinki and Turku. The governor declared that 'the dissolution was not meant as a counter-revolutionary step; it was meant to re-establish true rights, as an initiative towards the resumption of discussion'. But he acted to prevent the Diet from sitting, which some of its members had declared an intention of doing. There was a test of strength, with troops dispersing the deputies who tried to assemble despite the prohibition; but the confrontation was not as violent as Kerensky had feared, and authority remained with 'the Russian power' as the governor-general, Stakhovich, concluded.[39]

It was a short-lived victory, even though the defeat of the Finnish social democrats in the new elections was another apparent success for the Provisional Government. There was a non-socialist majority in the Seim – bourgeois and agrarians predominated, and the Swedish party re-emerged.[40] The overall situation was complicated and worsened by the German advance to the Gulf of Bothnia and the presence of the Finnish Legion in occupied Riga. It was composed essentially of members of the bourgeoisie, and was associated with the agrarian party. The Swedes also intervened, indirectly, in Finnish affairs, by allowing Finnish supporters of re-union with Sweden to enter Finland and by fostering an active clandestine traffic with Germany – in July 1917 fourteen kilograms of gold were confiscated by the Russian authorities at Oulu (Uleaborg) which had become a turn-table for such exchanges, the frontier being 'like a sieve since the Revolution'. The Russians worried both about the re-emergence of the Swedish party and the aid given from Stockholm, through the 'Private Central Bank', for the development of indirect German-Finnish links. It was obvious that Finnish bourgeois circles were increasingly hostile to Russia now that there was a real alternative, that of German-Swedish support.[41]

There were more and more incidents between Russians and Finns, usually between Russian workers, unemployed, and soldiers, and Finnish youths. The country slid towards civil war.[42] The social democrats, who had been beaten at the elections, declared that they 'have other ways of acting than elections conducted under a terror';[43] but in reality this 'terror' was less the act of the now disintegrating Russian authorities than of groups set up for self-defence by the agrarians and enemies of the social revolution, who were more or less in league with the Germans.[44] The social democrats set up in turn a 'Guard of Popular Liberty', in association with Russian Bolsheviks, especially Smilga, and, as against both Seim and Helsinki senate, a truly alternative power, seeking to establish soviets in Finland, was set up to Tampere.[45] It underlined its loyalty to October, whereas the Seim, without referring to the Act of 5 July, speedily proclaimed Finnish sovereignty.[46] This criss-crossing, like the ensuing events, appeared to be a straightforward demonstration of Marxist-Leninist theses on the association between the class struggle and nationalism.

The new Bolshevik régime met an embarrassing situation after 25 October. If it respected the proclaimed principles on self-determination, it would have to recognize Finland's independence; but which Finland? It could not be one that the Bolsheviks wanted to support, that of the working class; it would be a nationalist and bourgeois state, according to the results of the election 'conducted under terror'.[47] Stalin came to Helsinki as People's Commissar for the Nationalities on 14 November and called on the Finnish social democrats to follow the Russian example. But conditions were against this, for the left of the social democrats was popular only in so far as it stood in the vanguard of the nationalist movement, and for no other reason.

At the urgent request of the government set up by the Finnish Seim and supported by public opinion, the Soviet government was obliged to recognize the total independence of Finland, on 6 December 1917. According to Stalin, he had had 'to act against my own will, giving liberty not to the people but the bourgeoisie who, through a weird set of events, acquired independence at the hands of a socialist Russia'.[48] The recognition of Finland's right to independence, formulated just as negotiations started at Brest-Litovsk, lent reality to what the Bolsheviks said on the rights of peoples; it had exemplary significance. But the Bolsheviks had promised their 'Finnish comrades' help,[49] and, two months later, the Finnish social democrats' left wing, inspired by the neighbouring presence of the Soviet régime, and with the help of the Red Guard, tried to seize power. A Finnish Soviet government was set up which Moscow, paradoxically, also recognized. Russian forces — about a thousand men — came to the aid of Finnish Reds. Helsinki then called in the Germans. Within a few months the troops of Mannerheim and the Germans had drowned the revolt in blood, a true White Terror in which there were almost 80,000 victims. It appears that the Germans were of more help in crushing the movement after its defeat at White hands than in the military operations themselves, for they had to contend with the Red Navy: Russian ships, which held the passages in the Gulf of Bothnia, offered protracted and powerful resistance.[50]

The Red government vanished, and a token of this was the agreement of 1 March 1918 between Seim and soviets, which provided for arbitration by the Swedish social-democratic left in the event of a new conflict between Russia and Finland. A concession to the Bolshevik left was that a common Russo-Finnish citizenship was created, and recognized in the treaty. Two further acts completed the pattern of a policy that did not really abandon the Finnish Reds, and drew credits on the future: a Finnish communist party was set up in exile, and a separatist movement, fomented by the soviets, evolved in Finnish Karelia. At the same time Karelia was promoted to the status of Soviet Republic, constituting a Finno-Karelian territorial unit in the name of the workers' right to self-determination.[51]

The Finnish communist party (*SKP*) had been created in Moscow. Its founder, O. Kuusinen, had special links with the Russian Bolshevik party and played a part of particular importance in the *Komintern*. From Karelia, the *SKP* helped remnants of the party who fled from the White terror to survive, but it was prohibited when it went too far. By the 1930s, it seemed that the establishment of a Soviet régime in Finland was a purely historical problem. However, in November 1939, Stalin, who faced the threat of war with Germany, tried to strengthen the defences of Leningrad by acquiring the Vyborg neck. He had no other territorial ambitions, but, assured by the Finnish communists that the class-struggle was now ripe in Finland, he allowed the formation of a phantom Finnish government, called the Terjokki government, in the Karelian isthmus. The failure of this was still more bitter than in 1919, for the prime minister appointed by Stalin, Arvo Tuominen, escaped to the other camp and supported the Tanner government 'which defends Finland's independence'. The 'Winter War' was ended by a treaty that gave the Soviets the area they desired, and they did not even require the legalization of the Finnish communist party. The phantom Kuusinen government disappeared.[52]

It did not do so permanently. A year later, the Tanner government, encouraged by German might in the east, started a 'war of revenge' which ended in Finnish defeat. In 1944 the Finish communist party was legalized again, and helped set up a democratic union similar to those formed in western countries. The communists controlled this union, although they did not have a majority in it. In the general election it won 25 per cent of the seats, entered the government and obtained the ministries of defence and the interior, at the same time that Togliatti and Thorez had failed to do so in their countries.[53] In February 1948, just after the Prague coup, Stalin asked the Finnish government to sign a treaty of 'friendship, co-operation and assistance', similar in terms to those concluded with Hungary and Romania. The prime minister vacillated. Maybe the communist minister of the interior warned the chief of the general staff that a coup was forthcoming; maybe one was forthcoming. Whatever the case, the army disarmed the police, and the 'troubles' announced by the *SKP* did not occur.

There was no sequence to this, and in the next elections the communists lost votes, and then seats and ministries. The subsequent return to power of some communists owed nothing to the Soviet Union. She had once more stopped interfering in Finland's internal affairs, and in exchange was given guarantees as regards the foreign policy of Finland. This castrated form of independence, which its opponents call 'Finlandization', and which the problem of propinquity accounts for, created a kind of balance that both sides accepted. It has only recently been infringed when, at the USSR's explicit request, a measure in internal affairs was taken by the Finnish government to forbid translation into Finnish of certain works by Soviet dissidents.[54]

A model for relations with the non-integrated nationalities

The Finnish example illustrates both Soviet nationality and external policy, which can be summed up in a model.

1   The principle of the right to self-determination was recognized, to the benefit of the Seim, as long as Finland was emerging from the débris of the old order. The first modifications in nomenclature occurred once the 'state of bourgeois revolution' was started, for the right of self-determination passed from nation to working class, so that the Tampere government was recognized in its turn. In the same way, this made possible recognition of the soviet government in Khar'kov even though the Soviets had already recognized the sovereignty of the Rada. This was legitimized and made explicit by Stalin during the Ukrainian crisis, and the principle was later extended to Poland and the Baltic states. There was a second modification at the end of 1919, when at the 8th congress the proposal was adopted that the decision as regards self-determination lay, not with the working class, but with its party, i.e. the communists. According to Hélène Carrère d'Encausse, it was the same when Bokhara was attached to the USSR.[55]

2   As long as the most revolutionary body failed to carry out its task of reunification, state treaties became more important than relations between the communist parties. On two occasions the Finnish communist party had to sacrifice itself to the interests of the Russian Soviet Republic, as strategic reserve of the Revolution. Activity against a state with which

Moscow had concluded a pact of friendship weakened or endangered the position of the USSR as fortress of the Revolution, and so became counter-revolutionary. Communists who fought this need for 'repose' were expelled or liquidated, as happened with K. Manner in Finland and latterly to communist leaders from Latvia, Poland or Turkey.

3   The establishment of a communist party in exile, for Finland or Latvia for instance, could run parallel with the establishment of a second party when the policy of the one outside the USSR did not conform to Kremlin strategy and tactics or to the Soviet government's interests: after the Second World War this happened with Greece, India and elsewhere.

4   The creation of a national movement on the borders of the Soviet Union provided the scattered elements of the *SKP* (Finnish Communist Party) with a territorial base in Karelia, and, equally, provided for future claims to rectification of the frontier.[56] Before October 1917, there was no talk at all of a Karelian nationalist movement, and the state of Karelia was created latterly by the Soviet Republic. It was an *ad hoc* affair, based on a parochial patriotism that was dressed up as nationalism. The same method was used in Byelorussia, but with the variant that there was an existing Byelorussian movement – though an extremely small minority of the population supported it – which the Bolsheviks had attacked before October but none the less legitimized and revalued in 1918 in so far as it could be used to undermine the unrestricted expansionism of Poland and Lithuania. In Central Asia, the creation of states and several nationalities divided the Moslem movement into local movements.

5   The creation, though transitory, of a Karelian-Finnish federation, whether or not it was conceived of as a stage, was copied latterly in the Caucasus and was then made general in the constitution of the USSR.

6   The formation of an armed force such as the Red Finnish 'army' in Soviet territory was repeated several times especially in Poland during the Second World War. The help of Russian Soviet troops, which was obvious but limited in Finland, was more considerably used in the cases of Outer Mongolia, the Caucasus and elsewhere, and the conquest of Georgia was a military conquest, pure and simple, dictated by Lenin.

7   Intervention from abroad, which was real though limited in scope to start with although it was of great importance and was even vital for the survival of the Soviet Union, was used to justify and explain the direct engagement of Soviet forces abroad – against Germans and Swedes in Finland, Germans in the Ukraine, British and Canadians in the Caucasus, Japanese in Mongolia. It had protected the Baltic states' independence until 1939. But were there any foreign soldiers still left in Georgia when, in the name of this threat, the country was invaded and forced to sign an 'alliance'?[57]

A model for relations with the integrated nationalities

Finland resisted with energy and violence any direct interference from the USSR or the *Komintern*, and remained independent for many years, as it still largely does. Since October 1917, other nationalities were attached to or associated with the Soviet Union by a combination of methods. This is different from the Finnish case, especially where the nationalities were already integrated into the USSR. In proceeding towards reunification, Hélène Carrère d'Encausse shows that Lenin usually went through two stages.[58]

First there would be a bilateral alliance with the national state after recognition of it, or after Russia had lost her sovereignty over it. Then would come a process of reunification by which the state lost, one by one, various of the attributes of sovereignty — its own army, foreign policy, etc. For the Ukraine or Georgia, this process was over by 1923−4, i.e. before the era of Stalin, which was distinguished not so much by a specific approach to the problem as by the violent liquidation of all resistance, especially by bodies that proposed an alternative to Moscow's political system — Sultan Galev's pan-Islamic socialism, for instance, or *Poale Zion*.[59] Lenin would have preferred the reunification to come through freely-negotiated agreement for he never imagined that the nations, once free, could actually survive as entities and that they could only be reunited with the Soviet Union by force and constraint. When this hope proved wrong, he blamed the effects of Great-Russian chauvinism. In reality, the men who were responsible for this policy, themselves in any case seldom Russians, were obeying an authoritarian centralizing reflex, a kind of neo-Jacobinism, which tradition Bolshevism revived as soon as it triumphed in October, as the cases of Finland and the Ukraine show.

In all the cases of reunification, the Soviet government's action would, after successful reunification, effect a whole set of measures.

1   The bodies established to decide the status of the non-Russian territories would be de-russified, unless it could not be done. *Narkomnats*, from the beginning, was composed of non-Russians, though it was often difficult to find even a single Bolshevik among some nationalities.[60]

2   The regeneration of national cultures sometimes amounted to resurrection or even self-revelation. All the real or latent collective frustration was dispelled, and no régime has ever done so much for 'cultural minorities' and been able to use them in the interests of the state.[61]

3   Through the creation of a set of national and federal entities, a non-Russian intelligentsia was formed and it took over quasi-governmental tasks, at least in the area of representation.

4   There was an unwavering policy to set up more and more non-

Russian responsible bodies in the federal system of institutions, at the pan-Soviet level. The process was slow but irreversible, even if, in the mid-1920s, there came a reversal in the Russians' favour (see Chapter 7).

5   The creation of double nationality, federal and national, was regarded by most non-Russians as a promotion, but was an annoyance to people whose nationality had no territorial base, especially the Jews, but also the Black Sea Greeks.

6   The liberty accorded to each citizen to choose his nationality was barely used, even by Jews. If they wished to count as Jews they would be renouncing something; and if they wished to be Soviet citizens, their choice of nationality would have to contend with hostility from the anti-semitic civil servants of the territories they inhabited – especially in the Ukraine, but also in Russia.[62]

7   Legally, the existence of a Soviet Russian nationality that was open to all after 1918 permitted the sovietization of non-Russians, even abroad – thus the Poles and Jews who were not recognized as citizens of reactionary Estonia in 1919 were legally made into Russian citizens. Is this law, internationalist in spirit, still applied?

8   The gradual sovietization by law of Russians and non-Russians alike ended in a unification of cultures, and an equalization of status. Has the Marxist utopia been the last word on the nationality problem?[63]

Moreover, with the Stalinist reaction, and the violence that accompanied it, especially towards nationalities that, as a consequence of the Second World War, came in contact with the Germans – the Crimean Tatars, Ingush, Chechen, Volga Germans, etc. – sovietization was felt as a resumption of the old russification inasmuch as the higher elements of the hierarchy were steadily russified (see Chapter 7). This was the case in the Ukraine, and after the war, in the Baltic states and Kirghizstan. The increasing number of laws common to the whole of the USSR, though they were not necessarily marked with a Russian seal, showed the trend in so far as the harmonization of statutes might be taken as a subversion of separate national identities.[64]

9   Russian nationalism reacted, for its part, to the slow colonization of Soviet bodies by the nationalities, except at the top. It was often a reaction that was out of date, especially as far as the Jews were concerned, since the chief parts of the state had been in non-Russian hands only at the very beginning of the Soviet era (see Chapter 7). The resurgence of national sentiment was the obverse of the nationalities' resistance: it was a form of latent opposition to the régime.

CHAPTER 5

The Revolution
in the countryside

On 26 October, in the middle of the insurrection, Bolshevik delegates to
the second Congress of Soviets were asked to fill out a questionnaire. It
asked how far the soviet from which they had been delegated was representative, how many non-Bolshevik delegates there were, what the soviet
had done in the period of reaction, and much else. Most of the twenty-
eight questions received an answer from these delegates of 140 soviets,
but some got no answer – especially Question 19. It read, 'Have there
been agrarian disorders in your region? What is the soviet's influence over
the peasantry, and what part does it play in the rural movement?'

Out of 140 questionnaires, fifty left this space blank or said, 'We do not
know'. In the rest, the presence or absence of agrarian trouble is stated in
a single word without further elaboration. The soviet's role was only
mentioned fifteen times, sometimes merely to say that 'the former soviet
opposed land-seizure'. Its influence was stated to be important only in
four or five answers, those of the Nikolayev, Yelino, Vladimir and Gusev
soviets.[1] There is a problem here, for, if the soviet delegates' ignorance
about the countryside is so great, what was the relationship between the
peasant movement and the Revolution in the towns and the army? Was it
autonomous, or grafted on – part of a whole, or an inchoate *Jacquerie*?
The Russian past, the delegates' silence, the very expressions they use
('disorders', 'excesses') suggest that the two parts were relatively isolated. We have to consider the rural Revolution not in terms of the
political parties, or of the role of Lenin and the Bolsheviks, or even as the
government, in handling the agrarian question overall, saw it; we should
take other points of observation, such as a village at the heart of the area of
troubles, or the standpoint of the committees and assemblies where the
peasants underwent their political apprenticeship. This gives a clearer
picture of the difficulties at grass-roots level.

1 The geography and methods of the peasant Revolution: the isolation of the Russian village

In Russia, the isolation of the village, and the compartmentalizing of societies and cultures had a long history.[2] It was the outcome of a great war fought by the state against the peasantry to control it and pin it to the soil. The institution of serfdom in earlier days was intended to bind the peasant and force him to cultivate the land. Throughout their history afterwards, the peasants tried to free themselves, by revolt or by flight. Few histories show such frequent peasant revolt as Russia's – there were almost 300 such revolts from 1775 to 1800, almost 1,200 from 1826 to the reforms of 1861. In few nations did the peasantry so constantly try to run away from their old lands or were there such social alliances to prevent them. In 1658 an *ukaz* made such flight criminal: in 1682, at the merchants' request, another *ukaz* forbade the peasants from going to towns to sell their goods. In the emancipation two centuries later the merchants asked the Tsar to confirm this prohibition, wanting the buying and selling of rural products to be their monopoly. In the outcome, emancipation did allow many peasants to become itinerants or peddlers, and there were increasing numbers of them by the turn of the century. However, with the feebleness of the permanent network of distribution, the change of status did not bring the villagers out of their cultural isolation any more than did the emigration of many peasants to Siberia.[3]

The village community, the *obshchina*, reigned everywhere, except in the western provinces and the Ukraine which were more open to the outside world. It regulated the villagers' relationship with each other, the steward, the church and the Tsar's representatives. After the reform of 1861, it could purchase land that became available but, to pay for it, the members became indebted for life. There was little improvement in the peasants' lives, and in the relatively good land of central Russia they even lost land during the emancipation, which could hardly be seen as a liberation. Prophets spoke of another liberation – when land would be given *gratis* to the men who worked it. The *obshchina* periodically redistributed land, usually in accordance with the number of men in the family, but it was the *obshchina* that owned the land, and the peasants could not buy, sell or inherit it, or choose their plots. They remained fixed, and if each peasant dreamt of escape, of becoming his own master (*khozyain*) with his own land, peasants were none the less stolid, with the *mir*, or community, their only horizon.[4]

In 1905 there had been peasant troubles, generally in poverty-stricken areas where periodic distribution prevailed. The reforms of 1906 were designed to head off future risings, by breaking the peasants' unity through the creation of a class of better-off peasants. Those seeking to leave the *obshchina* were given benefits and guarantees, and there reform did have results, especially, as in the Ukraine, where the *obshchina* had already been weakened by the beginnings of social differentiation, and, again, where the vicinity of towns needing workers caused the poorest peasants to sell their plots to the better-off, as happened in the provinces of Moscow, Vladimir and the Baltic where links between town and country had always been closer. Equally, the most prosperous peasants would leave the commune and no longer have to submit to its constraints. These *otrubniki* were envied by peasants who could not buy, borrow or pay annual interest — i.e. most of them, at least in the central regions, the country's heart, where the communal economy still reigned in 1917.[5]

The irruption of capitalism was late, and brutal; it weakened the structural unity of the countryside in Great and Little Russia.[6] In some regions, social differentiation started earlier than in others, and the rural community disintegrated; but in the heart of the country the peasants waited in the messianic hope of change, with large parts of the rural economy remaining stagnant and isolated. The lord who rented out his surplus lands lived in a town, and the villages would be aware of the surrounding world, only to hate it, in the form of steward, tax-gatherer or Cossack arriving, when war broke out, to conscript men.[7] The state also ignored the ways and customs of the commune. The village was *terra incognita* and the church easily considered it heretical. There were indeed many *raskolniki*: at Viritiano, in Tambov province, the village priest could not even participate in the thirty holidays of the year, except Easter.[8] Some revolutionary notions did filter through the countryside, and in 1905 armed peasant bands appeared in the countryside of Saratov, Penza and Vladimir; the egalitarian propaganda of the Socialist Revolutionaries had some echo in the countryside, for redistribution of the land was desired for all of the peasants, not merely the poverty-stricken.[9]

The February Revolution in the countryside

Two sisters, who could be from a Chekhov short story, wrote a letter that says a great deal about the coming of the Revolution in the countryside. It was registered on 19 May in a set of documents on the province of Penza.

Everything has been quite orderly . . . we own about 3,000 *desyatins*, and employ nearly 100 people. . . . A few weeks ago the situation began to change. Letters from our steward show that the peasants have seized part of the land and left us forty-five *desyatins* only; they are themselves cultivating the rest. They use our meadows and pasture for their cattle. After a short time the 'village committee' prohibited us from selling cattle, and there is no point in feeding the cattle, because we have to sell it to keep our property going. Finally, following a decision of the '*volost* committee', our prisoners of war were removed as well as the day-labourers we had employed. The estate is in a hopeless position. Our stewards' speeches and objections have been fruitless, and the peasants are still aggressive.[10]

The peasants' timetable and their behaviour emerge in this account: first they waited, then individuals began to act, followed by the village and the *volost*; then comes discontent.

In the province of Penza, where the Prittwitz sisters had their estate, the peasants had thus hung back before acting. The *muzhiks* had got together since the news of the Tsar's abdication, and the heads of the *dvors* had assembled, the *mir* being revived. The peasants dictated their wishes and measures they thought to be for the salvation of the country to the notary or school-teacher, and then waited for an answer. The government said nothing about proper solution of the land question; the central land committee established by the government behaved as if the peasants had been silent, and ordered an enquiry into peasant desires. The villagers tamely repeated what they had already been saying for some months, that the land ought to belong to those who cultivated it, that each should have only as much land as he could cultivate with his family, that the distribution should be equal, given the opportunities open to each village, that the land should be given out for nothing, and that no compensation should be paid to people who had owned more than the average, even if – as with the *otrubniki* who had split off from the communes in Stolypin's reforms – they had taken over the land and not yet paid off their debt.[11] If, however, they themselves cultivated the land so onerously acquired, and not yet bought outright, they could continue to own it.

The peasants hoped for a confused mixture of collective and private land-use. They wanted to revive a distant past, before the 'reforms', when distribution of land regularly occurred under the *obshchina* according to the size of the household 'with regard to requirements and the hands available to it'. The peasants also wanted to have the land and not pay for it, as of right. They dreamt that the law would be equally fair-minded. The *muzhik* could extend his farm and become its true owner, *khozyain*. He could see no problem as to land ownership – it was God's or the Tsar's or whoever's property, but the peasantry had the right to enjoy the fruit of this land for nothing; the large estates' vast spaces should not remain uncultivated while high rents, poverty and death threatened the peasant's household because of the smallness of its plot.

The first response of the authorities was to forbid any illegal land-seizure,[12] and a further measure guaranteed landowners and other producers damages and interest for their losses in the initial disorders. Cases of land-seizure had been reported from the Kazan area, and on 21 April the government issued a decree to define the competence and organization of the land committees, and shortly thereafter decreed that the supply-committees, the composition of which it determined, had the sole right to dispose of improperly-used land. The first acts of the February revolutionaries were therefore meant to protect private property by depriving peasants of the right to occupy land. It was placed under the control of new institutions created in the towns. These steps appeared to the peasantry as conservative.[13]

As the capital saw them the first excesses, in March, were merely a settling of old scores. They could also be explained by the need for immediate improvement. That the local authorities failed to react, and were weak towards violation of the law, could only promote this, and at the time it was not intended to push through a radical change of the social and economic system of the countryside. Violence was also limited to where there had been excesses in 1905, and often occurred at the expense of great estate-owners with German names. But in the second half of March, impatience for real agrarian reform emerged. The authorities did manage, by and large, to convince the peasants to postpone the seizures they wanted to effect, but the peasants were now organized, and the structure of their committees was not what the government had prescribed.[14]

As the report ran,

> these soviets have multiplied, decreeing rules and regulations, defining the norms of peasant property . . . it is no longer a simple matter of drawing up an inventory of land, supervising the state of the land-register or giving peasants the right to do this.

It was designed to take over the landowners' property; the most active were men from outside the community, while the mass prudently hung back. In May the movement grew. The committees pretended loyalty to the government, but they flagrantly and consciously violated its decree forbidding confiscation and disregard for property rights until the constituent assembly had met, and their sphere of influence rapidly increased, forcing higher authorities to recognize their activities as legitimate.

The activities of soviets and committees caused the government to react, as explained by the civil servant responsible for this report (which omits to mention the effort at repression by troops, late in March). On 1 May Shingarev appealed: 'There must be no seizure of the lands of proprietors and *kulaks*'; on 3 and 28 June the ministry of the interior drafted a law against violation of property and seizure of land or forest. On 29 June, however, Chernov authorized the land committees to settle some matters. His efforts were not sustained by the government, though inevitably they were seen as a disavowal of his predecessor's circular. As the report ended, 'It fomented trouble, and had the effect of unleashing the peasantry.'[15]

The peasants, however, had not waited until these ministerial efforts before going ahead to effect decisions made at village or *volost* level; peasant committees had been set up at every level of government in the countryside. Deputies of the villages went to the *volost* and thence from *uezd* to *guberniya* – the current usually going from base to summit, though sometimes the other way about provided the peasants approved of what was decided.

The committees' activity and the function of their administration

In the province of Penza, the 'troubles' had started late in March. The commissioner, Kuguchev, who was chairman of the executive committee, immediately asked the government to send other commissioners to 'explain the position to the peasants'. One of them arrived and told the ministry by telegraph that the peasants had conducted *volost* elections without waiting for government instructions, and 'it is these committees that have authority over the peasants'.[16] Details as to one such, a superior jurisdiction, for Novochastky *uezd*, have survived. It contained twenty-eight *volost* representatives, all of them peasants, two representatives of the clergy, two large landowners, two teachers, nine representatives of small towns, and two of local commerce. They had all been elected, and forty-five members told the government commissioner that they would 'give effect to decisions taken in the capital, and organize the new society'.[17] However, in conducting an election and then meeting, they had not waited for the decree of 21 April on the constitution of land committees. The supposed 'government decisions' were in reality those of the peasants' assembly of Penza, which was held on 15 May; the decisions were at once applied.

The peasant convention of Penza agreed that 'the land question will be solved by the constituent assembly', but it took interim measures, to be applied at once: utilization of arable land, tools and animals; a redistribution of prisoners of war and workers who had taken refuge in the region; revaluation of farm leases: recovering of certain arrears. A commissioner who witnessed the deliberations reported that

> This committee is almost completely composed of illiterate peasants, except for a man and a woman teacher. It calls on owners to apply its decisions and freely give their property to the [*volost*] land committee so as to avoid illegal occupation by individual peasants. The committee has also decided to leave to the monasteries and private landowners what they need for sowing and the proper working of the part of their land they are allowed to keep, i.e. that which they can work, with their families, without outside assistance. The rest of the arable land is to be distributed to peasants who have too little, the price to be fixed by the committee, at between four and eight roubles, depending on quality. If the owners refuse, on the grounds that they have prisoners of war to work part of their land, then these prisoners would have to be removed, and put to work on tasks more immediate to military requirements. . . . Where the owners have already rented out some of their land, the rent is not to exceed eight roubles. There is also to be exact accounting of animals and tools, which are to be distributed in the general interest, in the same way as surpluses are to be distributed, by priority, to those who need them most, such as soldiers' wives. The committee will share out the tools, renting them out at between twenty-five kopecks and two roubles per day, according to implement; the income will go to a repair-fund. To avoid deterioration of stocks, the harvests and other products destined for sale, the committee will supervise the corn and rye harvests of owners with more than fifty *desyatins*. If the owner says he has not enough for sowing, the harvest will be taken over by the committee.[18]

These decisions were not unique to this *uezd* or the province of Penza. There was similar violation of property throughout the Black Earth area. According to a report compiled by the executive instances of the ministry of justice, violation of property by individuals fell from 100 per cent in March to 50 per cent in July, while that caused by committees grew considerably. In mid-August these instances drew up a list of such 'violations of rights', in forty-two categories. Nine concerned the method of seizure, seven the use of forest and similar seizures, ten the confiscations effected in the name of committees, and applying to harvests, animals, implements, etc., seven the violations of contracts and similar agreements between private persons, eight the non-payment of taxes, defaulting on debts, non-payment of rent or breach of contract with the civil or military authorities.[19]

The change in the peasant mentality: an eye-witness

At the second session of the Great Agrarian Committee that met at Petrograd in July, a representative of Penza province set out the change that had occurred among the peasantry. 'The newspapers have described our province as "the Kronstadt of the countryside".' It was the simple truth. There was, however, a difference, for at Kronstadt the workers and sailors were still stating demands, whereas in Penza the peasantry had already acted.

'Imagine what it is like in our province, with peasants so poor that they have only a few *sazhens* each; how can a man with a wife and three children live like that? It is no surprise that, with such small plots, the peasants wanted to improve their lot as soon as liberty was proclaimed, not only in their dignity but also in their conditions now that Tsarism, which everyone said was the cause of their misfortunes, has been swept away. It was for this reason that, following the decisions of our regional soviet on 15 May, the peasants have changed land ownership even before the meeting of the constituent assembly to legalize its decisions. . . . That is how the land of the proprietors, towns, monasteries, dynasty and the like came to be managed by local committees, which then shared them out among needy workers. That is what happened to sacrosanct private property.

'Obviously, not everyone was happy. Those who suffered material or moral damage were not pleased. A peasant will not bow down any more and say, "Have pity on me, Ivan Petrovich, my family is dying of hunger, give me half a *desyatin*"; that he will do no more, and instead he will tell you, "let me know how many *desyatins* you can cultivate by yourself, and with your children's help; come to our meeting tonight and we'll share out your land". Indeed, the owners are not happy, not at all [laughter] and they are showering the local and provincial authorities with complaints, threats of legal action and lamentations. They are trying to poison the atmosphere, frighten the government and convince it that anarchy has broken out. They shout for help and do nothing else.

'And what are the peasants after? Is it only poverty, or have they some great idea in their heads? I believe there is something of both. They want to safeguard and better their families, and escape from poverty, above all, but they also understand that the present government of Russia is threatened, and that only the working people can save it, especially the peasantry by taking action and then doing work in exemplary fashion. This, gentlemen, has to be said. What is happening among us in Penza is beautiful, artistically beautiful, and I willingly advise all Russia to copy us.'[20]

The assembly of Samara: a political apprenticeship

There was still a wall, for the peasants felt that there was at least some misunderstanding on the government side, in view of its declarations. They knew that within the government there was confusion: on the one side were the circulars of Shingarev, Prince L'vov and Tseretelli, which they more or less knew, and on the other were the declarations of Chernov, especially that of 15 May which allowed the local committees some liberty of action.[21] The representative of the assembly in Penza believed that, in going ahead, the peasants felt they were helping the socialist ministers. The reaction of peasant assemblies to government policy was in fact much more complicated, as is clear from the instance of the peasant assembly of Samara, bordering on Penza.[22]

It had decided, at its first session in March that, in accordance with government instructions, the buying and selling of land should be held over until there had been an overall decision for Russia as a whole. It did satisfy one of the peasants' urgent claims and decreed a reduction of land-rents. At the second session, in May, the delegates' impatience became clear: part of the assembly wanted the land question to be settled before the constituent assembly met. One speaker, of the Socialist Revolutionary party, opposed this 'because there is not enough land to go round, and an overall decision had to be taken'. He was booed, and had to give up speaking. Another speaker, this time social democratic, asserted that a decision not taken by the constituent assembly could not have legal force. He had the same reception – 'We always have to wait, you ass, don't play the fool with us.' The assembly then reversed its March decision, and the delegates shouted towards the administration that 'they want to stop us from getting land'. The minimalists who had been elected to the administration were forced to step aside. They proposed an interim arrangement, transferring all land to the *volost* committees, the lands to be divided according to people's individual needs, with tenants having a lease at a rate fixed in March, and all measures being regarded as provisional, in force only until the constituent assembly decided to give effect to them. The assembly again howled, 'that bunch of lawyers again, saying they're on our side, but we know different; they'll betray us'. During this session, the delegates took note of the Shingarev circular against seizure and occupation of land. One delegate wanted the assembly to approve the government's provisional arrangement, but he was out-voted.[23]

A few weeks later there came a delegate from Chernov's ministry, the Socialist Revolutionary P. Axel, to attend a meeting that was to prepare for the third session.[24] He reminded delegates of the government's opposition to any alteration of property-structures until the matter had been decided by the constituent assembly. He too was forced to leave. Just before the third session a Bolshevik newspaper *Povolzhskaya Pravda* rightly remarked 'it is certain that the decisions of the second session will be upheld despite the rush of circulars coming at us'.[25] At the third session, on 20 August, a government commissioner attended. He was proposed for the chair, but refused it. The morning was spent in discussion of the composition of the administration, and the agenda. Three points received stress: the activity of regional sessions, elections to the *volost zemstva* and to the constituent assembly. An angry woman delegate said, 'I can't see why we're wasting our time with this talk. Elections may well matter a lot, but the land question is more important. Our ploughs are not in use, the land isn't being farmed, and that deserves the priority [noise].'[26] The officers of the assembly ignored this, and decided to set up sub-commissions for finance, agitation, supply, strife, war-victims, information; general assemblies were to be held twice in the week from six o'clock p.m. until midnight.

The first report on the committee's activity revealed what it had done in three months: 370 matters had been dealt with, 119 concerning soldiers' families and poor peasants. Applying the decisions of the second session, the committee supplied them with land, according to what they were able to use in accordance with the number of hands in each household. Forty-five matters involved conflict between *otrubniki* and members of the *obshchina*, each time at the former's complaint. There were forty-nine conflicts between landlords and tenants, generally about rent. There were also conflicts between *volosts*, battles of competence between *volost* and *uezds*, all them about demarcation of land. Overall there had been no physical violence.[27]

The reporter then went on to discuss the Leontiev-Tseretelli circulars 'which go against our decisions'. The regional section believed that this had to be clarified, and decided to sent two representatives to Petrograd to meet the minister, Chernov. They concluded that 'the circular is meant to deal with unorganized activity, whereas those in our province cannot be described as such, because it is decided by local committees.'

A delegate   What did the minister answer?
The reporter   Brushvit and Klimuchkin can say better than I.
Klimuchkin   Yes, but the report could not give all the details, for it would have taken too much time.[28]

Kuzmin (maximalist★)   We ought to be discussing here only matters relating to the report, but it has . . .

Brushvit   You will have all the details in due course.

Chairman   Let us continue this discussion tomorrow, in connection with the land question.

On the next day, the following exchanges took place:

Kuzmin   In yesterday's report there was a matter that would allow us to see better how the land question is due to be solved. There was mention of a misunderstanding between Petrograd and ourselves, of a delegation to the ministry, but the report says nothing about what the delegation received at Petrograd.

The Chairman   Yesterday the debate proposed by Kuzmin was voted against.

Kuzmin   I am unable to decide about the activities of our commission, and I know nothing of the journey or the meeting with the minister; we have to be told about this, or we cannot know what the commission did.

Brushvit   I am surprised this is being asked again. The actions of the peasants' section are one thing, and the attitude of the government towards us and the land question something else again. You must judge only what we have done, whether it was right or not. That is what you have to make up your minds about, and vote [applause].

Getkold (maximalist)   Your report sets out matters — this or that conflict happened, etc., but does not say what happened. The section failed to deal with the price of grain. The report is emptier than a *zemstvo* one.

Kuzmin explained the maximalists' view that the committee had done nothing to put into effect the provisional regulations, or set up *volost* soviets where they did not yet exist; it had done nothing to get going and to promote agitation among the grass-roots; it had not fixed maximum prices for produce of essential necessity; it had not protested against measures such as the re-introduction of the death penalty or the calling of the Moscow conference. Kuzmin went on to demand the election of the supervisory commission. This proposal was adopted, despite the elected officers' opposition, and the commission was elected directly by the assembly without reference to party membership. Then the discussion was resumed.

★ I have kept the indications contained in these minutes as to party affiliation, etc. The 'maximalists' eventually became the left Socialist Revolutionaries. In the towns, bourgeois or non-militants lumped maximalism and Bolshevism together.

Lazarev (Socialist Revolutionary) insisted on the exceptional character of the constituency assembly elections, and stated that Samara would have the right to sixteen members, elected from a list for the whole province and not three or four per *uezd*.

A delegate How will the party representatives be chosen? By the party leadership in Petrograd or by the soviets?

A delegate from Buzuluk uezd The Bolsheviks want the constituent assembly not to work, and they must be prevented from speaking or acting.

A delegate What will happen to those who are not politically affiliated?

Getkold I will not necessarily be in agreement with what the assembly decides. If it restores the monarchy, must we give way? The land must belong, without compensation, to those who work it. The government is against this, as its circulars show. The Socialist Revolutionaries are silent. They have been denying their own programme since they became a government party. In the national land committee the chairman, Postnikov, even asserts that to avoid disruption of production and economic relationships, the land-question must be solved in the interest of *all* parties [noise].

A delegate then attacked the maximalists and Bolsheviks for being good at criticism but unable to act positively.

A delegate There are no political parties left, merely ruins of them. It is absurd for Socialist Revolutionaries, now that they are ministers, to be pushed about and made to behave like clowns. It is dishonest.

Stashenko (Bolshevik) We want to nationalize the land. It must be redistributed, and the peasants turned into paid workers, as in the factories. With such concentration, the land will be wholly the people's. The maximalists are for socialization, but they are unable to raise their voices even in their own party, which has in any case ceased to be one.

Svistikov The peasants will send only Socialist-Revolutionary delegates to the constituent assembly – no Bolsheviks, because only peasants can understand the peasants' viewpoint.

Khlopotkin And besides, many intellectuals do not understand it, even if they have lived in the country. Better elect peasants who at least are aware of it.

Kuzmin I have had to suffer a great deal for the victory of our programme, *zemlya i volya*, and now every peasant champions it. The maximalists call on the peasants to seize all the land, without indemnity, and transfer it to the people who cultivate it. . . . To defeat the sabotage of the economy by the capitalists, we must manage things ourselves. . . . If need be, we'll defend this on the barricades.

Fortunatov declares that the peasants have decided to vote Socialist Revolutionary.

Maslennikov What gives the minimalists the right to identify themselves with the peasantry?

Preobrazhensky (Menshevik) turns to the political context It is said that we need peace, but while we talk ourselves hoarse in saying we want it, the Germans advance, and it is not by slavery or under their heel that we can build our liberty. To make peace possible, the Revolution must be strong; it must organize; for it to organize, everyone must do his job. If the worker is at his lathe, the peasants will produce grain, and the soldiers, instead of kissing the girls, will get back to the front. I do not want to offend . . . but the capitalists must capitulate. The government is relying on our organizations to get the strength to combat anarchy. The country demands this, and awaits your commands [lengthy applause].[29]

The minutes of this session show that, at the end of the address, the Socialist Revolutionaries pushed through a resolution expressing confidence in the Provisional Government and requiring democratization of the command; improvement of the fighting soldiers' capacity for battle; supervision of the state administration; fixing of maximum prices; maintenance of the law on the grain monopoly; immediate confiscation of property belonging to the monasteries, the imperial family, etc.; transfer of people able to work, such as prisoners of war and refugees, to places where they were needed; the army to make possible a peace without annexations; greetings to the pacifist negotiators in Stockholm; immediate promulgation of a law giving land to the workers for nothing; dissolution of the Duma, pensions to be paid to soldiers' families; abolition of the death-penalty.[30] In other words, even though the debates had seriously challenged the government's policy, the peasant assembly still voted for the motion of confidence put forward by the Socialist Revolutionaries. The delegates did not feel that the government was stopping them from acting, and some believed it was relying on them. This was a semi-defeat for the maximalists who had not extracted an explicit statement — from Brushvit and Klimuchkin — that Chernov had refused to recognize as legal the decisions taken at Samara. However, they had a half-victory in that a supervisory commission was established, and also in their remaining initiators in the debates.

These clashes were of little interest to the peasant delegates, for whom the main thing was that the local committees should be able to act at will.

In the Nikolayevsky *uezd* the decision to share out land was taken on 2 August; the minimalists became associated with it on 2 September, and were prepared to risk disagreement with the leaders of their party – which soon came. There was a similar process in other provinces, and it was among the causes of the crisis in the Socialist Revolutionaries which led, after October, to the expulsion of the left and the establishment of a separate left Socialist Revolutionary party (under Maria Spiridonova and Boris Kamkov). These quarrels did not concern the peasants, and, as the author of a report on the land committees said, 'what matters to them is that the decisions and regulations now adopted should be irreversible. They no longer mention the constituent assembly in their resolutions.'[31]

2 Regional variation

In the province of Samara, and in so many other provinces, men no longer saw any sense in waiting for the constituent assembly: part of the land had already been seized, the committees had started with agrarian reform, and 'there was no question of debating as to these committees' activities'. After late July, 1,727 agrarian conflicts were counted, including 889 partial expropriations with redistribution; and this figure grew rapidly, such that, in September, in a single region, there were 750 seizures. These figures may appear modest, but only because they concealed realities. Proprietors could not always lodge a complaint, whether because the authorities had vanished, the roads were no longer safe or the landlords, as in some cases, were unsure of what to do.[32] An enquiry over twenty provinces reveals better than these figures do the extent of the initial peasant movement, which could be described as pacific. This official report, written early in September, distinguished between four types of troubled zone: the area where there were organized occupations, with the lands of peasants being redistributed to peasants who had little or no land, with old rent contracts being considered null and void – a radical transformation that caused total disruption of production, especially when the peasants substituted cereal and food crops for beetroot and industrial crops, with the beet land being generally the first to be seized. The second category included regions where redistribution affected not so much land as animals and machinery, even grain for sowing, to be used by the collective; which, the report said, had more or less the same disastrous result on production and yield. The third category consisted of villages and areas where the peasant rising was aimed not at a take-over of production, but to prevent economic life from pursuing its normal course – there would be sabotage of machinery and arson. The fourth type was made up of those areas where there was no real challenge to the economic and social structure, the peasants merely obtaining reductions in rent, regular wage-increases and an eight-hour day.

The author of this report failed to mention, in the third group, the farms and villages where landlords and priests themselves organized the sabotage. It was, in reality, not very fruitful to draw a map of these types of agrarian disturbance, for all could be found together in two well-defined zones. First, there was the great zone that stretched from the central region south-east of Moscow to the Volga, the provinces of Kursh, Voronezh, Penza, Ryazan, Tambov, Samara, Kazan, with enclaves further north like Pskov and Novgorod, and especially in Byelorussia. Here the peasantry was poor, and collective solidarity was still shown in the land committee as inheritor of the *obshchina*. The well-off peasant was he who had split off from the group.[33] Second, came the zone of troubles of the Ukraine, Bessarabia, which was traditionally 'individualist'; the situation here was different. The estate-owners were fewer, and were relatively less differentiated from the better-off peasants who had benefited from Stolypin's reforms. On both sides there was a capitalist-style spirit of enterprise. The most violent hostility set the landowners against the poor and landless peasants. In each area, the poor peasantry played with the old tradition of 'rural banditry', with the aim less of becoming landowners themselves than of abolishing large estates. It was here that Makhno's anarchism emerged and flourished; here too that landowners and *kulaks* organized to defend private property. The Ukraine, as against Red Russia, was the land of the White Banner and the Black Flag.[34] This model has to be completed with reference to Siberian agrarian troubles — there, there were no large landowners — and to those in the 'nationality' lands, where nationalism and the agrarian question interacted variably.[35]

3 The problems of the peasant Revolution

The land without men and without food

The land had thus been distributed. However, the peasant committees had not taken it over completely, or in conditions from which peasants could at once profit. The peasants had their own ideas as to fairness, and had not wholly dispossessed the landowners and *kulaks*, leaving them the greater part of the sown land. The share confiscated might be large in area, but it was low in value, producing at most 10 per cent of the grain yield, with the confiscation otherwise affecting forest, fallow land and pasture. The share of each family in arable land rose by very little.

Moreover, the land had been divided up according to the number of mouths to be fed, without concern for the means that each might have to exploit it. 'You cannot eat land', said Lenin; and without capital or animals, it could not be effectively exploited. Nothing could be done as long as the towns failed to supply the necessary machinery. Eighty per cent of the scythes and 90 per cent of the fertilizer were imported, and the war had interrupted supplies.[36] In the province of Tambov, for instance, 86 per cent of the peasantry had no metal tools. The peasantry especially lacked animals, and the mass of poor peasants constantly increased. Since 1914, the number of peasants who became landowners through the Stolypin laws rose by 7 per cent, but the number of peasant proprietors owning no cattle rose from 25.7 to 30.7 per cent. In the province of Kherson, peasants owning more than five *desyatins* managed to raise their landholding at the expense of the large landowners, but even more at that of the poor peasants; there was a similar change in the province of Penza, where the number of horseless farms rose from 31.6 to 36.8 per cent.[37] In these circumstances, the peasant's first concern would clearly be to take over the small amount of machinery and animals possessed by the landowners. The disappointment was great, because the landowners were not American farmers, and hardly 10 per cent of their land was farmed by modern methods; they had left the peasants renting the land the task of supplying their own animals and tools. Only a limited number of these existed for distribution, and there could, in the circumstances, be no question of increasing the sown area.[38] The only answer for the peasants was to have plenty of labour, but the war made lack of this more and more obvious. The call-up of healthy men struck at small and large properties without distinction, and in both the military and non-military zones.[39] In Bessarabia the working agricultural population fell from 560,000 to 200,000, and the decline was in reality greater, because the army used the remaining workers to dig trenches and build roads. At the other end of Russia, in Simbirsk, the governor reported that 'the military authorities send us 258 men in spring and 187 in autumn, but remove 8,000 on 1 October'. There were properties of 100 *desyatins* without a single worker; and those of fifteen *desyatins* without a worker could be counted in hundreds. In February 1917 the governor of the province of Kherson wrote to Rodzyanko, 'Here, hardly a third of the land can be sown, and people will die of hunger for want of labour.' In 1917, after three years of war, there was usually only one male worker for every two farms. The proportion of land unsown rose from 6.4 per cent in 1913 to 13.5 in 1917.[40]

The use of prisoners of war had allowed some amelioration of this situation, in so far as the army could release them from tasks with greater priority. Until the Revolution, it was the great estates that had benefited from the distribution of labour that to some extent held back the advance of disaster.[41] The prisoners, too, however, were affected by the ideals of February, and by April were demanding an increase 'and just stopped work when they were not given what they wanted'. One group of peasants complained about 'their lack of discipline' − 'They are fed but refuse to work.' There was a chorus of complaints from the large landowners, and the ministry instructed them to combine to form a guard, meanwhile warning the prisoners that their actions 'are in violation of international law, and they risk arrest'. However, before the ministry could make up its mind whether the ministry of war or the ministry of the interior was competent to deal with the violations, the prisoners dispersed. When on 1 August the ministry of war gave the peasant committees − no doubt imagining they had nothing much to do − the task of recovering the prisoners, the prisoners had already gone.[42]

The two stages of the peasant Revolution

'They take over the lands of the rich, and then they won't work,' complained a society of estate-owners, in indignation. Many noblemen had found it sensible to abandon their estates and take refuge in the towns: 'The troubles have been such [in the province of Kazan] that we cannot go on farming.'[43] There had been many such complaints to the Provisional Government, the commissioners, the governors, but they had been in vain. The state no longer existed, and, when they stopped lamenting, the estate-owners began to organize themselves. In the Zenkovsky *uezd*, for instance, a 'farmers' party' was set up. It demanded (1) that the government should be free of pressure by committees and parties, (2) that members of committees, soviets and the like should be conscripted into the armed forces, (3) that a declaration of soldiers' obligations should be substituted for that of soldiers' rights, and (4) that certain rights should be guaranteed to citizens, such as that to life and that to property. Since the early summer, 'Unions for the defence of estate-owners' of this type had existed in some thirty provinces (the Volga area, the Ukraine, Byelorussia and around Pskov).[44] At Ryazan they had a newspaper, *Zemledelets*, which said, 'The Tseretelli, Peshekhonov laws are being ignored . . . Chernov must go.' Some of the landowners 'demanded' representation in the land committees, but their plan was that suggested by the Kadets, to join the movement the better to put a brake on it.[45] Most of them tried to stop it, interrupting sowings, and deliberately not cultivating the greater part of their land, for 'there is no question of using machinery as long as local committees are deciding everything'. If need be they would allege that they lacked labour, that the prisoners of war had gone, or that the government's fixed prices for grain did not cover their costs. Since the land committees were forbidding labourers to hire themselves out to landlords to help them cultivate their large estates, it was better, they said, to halt production.[46]

Other members of the landowners' union, while trying to break the peasant movement, also wanted military intervention. After the July Days, Kornilov listened to them. On 8 July he issued a first *prikaz*, applying to the military zone of the south-western front, and including the Ukrainian regions of Vinnitsa and Zhitomir. He used the Cossacks to supervise its execution. On 17 July the commander of the western front followed his example, and on the 31st the arrangement was extended to the entire military zone. On 8 September, after the failure of the Putsch, Kerensky confirmed the *prikaz*, without even stipulating that it applied only to the army zone.[47]

The document was complemented by decrees from three socialist ministers. Tseretelli, in an instruction to the commissioners, condemned 'any measure spontaneously taken by land committees'; Peshekhonov as minister of supply warned the population 'against any confiscation of the harvest'; Chernov announced that 'land-rents arrived at by freely-given consent must be paid to the owner'. There was soon an established legal procedure to enable action to be taken against persons and committees that had infringed the law.[48]

The government commissioner in the province of Novgorod gave concrete expression to this. Using the old penal code as a basis, he issued a warning to those in contravention of the law that they risked a prison sentence of four to fifteen years, not merely of six months; and he called on the land committees immediately to give up the operations they had been conducting since February and give back what they had taken from the landowners. 'Such laws are not in order', replied some of the land committees. 'The peasants, despite your ordinances, have occupied our land, hired labour and ignored protests. We fear arson and the destruction of the harvest'. 'The laws of Tseretelli and Peshekhonov are being totally ignored', wrote landowners everywhere.[49] Then the troops would intervene – in the Baltic provinces, in Bessarabia, near Poltava, and even more in the zone of troubles. In the Ukraine the Rada acted similarly. In April and May the army intervened some twenty times, in September and October, over two hundred times.[50] Repression affected the Pskov area, Smolensk and Poltava; at Tula in September there were sixty imprisonments; soon, over 50,000 legal cases had been started. After the Kornilov affair, the peasant soviets' attitude became more radical and it needed little to trigger off a gigantic rising, especially in the Volga area.

Table 4   *Number of risings*[51]

Guberniya	July–August	September–October
Tula	66	162
Ryazan	60	165
Penza	104	184
Saratov	35	145
Tambov	90	281
Volhynia	39	157
Minsk	76	199
Total for seven *gubernii*	470	1,293

Between the two periods, there was a clear increase in these incidents (see Table 4). The difference was that this time there was bloodshed and arson: the Red Cock had crowed. To the west of Kozlovka a farmer who fired on *muzhiks* was killed, his farm was burned, and soon the same happened to manors in the whole region: 'the skies east of Kozlovka were black in the day, and red at night.' Twenty-four estates had been set alight in this way. On the 14th the army arrived, and that caused the movement of arson to extend over the whole region. The number of burned-down manors reached 105; in the Oryol region, ninety-eight manors, six distilleries and a sugar-mill were burned, and the movement soon spread to Saratov, Ryazan and Penza. In the Ranenbursky *uezd* of Ryazan there was virtually daily arson on one or more farms – on 20 September, twenty, and on the 30th, nine more, with the arson continuing on 1 and 3 October. *Den* said that the soldiers would not intervene. On the 13th their commander sent in the cavalry, and on the 18th confirmation came that on that day, from three to five estates had been set alight.[52]

To the south, the movement reached into the Ukraine, and 200 estates were destroyed in Podolia and Volhynia. In the Tambov region, in the heart of the troubles, Prince Vyazemsky, though 'very popular among the peasants', had his eyes put out, his chest pierced through and then his head cut off by *muzhiks* and soldiers because he refused to grant one of their demands. This case was not unique, and occurred some time before the Bolsheviks took power.[53] Not six months had elapsed since the heady days of February; the bitterness and anger of the summer gave way to the unleashing of pent-up rage in the autumn. It was a return to the feverish atmosphere of an old tradition, the *Pugachovshchina* (the rebellion of Pugachov and his peasant horde).

The class-struggle among the peasantry

The revolt, starting from the zone of troubles, extended all over Russia once again. This time it was the 'second line of defence' of the old order that crumbled. The great estates had been the first, and they had gone; the second, smaller properties, was also swept away. The hated *otrubniki*, who had often enriched themselves at the expense both of *pomeshchiki* and poor peasantry, had to unite to save themselves, as the struggle within the peasantry took over from that of peasants against land-owners.[54] The limit of the peasants' tolerance did not extend beyond eight to ten *desyatins* in the area of greatest trouble, or ten to sixteen elsewhere. Those with more land than that lost the part in excess, though, if they accepted the Revolution, the old owner might keep some part of his property as the peasants were loyal to their own concept of fairness. Table 5 (from *Agrarnaya Revolyutsia*) shows the extent of redistribution from 1917 to 1920. Compared with a table of changes in the sown surface in the province of Kherson from 1915 to 1916 (Table 6), it shows that the redistribution coincided with the enlargements of farms during the war.[55]

Table 5   *The extent of redistribution from 1917 to 1920*

| Size of farms (*desyatins*) | PERCENTAGE OF TOTAL NUMBER | | | |
| | District of Kandeyev (Penza) | | District of Abdulov (Tula) | |
	1917	1920	1917	1920
up to 2	8.82	3.09	6.46	4.12
2−4	12.38	16.98	15.44	15.95
4−6	9.5	29.74	22.64	26.2
6−8	10.71	25.02	19.58	26.65
8−10	16.59	14.26	14.27	17.67
10−16	26.94	10.21	14.95	7.52
over 16	15.06	0.7	6.66	1.39

Table 6   *Changes of sown surface in the province of Kherson 1915−16**

| Size of farms (*desyatins*) | Number of farms | Increase or decrease of sown surfaces | |
		desyatins	percentages
up to 5	9436	−2936	−12.8
5−10	5106	+ 297	+ 0.8
16−25	2641	+1219	+ 3.8
over 25	1225	−1081	− 0.5

* These figures are corroborated by other statistical studies, especially those taken from the *Ekonomicheskoye rassloyeniye krestyanstva v 1917 i 1919gg.* and published, with others, in Shanin (622c) pp. 53ff.

The rural movement and October

The rural movement had started in May, swelled in the autumn and went on before, during and after the October Days without a particular connection with the course of that revolt. Melgunov noted that the number of seizures did not much increase in October, and this was used to support the theory that the countryside had had no part in the revolt, which was made out to be 'the work of a small minority'. The rural movement did contribute only indirectly to the success of the revolt, but that did not mean the countryside was anti-Bolshevik. It went on independently, with little regard for what was happening in the towns or the army, though it sometimes proceeded by imitating what was going on in neighbouring provinces. Through the collapse of the exchange-structure, its mechanical consequences, like the psychological effect of this continual 'outrage' was inevitably very great, even though in October only 144 seizures were counted.[56] These seizures came at the end of many others, and were followed by more: there was no 'October wave', merely a constantly-swelling tide of troubles that went on for over a year, after October, and relatively independently of what happened in the capital's politics, especially after September. The size of the wave, if measured on a French scale, would reveal two seizures of large estates every month in every department – which, repeated month after month for over a year, and added to other 'outrages', would make up between 500 and 600 per department for the whole period of nine months preceding the Decree on Land of 26 October.

The effect of the Decree on Land

In publishing his Decree on Land the very day of the October revolt, Lenin was skilful enought to legalize a situation that already was partially existent, for he recognized the *fait accompli* and legalized it all over Russia.[57] In the provinces where Soviet authority was rapidly established (Tver, Ryazan, Vladimir, etc.) the transfer of land occurred in relatively orderly fashion, which was in contrast to the spontaneous movement in the central provinces and the rest of the country. For some time Lenin had said he would adapt the programme of the party to the needs of the hour and the 242 peasant-soviet resolutions that the Socialist Revolutionaries had summed up in a 'model decree' – 'Private land is hereby abolished without compensation and all land is to be put at the disposition of the local committees.' There was no question of nationalization, and this new goal, instead of being 'the last word in a bourgeois revolution' became the 'first step towards socialism'. Milyutin and Larin had been given the task by the party of drawing up a reform project, and they did not dare go so far as to overthrow the old programme wholly. Lenin seems to have been dissatisfied with their plan, for it disappeared without trace, and he substituted his own.

The Socialist Revolutionaries protested that the Bolsheviks were stealing their clothes. This was true enough; but Chernov, for six months, had not dared wear them.[58] To the objections that were raised, Lenin said:

'We are a democratic government, and cannot ignore what the masses decide for themselves, even if we do not agree with it. The peasants themselves will learn how things are when they put the law into effect. Life is the best school, and will show who is right. Let the peasants solve the problem in their own way, and we'll solve it in ours. It does not matter whether things go in our way or in the Socialist Revolutionaries' way; what matters is that the peasants should be assured there will be no landlords any more in the villages, and that the peasants can decide everything by themselves and organize their own lives.'[59]

One difference with the Socialist Revolutionary programme was that this reform was put through absolutely, without reference to approval by the constituent assembly. The reform also failed to state on what basis the land would be shared out by the committees – according to number of mouths or of hands. On this question the Socialist Revolutionaries themselves had been divided, and the peasants themselves usually decided things on lines of equity rather than on grounds of effectiveness. The Cossack lands, to avoid trouble and for tactical reasons, were not included. There were several *Vendées* just the same, since the decree did not specify that all land was at the committees' disposal or without compensation. *Otrubniki* and *kulaks*, who for over ten years had saved so as to pay their annual interest, now found that their efforts had been wasted and their land threatened with at least partial confiscation. The decree sharpened the class-struggle on the land, and Revolution there gave way to civil war.

The weight of the past: country versus *town*[60]

As far as the peasants were concerned, it was they, and not the Bolsheviks or Socialist Revolutionaries, who had achieved the agrarian revolution and the redistribution of the land. It was true that in regions near Petrograd, in the provinces of Tver, Ryazan and elsewhere, the October Decree had been the starting-point of change, but in the heart of the country it had been otherwise. This is clear from an enquiry conducted early in 1918 in the province of Voronezh, and affecting eighty-five *volosts*. Only five of the seventy peasant soviets that had by then partitioned the land actually alluded to the October Decree: the rest had acted before it.[61]

For the peasantry, it was clear that only the 'maximalists' — Bolsheviks and left Socialist Revolutionaries lumped together — really approved of what they had done. This situation became clarified after October, when the Bolsheviks made war on the peasants' traditional enemies, the landowners and the church. Very soon, the Bolsheviks took over from the left Socialist Revolutionaries because of the superiority of their organization; by spring 1918, in the province of Voronezh, the Bolsheviks were active in ten out of eighty-four *volosts*, and were being established in five others. This advance was remarkable, considering the isolation of the countryside.[62]

There was still, however, an element of ambiguity, in so far as anything emanating from the towns was suspicious, even the best-intentioned militants. There was mistrust of questions asked by them, or of the printed forms to be filled in. For instance, in the first questionnaire on the situation, sent out in March 1918, to the question 'Have there been disorders, looting or pogroms in your *volost*?', the peasants of the Rogovatsky *uezd* (province of Voronezh) replied, 'No troubles or looting', and yet, in the minutes of the first session of their soviet, held on 21 January, minutes which were scribbled down and turned up only later, there was a note that 'the formation of our soviet is designed to end anarchy and the pogroms prevailing in our *volost*, and to re-establish order'.[63] The peasants were suspicious, and preferred to conceal the truth from townsmen and the militia.

Towns, for them, had always been places where the peasants had been beaten, tricked, and forced to deal with traders, usurers, Jews, bankers, civil servants, and the state. Repression had come, even in 1917, from there, and once the peasants had been rid of the landlord, they were still fighting their ancestral enemy, the townsman. They had two reasons for their anger: either nothing could be bought with their so hardly-acquired roubles, or the price of the things they wanted had risen, whilst grain prices had been strictly controlled. Once again, as before February, the peasants' anger burst forth:

At Chukhloma, near Kostroma, on market-day, the peasants demanded that the merchants should sell them tobacco and tea instead of hiding it. To forestall trouble, the commissioners suggested that some of them should be elected to examine the state of each merchant's stock. No tea, tobacco, flour or sugar turned up . . . but some of the merchants were lynched nevertheless, and there was an investigation in all the small shops and stalls in Chukhloma. The next day, a commission of enquiry into the merchants was established . . . the ringleaders seized some chests of tea in transit through the state depots, and some chests of tobacco as well. They were sold off, and each soldier was given a packet of tobacco as well. The committee awarded a rouble each to its own members, taken from the proceeds of the sales. Later on, one of the ringleaders was arrested, and the crowd did not offer resistance.[64]

The trouble spread. At Yuryevets, agronomists who managed the supply office were arrested; at Nerekhta, a supply commission pillaged the merchants' shops; at Varnavino, stocks discovered in the depots of the *zemstvo* co-operative were seized. Early in October, it was recorded in the Kostroma region, discontent was still very great: the peasants protested against townsmen who raised prices while grain-prices were restrained and they stopped transport of timber to the towns. 'There was no political activity, and no great interest in politics. . . . There are continual protests against government policies and poor supply.'[65]

The situation was a very ancient one, which went back to long before the Revolution. It was more cause than consequence, and the events of 1917 merely completed what the war had started, the disruption of the system of production and exchange. A stock-taking by the Tsarist bureaucracy in 1916 revealed this breakdown, for in forty-six provinces, manufactures were in short supply. There was no cloth at all in the depots of twelve provinces, and similarly, in most provinces, with metalware (hardware, bazaar goods, etc.); when it was there, as for instance in the province of Nizhny Novgorod, it could be had only at a range from three to ten times pre-war prices. In the Almazny area in the Ukraine, there remained only a week's supply in the depots; at Maryevka, only three days' supply in summer 1917. Everywhere the peasants threatened force if need be to get what they required.[66]

There were many such incidents. They showed an atavistic mistrust of townsmen, who were suspected of concealing goods. The peasants' rage was all the greater since the Tsar and the great estate-owners had been chased out, because they imagined that the commercial circuits would start working again. If these townsmen, who were already highly suspect, set up committees to arrange supply, and supposed that they could take inventories of the stocks of grain, any peasants would imagine the worst. Writing to 'these gentlemen' they would say, 'Our grandfathers arrived barefoot, bought the land, paid the banks and the nobles. Our fathers also had to pay, and we are paying; and now you want to take away our harvest and our land. You tell us that people will come to remove them – let them

just try.'[67] The members of the supply committees, though all 'proletarians', would quite often be beaten. In the peasant's mind, revolutionaries were often confused with students, and students were suspect if the
peasants associated them with the towns, the source of all evil. 'Tell us,'
said a *muzhik* to a young militant who had arrived to organize the electoral
lists, 'Your nails are very long — you're not the Anti-Christ, are you?'
whereat 'Peasants started shouting, and attacked the poor man to see if he
didn't have a tail or whether he was covered in hair.'[68] On 9 September in
the region of Chernigov, soldiers accompanied the representative of the
supply committee who had come to investigate the harvest in the village
of Kuchinovka. The peasants collected near the school and threatened
the little group with axes, scythes and sticks. They would not let the
investigation go on. Something happened, and a soldier reached for his
rifle. He was at once assailed, and trampled to death.[69]

The weight of the past: town against country

The townsman's suspicions were equally great. He had always been afraid
of the peasantry: rural Russia had never been an Arcadia. For the townsman, peasants were savage, ignorant and 'dark as the night'. In the
committees, it was social democratic militants who predominated, and for
them the passivity and inability of the peasantry to act were felt as con-
stants that needed no discussion: indeed, they were part of the justification,
and accounted for the very existence, of social democracy, the truth of
which had been revealed by 1917. That there might be, within the
peasantry, some frustrated and alienated elements was certainly stated by
some theorists, such as Lenin, but this was not given a hearing. Although
there was some truth in these theorists' view of antagonistic social groupings, most militants either ignored it or failed to notice it. The committee
members also behaved very clumsily when, in their attempt to discover
hiding-places, they appealed to the poorest peasants, who were regarded
as traitors and good-for-nothings: they were unable to go back to the
village afterwards.[70]

Whenever the townsmen went into the countryside, it was something
of a *prodrazverstka* or punitive expedition. In declaring that 'supply of
grain must not depend on exchange of goods with the towns' the members
of supply committees took no note of peasant reasoning. If there was no
bread, they supposed, it must be the *muzhik*'s doing; they reasoned
much as did the authorities who had proclaimed that 'to fail to deliver is
the same as deserting'. There was no doubt a battle of authority and
power-rivalry between the Provisional Government's agents and the
popular committees, but both of them used the same methods — armed

force – against the peasantry. There was continuity rather than a break in this matter between the Provisional Government and its successor. The Bolsheviks did, however, appreciate that this was dangerous. Near Tambov, the small growers of vegetables and tobacco rose against the town committee for requisitioning their goods at a low price, for, as the farmers said, 'Our village has offered nearly 500,000 roubles for the Revolution' (presumably through subscription to the Liberty Loan). There was another revolt at Ishim, near Tobolsk, against a committee that had requisitioned all the grain. Thereafter the peasants could well wonder what the point of producing it was, or of having the land at all, if they were unable to sell at a good price, buy and consume.[71] It was a repetition of the situation 130 years before, in the French Revolution, when the 'dirty maximum' price was imposed on grain.

In some towns, soviets began to see that the supply committees could not be given their heads. It was the Bolshevik party that took the initiative in this stock-taking, in the reports it made at various sessions of the conference of factory committees in Petrograd on relations between town and country. It wanted to 'help the peasants with deeds and not with words.' It recommended that some of the factories should re-convert so as to get delivery of manufactured goods that the peasants could use. An agricultural commission laid the bases of an alliance between worker and peasant, the *smichka*. Other soviets (such as Kazan) did not go into the situation so carefully, but still 'advised against despatch of soldiers to the countryside for any purpose'. Soon, all the soviets which had Bolshevik or left Socialist Revolutionary majorities tried to reason with the townsmen, but it was wasted effort. The supply committees did as they pleased, and the townsmen supported them because they were hungry.[72]

This added a new conflict to the social unrest. Its origin was obvious: it was a war of town against country, and country against town. The peasants found, behind the townsmen, the state and its agents – soldiers, bureaucrats, oppressors, the enemies of time immemorial. This war was associated with, and continued, the war that had set the two societies of Russia against each other. There were as many rural revolts in the central provinces after 1917 as before. In Tambov, both after and before 1917, the peasants rebelled and did not always distinguish between 'soldiers, bandits and civil servants' (Singleton). The peasants' movement thus developed to a large extent independently of the conflicts in the town and the army. They came together only after October.[73]

In the villages, the first effect of the Revolution had been the restoration of old customs. The peasants, linked by a committee, brought back the old notion of individual possession associated within a property collective that distributed the land periodically in accordance with the number of mouths to be fed, and also divided up the animals and implements according to equity. Large landowners and *kulaks* had to submit to this common law which, to start with, only deprived them of land that they could not themselves cultivate. But as this common arrangement also covered other means of production – and here lay the great difference with 1905 – these landowners were hard hit, they resisted and were then forced to make do with the average share. In its first stage the Revolution thus affected all large estates, and in the second all landowners. It was a spontaneous movement that owed little to Bolsheviks or Socialist Revolutionaries. The October Decree merely extended the application of such decisions, or legitimized them. It accentuated conflicts within the peasantry, in so far as land was handed over to the committees without compensation, which put the richer peasants against the régime. The Bolsheviks were aware of the problem; nevertheless, they did not imagine that, if they relied on the poorest elements of the village they would alienate it as a whole, the members of the 'committees of the poor' being regarded as vagabonds and traitors, 'sprung from God knows where'. All of this accentuated the mistrust of townsmen and the state which, with new excuses, was trying to confiscate the fruit of peasant labour.

Traditionally, the rural Revolution had been seen as a test of strength, with two phases: in the first, peasants in general fought estate-owners who lived, for the greater part, in the towns, and in the second, *kulaks* and *otrubniki* were fought by lesser and landless peasantry. Analysis of what happened in the villages does show that these two phases occurred, but in a telescoped and confused way, often even before the victory of October. The documents show in particular that the villages displayed a solidarity that put those who failed to share the egalitarian vision of the poverty-stricken countryside beyond the pale. After October the rural labourer who belonged to the 'committee of the poor' was generally as disliked as the *kulak* when he failed to unite with the other peasants; and the hostility of the peasantry overall towards townsmen and delegates of the machinery of state (whatever its nature) counted for more than the conflicts among the peasants.

Later on, the state tried to set one section of the peasantry against another, the mythical conflict of which it had itself invented. The search for the *kulak* was partly false, a matter of chasing shadows, for the *kulaks* had often disappeared, or sunk to *muzhik* level, since the Revolution of October. As for the poorest peasants, far from dreaming of collectivization, they hoped like the others that they would have their own land and become its *khozyain* in the way New Economic Policy later promised would be possible. They did envy conditions of the better-off peasants, but always identified with them. (This assertion is of course a generaliza-tion, perhaps more general than for historical purposes it ought to be. Moreover, it applies only to the heart of Great Russia. The situation in the Ukraine, in Siberia, and among the nationalities was altogether different.)

The upheaval of 1917 brought no real solution to the peasant problem. In the first volume of this work, the wartime destruction of the economic relationship between town and country was explained. Here it has been shown that, although 1917 brought many immediate benefits to the peasantry, the economic advantage was an illusory one. Given that the towns were producing little, or badly, and that in October the requisition-ing of goods took over from conscription of manpower, the relationship between town and country remained strained, even if, because of fear that the landowners would return, the villages supported Reds against Whites. When reconstruction began, after some years of tension and con-straint, the New Economic Policy of the Soviets did at last allow the peasants to buy and sell more freely, to feed better, and have a breathing-space. The happy times of NEP were of short duration, because the problem of exchange with the towns had not been solved, since the towns had neither agricultural implements nor manufactures to give to the countryside. The coincidence of factors in 1916 was reappearing: 'Why bother getting roubles, why bother working at all if you can't buy any-thing with the roubles?'[74]

The state's reaction was to enforce the collectivization of agriculture. It was the great change in the peasant's way of life.[75] In a way, this revo-lution from above had its origin in the workshops, in the towns, among those engaged in industrial production. It was violently accomplished, and since then, the *muzhik*, now *kolkhoz* worker, has found his own response. It cannot be said that in Russia the harvest is necessarily a reflection of the weather.

CHAPTER 6

Labour against capital

'When I first went to a factory, and saw these unfortunates, I knew at once that I could not go on living or being happy so long as things had not changed.'

Alexandra Kollontai

The Revolution of 1917 was felt throughout the world as a victory for the working class, for it had the effect of expelling the boss from his factory and ending one of the harshest systems of exploitation that the capitalist world had ever known.

In October 1917, the régime that took over from the Provisional Government defined itself from the beginning as a socialist, soviet, workers' state. It owed its origin, in part at least, to the conditions in which the trial of strength had occurred between the workers of the towns and the system that they fought; its origin was also associated with the relationship between the workers and the organizations that represented them, and spoke in their name. This chapter will examine (1) what the Revolution in the factory was; (2) the response of the employers and the Provisional Government to the workers' efforts at self-management; (3) the ruin of the economy, the effects of the war and the sabotaging of output; (4) the response of different working-class institutions (socialist parties, trade unions, soviets of factory committees and the like) and of the October régime to the wish that workers expressed to organize production themselves.

1 The Revolution in the factory

The Russian factory before 1917

Table 7 is not demonstrating the Salic Law or a code of Kievan Russia.

It was put up on the walls of the workshops of the Obukhov factory in Saint Petersburg, some years before the October Revolution. It gives the details of compensation for accidents at work and is a transcription, written into the flesh of the people of Russia, of labour conditions in Tsarist times.[1] It was not simply the savagery of the times that was responsible, it was the system itself. The violence was no accident, but intrinsic to the capitalist relationship in the Russian context, and it was meant to break the workers' resistance. The violence could emerge without machinery or 'factory accidents' being involved. Some years before the Revolution, out of 325 murders committed in the factories, 257 were the work of members of the administrative side, and were carried out on workers.[2]

In Eisenstein's *Strike* there is a perfect analysis of the social workings of a factory under the old régime and of the relationship between capital, workers and state; a useful complement is formed by parts of Pudovkin's *Mother* (adapted from Gorky), for the social reality implicit in these films challenges many of the historian's assumptions.

Table 7   *Rates of compensation*

Head	1 Cerebral lesion, causing serious difficulties:		100 roubles
	2 Cerebral lesion, uncovering the flesh but without serious consequences		70 roubles
	3 Lighter cerebral wound		30 roubles
	4 Cerebral contusion		60–85 roubles
Eyes	1 Loss of sight in both eyes		100 roubles
	2 Loss of sight in one eye		35 roubles
Ears	1 Deafness in both ears		50 roubles
	2 Deafness in one ear		10 roubles
Face	1 Loss of speech		40 roubles
	2 Damage to the face, harmful to the working of the senses		35 roubles
Back	1 Broken vertebral column		100 roubles
	2 Damage generally to the back		10–50 roubles

Limbs		Right hand	Left hand
	1 Loss of a thumb	30 roubles	25 roubles
	2 Loss of index finger	25 roubles	15 roubles
	3 Loss of 3rd or 4th finger	10 roubles	5 roubles
	4 Loss of little finger	5 roubles	—
	5 Loss of all fingers	75 roubles	65 roubles
	6 Loss of hand	75 roubles	65 roubles
	7 Loss of both hands	100 roubles	

The workers are not seen to be quite united. Their divisions reflect hostilities that are not purely — as the written tradition would have it — ideological (Bolshevik *versus* Menshevik, Marxist *versus* populist) but associated with employment in the factory and with age. It is significant that the unity of the working class is shown against a fixed background of three generations of workers. The disunity is always caused by the oldest, who break the strike in *Mother* and act as double agents or provocateurs in *Strike*. The radical movement's leaders are all young, their children being at most six or seven years of age. These young workers have obviously just come in from the countryside: it is there that they can be themselves, be happy and relaxed, and do as they want — they were born there, they like the countryside, and they can play, make love, and return to die in it. By contrast, the 'blacklegs' and the informers come from the towns, and their realm is the street, the low dive, where they are at ease, and can win.

The second group of workers opposing the strikes in these films consists of foremen, whose wavering often shows the ambiguity of circumstances within the factory; and other proletarian opponents of the strike, inside and outside the factory, include porters, drivers (who sound the factory sirens), firemen ('the bastards, they're turning the hoses against their own people') and domestic servants, i.e. the people who, though workers, have some power, if not privilege, whether of opening and closing gates, supervising the workforce, putting people to work, approaching the boss or being responsible for safety precautions. They can be associated with the peasants who have been driven by poverty to seek work in the towns, and act as 'blacklegs'.

The process by which the strike breaks out and is crushed does not originate in a demand that has been refused, nor does it illustrate cause and effect. In *Strike* the workers are discontented and pamphlets are handed around, but nothing happens. The strike breaks out, completely and spontaneously, when a worker who has been wrongly accused of stealing a micrometer commits suicide in despair. The foreman who had accused him is roughed up and then mocked. He is not held responsible for his misdeeds — it is the system that men blame, hence the completeness of the strike. It is also crushed in an apparently illogical way, without any particular reference to the demands of the system and the requirements of the oppressors. The workers' demands have been rejected; they have beaten the police provocation, have demonstrated and finally been dispersed by the police: the incident could stop at that. The mounted police are guarding the area, and a small child slips under the hooves of a horse. Its mother runs in to save it, but the policeman whips her, and she shouts for help from the workers. There is an immediate battle, which ends in a massacre of the workers. The need for violence, the cruelty of the servants of the state, and the indifference of well-educated people are parts of the system which this apparently irrational process reveals.[3]

Between the situation described in these films and the Revolution, the condition of the workers hardly changed. The main modifications were that the number of women workers went up greatly after the men had been called up: in 1917 they made up 35 per cent of the workforce in Petrograd factories; it was the same with very young workers, under-age for the army. A further change was that links between workers and the land became weaker. Those who still had a small plot of land became very much a minority, especially at Petrograd — hence, in part, the hostility towards the countryside, where those who had stayed behind were able to enrich themselves.[4]

At the same time, the bulk of the working class had been won over to revolutionary ideologies. The workers of the large metal or textile works were, in the main, social democrats; only a minority of workers, often in semi-artisan workshops or small concerns, had more anarchist ideas. But in their war with the bourgeoisie and Tsarism, the workers saw little meaning in these distinctions, or those between Mensheviks and Bolsheviks, or, within anarchism, those between anarcho-syndicalists and anarcho-communists, which were of still less importance. The distinctions mattered mainly to the organizations, which wanted to count their strength. Since the historical tradition usually reflects such sources, it reflects more their obsession than the explicit choice of the workers, which emerged only gradually, and later on.[5]

These changes hardly altered the condition of the factory workers. When the Tsar fell, the workers' despair at their conditions, and the wishes they had, were revealed in the telegrams they drew up in March 1917. They ask for a life that is less inhuman. They do not challenge society. It was the revolutionary militants, who were ahead of the masses, who wanted to include socialism in the programme. In March, however, most of them, even, were convinced of the inevitability of the historical process, and believed that the length of each phase must be related to laws of economic development. Apart from Lenin and a few anarchists, they dismissed as illusory and frivolous — in fact 'unscientific' — any plans that failed to respect the inherent slowness of the process. In the Petrograd Soviet, they fought the bourgeoisie, but they did not realize that their own convictions served bourgeois ends, since the bourgeoisie could use them to justify their own right to govern untrammelled or even to refuse that minimum of supervision that the moderate socialists would have liked to exert in sharing power with the propertied classes. However, revolutionary pressures did force the bourgeoisie to concede, however minimally, and the militants then hesitated, once they were ministers, to demand more than that — they did not want to have to manage an economy that, they supposed, would collapse if the concessions went further. This amounted to evidence that the system could not satisfy even the most modest requirements of the workers, and the bourgeoisie used this as an argument for ceding nothing at all.

At the very moment when the workers expected and demanded change, their own intellectual guides paralysed them. As these guides saw things, economic problems and the antagonism of employers and workers were creating a situation in which the realization of the slightest demand of the workers would undermine the system of production and the proper pattern of the Revolution. These contradictions were resolved in a gigantic battle. In the course of it, the workers initiated self-management — as unexpected, as foreign to the claims initially set forth in the March 'grievances', and also to the plans of the socialist parties talking in the workers' name, and as 'illogical' as the outbreak of the *Strike* or its repression.[6]

February: from ancien régime to self-management

February brought immediate changes to the factories. The workers were now free to combine, discuss and petition without fear of informers or the police. The Tsarist state had collapsed, and with it the trials and prisons. The workers' first reaction was a simple and pitiful appeal: more humane treatment, an eight-hour day, something more than a subsistence wage, social insurance, and some help to wives and children in the event of an industrial accident to the husband.

The employers tossed these claims aside. They had their own problems, and expected that the change of régime would allow them to operate the government for their own advantage. They had taken on debts, they had orders to meet, and Russian industry was not competitive — to grant the eight-hour day would make it still less so, and for the moment there could therefore be no question of granting the workers' claims. The Revolution had already lasted a week, the factories were not working normally, and the workers, they felt, could not have any idea of what such interruption cost. Everything could be discussed later on, when life had returned to normal. However, it did not become normal, and, in the confusion, employers had to concede at least something. In the capital and some thirty cities, the eight-hour day was introduced. The largest factories agreed to some alterations in wages. This had not much effect, since the cost of living rose even faster.

The commotion had to be stopped: people should go back to work, the

Revolution was over – at least, so the newspapers said – and there was a war on, with soldiers needing guns and clothing. 'Return to normal' was presented as a patriotic necessity. In Petrograd and Moscow men on leave and men of the garrison applauded such talk and were irritated by the workers' demands, for the workers' lot was infinitely easier than the soldiers' in the trenches. It was also a good way for the soldiers to avoid returning to the front, if they carried out a patriotic task of supervising the workers and compelling them to produce for the country's effort.

The workers reacted, and organized themselves. They felt they had a just cause, and reasoned with the soldiers, but, being rather suspicious of these 'uniformed peasants', they also wanted to be safe, and established armed militias. Thus, almost unconsciously, the worker safeguarded his factory as he would have his home. As it was he was spending more time in the factory than usual – whether in voting on resolutions, electing soviet representatives, resuming trade-union activity, choosing delegates to send to barracks and district committees, or participating in meetings of the factory committee.[7] Factory committees had been set up in most works when the Revolution began. They were elected by the assembly of workers, sometimes partly also by the works administration, and the committees became a kind of alternative force in the factories. A dual-power system operated in the factories just as it had fought for political authority in the country as a whole. The government, with a law of 23 April, recognized these committees' existence, and defined their methods of election and their rights, which were to remain purely representative. Many committees had been set up with other arrangements, before the law had been passed; they had established labour-commissions, started negotiations with the bosses and applied the arbitration procedures recommended by soviet and government. There were even representatives of the ministry of the interior and the Petrograd Soviet in the first of the great assemblies of committees, organized by the large factories of the capital. The communiqué that they drafted in common even laid down the law: it was Menshevik in inspiration, and declared that 'the workers refused to participate in management as long as socialism has not been introduced'. This was 'prompted', and, as experience showed, it stood in no relation at all to what the workers really wanted.[8]

Whether or not the committees' competence was laid down by the law of 23 April, it was hated by the employer, for it compelled him to discuss, explain and justify his orders, which was anathema to him. Moreover, in the arbitration bodies, negotiations did not always go his way, since he could not at the same time explain the declarations of profit that were published in the financial press – and widely reproduced in the

Bolshevik papers – and his alleged inability to raise wages. The committees would seek information by every possible method, even investigating the offices of management, and employers would break off negotiations at the slightest opportunity. There would then be an immediate strike.[9]

The May strikes swelled to gigantic proportions. At other times, in Moscow, strikes would break out because the employer refused the mimimum wage suggested by the arbitration bodies, such that, as the employers saw it, 'supply is declining, production is collapsing and demand is rising; we cannot go on like that'. They had other reasons for their anger – the government gave no help, blocking price increases but not wages. It offered its good offices in mediation, and yet would call on the employer 'to part with money that is not the government's to give'. The state now claimed a right to control which would, despite its denials, amount in the bourgeois view to *de facto* nationalization.[10]

One bourgeois minister resigned, and others prepared to follow; conflicts increased at factory level. The workers, despite threats, 'go on agitating', while their productivity declined since they had the right to attend these 'talking-shops'. The employers were especially enraged that they had to pay the workers for not working, particularly in the 'commissions'. There were seventy-two committee members in the Obukhov factory and as many as 115 in the Treugolnik. 'We pay them by the day, and they are really being paid for doing nothing.' 'It can't go on.'[11]

As if in response to a word of command, the employers laid off many workers just after the great strikes, and soon 165,000 workers were on the streets. The soviets objected. The Moscow Soviet challenged the dismissals, and was told they were caused by poor supply; but was it not really blackmail, with poverty as the threat? Once more, the commissions, and the ministry of labour itself, were called in to mediate.[12] For instance the managing director of Vulkan had just dismissed 600 employees and would not pay them their month's notice: 'He told the minister that he

Table 8   *Statistics of disputes in the Moscow metal factories*[13]

Of 149 disputes submitted for mediation by the arbitration committees between May and July 1917
49 concerned wages
28 concerned the rights of factory committees and payment for hours spent
       in them by their members
20 concerned the division of labour in the factory, and working conditions
21 concerned dismissals
31 concerned inequality of wages (women, and piece-rate or daily payment)

---

could not afford to pay it, and, in the existing state of legislation, he was under no obligation to do so.' He was assured by the minister that he was under no obligation, for 'this meeting is purely consultative, and I shall content myself with warning you that you have a moral duty to pay the workmen; the factory will certainly not improve in overall atmosphere', a closure such as that of Prodameta must be avoided at all costs. The managing director Minkevich replied that he would pay if he could, but he had not the means to pay two weeks' notice unless the sum was got back through work, and output was actually in continual decline. The factory committee suggested a new way of paying piece-rates, and the managing director exploded, 'Why not ask for two months' notice, or three or four? The workers ought to demand only what is strictly necessary.' He was invited by the minister to reconsider his proposal, and answered, 'I'll think about it, but if output declines I can't pay.'[14]

He had agreed to the appeal for arbitration by the ministry. But not all did so. In the provincial towns, especially, where the strength of the two sides was not clear and where audiences with the minister were difficult to obtain, many employers underestimated the revolutionary pressure and felt that, by uniting, they could resist. Violence was the outcome. U. Rikatin was the first employer to suffer sequestration for refusing to execute the judgments of the commission of arbitration that looked into the function of foremen. The same happened to an employer in Kazan, the managing director of the General Electrical Company, who failed to raise wages, in defiance of the commission's proposals; there were several such cases. The employers of Moscow refused jointly to consider the mediation of the commissions, or to take part in their deliberations: they wanted to remain 'masters in their own houses'. The ministry threatened severe punishments for workers who sequestrated their employer. The conflict is shown in Tables 9 and 10. In the Russian context, it was mainly

Table 9   *Sequestrations that were the subject of a legal complaint*[15]

June	July	August	September	October (to 23rd)
4	5	17	21	16

Table 10   *Statistics of lock-outs in Petrograd*[16]

	March	April	May	June	July
no. of lockouts	74	55	108	128	206
workers affected (thousands)	6.646	2.816	8.701	38.455	47.754

the small and middle-sized factories that were involved. To these figures should be added the partial wholesale dismissals that affected much larger numbers of workers.

The situation worsened, and the bourgeoisie began to lose patience. Perhaps some of the workers' claims were fair enough, but they should increase, and not run down, their efforts at work, because this, the employers felt, was in their and in Russia's interest. Russian industry had to catch up with the other industrialized countries; Russian business would go bankrupt if, to the inherent economic problems, were added disruptions of output caused by the 'whims' of the workers. In such circumstances, the factory would have to be closed. Many employers decided to do this, and a second wave of lock-outs followed. To begin with, its significance was masked because supply difficulties, lack of fuel or raw materials, and the economy's bottlenecks were put forward as the main causes, but the employers' aims soon became clear. Ryabushinsky, in the industrialists' name, explained the position:[17] 'To get out of this situation we may have to employ the bony arm of hunger, and of national misery, to take these false friends of the people – the committees and the soviets – by the throat.' But whether the employer dismissed his men or closed down for whatever reason, the end result was the same – the man lost his job.

Gone were the hopes of February, for security of employment, wage rises and the like, and the allegedly socialist government provided only one disappointment after another – it had not signed the eight-hour day law, and left the soviets to negotiate separately with the employers in each town; it had not forced the employers to agree to wage rises; in particular, it displayed greater energy in threatening workers who did not adhere scrupulously to the judgments of the commissions of arbitration and who were then accused of 'betraying the Revolution'. In the name of national defence, it called on striking workers to start work again, but did nothing when the employers locked them out. The workers reacted, for whilst their leaders sought negotiation and compromise, the employers were refusing to submit, and were arbitrarily seeking to starve the workers out, thereby deliberately sacrificing the nation's defence. The workers began to question the legitimacy of private business – not explicitly, however, for they arrived at this conclusion slowly as the factory committees were forced, by the bosses' refusals, to take decisions on their own. It was in these circumstances that the first experiments in self-management started. They were not, initially, defined as such by the workers, who talked neither of socialism, nor of collectivism nor of self-management; they only said that they had been forced 'by the attitude of management, to undertake the proper working of the factory by themselves'.

An experiment in self-management[18]

The experiments in self-management came after a period of endurance. The workers were hungry; they would allow no delay and, with dismissal threatened, they knew that if they abandoned the factory no one would help them. Their conflict with the employer sometimes began even before the workers' organizations had met, for they had no time to waste and were perplexed as to what to do. The workers' section of the Petrograd Soviet had laid down procedures for arbitration, but they did not necessarily succeed, and the conflict would then become a political matter, for the executive committee of the soviet. The trade unions had not yet assembled their full strength at national level, and in March the trade-union representatives in the soviet, who were mostly Menshevik, had supported the policy of mediation. The factory committees, which emerged locally from each factory, at least in Petrograd, were quicker to hold their first conference.

This event, held in May, was the only one where factory conflicts were discussed in general. Not all the committees were represented, and not all the factories had committees, but the majority of participants were disappointed at the Mensheviks' conciliatory policies and especially the minister Skobelev's behaviour. Bolshevik speakers, particularly Zinoviev, were applauded for their outspoken condemnations. The final resolution was Bolshevik in inspiration, and called for the extension and systematization of workers' control. Resolutions did not mean food, however, and they had no legal force; there were firms which refused negotiation, demands or supervision. This happened in the Brenner factory where a conflict ended with an experiment in workers' self-management.[19]

The Brenner engineering firm was, in the Russian context, a small firm, employing about 200 people.[20] As elsewhere, the conflict concerned wages, hours and the competence of the factory committee. The two sides talked in different languages. They were equally watchful and energetic, and on both sides sought to put the issue to the test. On 21 May the management announced that the factory would close at the end of the month. The workers stayed on, sleeping in the place, and refused to move. It was difficult for them to appeal anywhere, for the soviet was too far off or too remote, and they did not have a representative in it. At the very least they wanted the support of the district committee, which was more representative than the workers of a single factory and could intervene with the competent bodies (see Figure 1).

On 8 June a member of the factory committee addressed the Peterhof district committee on the workers' situation. They wanted to have the

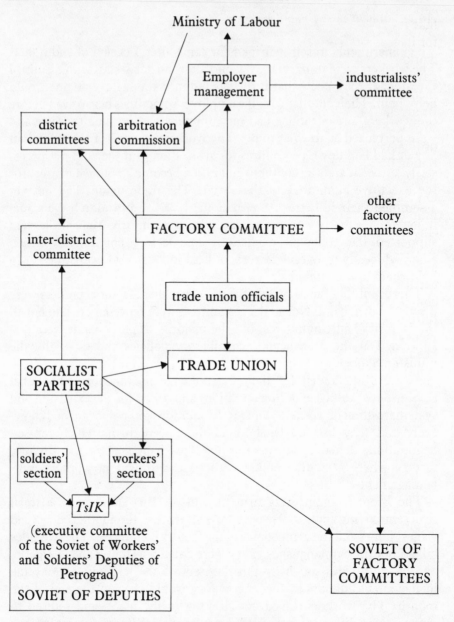

Figure 1   *External links of a factory committee*

factory produce, and wanted the district committee to approach the trade union. The committee felt somewhat lost, and needed people who could tell it what to do to get the factory going properly.[21] The problem was clear enough, that Brenner was doing all he could to stop deliveries and orders so as to justify the closure of his factory, they said, and wanted to take it over. The factory delegate asked the district committee to back it, for its support would have great moral importance and would stiffen the workers' will to fight. The Peterhof committee discussed the matter and gave its blessing to the Brenner workers. A first decision was for one of its members to go and find out the size of the Brenner family's property. Brenner received the man, and blamed him for taking his fifteen roubles so as to play the policeman – the sum he had been allotted in the place of ordinary wages. The man felt slandered, and complained.[22] All negotiation came to an end, and this time the factory's closure was irrevocably proclaimed for 3 July. The official reason was that it worked 'at a loss'. On 28 June the committee of the Brenner factory published a communiqué that marked an epoch in the history of the labour movement: 'In view of the management's refusal to go on with production, the workers' committee has decided, in general assembly, to fulfil the orders and to carry on working.'[23] In the presence of a legal official who could certify that the factory was working normally under the committee's control, it sent an appeal to the ministry of labour for authorization to fulfil the orders and continue the work for private persons and the government, for, without that authorization, the workers' position would have been difficult. Brenner complained to the ministry as well, and the committee appealed for help from the Putilov factory:[24]

We, workers and factory committee of the Brenner factory, hereby appeal to our comrades and foreman at the Putilov factory. On 19 May our employer told the factory committee that he had no money left and could not continue with the factory, and he asked the factory committee to help him by fulfilling orders as fast as possible. The committee agreed to do so, even prescribing immediate working on holidays. Brenner said on 24 May that he could pay the workforce for only two weeks more, and that the factory would have to close on 7 June. In reply, and knowing that the employer had received advances of 420,000 roubles on orders from the central war industries committee for goods still not produced even now, and of 100,000 roubles for infantry shields that have also not been produced, and yet was closing the factory, putting people out of work despite his huge advances, and even retaining the 2 per cent paid by the workers for their sickness fund, the workers, not having had their pay in full on 7 June, appealed to the soviet and the ministry for the factory to remain open. On 19 the committee resolved to start work again, even without the management. It has been going well. Although the employer made problems and obstacles, the work has gone ahead, but there is one difficulty, in supply of raw material, and that is why we are appealing to you at the Putilov factory, in the hope that you will help us in our conflict with the stealers of state funds, and violators of the law. We need money urgently, and without the raw materials we shall have to stop.[25]

A similar appeal was sent to the central committee of factory committees. The Putilov committee answered at once and referred the Brenner people to the assistance fund of the central committee of factory committees. This was done, the Brenner committee asking for an advance that would be repayable, to pay the wages of the workers who had nothing at all and were in the greatest need. On 29 July the Treugolnik committee agreed to give 15,000 roubles to their comrades at the Brenner factory, and the Putilov factory sent raw material.[26] Brenner himself intervened and complained to the war industries committee that

That committee has no legal ability to take on orders or receive money. The factory management was within its rights when it ignored the committee, for it had only to take on orders that came through the intermediary services of the committee for small and middle-sized business. The workers' accusation is quite without foundation: advances on orders allowed us to manufacture 4,000 cylinders.[27]

The conflict spread, and to stop it, the minister took a decision that marked a new departure: he ordered the Brenner factory to be sequestrated.

On 12 August there was great perturbation in the Peterhof district. The urban militia had been instructed by the government to evacuate the Brenner factory in view of its sequestration: the question was, whether there would now be a real battle.[28] The ministry also arranged negotiations between Brenner and the factory committee, Brenner agreeing to recognize the committee as representative, but wanting guarantees over wages, the more so as the metals industrialists aligned their wages with his.[29] The negotiations dragged on, and days went by. There were increasing difficulties inside the factory — raw materials arriving irregularly, if at all, and no money to pay the workforce. Some workers would not work for nothing, and others had nothing to do. Under-employment meant that idleness and drunkenness was on the increase; there seemed no solution. The factory's delegate at the Peterhof district committee, facing all of these problems, asked to be released, and gave his explanation. There was a discussion in the district committee, in which the importance of a failure on this scale was seen: 'it might discredit the whole movement'. One member said, 'Before you accuse the workers of negligence and drunkenness, you ought to feed them properly.'[30] But the solution was not obvious. Clearly, there was a link between the lack of income and the inadequate working – 90,000 roubles were received, of which 15,000 were at once paid to the Treugolnik committee. On 8 September the news was official that the ministry itself would take over the Brenner works, which brought the experiment of self-management to an end.[31]

Many factories went through the same tragic experience as the Brenner works. Thrown back on their own resources, they had lost an engagement, but the conflict over self-management was in itself only a frontier skirmish. The factory committees had not necessarily begun the struggle: the breaking-point at which they had decided on self-management had been the employers' decision to close down. As the Petrograd conference of factory committees' report said, 'at the moment, committees are forced to intervene in the economic functioning of businesses, otherwise they would have stopped working'.[32]

Supervising a factory, let alone managing it, seemed to be pointless if the employer, even where absent, could block orders and deliveries to stifle the business and put the workers out of their jobs. It was obvious that self-management, and even workers' control, would be possible only if the employers and the bankers were stripped of their control of the economic system. Only an 'organization representing the factory committees of all Russia can win a decisive victory', stated the final resolution of the Petrograd conference. Supervision would have to be made thorough with access to accounts, order-books and the like. Otherwise there would be no real achievement.[33]

The experiment in self-management had failed because it started at a time of economic difficulty, because the factories that attempted it were on their own, and because they were too small to threaten seriously the employers' power and the functioning of the economic system. The 576 factories in which workers' self-management was established had, on average, 335 workers each.[34] This was not much in the Russian context, and still less so in the capital, where there were giant enterprises: Putilov, with 27,033 workers, the Cannon Foundry with 19,046, Treugolnik with 15,338 and eighteen others with over 5,000 each. These, far from dismissing labour, took on increasing numbers – respectively 3,630, 1,501 and 1,102 from February to early July 1917.[35] Trade unions, the conference of factory committees, soviets and political parties – all the workers' organizations – had their eyes fixed on the workers in the large factories, and for them the time for self-management had not yet come.

Many factories were even then a long way from exerting any kind of control, and in many, especially in the Ukraine, there were not even trade unions or committees. Despite the decree of 23 April, joining one meant the sack. In these very large factories, the workers had still to fight to consolidate even the small concessions they had gained after February — greater wage increases, recognition of the committee by the board and the like. The workers' organizations tried to win concessions in succession, systematically — first the eight-hour day overall, then a minimum wage and recognition of factory committees.[36] When the Brenner workers had appealed to them, they had not intervened, and, of all the institutions, only the district committee had done so, and that was not a 'class' body. At this time the trade unions had hardly been revived, and the Brenner factory, because of its small size, was not represented in the first conference of factory committees. At the soviet, the workers' section did not often meet, while the executive committee of the soviet supported state control with the ministry compelling employers and workers to negotiate, rather than self-management. The Mensheviks Skobelev and Gvozdev, while waiting for control of production and management to come, recommended all kinds of mediation, and though they also supported the establishment of a committee, they wanted it to have only representative powers. If there were a breach, then the government could sequestrate — the manifestation of a new power, that of the state. It preferred sequestration because it could make government control effective, and reduce both the employers' omnipotence and the autonomy of the workers' committees. There was political reasoning here, too, for the institution that united the factory committees could make things difficult for government, trade unions and soviets, which were then run by Mensheviks. The leaders of the conference of factory committees sympathized with the Bolsheviks, which lent the practice of sequestration and the demarcation of factory committees' competence a political dimension.

In March or April, sequestration would have appeared as an act to dispossess the employer for the state's benefit. This was not the case three months later. Moreover, where workers requested it, as happened with Helfferich-Sade at Khar'kov, the government might refuse. Conversely, where it was proclaimed and carried out between July and September, and pushed through by troops only in places where workers' self-management had been started, the process looked like a defiance of the workers and a political stroke against the party of Lenin. Sequestration protected the bosses, because it ended workers' control.[37]

2 The response of the employers and the government

The bosses had always been against any kind of control. In February 1917, they had supposed that the hour of bourgeois revolution had come, and that they could therefore, at last, strip the state of the rights that it had acquired in the economy, especially in transport. These ideas had been opposed by Tsarist bureaucrats, and the employers, failing to see that, in essence, the bureaucracy had protected them from pressure from below, imagined that after the February Revolution, capitalist development in Russia could go ahead unhindered. Socialist ideas on state control struck them as far-fetched.[38]

When, however, the government began a policy of compromise and mediation under pressure from the Petrograd Soviet, the employers, while decrying it, pretended to give way. They did not at once realize that the second aspect of government policy, the rationalization of industry, would help them. They also failed to see that, if it came to a battle, sequestration really protected them. They supported it only after they had understood that the state, at least in a transitional period, would be more help than hindrance. 'We have no objection to supervision by the state, but it must not get in our way.' The main idea was to unify the activities of the ruling classes, and co-ordinate them with the government's, so that the state would serve them. There were other ideas, too, first among which was the creation of a powerful state machinery. The employers were sure that when it had been created, 'disorder' would come to an end, so that they were fundamentally unconcerned over political combinations with 'conciliatory' ministers.[39]

While waiting for political changes to terminate the 'anarchy', the employers called in the law, put forward technical arguments or the mysteries of finance to recover their control of the factories.

To achieve this, they meant to 'attack the evil at the root' and do away with the factory committees. However, not only were there more and more of these; increasingly, they frustrated the decisions of the boards. In the large factories, committees had been divided into commissions and sub-committees that controlled work at all levels. At the Mednoprokatny works, for instance, where metal was converted, there were nine commissions: fuel purchase, priority orders (army or navy), works management and conditions, employment and dismissal, the library, demobilization, and even one for the recovery of metal, because of short supply – it had been formed out of the purchasing commission. There were also commissions for co-ordination and control.[40] The reactions of a management partially divested of its authority and its business secrecy were foreseeable: as *Novoye Vremya* said, 'Engineers and managers are being put out, and the notion is "let's go ahead without the bourgeois".' The employers resisted, but it was not always possible for large factories with several thousand workers to close down, as the risks were too great; sequestration primarily benefited the bosses. They, blaming the workers for the economic run-down and the defeats at the front, used political arguments to get the government to intervene, and they also acted directly themselves. This twofold action became particularly energetic after the July Days.[41]

N. N. Kutler stated that the first priority was to end 'anarchy' and restore order in the factories. The socialist ministers reckoned it was their responsibility, and Prokopovich, minister of economic affairs, asked Avksentiev as minister of the interior to act against violence in the factories, especially that against sequestrations, which were becoming more numerous (see Table 9 above). The minister of labour, Skobelev, intervened, the starting-point being his circular of 28 August, which was published (hardly coincidentally) on the very day of the Kornilov Putsch. It was intended 'to clarify the law of 23 April on factory committees' and it declared that any meeting in working hours in the factories was illegal. The Skobelev circular was taken as a declaration of war. It had no direct effects, but the employers took it as permission to open fire. Since late July, some of them had agreed that they would not pay workers for hours put in in the workers' militia; now they decided not to pay them for time put in at meetings; next they forbade meetings on factory premises, which was taken as an infringement of the right of assembly.[42] The trade unions immediately objected to this 'restriction of our rights'.

The new factor after the July Days was that the minister of labour supported the employers.[43] The circular of late August could be read as a document stating the right to assemble, but its real effect was to give back to the employer his 'rights' inside the factory. There were other, later circulars that redefined the relationship between employers and workers. Skobelev, for instance, approved and even agreed to circulate a notice sent by the Urals industrialists and coal owners to the workers: it 'condemns any interference by the factory committees in management of an enterprise, for the workers' committees and soviets have only the authority to represent the professional interests of workers to the management or the board, and this excludes interference as regards decisions to be made or control of administration, accounting and output'.

The employers were again supported when the ministry of labour agreed to issue 'general regulations for the working of factories engaged on war work' — the competence of which could easily be extended at will, since the notion of war work was very flexible. Commissioners were appointed by the ministry to supervise the application of these regulations, and the idea of militarizing production was not one confined to the Kornilovites. The *Stock Exchange Gazette*[44] explained that 'if the economy is militarized, the workers will have to submit, because they will be treated as soldiers'. The government also used armed force, though it trod carefully, limiting such action to industrial works outside the large towns, for instance in the Ukraine. This zone of industry required particular attention from the government, because British and French capital had been invested there, more than elsewhere, and the government feared that, if the disorder continued, it would be withdrawn.[45]

These measures could not be applied in Petrograd, Moscow and other great cities. The employers considered transferring their work to calmer areas, where the forces of repression would function better. A further benefit here was that decentralization of industry would break the solidarity of workers in the mother-factory: in a new framework, they could be prevented from reorganizing. In Petrograd not only lack of fuel but also the German menace provided a patriotic alibi for shifting plant. With ministerial and military complicity it was easy to foster alarmism. The idea of shifting plant was very widespread about the same time – the last ten days of August – as the *Kornilovshchina* got under way. At the Petishev cable factory, for instance, the workers were told on 19 August that the plant would be shifted to Voronezh, and part of the workforce was dismissed with two weeks' notice. The factory committee answered that the management's reasons were inadequate, for there was enough fuel for three months and not all orders had been fulfilled. A delay was agreed. At Pulemyot the employer succeeded in evacuating plant without his workers' noticing: one morning they found the factory empty, the machinery having been removed in secrecy to near Moscow. The managing director of Vulkan tried to do this, but he was too late – evacuation in secrecy could succeed only once. At Dvigatel, in Riga, the workers forcibly opposed an evacuation, though this time it was more suitable because the factory lay near the front. Mistrust towards the employers and the government was such that, whether the ministry had ordered it or not, workers would stop evacuation.[46] It was expensive, and the industrialists soon saw that there was as much to be feared in the interior as in Petrograd. They thought again, and observed that

> in the enemy-occupied regions, because of the order established by the Germans, businesses have remained intact. Real estate fetches high prices. Houses in Warsaw can be sold in Moscow at five times their pre-war prices, and the securities of land-banks in Vilna, based on properties in German hands, are quoted above those secured on Russian territory.

This was in effect the shadow of a second *Kornilovshchina*, and on 13 October, Kutler spoke out against evacuation.[47]

The bosses were ready for anything, if possible with the government's help, to regain control of things. Lay-offs, closures and transfers of factories had been weapons of combat meant to bring the workers, as in western Europe, to their senses. It was felt that if hunger could be brought into play (the idea expressly stated by Ryabushinsky), it would be the final and absolute weapon against the working-class movement because 'in any case we cannot work the factories any more, we have ceased being boss there, so we might as well close down'. The weapon of closure could, however, become blunt if sequestrations went on and if the government did as many workers wanted and took measures of 'municipalization', i.e. nationalization. The government already talked of dividend limitation (the dividends were between 10 and 40 per cent annually), forced loans out of profits, and regulation of prices. It had to be frightened, by means, as it were, of an 'economic Riga'.

To hasten the advent of a Kadet government, without socialists, which would finally 'put an end to this play-acting', no sacrifice was reckoned too great. Some of the bosses went in for a sabotage expressly meant to 'discredit the Revolution', 'to put responsible men into power'; as the industrialist Fedorov said,[48] 'once the factories have stopped, it will be easier to deal with the "comrades".' The idea was not new. But it had to be effected in such a way that the government could not adopt the safe-guarding measures which it, as manager and inheritor, would not other-wise fail to take to stave off the economic disaster desired and worked for by financiers and industrialists. It was a narrow path to tread: they had to come close enough to economic disaster, but without provoking the workers into taking over or the government into intervening by sequest-ration or 'municipalization'. The path was taken, at the instance of 'French shareholders', in the Franco-Russian Factory, the Metallurgical Works of Donets-Yuryevka, where there were phased dismissals.[49] The most highly-concentrated part of finance and industry went in for calculated sabotage.

The aim was clearly a general lock-out to force the workers into surrender and the government into change. However, if this policy were not to rebound against its initiators, it was necessary for the factory closures to occur for ostensibly good reasons that would rule out a response from the workers. Theakston ordered the closure of Prodameta's Donets works, but not others; in the Urals some factories closed and others went on. Overall, the closure movement no longer appears to have any direct link with the specific demands of a factory — sometimes it was caused by breach of negotiations with the factory committee, sometimes by the committee's decision, for instance to introduce an eight-hour day; and sometimes factories closed even though 'all is well'. The main idea was to create an atmosphere of fear. It is not even too much to imagine that, given the structure of Russian industry, with its twenty or so large monopolies, there was some 'conductor behind the scenes': everything happened as if several banks had acted this part, even without the employers' knowing, by refusing credit to businesses and leaving them short of liquid cash. 'We can't find any new money, and can't pay the workers,' said people in the Urals, where the bosses were the spear-head· of the movement. It may not have been pure chance that the different firms associated with the International Bank closed down in succession. Besides, closure in successive waves affected well-defined areas of production – coal, railways – the bottle-necks of the whole economy. The Russian economy was very concentrated, and one or two actions of this kind could create general havoc. There were other ways – refusal of new orders, diminution of preparatory work, limitation of repairs and especially what the Russians called an 'Italian-style strike', i.e. constant postponement of decisions until finally the circuit of production in a factory becomes blocked. 'So long as this situation lasts, we have to be dilatory', said one industrialist. Works closed down, one after another – the Urals, then the Donbass, then Moscow. One hundred and fifty coal pits were closed at a stroke, and then five large converter factories of the same group, 'for want of fuel'.[50]

This organized sabotage came together with simultaneous mass closures in towns such as Kazan, with its leather factories, or in a single branch of the economy, such as coal, locomotive production, etc. It continued after October, and the employers, who were often assisted by part of their workforce, fought for as long as they could against the installation of 'workers' control' in the factories. There, Revolution turned into civil war, which ended only with the nationalization of industry. When Lenin did this on 14 December 1917 it was a death-blow to the bosses. Yet, as Chernov put it,[51] 'the Bolsheviks are at most playing the part of sextons, because the employers are already finished.' They had died from applying their principle: 'May the country perish if it no longer belongs to me.'

3 The economic collapse

Economic sabotage, strikes and lock-outs came together to cause a total collapse of production, as the conversion to a war economy had already brought about sufficient disruption to cause the February Revolution itself. Then, the shops had been empty and there had been no bread. Dearth, in both towns and country, had taken dramatic proportions. Failure in coal production and on the railways created, in Russia more than elsewhere, a bottle-neck for the whole economy. The condition of these industries gives a measure of the economic situation in general.[52]

The state of the railways was particularly grave. The inadequacy of network and rolling-stock was notorious for, despite the immense distances and a population of 170,000,000, Tsarist Russia had barely more locomotives than France. In January 1916 there were only 19,279, in February 1917, 20,600, and in the early summer, 20,884. Paradoxically, the number of engine drivers fell, in the same period, from 16,758 to 15,858; and the largest decline had been in mid-winter, with only 16,029 working on 1 March. This disproportion reflected the number of engines under repair, which had risen from 3,364 in June to 5,300 in September, or 25.3 per cent of the stock; and the number of waggons under repair had risen even more, from 25,810 in January to 51,076 in June 1917, or 9 per cent of the total number. In the Petrograd network, in September 1917, there were 3,500 waggons out of use, and nearly 4,000 in the southwestern zone that supplied grain from the Ukraine. In the Ukraine, moreover, forty places which usually despatched cereals had no locomotives. Of the 76,362 waggons used early in 1917 in the Petrograd region, only 43,429 were still working, such that the Petrograd factories were given only 16,500,000 *poods* of coal as against 23,500,000 in the equivalent months of the previous year: it was this decline that had been at the root of the February Revolution. Transport was an important factor in the overall decline, the gap between order and delivery in the Russian stations being of unprecedented scale. In May the army unloaded 24,932 waggons where it had expected 66,450. The number of waggons bringing foodstuffs to Petrograd declined from 351 in April 1916 to 230 in April 1917 and in May from 427 to 285 (per day). However, the supply of coal to the railways kept up, since they had priority: the shortfall here was under 15 per cent.

There was a similar situation in the provinces. At Tashkent, only 33 waggons came of 525 expected; at Moscow on 21 August there were 50 waggons with anthracite, whereas a year previously there had been 2,000.[53] Inevitably, given the paralysis of transport, stocks of fuel and raw materials built up at station platforms. However, lack of fuel could also cause a slow-down of transport; and by the autumn, it appears, the relationship between fuel and transport was reversed.[54] There were several reports to this effect: 'During the first half of 1917 the main cause of the shortfall was the decline in transport, circumstances changed in October, and output of fuel declined faster than transport, with fuel resources increasingly drying up.' Output of coal in the Donbass fell from 147,000,000 *poods* in June 1916 to 127,000,000 in June 1917 and 110,000,000 in October. The amount of Donbass coal reaching customers fell from 98,000,000 *poods* in June 1917 to 69,000,000 in October, as against 105,000,000 in the preceding October. Reality was dramatic for the consumers; the quota of the Petrograd area fell from 7,300,000 to 4,000,000, but actual unloadings declined from 3,800,000 to 1,600,000.[55]

There were many reasons for the fall. The decline in productivity had in fact started long before the Revolution, though it was often ascribed to it (Table 11). The decline started in the second half of 1915 and then

Table 11   *Productivity (per worker)*

1st half of 1914	4,514 *poods*
2nd half of 1914	4,543 *poods*
1st half of 1915	4,616 *poods*
2nd half of 1915	4,400 *poods*
1st half of 1916	3,888 *poods*
2nd half of 1916	3,537 *poods*
1st half of 1917	2,858 *poods*

accelerated. It amounted to 9.66 per cent per annum since the beginning of the war, and during the Revolution 12 per cent, an aggravation that showed the features of arithmetic progression.[56] It was not merely social conflict that caused the decline, for its origins went back some way, to the ruin of pits and galleries that had been frequently flooded. According to figures for the twenty-eight closed pits of the Shcherbinkovsky mine early in June 1917, the causes of closure were:[57]

flooded mines	13
boilers under repair	4
poor quality of the coal	2
worked out	1
abandoned shafts	1
digging of shafts	2
sickness of director	1
props shifted	1
excessive depth	1
undiscovered vein	1
unprofitability, because of high wages	1

Another engineer who investigated the reasons for the decline in productivity, suggested, above all, 'growing lack of skills, caused by the call-up'. Deterioration of the mines also counted, and also inadequate supplies, which meant that the workers' conditions were unsatisfactory. He gave other reasons, such as too much ash in the mineral, insufficient electricity, excessive use of tools that were too often, and too long, under repair. In an overall report to the Donbass producers the causes set out were: (1) substitution of unskilled workers (30,000 women, 70,000 prisoners of war, and children) for skilled miners called up by the army; (2) insufficient supply of goods of absolute necessity to the workers; (3) the poor condition of the mines, with premature dilapidation; (4) the decline in transport; (5) conflict between employers and workers, and the absence, to that date, of arbitration procedures; (6) absence of a government agency to rationalize production.[58] *Russkiye Vedomosti*, discussing the coal crisis, rightly referred to 'a vicious circle' that affected the entire economy of Russia:[59] 'It is clear that the decline in coal production is owing, not solely to disorders among the working class but to a whole series of causes affecting the mining industry. It would be wrong to seek out guilty men.'[60]

The Putilov factory in Petrograd provided a significant instance of the decline of the economy in the capital. It took nearly 10 per cent of the industrial fuel consumed in the Petrograd region, and in July it received 100,000 *poods* of coal whereas it had ordered 160,000; in August it received 47,000, or 4 per cent of its needs, and between 2 and 3 per cent in liquid fuel. By 9 October the factory could no longer continue, and most of the workshops were closed. The situation was hardly better in other factories: the Baranovsky had ordered 880 waggons of coal for the period November 1916 to February 1917, and received 125. In that quarter, output fell by 40 per cent. In August the factory had to close for a fortnight and in September it worked for only a week. There were a great many such cases.[61] In October the need for fuel became calamitous, to such an extent that in the capital even the electrified factories, which had priority, had to stagger their working hours: some received electricity on Mondays and Tuesdays, others on Wednesdays and Thursdays. A permit from the fuels committee was required to gain any exemption. On 19 September the paper factories of the capital declared that they had only two days' raw material left; the cotton factories were in a similar situation, and so were others. According to statistics covering 1917 as a whole, the national average for decline in production, calculated in gold roubles, was 30.5 per cent, with Moscow among the least affected places (−10.8 per cent) and Petrograd the most affected (−34.9 per cent). The greatest decline was in the metals industry (−65 per cent), chemicals (−45 per cent) and engineering (−25.7 per cent). The arms factories' output fell by roughly one-third.

The disintegration accelerated. Statistics, not for 1917 but for the fiscal year May 1917−May 1918 reveal that the quantity of coal reaching Petrograd was 30 per cent of the amount arriving in the previous fiscal year, the quantity of timber only 16 per cent. The lack of fuel soon affected domestic consumers. A circular of 6 June 1917 required owners of flats to convert their central-heating systems to timber for the winter; private consumption of electricity was cut by half, and from September the opening hours of shops, theatres, circuses and the like were restricted. On 3 October the capital's trams had to stop, at first for an hour and later for two, because there was no electricity. On 13 October Petrograd was plunged into darkness, since the turbines of the 1883 Company had not been supplied with petrol.[62]

Supply in the capital was worse than elsewhere because Baltic coastal traffic had been interrupted by the German advance, the railways had been blocked, and waterways had been allotted, as first priority, to petrol and coal. Thus, delivery of grain by water fell by nine-tenths in 1917. Early in March there had already been times when the depots held only enough grain for a day or two. The government, under pressure from the soviet, had proclaimed a grain monopoly, with fixed prices. The banks and the flour mills, which controlled trade, reduced their deliveries and hid their stocks; and transport problems completed the picture. Bread rationing was brought in in March, with 1½ lbs per day for heavy workers and 1 lb. for other consumers. By the end of April, the ration was universally reduced to ¾ lb. and possession of a card was no guarantee of supply, for these figures required monthly deliveries of grain that were never attained: in March the capital received 81 per cent of its needs, in April 34, in May 90, in June 62, and in the following months 50. Soon the same situation was to prevail with other foodstuffs: semolina, sugar, meat, eggs and fat were all rationed. Queues for these and other foodstuffs would begin to form at midnight, and sometimes even nine p.m. for an uncertain distribution the following morning. Deliveries of meat were half as much as the authorities had foreseen, fats were one-third less, and fish one-tenth. Deliveries of fresh milk stood at 8 per cent of their pre-war figure. Moreover, consumers had to travel long distances, because there was a continual decline in the number of properly-supplied shops. Prices, without any comparable movement of wages, rose dizzyingly, in consequence (see Table 12).[63]

The food crisis was threatening virtually the whole country. The Donbass workers, for instance, were getting in August 1917 only a quarter of the amount provided for.[64] Dittmar, president of the coal-owners' association, told the government that it was essential, if serious trouble was to be avoided, to allow the factories to obtain their own grain at free market prices, and an agent of the Provisional Government who enquired in the provinces of Kazan, Simbirsk, Samara, Ufa and Turgay discovered that the monopoly of grain was not working at all.

It was as if the various strata of the Russian economy were disintegrat-

Table 12   *Selected food prices in July 1917 and October 1917* (roubles)

Lard (1 lb.)	1.10	5.40
Cheese (1 lb.)	1.60	5.40
Cabbage (1)	1.60	2.20
Sausage	1.0	6.0
Meals in the Schlüsselburg canteen:		
Cabbage soup with meat	15 kopecks	58 kopecks
Cabbage soup without meat	8 kopecks	42 kopecks
Kasha	10 kopecks	32 kopecks

ing in the reverse order of their appearance. The disintegration started with the laws and regulations of the Provisional Government being virtually ignored; then army supply began to collapse; next came the patterns of output and trading derived from the industrial revolution: and finally the kind of commercial exchange that had been reflected in the very formation of the Russian empire. As it came apart at the seams, the economy disintegrated. Economic *seigneuries* came into being, and became autonomous. A barter agreement was made, late in August, between the provinces of Stavropol and Astrakhan, by which the one supplied grain and the other timber and petrol. It was the same between Chelyabinsk and Tashkent. The Berdzhansk soviet declared itself independent in matters of supply, and so did others. The government and the civil servants blamed these committees for their 'complete ignorance as to the workings of commerce'. The ignorance was no doubt there; but the fact was that commerce had ceased working.[65] The Russian economy was collapsing before the October Revolution took place:[66] 'the weakest link in the capitalist chain' met its great crash fourteen years before 'Black Friday' – it occurred in 1915, and February was one sign of a process that had been completed by October. The new régime had to rebuild from the ruins.

4   From self-management to nationalization

While the economic and social disintegration went ahead, in the autumn, and as the Mensheviks' policies of state control and conciliation were obviously failing, Lenin wrote that:

It takes very little to see that there are ways of coping with the disasters and famines, that the things to be done are quite obvious, simple, easy to achieve and quite within our capacity, and that, if such measures are not being taken, it is simply and solely because they would harm the huge profits made by a handful of big estate-owners and capitalists. That is a fact. It can be said with complete certainty that there is not a speech, not a newspaper article of whatever political persuasion, not a resolution by any assembly or institution whatever, which fails to state, in quite clear and precise terms, what is needed in the way of fundamental and essential measures to deal with calamity and famine. What is needed is control, supervision, stock-taking and regulation by the state, rational distribution of labour in production and retailing, and a prevention of all squandering of such vital resources. But that is not being done, out of fear that the omnipotence of great landowners and capitalists will be affected, together with the huge, scandalous and unprecedented profits that they can make from price inflation and war supply (and almost all of them claim to be 'working' indirectly or directly for the war effort) — profits which everyone knows about and can see, and about which everyone complains. The state does nothing at all to set up control, supervision or surveying. The government does not act. Everywhere, there is systematic and unrelenting sabotage of any effort at control, supervision, or surveying, or any state attempt in that direction. It needs incredible simple-mindedness not to see — or profound hypocrisy to pretend not to see — who is responsible for this, and how the sabotage is carried out. It is sabotage by bankers and capitalists, it is they who torpedo any control, supervision or stock-taking by the state, and they can adapt their tactics to the forms of state of our alleged 'democratic Republic' and its present institutions.[67]

Lenin's line was seemingly the antithesis of that propounded by the leaders of the February revolution, but even then it was not quite aligned with what the workers were doing by themselves. The Bolsheviks wanted control in every area; they accused their Menshevik rivals of neglecting the possibility, although in fact the Mensheviks' proposals did go in the same direction, towards control and eventual nationalization. But some of the workers, left on their own since the soviets and trade unions supported policies of conciliation and arbitration that were an obvious failure, went in a quite different direction, towards workers' self-management. They did still listen sympathetically to the Bolsheviks, because they were more radical than the Mensheviks, and because they had supported the factory committees in establishing workers' control in the factories; and they had also encouraged the creation of a body to unite all the factory committees in the capital, the first conference of factory committees. It was true that the Bolsheviks' motive was to use the factory committees to counterbalance the trade unions, which were then in Menshevik hands, but this hardly mattered to the workers, whose main concern was for support and organization, even if at the time they had not yet moved towards self-management.

In the conflict with the employers, which reached its height in the summer and autumn, the proletarian organizations were caught short both by the workers' actions at shop-floor level and the virulence of the employers' counter-attack. Moreover, in establishing their strategy, they were also, to some extent, prisoners of the policies of conciliation and arbitration that they had adopted since February and continued in June, through the Menshevik and Socialist Revolutionary majority in the soviets.

The conference of factory committees and the all-Russian trade union conference were arenas where the militants of different organizations clashed. As the lock-outs increased, and as workers lost their jobs, the militants would none the less fill their speeches with discussions of the nature of the Russian Revolution, the role and the aims of the government, the political parties, or the other proletarian organizations. Usually, simple workers, delegates from a factory or a trade, had their questions unanswered. One of them shouted at the Mensheviks and the Bolsheviks, 'I've had enough of all your talking, you never answer our questions – what are we to do if a boss threatens he'll close down? You're always ready with proclamations and words, but no one will ever tell us what to do in a real case . . . what do we do if the factory shuts down? We are here to decide that, and we've been sent here for that, and if you don't tell us, we'll go ahead on our own.'[68] There could be no clear answer to this question, because any definition of strategy and tactics here involved the respective competence of two rivals, the factory committees and the trade unions. It also involved the rivalry of anarchists, Bolsheviks and Mensheviks for leadership of the working-class movement. There was a majority response only on one point: the workers were not to act independently, as they had done over self-management.

The challenge to self-management as a principle

The debate was initiated by the factory committees themselves, or more precisely by their representatives at the conference of factory committees. They had condemned self-management even before it had started, by attacking the position of the factory committees that inclined towards it. These attacks were expressed within the first conference, in May 1917, in Petrograd.

At it, workers' control was defined – to meet the workers' essential wishes, to verify the employers' statements, prevent dismissals and deprive management of any pretext for closing down. The example of the Benoit factory showed what the consequences would be if there were a more modest interpretation of the committees' role: there, 500 workers were dismissed, and the committee protested that it had been without cause, because production had continually gone up from February to June despite the bosses' claim that the dismissals were owing to lack of money or raw materials. The committee's spokesman was received by the minister, Palchinsky, whom he asked for raw materials, only to be referred to the military commission. In fact no help had been given. The report concluded that 'it is pointless to continue in this way, with each committee going ahead on its own, each for itself; the whole working class must act together.' Another delegate felt that 'the aim of factory committees is not to go begging for machinery and money, and so assist capital. . . . We must set up a central office for the committees, as a kind of ministry of labour of the Russian proletariat. There must be some centralized collective management of industry; and as for finance, that must be taken from where it can be found, among the scoundrels who hypocritically talk of a Liberty Loan but then don't pay a penny for it while we, the workers, have to play the fool to go round begging for small sums in the factories in the name of the country's needs. The comedy has to stop: let's just take the money, and then see if the factories really have to close down.'[69]

Condemnation of 'individual initiatives' was re-stated more strongly at the trade union conference by Grohman, who, as a trade unionist and as a Menshevik, opposed the factory committees, which were considered Bolshevik. His arguments were sometimes even used, later on, by the Bolsheviks themselves. Self-management, and agreements struck between factory committees and employers, thought Grohman, 'can solve only an individual problem, and are therefore questionable. They aggravate divisions within the working class because people who strike an agreement like this will lose interest in the condition of the workers: it is each for himself, with a sort of "factory patriotism" developing, in which each man fights for his own, whatever the means.' Agreements of this kind could harm workers who had not managed to get such arbitration; the bosses of Russia must accept the conditions of the whole proletariat, point for point. Through Milyutin, the Bolsheviks in the trade unions also attacked occupation of factories 'so long as the movement is not general and organized'. To distinguish their position from that of the Mensheviks, they stated that 'workers' control is more suitable than the paper laws of an impotent and useless government'.[70]

At the second factory-committee conference, in August, when the failure of the self-management movement was manifest, the Bolsheviks declared that the committees' job in the factories was to supervise, not to take decisions. Only the anarchists, through Volin, defended self-management. For them, the factory committees should be 'the kernel of proletarian power, and the committee will show themselves as the motive-force of the revolutionary movement'. The recent defeats of self-management and the condemnation of factory occupations by the chairman of this conference, Levin, were as much responsible as the under-representation of the small factories for the total failure of the anarchists' motion, which received only eight votes. The failure in practice and the institutional defeat of the advocates of workers' self-management were to have powerful effects on the committees themselves.[71]

Trade unions against factory committees: the Bolshevik volte-face

When in their first, May, conference the factory committees had attacked 'individual initiatives and lack of co-ordination', they wanted a centralized, collective management of all industry. They had talked of the need to end the war, to convert the economy back to its peacetime basis, to give the population's needs priority, and, though these ideas were premature in May, they were successfully upheld at the second conference of factory committees by Larin, a Menshevik who had come over to Bolshevism. Henceforth, he said, 'the factory committees cannot only be seen as an institution safeguarding and guaranteeing the rights that the workers have gained in the Revolution. Workers' control in the factories is changing into a countervailing collective force that aims at managing the economy as a whole.'

This aim was contrary to that of the rival trade unions, who claimed competence at the national level.[72] However, the trade unions' machinery was clumsy because of their cumbersome structure and the multiplicity of their aims, which made them a veritable tower of Babel; they were also paralysed by demarcation disputes, for instance, in the railways, and by internal rivalries (with four metal-workers' unions at Yekaterinoslav and four unions in transport). They were even more paralysed by the wrangling that broke out at every turn, and at every level, between Bolsheviks and Mensheviks. It was only in June, at the height of the class struggle, that their first all-Russian conference took place, just as giant strikes began in the textile and furniture industries and, later, railways, and when, in the metals industries, the spread of lock-outs was prompting workers towards self-management.[73]

In the national trade union council, the Mensheviks, under Grohman,

Grinevich and Astrov, had a small majority against the Bolsheviks Ryazanov, Milyutin and Lozovsky. But there was a gulf between them and Skobelev, the Menshevik minister, because they blamed not so much the war, the failure to rationalize the economy, or the factory occupations ('we have condemned this, so lock-outs are unnecessary') for the economic problems, as the employers' doings, refusal to accept arbitration procedures and lock-outs. The Menshevik trade union council wanted to institute compulsory recourse to tripartite tribunals, where employers, workers and state would be represented. But, said Grinevich, 'the workers must show moderation, and circumstances have to be taken into account. Russia has been infected by past errors, and an unhealthy basis that the war has worsened. We must wait for the Economic Council to rationalize industry in the nation's interest as a whole, to guarantee the right to work, and to set up the employment offices that will put it into effect.'[74]

This, a few months later, would have been Bolshevik language, but only after October. Milyutin disapproved, for Grohman and Grinevich had condemned 'individual initiatives' and 'excessive' claims; they had told people 'what not to do, not what to do'. The Mensheviks told people to wait patiently because rules and regulations from above would at some time decide the future of the workers, but greater 'activism' was wanted. As Lozovsky said, 'This is a castration of the workers: compulsory recourse to arbitration procedures will prevent the workers from being more aggressive when things improve because they will be tied by these agreements.' But even he recommended prudence, because the employers' intransigence could possibly prove to be a provocation towards strikes and then lock-outs. The supreme weapon of the workers must remain the strike. The Menshevik resolution was that the arbitration tribunals should be a permanent instance, with strikes forming an exception. It was upheld, although so too were Bolshevik amendments that maintained the priority of the strike as a combat weapon.[75]

The essential problem was a definition of competence: who would decide on a strike, trade union or factory committee? Who was to have the authority in supervising the factory and the application of proper procedures or in safeguarding workers' control? Who would supervise the nature of production at municipal or provincial level, and who would be represented in state bodies such as the Economic Council to organize collective management of the economy? The majority of trade unionists were annoyed by the factory committees' doings, and condemned 'individual initiatives'; they were against such actions as the 'imprisonment or expulsion of factory administrators, haphazard methods and sabotage'. Trade unions were to 'fight to take over the leadership of the labour movement, so as then to take over the control of economy. Only it a national trade union can exercise an effective and universal control; it must come not over single factories, but everywhere.'[76]

Additions to the Menshevik resolution that was adopted showed the anger of the workers and the trade unionists. They stated that, for the state's and workers' control to be effective, the workers' delegates must be in the majority in the Economic Council; moreover, in view of the prevailing anarchy, the state must step into the economy. The roles of trade unions and factory committees were stated in these terms: (1) the factory committee will supervise production within the factory, and make sure that workers' rights are respected, whereas the trade unions will organize the workers' struggle for these rights; (2) the trade unions will defend these rights under whatever form of social organization, even if the economy is government-controlled; (3) factory committees will not take control or manage the administration of a factory; the trade unions must work to strengthen them . . . and, using them as intermediaries, make a reality of trade-union power; (4) trade unions will organize elections for factory committees; (5) factory committees are to leave to the trade union the leadership of any fighting action by the workers.[77]

The trade unions' majority resolution was therefore to reduce considerably the competence of factory committees, which were given only a partial right of control in the factories, and which were systematically left out of account at the level of the capital, let alone that of the country. Yet the factory committees' bodies at these levels were meant to organize control and planning of the economy within the framework of state institutions. Whereas the factory committees had laid down the nature of self- and collective management at several levels – factory, town, country – the trade unions wanted a centralized control, with the factory committees having only supervisory rights at a local level.

The Bolsheviks in the trade unions were not so unfavourable towards the committees, but even so they were very much less charitable towards them than they had been in the committees' conference. In their report on relations between unions and committees they stated that control of production must not be exercised bureaucratically by institutions where capital had a majority, and added, first, that through the mediation of the committees, the unions must have a right to take part in the control of firms, with a right to see the books and accounts, which the management would be required to show, and, second, that it was essential to stress, once and for all, that control of production was a matter for the unions. Up till then the trade unions had been the working-class organization for economic combat, and they now should have new tasks, to control and regulate industry. The Bolshevik reporter went on that 'latterly, there

has been discord between trade unions and factory committees, instead
of a spirit of unity; the Petrograd factory committees have called an
assembly and are trying to control production. Two quite separate
approaches have been outlined. In acting in this way, the committees are
taking decisions that really are matters for the unions – wages, relations
between bosses and workers in the factory, length of the working day and
the like.'[78] He wanted the factory committee to have only the well-defined
function of calling a strike, but only inasmuch as the unions had not yet
been able to organize at national level.

At the second factory-committee conference in the capital, the
Bolsheviks went further towards the committees, but they also reached
out to the unions. They recognized that committees should have the
function of control that the trade unions were refusing to them; but they
also decided that, from then on, it was the union that should have the job
of starting strikes. Ideally, the central committee of factory committees
would have a right of control at municipal level; and even the Mensheviks
allowed the committees some rights of control. However, Levin, chairman of the committees' conference, who had already condemned self-
management, also saw that in the long run the committees would not
succeed, and he recommended co-ordination between them and the
unions. He also supported a Bolshevik proposal calling for recognition of
the federal-level body of the factory committees, about which the
Mensheviks were silent. Lozovsky's motion easily defeated Volin's and
Cherevanin's. The committees' activity might therefore be extended in
space, but it would not be deepened; supervisory rights, it was understood, stopped short of decision.[79]

The Bolsheviks' *volte-face* towards the trade unions just before October
was a product of both basic and tactical reasoning. At bottom, the
committees' position was contrary to what the Bolsheviks argued as
regards self-management, even in collective form, which to them was not
socialism: what the committees wanted was something like anarcho-
syndicalism in the Bolshevik view. Moreover, on a tactical level, the
Bolsheviks, who now enjoyed a majority in the trade unions, which were
also growing stronger, no longer needed to support the factory-committee
organization as they had done in June. The trade unions were more
centralized, and would be a better intermediary for nationalization now
that the party could envisage conquering the apparatus of state.[80]

The defeat of the factory-committee movement and the defining of workers'
control

When the all-Russian factory-committee conference met in October 1917, the Revolution had made a gigantic stride forward. The Kornilov Putsch had had the extraordinary result, in Schapiro's words, of 'expelling the bourgeoisie from interference in public affairs'. The majority of the working-class organizations were now Bolshevik, and the moment to prepare for the overthrow of the Provisional Government had come.[81]

Trotsky and Kamenev attended the conference; they declared that the taking of power by the soviets was essential if a further attempt at counter-revolution, a new *Kornilovshchina*, were to be avoided. The workers now linked the return of normal life, the demobilization of industry, with peace, and hence also with soviet power. The network of factory committees at this time extended throughout the country, but it was loose, and lacked structure. These committees usually acted in isolation, without even co-ordinating their activities at municipal level − this was achieved at Narva, Yelizavetgrad and Tsaritsyn, but not until September/October. In large industrial areas like the Urals, Tver and Kostroma, even in October they had no central organization.[82] The factory committees' activities were also more restricted there than in the two capitals. The committees complained at Petrograd that managements were not recognizing their rights, were failing to allow workers' supervision, or to pay committee members their wages − in some cases they themselves would appoint the supervisory commission. The committees therefore had still to fight for their existence, to stop or delay the closing-down of factories, and to win reasonable compensation for the workers. The provincial committees were limited to defensive action, and could hardly claim to organize production, even if this aim figured in their statutes, as was the case in Ivanovo-Voznesensk. The weakness of the movement had become quite clear to the preparatory regional conferences: at Saratov only 81,000 workers were represented, with 209 factory committees, at Archangel only 27,000 workers with 34 committees.[83]

At the all-Russian conference of factory committees between 17 and 22 October, the agenda was dominated by questions of workers' control and co-ordination between unions and committees. The Menshevik element, with eight delegates out of 137, was completely eliminated and impotent. The Bolsheviks, who were masters of the Petrograd Soviet and the unions, and who already had a majority in the regional conferences, had no difficulty in asserting their viewpoint, having 86 out of 137 delegates. Milyutin, yet again, stated that proper workers' control could only be realized through a soviet take-over. True workers' control would mean the nationalization of several branches of industry and the control or nationalization of the banks: otherwise it would be meaningless. It might have been reasonable to object that the soviet take-over would be premature, if the old economic system had saved the country from economic disintegration: but the system had only hastened the coming of disaster. 'The idea of workers' control', said Larin, 'is the transposition of democracy into the economic field. Through workers' control, the nature of labour would change, for, once the workers have taken over, it would be more productive because the workers would have a sense of responsibility. Germany has set up a national economic programme, but it has been conceived in the interests of the ruling class: we must do the same, only in the workers' interest. The Economic Council must have a workers' majority, with the distribution of labour decided at national level, and wages determined by trade unions. The factory committees' function will be to guarantee control of production at factory or municipal level.' These proposals left the Economic Council, on the one side, and the factory management, on the other, in full charge of things, and the factory committees were left standing. The anarcho-syndicalists objected and proposed self-management 'because there could never be any harmony between the aims of bodies representing the workers and those of the firms' management'. The Bolsheviks pointed out that there would need to be some intermediary stage; it was clear that they mistrusted a self-management that left administration to the workers themselves. The anarcho-syndicalists had only a few delegates, and so the Bolsheviks won a crushing victory. Larin's report was adopted by a huge majority.[84]

This retreat showed how worried the factory committees were, for the formula of self-management which they had thought up had failed, as had attempts to establish even partial workers' control. The employers had proved combative, unemployment was growing, and the collapse of the economy was accelerating; it was now vital to convert industry as a whole. Workers' power at the shop-floor level appeared quite utopian; Larin's proposals did give the workers' bodies a competence that guaranteed security of employment, maintenance of overall interests and supervision from the shop floor; it seemed to be the only way to prevent the employers from winning at the national level, to guarantee workers' rights and demobilize industry. Larin put forward workers' supervisory rights, economic planning and rationalization of production, all of which foreshadowed the achievements of Bolshevism.

Another report, by the Bolshevik Schmidt, suggested that these proposals would mark the end of the self-management experiment. The committees had fought in the vanguard of the proletarian cause against the employers, and had done so when the trade unions had hardly begun to revive. They had acted as 'substitutes', he said, but their chance of acting at a national level was limited, given that their organization was of recent origin, while, by contrast, the trade unions had a better structure and now developed as in no other country. They alone could act effectively at all levels; the factory committees might act as their local branches in individual firms, but any decision as to production and wages was a matter for the national level. The anarchist Piotrkovsky made a final appeal for the committees: 'the unions are trying to throttle us . . . their members are not actually in the factory . . . they are always ready to compromise . . . the committees hold the key to the future.' Ryazanov intervened, to the effect that committees could not stand comparison with unions, for they lacked an overall view of the economy and exhibited only a parochial patriotism; the all-Russian conference was, he said, a fiasco, and an attempt to unify the workers on the basis of a federation of committees was bound to fail. The unions would fight capital as a whole, whereas committees defended the interests only of a single enterprise. He proposed union, and even fusion. The final resolution recommended only co-operation which, in reality, made the committees dependent on the unions' council. The vote was very close, and Levin, the chairman, only supported it because the leadership (now Bolshevik) of the trade unions could give the working-class movement the unity it had hitherto lacked. In the name of that unity, and in view of the Bolshevization of all labour organizations, the committees accepted with little ill will − except in the anarcho-syndicalists' case − subordination to the unions. Every committee was allowed some autonomy in its own firm, and at the national level the committees were allotted representation in the unions' national council; they could also be the nucleus of the labour movement in individual businesses.[85]

Nationalization: the dichotomy between management and control

On the very day of the October Revolution, Lenin announced that the new régime would be based on workers' control. The soviets approved, and by November there was a decree on workers' control. A new age had opened.

At the end of this decree there was a statement to the effect that, at shop-floor level, workers' control would be exercised by all the workers through elected institutions − factory committee, council of elders and the like, which would include representatives of management and the technical staff. They would have access to accounts and stocks − a legalization of what many factory committees had already done. At Point 5, however, there came a statement that decisions made at factory level by the workers' institutions could be reversed by higher institutions: in the towns, there would be councils for workers' control, to form a section of the town soviet, and to include representatives of the trade unions, factory committees and workers' co-operatives. At national level there would be an all-Russian soviet for workers' control, associated with the supreme Economic Council. Its composition completed the defeat of the councils of factory committees, which could nominate 5 representatives, as against 10 for the soviets, 2 for the co-operatives, 7 for the engineers and technicians, and 7 for the trade union council. Each trade union with over 100,000 members had the right to 2 further representatives, and smaller unions had another 1 representative. In the heart of the all-Russian soviet, delegates of the council of factory committees formed only a small minority.[86]

The conference of factory committees, as rival to the unions and as claimant for management at the national level, struck its flag; its leading bodies were absorbed. Given the political revolution that had just occurred, and its relevance in the social field, neither the workers nor the committees were very perturbed, for it was a question of essentials: four days after the Revolution, the eight-hour day was recognized as a principle, and the forty-eight-hour week. Child labour was outlawed; inequalities regarding working women were abolished; unemployment and sickness insurance became compulsory.[87] Workers' control became equally obligatory, and in concrete terms the committee became master (khozyain) of the factory, as far as the workers were concerned, because the national and regional institutions as yet existed only on paper. The movement here went so deep that the government made no attempt to check it:[88] a government statement urged, 'Take the factories and guard them as the apple of your eye.' Lenin and his colleagues needed massive help from the workers; and since, in the heart of the labour organizations the chief resistance to Bolshevism came from some of the unions, they allowed something of a self-management movement to continue, Lenin encouraged it as a 'stage' on the way to socialism. He took this attitude despite the misgivings of the People's Commissar for Labour, that same Shlyapnikov who later became a leader of the 'Workers' Opposition', despite the trade-union Bolsheviks Lozovsky and Ryazanov, and despite the national Economic Council (Vesenkha) including Bukharin, Larin, Milyutin and Schmidt. Under the imprint of the soviet for workers' control, a pamphlet that had been written by Larin and Severdin was sent out to the factory committees. This 'directive' told workers in all parts of industry in full what they should do to effect a supervision that was in reality close to complete management, with sets of regulations and guidelines for the drawing-up of balance-sheets.

However, even with this second wind, self-management did little better than in the summer, and it ended in much the same way. Conditions overall were even worse than some months previously, and the government lacked the means to overcome them, while the general depression was worsened because of strikes by political enemies such as bank clerks and civil servants. The Russian economy was almost a corpse, with almost all its circuits in collapse and the employers doing nothing — quite the reverse — to revive them. For the workers, it was meaningless to have to manage a situation of dearth — how could they, after so much suffering, with poor food and housing, successfully launch a new method of labour-organization in a few weeks? Who could manage it? From now on, workers of the Alexandrovsky railway-station, who produced waggons, and thereby more or less had a guaranteed wage, used them to house their families, since the waggons no longer had to travel. Elsewhere workers would sell plant, in the belief that it was now their property, and was otherwise not being used. At least it could feed them for a few days. No doubt these were extreme cases, and they were attacked by enemies of the régime who were still in a position to do so; equally, they were con- demned by the new leaders. These 'excesses' were of course explicable in terms of the exceptional circumstances, but there was no sign that things would be different so long as the employers continued to fight against their own businesses, and so long as this war was associated with the civil war that was just starting. The new leaders did not intend to be discredited before they had even begun.[89]

The trade-union Bolsheviks attacked the factory committees, Tomsky, chairman of the trade unions, already used managerial language and observed that 'productivity has fallen so low that workers are producing less in value than they get as a wage'. Was it bad feeding, lack of ability, incompetence by committee members who could not keep the books, or was it a reflection of the workers' unwillingness to work? Bolsheviks in charge of the economy did attack the employers as chiefly responsible, but they also talked, as Gostiev did, of 'economic sabotage, no longer solely by the bourgeoisie . . . but by the whole nation, the working class'. To parody a famous saying, these leaders seemed to imagine that, since the working class no longer enjoyed the confidence of the party of the working class, it was up to the working class to regain it.[90]

On 14 December 1917 Marx won his revenge on Bakunin. Lenin signed the first decree on nationalization of businesses on that day, and there were other decrees, later, which ended in partial or total expropria- tion of the employers. The composition of the first 81 nationalizations demonstrates that the intention was essentially against the employers, for they occurred mainly where working-class pressure was strongest, and where self-management had not been pushed through, rather than in places where it had been effected (there were 48 nationalizations in the Urals, 14 in Moscow, 8 in the Ukraine, as against 11 in Petrograd).

Nationalization was much like the sequestration that the workers and many labour organizations had demanded.[91] Still it was in the nature of this measure to terminate self-management, which satisfied organizations rather than workers or committees.

Management of the industries, which was clearly distinguished in the decree from control of them, now became a government matter. In the factories, it was taken over by a new board on which the former management and the committee were represented. In such factories it was clearly laid down by the new board (*rukovodstvo*) that 'decisions concerning management and the activity of the industry belong to management. The control commission will not take any part in this management, and will not be responsible for its functioning, which remains a managerial matter.'[92] The real new era for the factories began on that day. Although the workers hardly noticed it – and there were no positive signs, it was on that day that there ended, at all levels, a unique experiment in which the workers had tried to manage factories on their own.[93]

In the class struggle, from February to October, the workers had proceeded from a reformist stance, with various claims proposed, to a revolutionary one. In February they had hoped only that, with the fall of Tsarism, conditions would improve. By October, they half-controlled the factories, and meant to run them as well. In their resolutions, they no longer talked of labour conditions and wages but of sanctions against the bosses and obligatory labour for the bourgeoisie.[94] It was the workers of small and middle-sized firms that headed the movement and wished to go furthest; but even when they started self-management, they did so not because of principle, as anarchists or socialists, but because they were driven to it for survival, as a response to the challenge of the employers who were prepared to sabotage production so as to break the workers' demands and push the workers into a corner. The workers replied by establishing in the factories the rural model that they knew, the general assembly of workers, corresponding to the village *obshchestvo*, for collective self-management was a form of *mir* or *artel*.[95] One factory collectivity could appeal to another, just as one village could call in another to defeat the *pomeshchik*. The workers wished to be masters of their factory in much the same way as they thought the land should belong to the people who cultivated it. The peasants' individualism and dreams of becoming master or *khozyain* of land were reflected in the collective individualism of the workers of a business, who were inspired by a kind of local patriotism (*skrypnik*).[96] It was natural enough that the self-management movement would be the more lively the smaller the factory, because it was easier to take charge, and easier also for all workers to take part. This was not so in the large factories which, because of their size, took the leadership of the factory-committee movement without actually wanting self-management. To them, self-management was utopian or anarchic; the notion of workers' control, which was apparently close to what the Bolsheviks wanted, was as far as workers in the large factories would go. They interpreted it as a system of procedures to be established by themselves, a control to preserve them from abuses, protect their jobs and more, and transform them, at factory level, into full participants with their due rights. The Bolsheviks, to whom 'management by several is no more socialism than management by one', favoured control, but they were hostile to the idea of workers' taking decisions in the factories: they believed that a takeover of the factories by a 'workers' state', i.e. by institutions that stemmed from labour, was the only way of guaranteeing people against exploitation. At bottom all the militants except the anarchists took this view.

The centralizing Bolshevik plan was quite the opposite to self-management. But for some weeks, while Russian capitalism was still fighting, and the rallying of support from labour was a matter of urgency, experiments in self-management still received tolerance, and even benevolent tolerance, from Lenin himself. The action against it was started by Lozovsky in the trade unions, and it was given theoretical justification by Bukharin. To them, self-management was obviously an experiment in the anarchist ideology that was latent in the world of labour.[97]

That self-management failed both before and after October, had an infinite number of causes. But the failure had to be conceded, such that, willy-nilly, workers had to support the formula of nationalization with workers' control. It seemed better adapted to the fight against capital, and, since it was accompanied by immediate measures against the employers and in the workers' favour, it was felt as a victory for the Revolution. In this sense, so it was. Management of factories became, however, a matter for the organizations rather than the workers – soviet for workers' control, trade unions, soviet of deputies, ministries, all under Bolshevik control.[98] The story thereafter is not labour history; it was the story of men who, having won labour's confidence, now spoke and acted in its name.

CHAPTER 7

The state-from soviets to bureaucracy

In its various ways, the Revolution of 1917 had caused the disintegration of the state, the secession of the nationalities, the flowering of peasant radicalism and the attack on the capital. The experience of 1917 bore out what Friedrich Engels had argued, and Lenin, in *The State and Revolution*, stressed Engels's relevance. The experience also confirmed the view that Lenin and the anarchists shared as to the role and function of soviets, as the centre of a new force that had emerged in February. They were the Revolution incorporated, and not merely the 'counter-balancing power' or 'proletarian fortress in a bourgeois land' that social-democratic tradition imagined them to be, and which the Petrograd Soviet, to begin with, had been. They were both an instrument with which the old state could be destroyed and, in the towns and the army, the embryo of a new workers' state, on lines not unlike those of the Paris Commune.

There was a striking contrast between the extraordinary growth of these multifarious centres of power and, later on, the ordered centralization of the Soviet state. The causes and methods of this transformation have for long been an object of wonder. Did it have to do, as Trotsky said, with the emergence and triumph of Stalinism? Are we to accept his view that bureaucracy and Stalinism were two aspects of the same parasitical phenomenon which grew in the wings of Bolshevism, and against which Lenin is said to have warned his colleagues, apparently from October until his death? Or was it associated with Bolshevism as Lenin defined it in *What is to be Done* and as Plekhanov condemned it in 1903?

The principle of the one-party state is certainly present in *What is to be Done*, but not the bureaucratic phenomenon. One of the specific features of the Soviet state, which official histories gloss over, is the special relationship between these two.* Here we examine the emergence of the Soviet state, as it started to function. Contrary to both the Trotskyist and the anti-Bolshevik interpretations, it will be shown that the nucleus of this

179

state existed before October, already working with its own special features. The Soviet régime was as much the child of the Revolution as the Bolshevism that reinforced its specific character. In succession, there will be considered: (1) the constitution of an embryonic proletarian state, and the ways in which real power was transformed from one of its limbs, the soviet of deputies, to other institutions that are normally simply lumped together with it, such as soviets of factory committees, district soviets and the like; (2) the emergence of the bureaucratic phenomenon, in association with the political parties and institutions, and the formation of a new social group, the existence of which was a consequence of the disappearance of the old state; (3) the place and function of the Bolshevik party in this embryonic state; the forms of Bolshevization of this state before the October Revolt.

1 The constitution of an embryonic proletarian state

The disintegration of the soviet of deputies as counter-balancing force

There were several kinds of soviet. A veteran, freed after forty-five years' service, wrote to the Petrograd Soviet that 'I must point out how far a will to self-government (*svoyevoliye vlasti*) prevails in the provinces. There are political, agricultural, supply, and land committees, justices of the peace, administrative tribunals, soviets, liaison bodies, and no one knows where to address complaints. Discontent is mounting all the time; it is complete disorder, and must not go on.'[1] This letter, though dating from the summer of 1917, makes no mention of the Provisional Government or the all-Russian congress of soviets; the local soviet is mentioned only for the record, among other committees, which themselves might be described as soviets. The centres of power had multiplied, and there were different, rival soviets. Each one stood for the various identities that a citizen could have. As a wage-earner, the worker could be in a trade union or not, if he preferred. He was part of the factory, and could sit on its committee. As a proletarian, he elected representatives to the soviet of workers' deputies; as a citizen, he voted in elections to the municipal council or the town's political committee; as a resident, he could belong to his district committee, and as a consumer he could be present at the supply committee. Finally, he might also be a militant in a party; and the natural outcome of these ambiguities and of the varieties of status and activity was that capacities and representative functions could coincide.

To begin with, the situation was simple. A soviet of workers' and soldiers' deputies had been established in Petrograd. According to its

Menshevik and Socialist Revolutionary leaders, it was the political representative of the workers and soldiers in the capital. At its appeal, identical soviets were formed in other Russian towns, to represent the masses against the town councils and the *zemstva*, as 'bourgeois' institutions. In June 1917 there were 319 soviets of deputies, with thirteen regional bodies (northern region, centred on Vologda; Volga region, centred on Saratov, etc). At the summit, acting as a veritable workers' and soldiers' parliament, sat the congress of soviets, and it was the true counterpart to the government, with negotiation going on through its executive council, the *TsIK*. Here sat the members of the executive committee of the Petrograd Soviet, the 'founding fathers' of the Revolution.[2] As the Russian socialists saw it, the soviet of deputies, and each institution, had its principle of representation and its proper function.[3]

The principle of representation of the soviet of deputies was class; that of the district committee, residence; trade unions had employment, and factory committees, place of employment. The soviet of deputies, the political representative of the working class, upheld the overall interests of the workers as against the government, the state and the employers. The trade unions and factory committees maintained their economic claims, the former at national level, the latter within each firm. The function of district committees was to preserve the alliance of the lower middle class and the working class. The political parties were to be a vanguard (see Table 13).

Table 13 *Principles of representation*

Function	Class	Domicile or place of work	
Vanguard	social democratic workers' party	party section	
Political	soviet of deputies ⟷	soviet of district committees ⟵	district committees
Economic	trade union ⟷	soviet of factory committees ⟵	factory committees
Defence	workers' militia ⟷	Red Guard	

(Institutional expansion = ⟵; conflict zone = ⟷)
institutions of the embryo proletarian state

However, as the revolutionary struggle developed, neither these organizing principles nor the definition of competence and function were respected for long. The political parties which had determined them indeed challenged them themselves, and the fact was that, until September, when there were new elections, the soviet of deputies lost its uncontested pre-eminence. Other institutions took over, although the soviet retained some of its prestige.

At the very beginning of the Revolution the authority of the soviet and its executive committee, as against the government, had no rivals. At a single call, appearing in *Izvestiya*, all Russia had produced soviets, and, again at its appeal, hundreds of trade unions were set up. At a time when the Provisional Government could neither do nor say anything without first consulting the soviet, factories, regiments and villages addressed their wishes and loyalties to it, and frequently to it alone. The Petrograd Soviet was the unchallenged guide of the Revolution, it alone could discuss peace and war, and at a word from it, the soldiers stopped fraternizing and, in the April Crisis, restored order. June, when the first congress of soviets was held, appeared to be the soviet at its zenith. It was, however, largely an illusion for the demonstration of 18 June brutally reminded the soviet leaders of the reality, that they had lost their prestige. In July, demonstrators failed to respond to an appeal from the soviet, and demonstrated against it; now, they followed the watchwords of institutions that called themselves soviets of factory committees or of district committees. The *TsIK* leaders were taken by surprise and overwhelmed — the chairman, Chkeidze, in particular. Although he had been elected by the people and by the congress, and was acclaimed within his own preserve, he had, at each crisis, to go out to meet the demonstrators — not to guide them and to show himself, but to calm them down and face insults. Others had been roughly treated, Chernov almost being lynched in July. The discomfited leaders could only wonder as to why they had fallen from grace, why the soviet's authority was melting away, with other committees inheriting its mantle.

From 1917 onwards, explanations were offered for this. Bukharin said that

> At the start of the Revolution, the soviets were one of the centres of power. The other was the Provisional Government. The local soviets and the Petrograd Soviet had as yet no structure; they had authority and prestige, though not all the power. No one dared to oppose them. Then, the coalition government was set up, in May, with the leaders of the congress of soviets taking part in it. The congress of soviets and the local soviets became auxiliaries of the government, their representatives being assimilated into the ruling class. Just as, at the start of the Revolution, the Petrograd Soviet collaborated with the government only in so far as it approved of government policies, the grass-roots committees now took account of its decisions only in so far as they did not disapprove of them.[4]

To this reason, Trotsky added a further one, which had to do with the very nature of representative systems, including the soviet one:

There was little chance that, at ground level, decisions made by political representatives at a secondary level would suit, because the demands of workers and soldiers had had to be negotiated, and haggled over with the ruling classes and other social groups; they could not be wholly and simultaneously satisfied. Thus in the large towns the factory committees frequently came into conflict with the soviet and became radicalized; just like the village committees, they expressed the citizens' direct will, whereas the resolutions adopted in assemblies with multiple social representation had not been determined by them directly.[5]

Trotsky and Bukharin saw the reason for the fall from grace in the policy of conciliation, for it affected the soviet administration and the *TsIK* alike. In February, there had been a few soviets with Bolshevik majorities that condemned the policy, although the minority grew. When, early in May, the coalition was formed, the Petrograd Soviet received seventy-six telegrams of approval, which was not much; seventeen of them came from soviets. The Yekaterinburg Soviet's reasons for disapproving are documented, and were accepted by 100 votes to 51: 'The participation of soviet deputies in the government is a mistake, because it diminishes the role of the soviets.' The condemnation did not solely affect the nature of the policies, and was more than a simple questioning of them: 'Our soviet has lost the masses' confidence', wrote a deputy from the Urals when he returned to his factory after the session of the congress of soviets, 'and that is because of agitation by a handful of anarchists and Bolsheviks who call our soviet "bourgeois" . . . these maximalists boycott it, so that it has lost the masses' trust.' A commission of the congress of soviets, that dealing with relations with local soviets, preserved many reports on this divorce. The delegates believed that the role of soviets was increasing because they had participated in government, but the workers and soldiers believed the contrary. They felt that the policy of conciliation was depriving the soviets of their function, for they were reduced to the role of electors in a primary and, more importantly, the parliament they elected had neither the will nor the power to accomplish the social transformation that the people wanted.[6] Lenin ably analysed this in *The State and Revolution*:

The way of escaping from parliamentarism does not consist in destroying the representative principle and the representative bodies, but in turning these word-mills into active assemblies . . . not

parliamentary organisms, but active ones like the Paris Commune.
. . . Even in the Russian Republic, which is a bourgeois democratic
republic, all the vices of parliamentarism have turned up even before
a real parliament has assembled, and the rotten philistines, the
Skobelevs, Tseretellis, Chernovs and Avksentievs, have even
managed to inject their gangrene into the soviets, which have turned
into sterile word-mills . . . while 'the work of state' is carried on
elsewhere, in the chancelleries and the staffs. The rage of the
workers and soldiers comes from this dispossession, for they have
been done out of their right to act, which, in everyone's mind, is
associated with the success of the Revolution.[7]

Moreover, they had been dispossessed of this right by representatives
who themselves had abandoned their own right to decide and act. In fact,
there had been a two-stage abdication by the soviet of its right to exercise
governmental powers. The agreement on dual power had been the first
abdication, though it was incomplete, since the 'poskolko-postolku' clause
had left the soviet as guarantor of revolutionary legitimacy. But there was
soon a second abdication: the soviet summoned the workers to resume
work, so as to reassure the bourgeoisie. The workers answered that they
would not become 'convicts, as under the old order', and they demanded
at least the eight-hour day and improvements in their conditions. The
soviet did not dare decree the eight-hour day as the Bolsheviks proposed.
It appealed to the government, which refused to issue such a decree, but
mandated the soviet to negotiate with the employers of the capital:
government and soviet thereby reversed their roles. In a further self-
dispossession, the soviet abdicated its national representative character.[8]
The Petrograd Soviet did extract from the employers, in the emotion
of the February Days, an agreement to accept the decree of the eight-hour
day. But the very manner in which the success was achieved discredited
the soviet's leaders. 'Men are suspicious of us', noted the Menshevik
Bogdanov as early as 10 March: he had taken part in negotiations, under
pressure from workers who remained on strike. Other workers, more
radical, simply effected the eight-hour day by themselves.[9] The workers
of the large provincial towns were still more bitter, feeling that the capital
was forgetting them. The provincial soviets did not wait for any mandate
from the government, and locally decreed the eight-hour day: of twenty-
nine towns where it was introduced, sixteen experienced it as a unilateral
decision, without even negotiation with the employers.[10] Locally, the
soviets' prestige was higher than that of the Petrograd Soviet or even its
inheritor, the congress of soviets, which, from now on, had little real
authority over the workers.[11] This case demonstrated to what extent

power, though remaining in the framework of the same institution – soviets of deputies – could change level, and shift from centre to local body. Other cases demonstrated how the counterbalancing power of the *TsIK* disintegrated, and shifted from the institution of soviets of deputies to conference of factory committees, trade union federation, or political party. 'There is increasing hostility towards soviets', recorded Bolshakov in his report on the activities of soviets in southern Russia, and 'in parallel to the soviets, a series of special organizations has been created – arbitration-tribunals, trade unions and the like, to whose advantage the soviets have been neglected'.[12]

To these reasons there could have been added others that were not formulated at the time because they called in question the very principle of revolutionary parties and the representative institutions established in February – their class composition and the class of their leaders. Of the 519 soviets of deputies existing in June 1917, only 28 were purely working class; there were 101 soviets of workers and soldiers, and 305 of workers, soldiers and peasants. The extreme case was Reval, where the soviet was elected by every class. The soviets, though founded by labour parties, were not so much the expression of a single class than representatives of various social groups with different interests.[13] A further point distinguished the soviets of 1917 from those of 1905, for most of the 1917 soviets were dominated by militants who were not of lower-class origin. In the executive committee of the Petrograd Soviet, for instance, out of 42 members, 7 were workers and 8 were soldiers, and they were soon knocked out. It was the same at Tula and in the Volga region. In the first congress of soviets, for which over 13,000,000 workers and soldiers had voted, the 57 executive officers included only 4 workers, 1 sailor and 6 soldiers. Not a single worker delegated by a factory, and not a single soldier spoke even once – the speeches were made by representatives of the political parties, and not one of them was of working-class origin.[14]

In the circumstances, as long as the soviets' composition remained as it was – which was so until October – it was unlikely that the leaders' behaviour would conform to the social groups they were supposed to represent, especially the workers. None the less, the workers persisted in their demand, 'All power to the soviets'. The illogicality of this was only on the surface, for the congress of soviets and the *TsIK*, even though discredited and associated with the government, could still seem to be a counterbalancing power to a bourgeois-military régime. In the slogan, the plural had been substituted for the singular, for not only the soviet of deputies was involved, but other soviets as well, i.e. those established by the workers themselves. Before they were absorbed by the trade unions and the Bolshevik party, many institutional systems different from soviets of deputies had been created on the basis of factory and district committees, which acted, in a way, as nuclei of institutions. Their mutual impact had also created a section of the working-class armed forces, the Red Guard.

In February the workers had first of all identified with their soviet. Its abdication created a void that the trade unions, which were slow to organize, could not fill. The factory committees therefore took over. As the revolutionaries saw things, these bodies, as a counterbalancing force at factory level, were to have only restricted competence, but the logic of the struggle with the employers was such that their competence received a twofold extension. The first type – horizontal – was the creation, at the level of the capital, of the Petrograd conference of factory committees, then at regional level of similar bodies (Saratov, etc.) and finally at national level of the all-Russian conference of factory committees. This last caused conflict with the trade unions, which claimed such competence at national level for themselves. The Bolsheviks for some time advocated this extension of factory committees' power, because the soviets had abdicated and the trade unions were weak, but, later, they condemned such 'factory patriotism', and, when self-management failed, supported the unions, whose influence grew and who became more radical.[15]

There was a second, vertical, extension of the factory committees, too, in that the nature of the problems they faced grew more complex. To start with, their statutes, resolutions and actions were circumscribed by a single firm's concerns. However, the employers' refusal to negotiate over such matters, or to admit the factory committees as a valid partner, caused the committees to adopt political activity, in the belief that, as the leaders of the soviet of deputies said, the employers' refusal reflected the principle of the régime, the participation of the propertied classes in the government: should they not be expelled, and the nature of the régime changed? By June the Petrograd conference of factory committees was demanding 'All power to the soviets', and sent a warning to the government against arrests at the Villa Durnovo, the headquarters of the anarchists. On 1 July it supported the Bolshevik party's central committee and disapproved of the setting-up of a political centre at the same Villa Durnovo.[16]

The horizontal extension of the factory committees' activity had brought about conflict with the unions; the vertical extension led to rivalry with the soviet. Through the principle of separation of function, the soviet took no note of the conference's existence, and its workers' section did not invite conference members to attend debates. The committees were 'ghettoized' and felt that 'counter-revolution has reached even the soviet of deputies'; they claimed that the factories should take over from it, and become 'fortress of the revolution' in enemy territory. They became a true working-class countervailing force, and self-defence, based on the districts, was soon organized.[17] But the defeat of the self-management movement meant the end of the committees as nucleus of a true proletarian counterbalancing force. The idea had its defenders, anarchists for the most part, but it seemed utopian; and the committees, accepting Bolshevik mediation, bowed to the unions and the soviet, at least inasmuch as these, in the meantime, had become Bolshevized. Similarly, they put the Red Guard which they had established at the disposal of unions and soviet, much as had happened with the district committees already.

These latter, although set up at an appeal from the Petrograd Soviet, had no organizational link with it. Their function was simply to bring together all, without distinction of class, who meant to defend the Revolution at the soviet's side. Such committees were immediately set up in most of the capital's districts. Whereas the soviet was concerned with general political questions, the district committees' task was to make sure that soviet decisions were respected, that the city was properly defended, and that a new life was organized in the districts.[18] Soon, it was the last that took priority, and the committees' secretariat was swamped in demands – workers who were unemployed or badly housed, war widows, delegates of businesses turned to the new authority for help. The committees set up crèches and canteens, combated drunkenness and gambling, formed communal hostels and cultural centres, requisitioned empty houses, and tried to improve the situation as regards food supply.

To begin with, such concrete tasks mattered more than politics to these committees; and in any case, since different social classes were involved in them, 'we must avoid any question that divides us'. They scarcely talked, for instance, of peace or the attitude that should be adopted towards establishment of coalition governments. However, the question of the committees' political and legal status was always being posed, and it split the participants almost despite themselves: did their leaders, for instance, have a 'right' to take decisions over requisitioning of houses or to organize food distribution independently of ordinary commerce? The committees wanted to strengthen their position by having a link with the soviet, but were turned down by it, for its principle of organization was class, whereas the committees' main justification was residence.[19]

With a horizontal extension similar to that of the factory committees, the districts set up an inter-district conference in April. It assembled at the initiative of soldiers who, after the April Crisis, believed that these committees should co-ordinate in the event of military reaction. A

member of the Petrograd Soviet, the Menshevik Anisimov, was elected
chairman of the conference; in the name of all of the districts, it wanted
to have a right to take part in soviet debates, though not necessarily with
the right to vote. The soviet again refused, but for a different reason – the
district committees, out of discontent at soviet policy, had started being
more radical.[20]

After the July Days, Anisimov intervened as member of the Petrograd
Soviet, asking the conference of district committees to collaborate in disarming the workers. He emphasized that the request was made only to
forestall intervention by the military, but his proposal was indignantly
rejected, for the soviet, having repeatedly ignored requests from the
district committees, now appeared to want their conference's authority to
carry out an 'anti-proletarian policy'. There was a breach, and Anisimov,
as chairman, was compelled to make way for two Internationalists and a
Bolshevik, Rappoport, Manuilsky and Gorin. The inter-district conference in its turn became a counterbalancing force to the soviet of
deputies, turning more and more to politics, and acting at two levels –
supporting the Bolsheviks and Chernov, who was held to have been
'slandered' by the bourgeoisie, and building up defence against the
increasing threat of a military putsch. As the Petrograd conference of
factory committees' authority declined, the district committees to some
extent took over.[21]

During the Kornilov Putsch, the district committees' conference
became allied with the local soviets that Bolsheviks set up, those of
Schlüsselburg, Kolpinsk and Sestroretsk. These two institutions formed,
together, a nucleus of popular resistance, and on 28 August they
sent representatives to the 'committee for struggle against the counter-
revolution' (KNBK), which approved of their action and encouraged
them to distribute arms to the workers. The district committees' militia
supervised the commissariats, which were of dubious loyalty; and the
Bolshevik party, through the conference that it partly controlled, was able
to lead the capital's revolutionary action. In a sense, the resistance to
Kornilov was, at this level, a dress-rehearsal for the October Days.[22]

The defensive function and the area of competence of the district
committees had been extended; but the committees no longer discharged
their initial function of maintaining an alliance between the proletariat
and the progressive-minded bourgeoisie. Bourgeois who took part in the
district committees' activities were in a small minority, and the districts
that did have a bourgeois majority were themselves in a minority. At the
committees' conference, representation was such that the most moderate
elements were swamped: just after the Putsch, when the conference
refused to disarm the district militia at Kerensky's request, they opposed

the decision, which they described as 'illegal', and they also protested against the district of Vyborg's prohibition of the dissemination of 'bourgeois' newspapers. On this latter point the conference gave way, and the decision was cancelled, but it was the last act of resistance by delegates of the middle-class districts to the law of the majority.[23]

The committees stemmed directly from factories and barracks, and they became radical, gradually turning Bolshevik. When, in mid-September, the Petrograd Soviet turned Bolshevik, the administration of the soviet of district committees was allowed to set up office at Smolny, on the second floor, just next to the Petrograd Soviet's executive committee. This was symptomatic in two ways: in allowing the district representatives to sit next door to class representatives, the Bolsheviks showed that it was more important to them to meet popular claims than to respect legal and doctrinal fictions; moreover, the delegates of the bourgeois districts, who were under-represented in the administration, found themselves integrated into the soviet system. At least in the district administration, and some weeks before October, representative democracy had given way to a 'dictatorship of the proletariat'.[24]

The emergence of a proletarian armed force

In February, the dual-power system was reflected in the existence of two militias: a government force and one stemming from the population at large. Both urban militia and working-class guard had been set up at the same time as the new régime, which they were designed to protect. In Petrograd, both of them were soon taken over by the municipality, which caused the working-class *druzhiny* to secede, since their idea of order was not the same as their rivals'. They remained under arms, but they were no longer paid, and changed their status and outward appearance.[25] When the workers' militia was set up, it was also concerned with defence of the factory against the army or the government which, if an employer called them in, might try to restore order and disperse the factory committee. These units were the nucleus of the Red Guard that later appeared, as an armed proletarian force, encouraged in its creation by Lenin, Nevsky and Bonch-Bruyevich. Lenin wanted this force ultimately to replace the police, the administration and the army. It was started by the printers' trade union and a collective action by some factories, which appointed a preparatory commission to set up the Guard at town level. It was done secretly, often at the instigation of workers who had no formal party affiliation and counted as anarchists.[26] The Bolsheviks encouraged a movement that developed in spite of the veto of urban militia, Petrograd Soviet and the Menshevik-Socialist Revolutionary leadership. In October the Guard, according to Startsev, contained between 10,000 and 12,000 men.[27]

The Red Guard, like the urban working-class militia, was associated with factories. To start with, it was difficult to distinguish between the two — militiamen of the factory guard did their jobs daily, and were paid for this; those who belonged to the Red Guard took up arms after work and on Sundays. Although all factory guards were not Red Guards, all Red Guards none the less were factory guards, and management was required to pay them. In the Russky Renault factory, for instance, the Bolshevik Babrar was elected commander of the Red Guard, but he was also responsible for the factory militia, and in the management's archives his pay-slip as leader of this latter has survived, for he was paid as such until September. In some factories, Red Guard might therefore be confused with factory guard, while, elsewhere, it was formed out of part of the factory guard.[28]

2 Forms of bureaucratization; the constitution of a new social grouping

In the Revolution of 1917, bureaucratization was one way in which various institutions fought for hegemony: political parties, soviets of deputies, factory and district committees were involved in it. But bureaucratization differed in form and function, depending on whether the institutions that produced it were 'mother' or 'daughter' or non-institutionalized groupings such as those representing the young. Between February and October, bureaucratization from the top downwards was designed to prevent the disruption of representative bodies that were based on class, for it strengthened the hold of the political parties — the only institutions to have a real existence in February — over the soviets of deputies, and that of these soviets over citizens who tried to organize on a different basis, whether of generation, sex, or nationality. Bureaucratization from below came as people tried to consolidate and promote a new institution. This dual process of bureaucratization brought about and solidified a new social grouping that owed its existence to the Revolution. It was not fully formed in 1917, but most of its elements were already present then.

The forms of bureaucratization[29]

A   The first method of bureaucratization from above came when the Petrograd Soviet was established, on the day the Revolution succeeded.

The Bolshevik Shlyapnikov addressed the assembly in the Tauride Palace and proposed that each socialist party should have the right to two seats in the provisional executive committee of the soviet. This proposal was designed, initially, to give the Bolsheviks a decent showing, for they were only a small minority of the initiating group; and the proposal went through, in the absence of certain other parties and organizations, without difficulty.

The result was that members of a dozen different parties and organizations (trade unions, co-operative movements, etc.) entered the executive committee. They called themselves 'representatives' (of their organizations) and, by virtue of this, they speedily eliminated from their discussions the committee members chosen by the general assembly although they were the true founders of the soviet, even if they were not prominent members of their own parties, and sometimes did not belong to one at all. Men like Sokolov and Pankov were knocked out, and even the Bolshevik co-founders of the Soviet, Shlyapnikov, Zalutsky and Molotov, had to make way for Kamenev and Stalin, as delegates of the party. The eight soldiers who had been elected by the garrison had no political affiliation and were therefore excluded, vanishing for ever. In this first case, bureaucratization was shown, not in the right to have two seats for each organization in the executive committee, since this proposal had been discussed and accepted in the general assembly, but only later, in that the choice of the two members lay with the leadership of each organization, its executive officers, and not with the assembly. The assembly had lost its right to control.

This first form of bureaucratization by the parties (a 'mother institution') was practised at Archangel, Astrakhan, Vologda, Ivanovo-Vosnesensk, Kostroma, Saratov, Poltava and some other places, but not universally − not in Ryazan, Kishinev, Vyatka or Baku. Rather more than two-thirds of the soviets practised it.[30]

Traces of a further form of bureaucratization from above emerge in a complaint lodged by the Bolsheviks: late in July, in Petrograd, the Bolshevik members of the *TsIK*, or executive committee of the all-Russian congress of soviets, protested that 'neither the workers' section nor the executive committee of the Petrograd Soviet had met for two months'. The Bolshevik members of these two committees did meet, but only as members of the *TsIK* and not in other capacities; and it was the same with Chkeidze, Dan, Gots and Filipovsky. In the national committee, the *TsIK*, these Menshevik or Socialist Revolutionary deputies could muster forty-six 'conciliatory' votes as against about ten for the extreme left, whereas in the Petrograd Soviet's executive, Kamenev and his friends had a larger minority, so that, as time went by, the majority became much less interested in the proper development of the Petrograd Soviet and its workers' section: the majority refrained from calling executive and general meetings. As they controlled the all-Russian movement, they tried to fend off the pressure from below, in the factories, which, as they grew more radical, demanded, through the workers' section, that there should be new elections.[31]

This procedure, typical of all political systems, enabled the *TsIK* to gain time. There was a rather similar movement in the countryside where the ministry of agriculture, which was controlled by Socialist Revolutionaries, tried to organize the land committees from above, at *guberniya* level, whereas at the base, the peasants wanted to gain control, through their own chosen representatives. A battle followed. On 1 July 1917 twenty-nine *guberniya* committees had been established on the government's pattern, with another eighteen planned; at *uezd* level, less than half of the required total had been set up; but the number of *volost*, or base, committees grew very rapidly, from 650 to 2,871, in July. Just before the October insurrection, in the *guberniya* of Voronezh, for instance, all of the *volosty* had committees. It was only the *volost* committees that were elected wholly by the peasants. As Lenin wrote, 'the *volost* committee is more democratic than the *uezd* one, the *uezd* one than the *guberniya* one, which in turn is endlessly more democratic than the great Agrarian Committee in Petrograd.'[32]

In the eyes of peasants and workers, assemblies with complicated representation, the composition of which had been determined from above, merely slowed the pace of reform; and, as was shown in the case of Samara province (chapter 5), the citizenry acted in their base committees before the higher ones had even met, for they had had to wait too long. They also could not understand how such bodies could be representative, given that they were called by an executive council whose method of recruitment remained a mystery.[33] They did recognize formally the authority of the *guberniya* committee or the congress of peasants' soviets, and sent their delegates, but the fact was that the committees acted autonomously, as in the provinces of Samara, Kazan or Voronezh. The representative system was certainly there, but void of content.

In its third form, bureaucratization from above reflected the majority principle, and advanced by abuse of it. For instance, the Menshevik and Socialist Revolutionary 'majority' in the soviets of deputies, which were already controlled by the parties, seized all the strategic posts that the soviet could command. In 1917, Gots and Avksentiev for the Socialist Revolutionaries and Dan and Gvozdev for the Mensheviks played the part that Sverdlov and Stalin later took over, of 'controlling' appointments to all of the important posts: departments of the ministries, staff jobs in the workers' militia and the like. The case of Anisimov, chairman of the soviet of district committees, was one in point. In truly democratic style, Anisimov ought to have been at least a deputy for his own district before he could be elected to the chairmanship of all of the districts. But his name does not figure in any of the minutes of the Petersburg district where he resided. He was 'selected' for the chair through the Mensheviks of the soviet of deputies and the Petrograd committee of the Menshevik party. This was a bureaucratic form of appointment, endorsed, at the executive council's proposal, by mass approbation − a method later practised, systematically, by the Bolsheviks.[34]

Statistics can show the extent to which these different practices went on. They concern the conference of Petrograd factory committees, a list of members of which, for the first, second and fourth conferences, is extant. Between June and October, the number of members who had not been directly elected by a factory but figured in the list of soviet-appointed members by virtue of this type of bureaucratic procedure rose from 4 to 12 per cent (see Table 14).[35]

Table 14 *Members of conferences of Petrograd factory committees*

	First conference (June 1917)	Second conference (August)	Fourth conference (October)
Total no. of members	585	326	174
No. of members chosen by trade unions	10	9	2
No. of members chosen by parties and soviet executive offices	6	11	18
Total	16	20	20
Hence: Elected by factories	96%	93%	88%
Bureaucratically appointed	4%	7%	12%

Bureaucratization from above was one of the ways in which the institutions could fight for the conquest of power; and the same feature is borne out by the specific forms of bureaucratization from below as well.

B   In the popular institutions of 1917, where there was direct democracy, other, virtually spontaneous, forms of bureaucratization can be found. It may be described as bureaucratization from below.

As with the earlier cases, it was a procedure that strengthened or consolidated power, possible even as a single person's, but in a 'daughter' rather than a 'mother' institution or even in embryonic institutions not, as yet, recognized. This explains why bureaucratization from below was less obvious than other forms, because it could emerge from institutions that were stillborn and left no archives – bureaucratization obviously presupposing an institution. This happened, for instance, with the young workers of Vyborg who tried to set up autonomous youth groups and to form a procession separate from that of the other Vyborg workers. The only trace of their initial attempt at institutionalization is the existence of streamers, carrying their specific slogans. A second element is the conference of youth that they organized. They took part in the October Insurrection and then, at the instigation of one of their members, such a body appeared in the Bolshevik organizations. They thus received bureaucratization from above even before they existed institutionally.[36] Here, there could not have been bureaucratization from below.

However, in the case of the factory committees there was something like it, at least in the most obvious meaning of the term for, in the few photographs that have survived, the separation of committee and factory assembly emerges from the fact that the committee is, aptly, seated around a bureau, while the workers remain standing. The bureaucratizing emerged properly when – in spite of the statutes, which were quite explicit – the partial replacement of the committee's membership was no longer observed, as can be seen with the factory-committee delegates to the three Petrograd conferences. Similarly, the existence of assemblies that took decisions, though inquorate, is demonstrable. The committees noted the fact in their minutes, and still took decisions although expressly forbidden to do so by the statutes. This perpetuated their authority in a different way.[37]

The case of district committees is an exemplary illustration of bureaucratization from below. It came as political activity was taken over by permanent members. In the beginning, in February, the permanent members were not working-class militants, a few trade unionists apart, but rather residents of the districts who, once they had a permanent post in the committee's office, would gradually abandon their ordinary jobs. Since they now drew no wages, the assembly of the district committee would agree to give them a small sum from the money received by subscription. Thereafter there was a clear correlation between the elections of permanent members and the regular diminutions of attendance at general assemblies (except in the July Days, when it revived). Attendance at the Petrograd Peterhof district, for instance, went down from forty to twenty-two, on average, between March and October. Meetings of the officers of the executive council rose from two per month in April 1917 to three or four per week in the summer and autumn, with the general assemblies called by the officers becoming fewer and fewer – six in September, and four in October. Attendance was sparse, and the people, ill-informed, took no further part in the discussion. It was left to members of the board, who would suggest motions that the assembly could vote for or against (see Table 15).[38] Thus, in the districts, the citizenry had lost

Table 15   *Attendance at Petrograd Peterhof district*

	March	April	May	June	July	August	September	October
General assemblies	20	18	11	11	15	11	6	4
Meetings of the political committee (board)	0	3	2	0	6	6	6	4

their right to speak, and a board did so in their name. The relationship of governor and governed had reappeared, to the advantage of people who were allowed to maintain it only in so far as they presented themselves as a branch of legitimate authority. As the district committees and the Petrograd Soviet became radical and Bolshevized, they arrived at this sought-after legitimacy when the administrative council of the soviet was set up at Smolny, near the Petrograd Soviet; and the Bolsheviks, on their side, started their own first act of bureaucratization from above – they simply nominated A. A. Yoffe, a member of their central committee, to the presidium of the soviet of district committees, where they and their allies had acquired a majority in the most democratic possible way. This strengthened the position of Manuilsky, who was the only Bolshevik on the presidium, at the expense of his two 'Internationalist allies', Gorin and Rappoport.[39] The institution of district committees was thus bureaucratized both from above and below, to the Bolshevik party's double advantage. There was a similar process elsewhere, particularly with the small-town soviets. After October, the Bolsheviks were more systematic in their use of these methods, but there was a difference: there were now no more truly free elections that might have put a brake to a procedure that could benefit only the Bolshevik party. The framework of one-party and bureaucratic state was coming into existence.

The formation of a new social grouping

The process of twofold bureaucratization underlay the creation of a new social grouping, the Soviet bureaucracy of the future.

(a) With the excellent index drawn up by the Leningrad archivist B. D. Galperina, it is possible for us to tell the social origins and the political identity of the district-committee members and their officers. Some 60 per cent of them were workers of the district, 25 per cent were soldiers stationed in the vicinity, 10 per cent were trade-union militants and 5 per cent were clerks or members of the liberal professions – a doctor, a priest or two, etc. Half had no political affiliation, while 30 per cent described themselves as Bolshevik, the rest Menshevik or Socialist Revolutionary.[40]

From the minutes of the assemblies it is clear that the committee members did not, for some time, separate from their class: they spent part of the day in the factories or barracks, and another part in the committee. Later, when they began to get a payment out of subscriptions, they were no longer wholly workers or soldiers, but leaders who fought, not for a party, but for their fellow-citizens – finding them a place to live, obtaining a pension for them and the like. In time, they split off more and more from their original social group, and their way of life became different from that of their former comrades.[41] For them to avoid having to go back to the factory and to remain as leaders, two conditions were required: first, that the old state should be abolished, for if it defeated the committees and soviets, the leaders would inevitably be dispossessed. Thus there was a kind of functional solidarity between the members of the committees, not necessarily the Bolshevik ones, and Lenin's party. In the districts, moreover, the committee members had to be more energetic, devoted and radical than most of the assembly members, otherwise the assembly would simply choose different leaders. Lunacharsky's first film, *Uplotneniye*,[42] demonstrates this: in the Petrograd district the district-committee member is more radical and Bolshevik than the worker who wants somewhere to live. The worker does not dare occupy the rooms of the professor's house, although he has a permit to requisition them. 'But you've got the right', says the delegate, and, even though one room is said to be enough for the worker and his daughter, he goes on, 'You've got the right to two rooms', ostentatiously spitting on the staircase carpet while the worker, cap in hand, is careful not to dirty it. It is impossible to tell how many of these committee members were permanently freed from having to go to the factories, at least as workers, but they formed the first element of a new social grouping.[43] Its characteristics were (1) a new source of income, (2) a new social activity, (3) a break with their original class, (4) necessary solidarity with the Bolshevik party, (5) dependence on their leading institutions. The district-committee members were not alone in this category: there was a similar development among most trade-union delegates and members of other local committees.

(b) A second constituent element of the new social grouping emerged with the Red Guard. The destiny of these was of course different from that of the first element, but less than might be supposed. What happened with the Red Guard of the capital is clear from the stated conditions of recruitment. There is, in the archives, a questionnaire filled out by 3,663 of the Red Guards, which, for Petrograd, was a quarter of the effective strength at the time of the enquiry (March 1918). An obvious feature is their youth: out of the sample of 3,663, 280 were under twenty, and more than half were under twenty-five. Only 153, or 4 per cent, were over forty. Moreover, 3,513 were of working-class origin – 96 per cent of the total sample. Seventy-seven per cent came from the large metal-working factories, such as Putilov, Arsenal and Promet, though the Guards were supplied by a large number of factories – 180 in this sample. Among the 150 Guards who were not of working-class origin, there were teachers, doctors, some twenty demobilized officers, a handful of students (most students were in the urban militia); there were few textile workers, and few bakers or food-workers, if any. 'Birthplace' showed that 29 per cent of the Guards came from the capital, 44 per cent had been born in towns generally, and 56 per cent in the countryside. These proportions confirm what was stated above as to the recent origin of the working class in the large factories, most of the workers having been born in the country. Years ago, before the historians and sociologists, Eisenstein guessed as much in *Strike*.

No more than a quarter of the Red Guards were ever involved in fighting. Of this sample, 137 had taken part in the July Days (out of 3,663), 241 in the action against Kornilov, 126 in the October Insurrection and 413 in the taking of the Winter Palace, the two latter events being considered separately in the questionnaire distributed to the Guards. If we multiply the figures by four, we have a useful clue to the real extent of the fighting in the Revolution. The political tendencies of the Red Guard are equally clear: 44 per cent described themselves as Bolshevik while 53 per cent declared no party affiliation. The remaining 3 per cent (and this was for a quarter of the total membership) consisted of 34 left Socialist Revolutionaries, 11 maximalists, 10 anarchists and 10 Mensheviks. Among the 1,603 Bolsheviks, only 258 declared that they had been Bolsheviks in February, which demonstrates, once more, how the masses became Bolshevized between February and October.[44]

As an element of a new social grouping, the Guards resembled the district-committee members in several ways other than in social origin: they too changed their way of life, and soon, for those who entered the Red Army, the source of income also changed. Before October they had more than a functional solidarity with the Bolsheviks, too, because if Kornilov had won they would have been shot.

The Guards did differ from the *apparatchiki* in some important ways. Their relationship with the Bolshevik party bodies was the inverse of the district committees' relationship with them. In the district committees, given the social mixture of the participants, only part of the assembly was radical; but the officers were more radical, and Bolshevik, and the central committee of the soviet of district deputies became an agency of the Bolshevik party itself. The Red Guards, on the contrary, were often paid by their employers (see above) so that their relative independence was greater, and they were less anxious to maintain organizational links with any institution, even the Bolshevik party. The Petersburg committee of the Bolshevik party did not manage to create an effective link with the Red Guard, which remained a federation of units based on the districts and the factory committees, not a centralized corps. Its statutes provided for an elected command, the staff of which was to include, among others, a representative of the Petrograd Soviet, and members of the central committee of factory committees, and of the trade union council, but these arrangements remained merely on paper (see Figure 2).

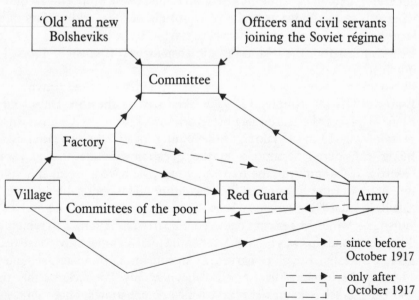

Figure 2   *Social mobility and construction of* apparatchiki *groups 1917*

The Red Guard was bureaucratized neither from above nor from below, and had a reputation for instability and lack of discipline. Photographs and statistics show that they were composed of very young people, violent and unruly in the way of the young. The Bolshevik party had little confidence in these volunteers not controlled by it and, wrongly, regarded them as anarchists. It is significant that, during the first days of the October Rising, Trotsky and his colleagues on the *PVRK* sent fourteen times fewer messages to the Red Guard than to the soldiers,[45] as will be shown in the following chapter. This discrepancy explains the relative disappearance from official ceremonies of the Revolution of the Red Guard, for it appears only collectively and symbolically. Trifonov, Yurkin and Pavlov are not names that figure in the official history of the Revolution, and it is Startsev's achievement to have noted them. After October, the Bolsheviks rejected Trifonov's plan to broaden the Guard into a militia through which workers could rotate, under the control of factory committees. The committees, who were already suspected of aiming at self-management, found this proposal turned down: Lenin said that 'the place for the best workers is the factory'. Guards who wanted to serve the new state with armed force soon got instructions to join the Red Army, which 25 per cent of them accepted. The others remained Guards for some time, but the new régime showed as much zeal in dissolving this institution as earlier it had in creating it.[46]

In 1918, when the Red Guard was dissolved, many workers went straight from the factories to the army. The factories, in consequence both of the sabotage of the economy by the middle classes and of the economic collapse, emptied; young workers, turned out into the streets, enlisted, and took part in raids against the countryside to feed the towns. Some of them settled down in the villages to form the nucleus of committees of the poor, which soon came to rule the villages with Bolshevik party help. Thus, part of the Red Guard, like some of the workers and soldiers, joined in the administration and defence of the régime. They had in common with the first group the fact that they brought new blood, of working-class origin, to the developing state; and the members of these two groups became associated with two other elements that constituted the Soviet state:

(c) Members of the old administration and the officers' corps which, latterly, joined the new state although just after October the old Tsarist bureaucracy carried out a sort of staggered strike; and

(d) The leadership of the Bolshevik party, which became head of state.

Who were these Bolshevik leaders in 1917? It has perhaps been insufficiently stressed that revolution and emigration was associated and rooted in the same humiliation and anger. From Livonia to the Black Sea and the ghetto of Yekaterinoslav, discontent, persecution and poverty caused several million subjects of the Tsar to emigrate to Siberia and take refuge in a soil less harsh where, as in America, there was a chance to lead a life worth living if one forgot the past and settled down to work.[47]

The number of old-style Bolsheviks, like the number of emigrants, grew with increasing distance from the capital. The greater number was born in the Ukraine, in the marginal areas peopled by minority races whose experience of Tsarism and Holy Russia was only through civil servants, Cossacks' whips and harassment. The arrival of railways had made them more sensitive than others to the effects of modernization in the capital.

Among the 264 most prominent Bolsheviks of whom *Granat* took a census in 1920−4, only 12 came from the capital and 35 from distant provinces, as against 119 from minority peoples and almost one-sixth from the ghettos. The proportions are still more significant in 1917, before the new blood from the masses had given the party its definite shape: the proportion of Ukrainian Jews, most of whom were petty-bourgeois, was greater, as was also true of the Mensheviks.[48] They too had left their homes to become professional revolutionaries, and they did not feel they were Jews or minority peoples; nor were they considered as such, except of course by the right, but more as revolutionary fighters who were listened to because they, more than others, could express the humiliation that afflicted all the poor and the persecuted.

The Bolshevik militants were much older than the people who joined the party in 1917 and later. Their average age was 36 (as against 22 to 25 later) and Lenin, at 47 in 1917, was nicknamed 'the old man'. They were also better-educated, and among the holders of leading party offices in 1917 virtually all had had secondary education, the majority having had higher education either in Russia or abroad. Many had already written articles or books. The leaders were sufficiently homogeneous as a group, culturally and socially, even though some were of aristocratic (Chicherin), higher industrial bourgeois (Pyatakov), landed bourgeois (Smilga), commercial bourgeois (Yoffe) or bureaucratic (Lenin and Kollontai) origins. They put all their energy into the revolutionary transformation of society, and otherwise led a modest existence. As individuals, however, they obviously had personal means and did not have to work. When they took a job, it was not, except in Frunze's case, because they had to but because they had chosen to make a break with their families, as in Antonov-Ovseyenko's case, or because they had to take on a worker's job to defend the cause and indoctrinate the workers. As L. S. Feuer said, for them 'existence did not determine consciousness'.[49] When their families' means did not suffice, the party chest helped out, and it was supplied with gifts from men such as Yoffe who handed over his whole inheritance to the party, or from more or less disinterested sympathizers.

In this sense, the Bolsheviks formed a kind of counter-society the basic regulation of which was total devotion to the party, while social conduct and morality had to be exemplary, and disinterestedness equally complete. Responsibility was regarded not as an advantage and as power, but as a burden and an act of self-sacrifice. The consequence was indifference to personal advantage, which was considered 'bourgeois', individualist in nature, and hence the political militants' hostility to all other demands, which they wrote off as petty-bourgeois and not social — for example, women's or nationalities' demands. This attitude reinforced the group's identity and the identity of its representative, the party.

With its twenty-five newspapers and three weeklies, and its network of 24,000 members in August (and 40,000 in October), the Bolshevik party became a force, a state within the proletarian state. It had its deputies and specialist spokesmen in all institutions; the minutes of the central committee show the extreme centralization of the system and the specialist knowledge of the various leaders, as well as the great freedom of choice as regards decisions (as exemplified by events between July and October) at least within the central committee, with Kamenev frequently challenging Lenin's line. This major conflict over the strategy and nature of Bolshevism was associated with a further one that reached its height in July, that between party leadership and militant vanguard. The failure of the latter in July strengthened the authority of the central committee, with Sverdlov enforcing discipline and playing the role of 'night-watchman' that Rosa Luxemburg attributed to Lenin. The central committee of the party acted as 'brain', omnipresent, and affecting a whole section of society. Its members sat in different sections of the popular institutions: Kamenev in the *TsIK* of the congress of soviets. Trotsky in the Petrograd Soviet (after September), Yoffe at the soviet of district committees, Skrypnik in the trade union administrative council. The grafting-on of groups (a), (b) and (d) (see Table 16) occurred before October, with the 'new men' of popular origin appearing in the middle ranks of the party or the institutions it more or less controlled. These were the 'leather-jackets', committee members who, after 1918, frequently shifted to the army or the administration.

Groups (c) and (d) belonged to the lesser nobility, the bourgeoisie and the intelligentsia. At the decisive point in their lives, between twenty and thirty, in the years 1895–1905, they had chosen two different directions: some of them, as civil servants or officers, entered the service of the state while others became revolutionary and took up a position in the 'vanguard' of society. The latent and explicit aims were the same —

Table 16   *The structure of Soviet bureaucracy*

| | Popular classes | | Intelligentsia | |
	Group (a)	Group (b)	Group (c)	Group (d)
1917	+	+		+
1918–24	+	+	+	+
1928 (bureaucracy of nationalities)	+	+		

Definition of the groups in 1917

(a) Members of committees and soviets (urbanized resident workers, militants, soldiers of the garrison, etc).

(b) Red Guards (very young workers, newly in from the countryside), and later veterans of the Red Army, committees of the poor, etc.

(c) Former Tsarist officials, officers who came over to the soviets, and non-militant intelligentsia who joined the revolutionary régime.

(d) The Bolshevik Old Guard (between ten and twenty years older than group (b)).

The social and cultural turn-about of the Stalin era was associated with the ruin of the old intelligentsia, with purges and show-trials, and the absorption of its surviving elements into the popular classes, where gradually elements of rural origin came to predominate.

leadership and reform. They were revolutionaries and reformers in their ideals and ambitions, and they represented the values of the town, of reason, of the European Enlightenment. In 1917 there was a battle, but a transitory one, between groups (c) and (d), after which the old Guard called in some members of the group it supplanted. But both of them were soon submerged in the advance of groups (a) and (b) which, being younger, ultimately took over. It may be suggested, as a hypothesis, that the Stalin era corresponded to the slow transfer of power from groups (c) and (d) to groups (a) and (b), the latter being essentially of peasant origin. Stalin relied on them, increased their numbers and their importance, and they represented a more conservative cultural tradition which was attached to the values of family, of authority, of academicism. One function of the purges and show-trials was to eliminate the former privileged groups to whom even the 'old style' Bolsheviks had belonged despite their being, historically, in the 'vanguard'. The rise of popular elements could quite easily be adapted to the elimination, both at the top and at lower levels, of these formerly privileged elements, 'these men with their knowledge, all these swine', as Gorky said.

3 The Bolsheviks and the future of the state

The Bolshevization of the soviets

Bolshevization of the popular institutions came, essentially, in two ways:
the radicalization of the masses, who followed different watchwords of the
extreme left and showed their radicalization instantly, through direct
democracy; and the increase in organizational links between these institutions and the Bolshevik party. The dependency relationship with the
party reflected both the extent of radicalization and of bureaucratization.
For instance, the Red Guards, though completely radicalized and also
half-Bolshevik, had few organizational links with the party: some units
did of course have links with a Bolshevik party cell in a district, factory
or whatever, but there was never a link at a higher level. With the district
committees, it was the other way about: because of their social composition they were only partially radicalized, but the administrative boards
of most districts were Bolshevized and, at the top, the soviets of district
committees were controlled by the central committee: links with the party
became very close.

The trade unions and factory committees stood half way between these
extreme positions. However, although the evolution was not everywhere
exactly similar, it did go in the same direction, towards overall Bolshevization. It was natural enough for Lenin's party to demand that there
should be new elections to the soviets of deputies so that the changes
could be translated into the top level of the institutional edifice, the
congress of soviets of deputies and its executive committee, the *TsIK*.[50]

Even in February the Bolsheviks had contested the electoral system
established by the first provisional executive committee of the Petrograd
Soviet on the grounds that it put the large factories, which were alleged to
be Bolshevik, at a disadvantage. Since then they had always demanded
new elections because the February ones had been carried out 'in the old
way'. In some cases there had been grass-roots revolt, as in Orekhovo-
Zuyevo, where the executive committee had been chased out after three
weeks – the leader of the administrative board had been a private-school
headmaster and a factory inspector, who had put through a motion
declaring in favour of 'war until final victory'. In another case, the
electorate had disavowed a delegate who had not respected their
decisions; and similarly with the delegate of the Milevsky factory at
Moscow who had flouted a resolution by 1,500 workers of twelve
factories, and spoken in favour of the Liberty Loan. By May partial re-
elections were occurring in the provinces of Oryol and Moscow, and on
each occasion there was a clear advance by the Bolsheviks, whose

delegates rose from 5 to 40 in Oryol, out of 160, and from 15 to 30 in Tula (total unknown). The Bolshevik party was encouraged by these results, and fought on a platform of re-election to the soviet of deputies. The Menshevik Socialist Revolutionary *TsIK* tried to temporize. Initially it agreed, and then had commissions elected which decided, despite Bolshevik protests, that the re-elections would have to be approved by at least a quarter of the electors present in the factory assemblies, in which a quorum of 60 per cent of the possible voters would be necessary — a clause that figured in the statutes of most factory committees. In the then condition of Russian industry, with lock-outs, dismissals and strikes adding to the instability of working-class numbers, all this really meant postponing the elections indefinitely.[51]

But after the Kornilov Putsch it became all the more difficult to oppose re-elections because the left Socialist Revolutionaries and a majority of the Menshevik Internationalists agreed with most of Lenin's slogans, and this, to some extent, could count as the third form of Bolshevization. On 31 August, in the middle of the Kornilov crisis, the Petrograd Soviet passed a resolution which was not much noticed at the time, but was still of historic significance: 'Not only the accomplices of Kornilov, but representatives of the propertied classes generally, must be expelled from power.'[52] In a completely unexpected way, and impelled by the fight against the Kornilovite reaction, the body that symbolized the Revolution thus adopted a resolution that ran counter to what it had been saying for the past six months; and this was also the first Bolshevik motion that had won a majority since the very beginning of the Revolution. A few days later the same resolution went through the Moscow Soviet by 354 votes to 252. Chkeidze accurately gauged the extent of the defeat and gave up the presidency of the Petrograd Soviet on 6 September, retaining only the chairmanship of the executive committee of the all-Russian congress of soviets. Some days later the Bolsheviks won a majority in the workers' section of the Petrograd Soviet; and in the administrative council of the soldiers' section there were 9 Bolsheviks to 10 Socialist Revolutionaries and 2 Mensheviks — the president, Fedorov, was a Bolshevik. Later still the Petrograd Soviet went left, Trotsky being elected president, and no-confidence in the former council being voted with 519 votes to 414. The historic council resigned — Chkeidze, Tseretelli, Skobelev, Gots, Chernov, Dan and Anisimov.[53]

The Moscow Soviet also went in this direction: in the *TsIK* the Bolskeviks rose from 10 to 16 in number. The movement soon affected the peasant soviets, and their congress resolved that all power should be transferred to the soviets.[54] It is easy, in the circumstances, to understand why Martov should have said that the leaders were becoming 'more and more irresponsible with regard to the democratic organizations'.[55] A breach between the provincial soviets and the Petrograd Soviet on the one hand and the *TsIK* on the other was becoming unavoidable: a second congress was urgently required. On 21 September Trotsky and Bukharin, in the name of the Moscow and Petrograd Soviets, tabled this question. Dan wanted to put it off, and the Socialist Revolutionaries asserted, like him, that Kerensky would not in any case submit to the congress in any event. It was a trial of strength: the Bolsheviks stepped up their pressure, with the Revel and Moscow Soviets threatening to take away from the *TsIK* its responsibility for calling a second congress, and Trotsky declaring that 'if need be we will call it in a revolutionary way'. The *TsIK* finally gave way, and the date of the meeting was fixed for 20 October.[56]

The preparations for this second congress of soviets showed how quickly the radicalization of the workers and soldiers had gone ahead: Bolshevik representation went up, and there was a leftward shift in the type of resolutions voted.[57] The example of the conference of soviets of the Petrograd region, early in October, was significant, for it resolved that 'the soviets are the only institutions that can guarantee the victory of the Revolution; only they constitute the power that will give the country peace and the policies desired by a majority of its people'. Identical resolutions went through the regional assembly of the soviets of the Volga region in the first third of October. These assemblies were held as part of the preparation for the second congress of soviets, and the Bolsheviks won success after success. At Petrograd they took 443 seats to the Mensheviks' 44; in the Urals they also won an absolute majority, with 80 delegates out of 110, and they took the largest number of votes at Smolensk and several towns in Siberia. Even where they were not in the majority, the resolutions passed showed to what extent they were the leaders: at Kiev, for instance, the sovereignty of the second congress was proclaimed by 159 votes to 29.[58] It was clear that this congress would have a Bolshevik majority, and that the majority would also declare that the congress should take power. The government could not let this happen, so that a second *Kornilovshchina* was inevitable, with the military attempting to dissolve the soviets. Men asked whether the Bolsheviks would be strong enough to forestall this, and what kind of power would be installed once the principle of taking power had been proclaimed.

It was not thought that the party could do it, being too weak in structure — a situation that the leaders continually deplored. How the Bolsheviks judged their own strength is revealed in the repots of Boky, which were read to the capital's committee on the morning of the July Days and on 16 October, a week before the uprising. The reports are interesting in that they reveal how, Lenin apart, the Bolsheviks under-estimated the revolutionary will of the masses and their ability to carry out a complete social change because they associated strength with the number of militants formally controlled by the party. The Bolsheviks themselves contributed in this way to the legend that the Revolution of October, if not the October Days themselves, was the work of a minority.

Boky's report calculated that on 1 July there were, depending on geographical definition, either 32,220 or 30,610 mandates in the capital: the Vyborg district came top, with 6,632, followed by the Narva district with 5,274, and then by Vasilevsky Island. The great defect was, Boky said, absenteeism: even in the municipal committee, the chief body in the capital, only thirty, on average, of the fifty delegates would be present, and another factor of insecurity was the military organization of the Bolsheviks, which had only 1,600 members. Nevsky felt that the 4,000 members of the *Pravda* club could be added: 'Ninety per cent of them are peasants, but without them the Revolution cannot succeed. They are difficult to control'; he went on that the party's influence was strong only in the 1st machine-gun regiment, the sappers, and the 180th infantry regiment, 'where there are many artisans'; moreover, workers had to subsidize *Soldatskaya Pravda*; and Slutsky was not even convinced that in these units Bolshevik influence was predominant. Rakhia remarked 'the mood is certainly Bolshevik, but there is no organization'; to which Bogateva answered, 'We cannot even send three representatives of the military organization to the district committees'. There was a complaint that no fixed relationship between them had been created.[59]

Three and a half months later, during the discussions as to whether the time was right for insurrection – eight days before it – the Bolsheviks were still considering the strength of the revolutionary movement in the light of their own possibilities of leading it; and they still under-estimated their own strength, despite their extraordinary progress. According to the delegates, only the Moscow district was 'bold' in mood: elsewhere there was 'no fighting spirit', not even in Vasilevsky Island or Vyborg. It was true that the party was 'gaining influence', and 'the troops are at one with us', but 'they will not act unless really provoked into it'. This passivity was explained by fear of the sack, and of universal lock-outs. There are two further noteworthy features in the Bolshevik delegates' reports: the anarchists' influence seems to be increasing, and the workers and soldiers would take to the streets at an appeal from the soviet, but not at an appeal from the Bolshevik party.[60]

The Bolsheviks, persuaded of their own weakness, dared not rely only on their own strength. Organizationally, they would have to mobilize the revolutionary body of all revolutionary bodies, the soviets, which had now been invigorated by an infusion of new blood in the elections. In Petrograd, they set up a new agency in October, the *VRK*, or Military Revolutionary Committee, attached to the soldiers' section of the soviet. Cleverly, they left a left Socialist Revolutionary as head of the organization, but the nature of the committee was really dictated by Podvoysky's Bolshevik military organization. In accordance with custom, a member of the trade union council (a Bolshevik), a member of the soviet of factory committees (a Bolshevik) and *ex-officio* members of the military organizations of the political parties (Bolsheviks and left Socialist Revolutionaries) and the presidium of the Petrograd Soviet (Bolshevik), with army representatives, were included. *VRK*s were soon set up in sixty Russian towns, and they were to be the military brain of revolt.

Unlike the *KNBK*, established in August spontaneously under the impact of Kornilov's revolt, and even then only at Bolshevik initiative, the *VRK*s were an emanation of the Bolshevik party itself, though generally *via* the initiative of a Bolshevik soviet. Khesin has shown that, out of 53 *VRK*s examined by him, only 9 were set up not on party initiative but by a soviet; 43 *VRK*s for which such information is available were wholly Bolshevik, while a further 32 were inter-party with a Bolshevik majority, and 20 more had the Bolsheviks as the largest party in them.[61] The Bolshevization of this, as of other institutions, was possible only because it was accompanied by a wide popular consensus.

The Revolution, the soviets and the constitution of the state

The masses' radicalization, the advance of Bolshevism and the collapse of the February régime called in question the functions of the various institutions on which the Revolution had been based. It altered the relationship of the socialist parties to these institutions.

The historical and political tradition naturally reflects the documents on which it is based; and, since it has accorded a privileged place to the archives of the parties (or the soviets that were their expression) it necessarily sees things from their viewpoint, and therefore has failed, on the whole, to cover this problem adequately. For instance, as regards the role of soviets in the struggle for power from February to October, traditional history has considered it by discussing the function that the socialist parties expected soviets to have, or by analysing the rivalry of the parties as they fought to control it. This is legitimate enough, but it is still one-sided, for there was an aspect of political struggle that was not a matter of party against party, anarchist against socialist, but of institution against institution, quite independently of ideological or party-political orientations. These institutions fought to extend their range – trade unions fought factory committees, district committees fought soviets of deputies, and each institution constructed, as the political parties did, a theory of politics that legitimated its right to a pre-eminent place.

The strife weakened the institutions, to the profit of the political parties and especially the Bolsheviks who, with the radicalization of opinion and the organizations, figured at the heart of every institution. The Bolsheviks could offer to help and mediate. The offer, as was shown in the preceding chapter, was accepted, in so far as both party and organizations aimed at the same thing, to overthrow the Provisional Government and the institutions of the past, and to take their place. By agreeing to the party's making the interim arrangements, the organizations gradually gave up their separate identities. Their leaders, often Bolshevik themselves, could more or less accommodate themselves to the loss of identity; but it also meant abandoning the particular plan of each organization, which involved a fourth form of Bolshevization.

This happened in the field of political theory. The first such theory to collapse was the theory of workers' power, upheld by factory committees. Then it was the turn of the trade union's plan, after October, when Reisner was out-voted during the drafting of the new constitution of the Republic. Tugan-Baranovsky's co-operative theory also fell down: co-operatives, in his project, were meant to 'overtake' the class struggle at a time when that struggle was too much of a reality for anyone seriously to contemplate 'surmounting' it.[62]

The soviets of deputies had not worked out their own political theory because, at least to begin with, in 1917, they stemmed from socialist parties. When the relationship of parties and institutions were inverted, soviets remained the only agency in the proletarian state whose function had not been subject to compromise. The Mensheviks and anarchists had their own ideas as to the role of soviets, but they were defeated in the political struggle and had to leave to the Bolsheviks the task of defining what soviets were to do in the new state. The Bolsheviks achieved this after a lengthy process, ending only with the promulgation of the Soviet constitution.

A   Paradoxically, the Mensheviks and populists, having been the great advocates and founders of soviets, constantly sought to reduce their role and stressed the sovereignty of the constituent assembly. In February they had adopted arguments of revolutionary strategy — having become masters of the soviets, they would not take power so as not to discredit the socialist ideal which they represented for, given that the condition of Russia was such as to rule out any satisfaction of the people's demands, the bourgeoisie would have to take power while the soviets would supervise, safeguard the transition from autocracy to democracy and guarantee that a constituent assembly would be convoked. Next, after April, when Lenin popularized the slogan of 'All power to the soviets', the Mensheviks and populists opposed it in the name of democratic principle, saying that soviet power was not legitimate, because the soviets represented classes and not the nation, so that only the constituent assembly could have legitimate authority.

After May, moreover, with soviet delegates taking part in the government, the Mensheviks and Socialist Revolutionaries made out that the soviets must no longer play the part of a counterbalancing force, for they would weaken the state's authority at a time when the government was fighting the last adherents of the old order. To them, the extremist slogans of 'All power to the soviets' were sheer adventurism, substituting a class-tyranny for the old autocracy: they were anti-democratic, would destroy all democracy, as incarnated in the conciliatory elements and the progressive wing of the bourgeoisie, and had to be opposed by force, which happened in July. The Socialist Revolutionaries, socialist-populists, Mensheviks and supporters of Plekhanov were easily led to assume that the soviets had outlived their usefulness – now that they had helped to destroy the old order, they should go. Anweiler has rightly noted that the Menshevik resolution on the most urgent problems of the Revolution and the state at the State Conference in August said not a word as to soviets. As Kerensky had always said, it looked as if the soviets would simply die of natural causes. Fifty years later, confronting the reality rather than the dream, he did not even remember that he had been both the godfather and the vice-president of the Petrograd Soviet.

For six months, the Mensheviks and Socialist Revolutionaries who controlled the soviets stubbornly resisted the proposal that the soviets should take power. On the very day they lost their majority in the soviets they resisted it, inevitably, still more stoutly. They put all their hopes in the constituent assembly, the electoral procedure of which they controlled. The right Socialist Revolutionaries associated with the socialist-populists even wondering whether it was necessary to call a second congress of soviets: the main socialist newspaper, *Delo Naroda*, produced a headline on 5 September 'Long Live the Constituent Assembly'.[63]

B   Since February the Bolsheviks had also been rather unclear as to soviet power. In most of the resolutions adopted by soviets and other institutions that the Bolsheviks controlled, there was also a demand for the date of the meeting of the constituent assembly to be fixed. Sometimes the demand was simply added, without comment, to the list; sometimes, as at Yaroslavl and Rostov, there was an explicit statement that 'only soviet power can guarantee that there will be a constituent assembly, which the government is trying to subvert and postpone indefinitely'.

Convocation of the constituent assembly once more became the final aim, with soviet power only a means of achieving it. In other words, as *Rabochy Put* explained on 4 October, 'In the name of the Constituent Assembly, long live the Soviets'.

Lenin argued against this constitutionalism. It did not concern him that Bolshevik revolutionary action might profit anyone other than the Bolshevik soviets, for it was obvious that the Bolsheviks would not win a majority in the general election. From the beginning he fought a hard battle, initially within his own party, over the function of soviets, the constituent assembly, the Bolshevik party itself and the nature of the state in the transitional period; it was also a battle about the tactics and strategy of take-over. It began right at the start of the Revolution.

In February the Bolsheviks had not displayed much enthusiasm for the creation of the Petrograd Soviet but then, in opposition to the Soviet–Duma agreement, they launched the slogan of 'All power to the soviets'. They were sure that the conciliatory policies of the Socialist Revolutionaries and Mensheviks would fail, and they hoped to win a majority in the end. Stalin, in agreement with Kamenev, wrote at this time that

> It is essential to have, for the whole country, an institution for revolutionary struggle by the whole of Russian democracy, and to turn it, when necessary, from an institution for revolutionary struggle into an institution for revolutionary power. . . . It can only be an all-Russian soviet of deputies, a kind of proletarian parliament that can turn itself into a convention. This clearly will not mean the dictatorship of the proletariat, but it will undoubtedly facilitate the preconditions necessary for the creation of such a dictatorship because, even though it will put Mensheviks and Socialist Revolutionaries into power, they will be obliged to carry out their counter-revolutionary programme which must hasten the revelation of their true nature, isolate them and cause the masses to break with them.

Lenin criticized this as soon as he came back to Russia. The Leninist revolution, as far as soviet power was concerned, was twofold. First, although Lenin used the slogan 'All power to the soviets', he ruled out collaboration with 'defensist' socialists and stressed the claims of his own party, however much in the minority, to sole power. Moreover, unlike the other Bolsheviks, Lenin envisaged the various soviets not merely as institutions to represent the people and designed to become a convention, but as an embryo of the future proletarian state. To Lenin, the important thing was not to win a representative majority and take legitimate power so as to inherit the old, moribund, apparatus of state; it was rather to destroy that apparatus and create a new one. Here, as over the vital agrarian question, what he said echoed anarchist statements, and the anarchists wanted a soviet republic. The other Bolsheviks accused Lenin of seeking to occupy the throne of Bakunin; but the reality was that Lenin wanted to launch the proletarian state, to be its leader and guide: the soviets were to become the reins by which the party would manage things. He propagated these ideas, and invited the soviets to take power. Lenin always kept his ear close to the popular ground, and was able to put popular aspirations before his party's programme. He knew, too, that the Mensheviks and Socialist Revolutionaries would go against them, and would be swept out, so that the Bolsheviks could take their place in the different kinds of soviets that would constitute the new power.

Lenin abandoned the slogan of soviet power only in June when, like Milyukov and Kerensky, he supposed that the soviets were as finished as democracy itself. The fact was that, as they stood, the soviets did not interest Lenin.[64] However, in August there was a further switch, for Lenin once more took up the slogan when the soviets revived, under the impact of the Kornilov Putsch. Because of the workers' and soldiers' anger and impatience, Bolsheviks had been able to take over the leadership of local soviets, so that 'soviet power' henceforth would apply to Bolshevized soviets. From then on, the slogan concerning the constituent assembly was meaningless; but an abandonment of it would be misunderstood, at least as long as legitimate authority lay with the Provisional Government. Also there were left-wing Mensheviks like Martov, Internationalists like Lunacharsky and even Bolshevik democrats like Kamenev and Rykov who hoped for a chance to define some new form of state, in which legitimate power could lie both with the soviets and a constituent assembly. Lenin did not want to offend them and alienate their sympathies in advance, so that, up to the taking of power, the Bolsheviks left the constituent assembly on their agenda. To his intimates, however, Lenin confided that when soviet power had been established, to convoke a constituent assembly would be to step back: the assembly was 'a liberal joke'. He added that 'Events may carry us into power, and when we have got it, we will not let it go.'

C   The anarchists, like the maximalist Socialist Revolutionaries, were openly against any parliamentary system, even a representative one, and wanted soviet power, though not in centralized form. They could see that such a power risked becoming merely the fig-leaf of Bolshevik power. To them, the essential was that power should disintegrate, and they appreciated that the Bolsheviks championed the soviets only for tactical reasons, because, at bottom, the Bolsheviks were centralizers. No agreement with them could be lasting, therefore, and four days before the

October Uprising, Volin wrote in *Golos Truda* an article that revealed the nature of the anarchists' and Bolsheviks' relationship. He displayed the points of resemblance and also the divergencies between the two revolutionary visions, foresaw in prophetic fashion the 'capture of power' by the Bolsheviks after an insurrection, but still hoped that the social revolution would succeed, even though he had reservations as to its possible outcome.

The anarchists had made their choice. Certainly they had their reservations: but how could they imagine that, with Kerensky overthrown, they would be able to hinder a centralized party from keeping power, all power, to itself? They had been hard hit by the repression after the July Days, and no political party had made even a gesture of support for the anarchist prisoners. They were discredited by the July failure and by their defeat in the factory committees, and, as against Lenin's party, they did not have that unity of vision that, at least apparently, turned Bolshevism into a real force. In September, for instance, Kropotkin published a new Letter in support of patriotic defence, and advised Kerensky to turn Chernov out of the government because he was 'too far left', whereas Volin and most of the anarchists talked on lines similar to Lenin's. At the Kharkov congress in June, the anarcho-syndicalists and the anarcho-communists fought over all the issues – pursuit of the war, workers' control, participation in the soviets, means of federating committees and the like. At the end of the session they could not even agree on a joint communiqué. After October, the anarchists of the Ukrainian countryside, under Nestor Makhno, were much more suspicious than the urban anarchists were towards 'soviet power'.

The anarchists had an important part in the revolutionary struggle and then, after October, in the armed contest in the towns. More than the Bolsheviks they were the advocates of workers' control and not of delegation of power. Better than others, they understood the implications of Bolshevik doctrine; however, as they had regained some of their popularity just before October, they had delusions as to their capacity to neutralize the Bolsheviks' will to power.[65] On the evening before the revolt, on 25 October 1917, the leading groups of the Bolshevik party had no plan for their own metamorphosis into an apparatus of state. The soviets had overthrown the Provisional Government by the action of the *PVRK* (see chapter 8) and a council of people's commissars, all of them Bolshevik, constituted itself as a government. This was universally thought to be provisional, because the constituent assembly, as sovereign body, would oblige the victors to form a representative socialist régime.

Since February the Bolsheviks had constantly accused the government of postponing the constituent assembly: they could hardly fail to summon it. However, Lenin had said that 'to recognize the constituent assembly as sovereign would be to step back as regards soviet power'. It was clear in advance that the method of election chosen by the Mensheviks and Socialist Revolutionaries would be unfavourable to Bolshevik represent-ation, and Volodarsky said, before the constituent assembly met, that 'we might have to dissolve it'. In the elections of November 1917, the Socialist Revolutionaries alone had over 16,000,000 votes, the Bolsheviks 9,000,000, other, moderate, socialist elements rather fewer, and the Kadets and other bourgeois parties less than 2,000,000. The Bolsheviks had 175 seats out of 707, a very clear minority, even with the alliance of forty left Socialist Revolutionaries.

Sverdlov, at the opening of the session, shoved aside the father of the assembly, an elderly Socialist Revolutionary due to make the customary speech, and he read a declaration of the 'rights of the exploited people', requiring the assembly to vote immediately on this document, which recognized soviet power, a democratic peace, land for the peasants and the like. The assembly refused, and elected Chernov as president, by 244 votes to the 153 for Maria Spiridonova, a left Socialist Revolutionary supported by the Bolsheviks. Chernov and Tseretelli in succession attacked the Bolsheviks' *coup d'état*. The assembly in principle cancelled the October decrees, and, the chance being given, substituted different ones. The assembly guard, presumably pushed by the new rulers, showed its impatience at these 'useless speeches' − 'let this gossiping stop, the guards are sleepy'. The hall was evacuated. There was no further session, and the *TsIK* of the second congress ordered dissolution of an assembly 'that only serves to cover the bourgeois counter-revolution and has the job of overthrowing soviet power'. The Red Guard barred access to the assembly when the deputies turned up again. Their appeals to the public had no answer and they dispersed. Militants of all socialist organizations were scandalized by the dissolution, and so were many Bolsheviks. The citizenry remained quite indifferent.[66] The experiment in parliamentary democracy had lasted for only a few hours (January 1918).

Once the constituent assembly had been dissolved, a constitution had to be drawn up. This was a problem that Lenin and the Bolsheviks had not seriously considered until then. *The State and Revolution* had of course been a set of reflections on the nature of popular power, but it was written at a time when the party was crushed by repression and unlikely to take power at all. In a way, *The State and Revolution* even laid the found-ations and sketched out the essential features of an alternative to Bol-shevik power, and only the pro-Leninist tradition has used it, almost to quieten its conscience, because Lenin, once in power, ignored its con-clusions. The Bolsheviks, far from causing the state to wither away, found endless reasons for justifying its reinforcement.

To achieve this they had to find the best form, and solve the problem as to what the respective functions of soviets and party should be. The Bolsheviks, once they had mastered the soviets, were in all the executive committees. The party on the one hand controlled the soviets, and on the other the governmental institutions created in October. Party members being in the command-posts of the state, what then should be the role of the party itself? Preobrazhensky believed that, now that the Bolsheviks had mastered the soviets, their party had lost its reason for existence – an extreme position. At the other extreme, Sverdlov, who was responsible for party organization, regarded the party as the kernel of the state, with the soviets arranging its relationship with society in general. His viewpoint prevailed, for Lenin preferred a disciplined party, with recruitment and function controlled by him[67] to democratically-recruited soviets that would inevitably be uncertain factors. The constitution ratified by the second congress of soviets in July 1918 laid down that 'the party leads and dominates the entire apparatus of state'; and it is legitimate to wonder, as Feuer does, how far Lenin really was against the bureaucratic system itself, as distinct from the authoritarianism or negligence of its leaders. In relation to real democratic working, the system meant centralism as against autonomy.[68]

The state, women's emancipation and the problem of the family

1 The revolutionary leaders and the feminist movement

The leaders of the revolutionary movement felt that the construction of a new society would have to involve the withering-away of the family, because it had sustained the old order. Marxists adopted much the same attitude towards the family as to religion: they were against it, and regarded the disappearance of its remnants as inevitable; but they did not want to attack it frontally, as did the anarchists, because of the masses' attachment to these social forms and beliefs. They had learnt the lessons of the French Revolution, and saw no reason to be offensive. They had 'more pressing problems' so that, Alexandra Kollontai's apart, there are no Russian Marxist theoretical writings on the family – no application to Russian circumstances of the essays by Engels or Bebel similar to that carried out on the agrarian question or on the question of nationalities. It is also significant that whenever Lenin dealt with the family, he related it to the nationality problem. Implicitly, this meant that under socialism great differences between classes and nationalities would disappear, and with them the habits and beliefs of the 'pre-scientific' era.[69]

This, until October 1917 and even later, was one aspect of Bolshevik policy towards the family. The other involved the pursuit of the main objective, the conquest of the masses and their subjection to the party and to it alone. This latter meant supporting any claim that could weaken the existing order, in particular the aspirations of women. The problem of the family's function and relationship to the social order was posed by this tactic; Lenin himself said that he concerned himself with the problem of women only with the attention needed to strengthen the party through it − 'We cannot win over the masses to political life if we exclude women. . . . We must win the millions of women to work for our cause and our fight.' This attitude had been consistent since 1908, when Klara Zetkin had introduced Lenin to the problem of women's demands. Thereafter the party press always had a women's feature, and in 1917 Lenin initiated the publication of *Rabotnitsa*.[70]

But there was still some ambiguity, and Inessa Armand failed to clear it up in her correspondence with Lenin. The problem of women and the family was never dealt with specifically, and it was even to some extent denied altogether, or at least regarded as of secondary importance. This attitude was not unique to Lenin, and could be found each time the Marxists concerned themselves with the question. The militants' dogma and law subordinated everything to the class struggle, which was the very reason for the existence of social democracy. Recognition of any legitimate identity that was not to do with class − whether of nationality, sex, or generation − could only weaken the party and deny its reason for being.[71]

The ambiguity of attitude towards women and the family had to do with the role that women of the intelligentsia and elsewhere had played in Russian social life and the revolutionary movement in particular, long before the introduction and diffusion of Marxism. The contrast between the status of these women and the status of other women was the result of a cultural gap little known in European society. This gap accounted for the proposals made by Alexandra Kollontai, the initial application of her ideas and the reaction to them in the party and the country both in and after 1917.

A Georgian, Dzabadari, revealed the part played by women of the Russian intelligentsia in the revolutionary movement when, in the 1870s, he led a delegation of Georgian populists to negotiate alliance with the Russians against autocracy, and noted: 'We were quite surprised to find a delegation of some ten young women, all dressed in an elegant simplicity that caught the eye. . . . Seeing them, you might have thought they all belonged to the same family, and so they did, though by comradeship rather than sisterhood.' The sister of one of these young women, Vera Figner, wrote how, in the atmosphere of the revolutionary movement, these girls introduced a new element of equality which she called 'ascetic and religious': 'The idea of equality seemed to us irrefutable, and any reservation or objection inspired solely by egoism or fear. To be up to our task, we had to prepare for all possible blows and . . . renounce our worldly goods, practising true asceticism, otherwise we should be thought "bourgeoise".' When the Georgians and the Russians discussed the statutes of the future revolutionary organization, the girls wanted them to include renunciation of marriage, but the men objected, and the point was not taken up.[72]

This account reveals the tradition of the movement: it had little place for feminine demands, or 'Sandism' as they were called, and when some years later these demands emerged, with the feminist leagues, their bourgeois character disqualified them almost by implication. To have the question aired within the revolutionary movement, Alexandra Kollontai had to base herself on Lassalle, Engels and others, and she was hardly more successful than Inessa Armand or Klara Zetkin had been. In Russia the matter was not so urgent as elsewhere in Europe because the women of the bourgeoisie, whether militant or not, did not need to justify their right to equality, for it was, as reality demonstrated, an agreed principle. Russian literature displayed the feminine intelligentsia's virtues of energy, a contrast with the indolence and *oblomovshchina* of the men – the tradition is too well-attested not to have some element of truth in it. In the 1860s, five out of twenty-three revolutionary groups were led by women, and the Pahlen report showed that in 1877, 158 women were arrested for various criminal acts against the Tsar, which made up a quarter of such arrests.[73]

These revolutionary women were only a sample. In other fields of social life, bourgeois women had a position without rival either in Europe or America, and in this sense the autocracy had done more, since the time of Peter the Great, for the emancipation of women (naturally, women of the bourgeoisie) than western democracies, including the Third Republic. By 1917 12 per cent of the doctors, 26 per cent of the medical personnel and teachers, and in all 11 per cent of the technical staff of the country were women. Integrated in this way, they had an impact on society that was especially marked in the countryside, where the *muzhiks* would trust women doctors more than the men, whom, traditionally, they suspected of being agents of the state entrusted with the task of conscription.[74]

Women's organized activity was a kind of general alternative to the revolutionary vision. To the political parties, especially the Bolsheviks,

the Women's Leagues were suspicious, much as the co-operative movement was, for their organizations competed with the party's and their
activities, particularly in the countryside, stole some of the revolutionaries' limelight. During the February Revolution the women workers
had had a decisive role: 'they lit the fire, and Revolution triumphed.' The
women had acted, not as women, but at the side of their brothers and
husbands, and, latterly, as wives and sisters of the combatants.[75] It was
different with the Women's Leagues that were set up after the abdication
of the Tsar, and frequently demonstrated for equality. There exist many
cinematic records of their disciplined processions, in which women –
well-dressed, and not in blouses and head-scarves – carried placards
reading 'There is no real equality without women's equality'. At the head
of the movement was the *Soyuz ravnopravil zhenshchin* which wanted
especially the vote and equal wages, right to divorce, improvement in the
status of single mothers and so on. The movement was not limited to the
capital, but it had little impact on the countryside. It even had links with
the nationalities.[76]

The Provisional Government, in particular Kerensky himself, was not
against the women's demands, and showed this by giving a secretaryship
of state to a woman, Countess Panin, by allowing women to become civil
servants on the same terms as men, and by offering the presidency of the
inaugural session of the Council of the Republic to Yekaterina Breshko-
Breshkovskaya. These symbolic gestures account for the attachment of
the Women's Leagues to Kerensky, and the urgency with which many
volunteers in all classes joined the women's battalions for the defence of
the régime. In the constituent assembly elections the women of the
leagues intended, following the English suffragette example, to present
lists of their own, the only way, they felt, in which their rights would
be enforced.[77]

The working-class women's movements were less numerous, less old
and less well-organized; they were part of the working-class movement
and remained in the Lassalle tradition, more feminine than feminist. In
1917 a union of seamstresses was set up, the first such, with 300 members,
and soon there were others, especially in the tobacco trade where the
workers were mainly women. Their aim was to extend party activity to
places where women had a decisive part to play, and to uphold their
claims. In these working-class circles the women's aspirations were not
specifically feminist, and were directed towards wages, labour conditions
and hygiene. The demand for equal wages did not often figure, though it
did among the washerwomen.[78] Their strike was an important point.
They had demanded a rise in wages, and the employers, to stop them,
closed forty-five laundries. In the meantime, the laundrywomen's action

changed its nature, for they now substituted the general claims of the working class, for an eight-hour day, trade-union control of hiring and dismissal, two weeks' paid holiday a year and the like, for the first demand, equality of wages with the men. This last they were to only demand later on.[79] A cause of their provisional abandonment of this, their principal claim, was that the Bolsheviks had become involved, and they wanted to dissociate the social struggle of women from the feminist movement. The great breach occurred at a meeting of the League for the Rights of Women, in April. Inessa Armand, who headed the Bolshevik delegation, first announced that 'the time has now passed when women's only job was to take an inventory of household goods' and then said that 'working-class women have no problems in common with middle-class ones, only with their own brothers and husbands'. She refused to examine the league's programme and left the hall, followed by the Bolshevik delegation.[80]

The Bolsheviks' hostility stemmed from the fact that the women in the leagues, were not fighting under Bolshevik control; and there was an ill-concealed attitude, except among the women in the Bolshevik leadership, of indifference or even latent hostility to feminist claims as such. In *Rabotnitsa* and *Zhizn Rabotnits*, the party newspapers, not a word was said of demands that could not be called class issues; there was little concerning marriage or free union, and apparently even Lunacharsky, though counting as a defender of women's rights, did not believe it was opportune to assert them, except perhaps for the intelligentsia. In October Lenin did, however, appoint Alexandra Kollontai as people's commissar for social security, and her ideas on the sexual emancipation of women were well known. The consequences were immediate.[81]

2 October and the emancipation of women

Alexandra Kollontai made radical changes in the legal status of women, and legalized most of the measures that the league had wanted. The Bolsheviks, for all their circumspection concerning feminism, did more for women's real rights than people who had been ostensibly more sympathetic to feminism had done. By the end of 1917 the Bolsheviks had recognized working women's rights, (1) to the eight-hour day, (2) to discuss wage-levels, (3) to keep a job during pregnancy, labour and the infant's first months, (4) to divorce, (5) to improvements in the status of single mothers and illegitimate children, (6) to have their children looked after during working hours, and (7) to political rights equal to men's. The proclaimed ideal was monogamous, the working-class family, and not the 'free unions of free individuals' that Kollontai had imagined.[82]

These measures were essentially part and parcel of the defence of women's rights. Other measures, taken later, stemmed both from Marxist ideas as to the inevitability of the disintegration of the family, and from the emancipatory tradition of feminism. By 20 December 1917 a decree abolished religious marriage and deprived the church of its right to register marriages, which became a private matter to be registered only with the civil authorities. Divorce became much the same, and was automatically granted if both parties requested it; if only one party requested it, it could be granted after very simple legal formalities. Soon registration was not needed for a union to be recognized, unless there were a need for such recognition, as for instance if the couple had a child and a question of maintenance arose.[83]

After religious marriage, the common-property system of marriage was also abolished, 'so that marriage shall no longer be dictated by financial interest'; a further blow to 'bourgeois' ideas of the family was the prohibition of adoption, to avoid the harsh treatment by parents of any adopted child.[84] Emancipation of women and destruction of the family soon met another objective, the more rational employment of labour. The régime declared that 'women, if they are chained to the home, cannot be the equals of men' and regarded this as an unpardonable squandering of productive labour and of the strength of the new state. In 1920, for instance, calculations were made in Moscow of the number of hours of labour lost through the simple fact that women remained housewives. The liberation of women became a condition for economic growth: by increasing the number of crèches and canteens still further, women might work, become men's equals and so, the leadership being convinced that superstructure was determined by infrastructure, would have the same ideas as their husbands and become good Communists. 'The tragedy of many households comes about because the man is Communist and the woman is non-party,' thought Trotsky.[85]

Increasing numbers of crèches and canteens, a dominant party theme in the early years, had to do with a new concept of the function of the family and of relations between parents and children. 'We must save the children from the evil influence of the family,' said Z. I. Lilina, the wife of Zinoviev, 'and we must nationalize them, teaching them the ABC of Communism for them to become true Communists. We must force mothers to give up their children to us, the state.' The memory and image of the traditional family were still terrifyingly present: hence, in some degree, the convictions that most of the leaders shared. The idea was not yet to control the family, but to liberate it, and translate it, in Engels's phrase 'from the realm of necessity to that of liberty'. However, there was a very thin line between Krupskaya, who wanted 'the pioneer detachment to be henceforth what the family has been for the young', and A. B. Zalkin, who thought that 'Children should respect their parents only if they have Communist opinions. Respect and obedience are not due to a reactionary father.' The time was not far off when a boy would denounce his father as a bad Communist. The boy was killed by his father's friends, and became an official martyr of the régime.[86]

In 1920 Lenin told Kollontai, the theorist of 'free love', that he disagreed with her, disapproving of the 'glass of water' allegory and saying that he could not dissociate the sexual act from 'true', i.e. lasting love. But many important measures were taken towards the liberalization of sexual relations, such as legislation on abortion. The legislation did not mean that the authorities were in favour of it: they praised birth control, and did much to encourage it, but they wanted to substitute legal abortion in specialized clinics for back-streets operations that would damage a woman's health and self-respect. This transitional policy was all the easier to put into practice because a large part of the medical personnel were made up of women. Young women, who had greater confidence in the women doctors than in their male colleagues, attended the clinics in large numbers, and films of the 1920s, particularly Ermler's, show better than statistics can how simple the procedure was, and how good-humoured the atmosphere was in this unique liberation. It opened the way for a new concept of human relations. Already the urban utopias, such as those of the architect L. M. Samsonovich, foresaw a new type of city, with communal nurseries for the children, restaurants, dwellings for couples, and cultural areas.[87]

3 1917: resistance and reaction to it

Resistance surfaced early in the 1920s, and it came up from the depths. Leninist legislation had hardly affected the large cities, and even in 1924, 71 per cent of marriages in Moscow were religious.[88] In the countryside, as *The Good Women of Ryazan* shows, nothing had changed for centuries: the reforms of Peter the Great had not even reached it. The young girl in Olga Preobrazhenskaya's film is the subject of negotiation between her father and intermediaries, and she does not know who her future husband will be. In 1915, when her husband goes off to war, she is raped by her father-in-law; the village condemns her for rebelling and she kills herself. This case makes some of the young women sensitive to new ideas; one of them becomes a teacher, but, as she has a common-law union, opinion is against her, and from then on she devotes her time to the fight for women's emancipation.[89]

Between the status of women in the province of Ryazan and that of the young Kirghiz girl in Konchalovsky's *First Teacher* there is hardly a difference – certainly not the practice of *kalym*. To the women, and the peasant in particular, the Orient began at Moscow.[90] A Russian proverb ran, 'Master in his own house like a Khan in the Crimea', and there were others that defined equally well the status and condition of the Russian peasant woman early in this century: 'Take for wife her who pulls the plough, not her who decorates the garden'; 'Better a poor wife than a rich one who won't let you be master in your own house.'[91] The peasant-workers who flooded to the towns in the wave of industrialization that preceded and accompanied the war hardly changed in outlook. The men behaved in the towns as they had done in the countryside. Workers petitioned for soldiers, and vice versa, but no one pleaded the women's cause in the Revolution of 1917 except the women themselves. They were present in the fighting, but they were still not elected to leading offices. I can count only 2, Krupskaya and Fedorova, out of 34 Bolshevik deputies in the district councils, and the example is not unique – there were 22 women out of 585 delegates at the first Petrograd conference of factory committees, 10 out of 484 at the workers' soviet of the Nikolayevsky district, and 259 out of 4,743 delegates of the assemblies of the Moscow soviets.[92]

It was these assemblies that gave a structure, after October, to the new régime; such delegates were soon to swamp the revolution intelligentsia. There were four different movements, tending away from the emancipation of women: (1) popular elements, more conservative in their view of family morality, were grafted into the Bolshevik body, the officers of which were emancipated, and gradually, the new element took over; (2) within this popular element, the ratio of men to women remained after October what it had been before: during the elections to the Russian soviets in 1923, 16,000,000 men voted and only 3,000,000 women, and out of 80,000 rural soviets constituted at this time, women formed only between 3 and 5 per cent of the elected delegates;[93] (3) in the women's own assemblies and delegations, rural elements, which were more traditionalist, gradually took over from urban ones (and *a fortiori* the intelligentsia) as Table 17 shows, and thus, in three years the number of

Table 17   *Participation in assemblies of women workers*

	Total	Working-class women	Peasant women
1923	208,704	51,244	121,511
1926	620,000	96,610	385,890

women elected who lived in towns declined from half of the number of the country-women to one quarter;[94] (4) in the all-soviet (mixed) assemblies, rural, popular elements, already in the majority, discovered an objective ally in delegates of the nationalities, who were also becoming increasingly numerous. By 1927 the Communist party of the USSR contained 12 per cent women, but among the Tatar delegates, women were 4.7 per cent, among the Bashkir ones 2.5 per cent, and among the Tadzhiks 0.7 per cent.[95]

Progress in women's representation was regular enough after 1922; but, as regards the ratio of forces for and against emancipation, the liberals were soon reduced in strength as the party increased in size and the Old Bolsheviks became a small minority. Even most women were now hostile to the measures suggested by Kollontai: at their stage of cultural development, with families broken up or destroyed by war and civil war, they looked to marriage for guarantees and not liberty. They would not take advantage of the law on non-registration of marriages, and did not want a fund to help single mothers or abandoned wives, which would simply salve the consciences of men escaping from their responsibilities. They wanted fathers to have to pay maintenance; during the great debate on marriage in 1925, Kollontai was defeated, and Ryazanov became the champion of compulsory registration of marriage. The great turning-point had been reached.[96]

Even in 1918, the régime had sensed resistance.[97] It had had to abandon the first draft law abolishing inheritance, to authorize the bequeathing of sums of less than 10,000 roubles, to make exceptions in favour of *muzhik* farms, and then to forget about the limit of 10,000. It had, similarly, to forget its prohibition of adoption during the great famine of 1921. At all stages it is clear that, as regards the problems of women and the family, the Old Bolshevik leaders were on the retreat; and in sexual matters, the retreat was even quite voluntary. Within the party there was a great gap between the women of the Russian intelligentsia who inspired the liberationist movement, and the men who, for the greater part, belonged to marginal areas and were more open to the influence of Jewish or Christian morality.[98]

The wave of reaction reached its peak and overflowed in 1926, the laws of 1936 being even more reactionary by contrast with those preceding. In 1968, fifty years after Lenin's decree on freedom of divorce, the divorce rate in the USSR was exactly the same as that in 1919. The darkest areas corresponded to cities with citizens drawn from the old stock, Leningrad and Odessa; the lowest rate was in the countryside and the highest in the intelligentsia and the bureaucracy.[99]

The blockage could reverse or slow down the irreversible evolution that occurred in other fields of women's emancipation, but could not halt it for ever. The Communist party had 7.8 per cent women in 1922, 12 per cent in 1927 and 20.9 per cent in 1967. The number of responsible women officers also rose regularly, except at the very top, and the social origin of these women also became diversified after the Revolution; the general tendency towards equal status was even noticeable among the nationalities.[100]

CHAPTER 8

The October Rising

1 Violence and Revolution

'Proletarian Revolution is not terror. The Revolution is against institutions, not human beings, and it abhors killing.' This Spartakist declaration would have been endorsed by the Russian revolutionaries[1] but whether the workers and soldiers in whose name these revolutionaries spoke would also have endorsed it is another matter. In 1917, things went differently: terror began in the countryside and in the army, where the militants were not so prominent, whereas in the towns and factories, where they led the Revolution, they intervened so that, before October, physical violence was rare.[2]

The intelligentsia took a moderating and mediating role from the start, for it had absorbed the humanist principles of the socialist tradition, and it applied them naturally. The intention was to replace the old leaders, not to destroy them physically; and besides, for the sake of their own rule, the new leaders had to show their moral superiority to the old ones; they had to be generous and incorruptible. Kerensky set the example in February when he protected the lives of his own jailers; and Trotsky saved his rival, Chernov, from the people's rage, while Zinoviev told a group of soldiers ready to butcher everyone to go back to their barracks. The Russians trusted these 'just men' who, like themselves, had been victims of a detested régime, and they saw the militants' message as one of hope. They had curbed their own violent leanings.

However, six months of frustration, the Putsch and its failure, had a traumatic effect, for the accumulated resentments and pent-up energies were released, and the republic of orators came to an end. That was when the violence began. In August 1917, at the Moscow conference, the industrialist Bublikov had given his hand to the socialist Tseretelli; in September, after the arrest of Kornilov, Kerensky embraced Kamenev, who returned the affection. It was the last effusion of the February Revolution. In 1922 Sukhanov asked Trotsky, 'Do you remember the days when you promised us that the Bolsheviks would respect democratic liberties?' 'Yes', said Trotsky. 'That was in the old days.'[3]

After the Kornilov Putsch the time had passed for gestures of love and for fine speeches. The officers of the Revolution could no longer contain their troops, and from factory and army came a cry for vengeance, the arrest, trial and expulsion from Russia of the bourgeoisie, with compulsory labour for those who remained, and the arming of the working class. In the towns and the countryside there were apparently 'irrational' activities, replacing political work. At Tsarskoye Selo the populace 'suddenly' began pillaging the Tsar's palace, six months after his abdication and long after he had gone to Tobolsk – but only just after the Kornilov affair. At Gatchina, the military committee arrested Grand Duke Michael – the newspapers absurdly saying that it all had 'nothing to do with the Putsch' – while at Helsinki and Kronstadt there were massacres of officers and in the countryside and the army September and October were marked with bloodshed and a new wave of pogroms.[4] The new factor was that soldiers, acting outside the framework of the army, took a massive part in the violence. In the countryside, for instance, seventy-five risings in which soldiers took part were counted in the rear areas of the south-western front;[5] in Podolia peasants even disguised themselves as soldiers in order to go looting. In Oryol, Yelizavetgrad, Irkutsk, Samara and Ufa, soldiers took part in isolated actions against merchants and magistrates were molested; and now, the violence also affected people who, in the heady days of February, had been spared – former policemen, civil servants, common-law criminals.[6] The Bolsheviks were not much involved.[7]

Similarly among the working class it was not the Bolsheviks but the grass-roots who wanted, for instance, the closing-down of bourgeois newspapers (demanded collectively by over twenty factories early in September) or compulsory labour for the bourgeoisie, or expulsion of it from Russia. The workers used Bolshevik watchwords and phrases where they wanted to, including the call for measures against bourgeois leaders, but not those relating to planning and nationalization (see Table 18).

Before September the masses' vanguard was more Bolshevik than the Bolsheviks, but after September the masses were more Bolshevik than their own vanguard. Few of the Bolshevik leaders perceived this, probably because they were too busy in the leading institutions – Kamenev in the *TsIK*, Zinoviev in the trade unions, and even Trotsky, whose attitude in the congress of the armies of the northern front was more radical than in the Petrograd Soviet. It was different among those Bolsheviks who

Table 18   *Factory workers and the Bolshevik party: convergences and differences (September–October 1917)*

Claims and slogans in common	Purely Bolshevik	Purely working-class
No agreement with the bourgeoisie, all power to the soviets.		
Workers' control of production.	Nationalization of the main branches of industry.	Control under the trade unions and factory committees; unity of the firm.
Merciless taxation of large capital and landowners; confiscation of war profits.		Law against lock-outs; death-penalty for those responsible.
Dissolution of the Duma and the State Council.		Suppression of bourgeois press.
Arming of the workers.		Disarmament and arrest of counter-revolutionaries.
End repression of the workers and the Bolsheviks.		
Supply industrial goods at fixed prices to peasants.		
Eight-hour day and social insurance.		
Democratic peace.	Publication of the Secret Treaties.	Obligatory labour for bourgeoisie.
Abolish the death penalty.		Expulsion of British and French agents from Russia.
	Local election of commissioners.	
	Equal pensions for officers and soldiers.	Improvement of conditions and wages.
	Right of self-determination for nationalities, particularly Ukraine and Finland.	
	Constituent assembly and democratic republic.	If necessary, we'll act on our own.

were active at the base, and especially among those who had converted to Bolshevism and ruled their local soviets; to survive, they had to be very radical.

Taking power by violence, even though it might have been seized peacefully, was probably Lenin's notion of exorcizing the violent streak when he tried to convince his colleagues to prepare for an armed rising, in the face of Kamenev's and Trotsky's arguments that the régime would in any event disintegrate. This notion reflected, in all probability, the very basis of Lenin's thought.[8] Until then, as Geyer has said, 'the concept of insurrection had been very vague, with memories persisting of the July disorders and the repression'; Lenin suggested a different kind of insurrection – not one linked with a mass demonstration, but one associated with military art.[9] The idea of insurrection as an art came from Marx, and Lenin had given it a political translation when he conceived the Bolshevik party as a centralized military force. Since then, even Clausewitz had been read in this sense.

No doubt Lenin had other reasons, which emerged only later; perhaps he felt that the change of power would be misunderstood, and be regarded as illegitimate if, at least in appearance, it did not come through violence. He lived at the centre of the conflict, but at the same time, being in hiding after July, he could also see it from a distance, and he could analyse it with corresponding clarity. The violence he had in mind was purely tactical and institutional, although it was his movement which in the event institutionalized terror. Six months after the Tsar's fall, i.e. before October, the traditional institutions no longer functioned, and others had taken their places. Economic life was paralysed, and social relationships had been overturned. The country was in the throes of a complete

---

This table brings out several points:
1 There is an overall convergence.
2 There is divergence over problems of workers' control and factory management as analysed in chapter 6.
3 There is a difference in interpretation of the nature of the revolutionary upheaval: measures against persons or against 'bourgeois' liberties are demanded by the masses rather than the Bolshevik party.

Compared with the working-class aspirations, on the fall of Tsarism this table shows how far the working class had become radicalized between February and October. In February it had wanted only improvement in living conditions, whereas in October it wanted complete change in them, and wage-demands became secondary. There is also a striking difference if the soldiers' slogans on the eve of the October rising are compared, for the soldiers' adoption of the Bolshevik programme is obvious, the workers' adoption not so. Bolshevization of the army was at its height, whereas conflict between the working class and the party was already on the horizon.

transformation. It was a picture of great complexity, which no simple map of zones of resistance and zones of movement could convey, for some changes happened more rapidly and others more deeply. There were villages where the peasantry confined their action to non-payment of rent, and otherwise passively waited for reform from above; but elsewhere, in their impatience, they themselves carried out the rural revolution. They applied the principle of 'to each according to his needs' and parcelled out the land according to the number of mouths that had to be fed. None the less, these same peasants who set up a new method of production based on ethical principles went on massacring Jews, lording it over their own families and beating up townsmen, whether gentlemen or proletarian, at the first opportunity; while, in other areas, they were capable of giving food to the hungry 'without distinction of race or religion', and without any committee resolution or the like to require it. The countryside's various areas each produced their own pattern; relationships with government or soviets might alter the rural movement's pace, but they did not change its nature.

The impact and significance of October could not, therefore, be the same everywhere: in some areas the Decree on Land came as an act of liberation, but in others, October meant merely a change of government. In the province of Tambov, where peasant rioting was as frequent after October as before it, October was only an episode in this long history of peasant unrest, and did not affect loyalties towards the régime – Tsar before 1917, Bolsheviks thereafter. Here, as elsewhere, the great caesura was not the Decree on Land, but collectivization, ten years later.

This was still more the case with the minority peoples who were not wholly integrated into the empire. The movements that they threw up in 1917 did not necessarily have the same pattern as occurred elsewhere in the country. National and social conflicts intermingled in a confused way: in the Moslem-Russian regions, even emancipation of women predominated for a time. In Kiev, October was greeted as an act of liberation from foreign occupation as soon as the Decree on Nationalities was appreciated; but the October rising could quite easily be carefully ignored, and regarded as a change of government in a foreign country; while, for other non-Russian social groups that participated in October, such as the Lettish riflemen, October was regarded as the start of an era of Soviet Republics. All of them had an eye on what happened in Petrograd, but the various social groups were not necessarily or equally involved in the test of strength between the Provisional Government and the Bolshevized Soviet.

In the army, the soldiers wanted an end to the war. It had been clear, since the failure of the fraternization movement, that peace could only be determined by the government, not the soldiers; therefore it had to be forced to make peace, or changed. This brought the soldiers directly into politics in April, July and October. They were always in the vanguard − a fact that Marxists could not take in, because they always saw the soldiers simply as uniformed peasants, to them the most reactionary group in the Revolution. But the fact was that, since February, the soldiers − in particular as a result of Bolshevik teachings − had learned how to distinguish between the army's repressive and patriotic functions. They also appreciated the relationship these functions had, for, behind the colonel's uniform lurked the old landowner whom they detested, the oppressor they feared. Thereafter, every single order from the military commanders was scrutinized and questioned. In October, the soldiers, as soldiers, were in the forefront of the fight for peace, and as peasants they broke the apparatus of repression that might have stopped popular power.

The workers' struggle was just as relentless. However, in October, the final battle was not that which Marxist tradition had imagined. The workers' actions had been offensive in the spring, but became defensive because of the patriotic resistance that answered strikes with lock-outs and a conscious, organized sabotage of production. This, combined with the disruption and decline of the economy brought about by war, threw many thousands of workers onto the streets, while thousands of others feared the sack. In these conditions, efforts at factory occupation and self-management were a failure, even threatening the unity of the proletariat, for they added to the divisions of workers already pulled between Menshevik, Bolshevik and anarchist propaganda. They also did not know which form of organization to prefer − soviet of deputies, factory committee, or trade union. The successive radicalization and Bolshevization of each of these institutions led to the adoption of a synthetic, and also an ill-defined, platform − workers' control of production, implying the take-over of the economy by workers' organizations and hence also a political revolution for the soviets to take power. The great change since the start of the Revolution was the politicization of strikes: workers and soldiers alike felt that the overthrow of the Provisional Government was a vital necessity.[10]

There was a third force, the direct outcome of the Revolution, that also acted in favour of a test of strength with the men of February − armed force and the new bureaucracy, which constituted the staff and leading personnel of the embryonic proletarian state. Its members were essentially popular in origin; they had changed status with the Revolution, and therefore formed a kind of new social group, made up of leading militants, salaried, and committed to victory in order to survive. The new social group was grafted on to the traditional body of militants, in the main the

Bolshevik group, with which the new men could see they had much in common, as the Bolsheviks identified themselves with the workers, largely through Lenin's influence, for since April he had fought a hard battle with his colleagues to radicalize the party line.

The October Rising was the outcome of this coincidence of factors – on the one hand, social pressures towards disequilibrium, and on the other the chronic incapacity of the Provisional Government to head off a rising, with Lenin's awareness of this incapacity, and his conviction that a rising was opportune, necessary and beneficial to his own party. His success in convincing the party leaders is one of the best-known episodes in the insurrection, but it is also one of the most falsified in historical tradition. Until publication of the *PVRK* documents, little was known of the conflicts, tactical rather than strategic, that set Lenin and other activists against various members of the *PVRK*. It was particularly difficult to analyse the various factors that produced the October victory and also predetermined the terror dictatorship – the introduction of violence, Lenin's coup and the split within the Bolshevik party.

2 The October Rising

'Before Kornilov, anything could have happened, but after him there was nothing that could have been done'[11] – Kerensky's verdict, fifty years later. It was redolent of a quite imaginary political world, in which, in Kerensky's mind, the law was still the law, and in the army an order was still an order. The fact was that the Putsch revealed rather than caused the paralysis of the régime. It was illusory to claim that the Putsch deprived the government of army support in the case of a Bolshevik uprising, for the army would intervene in politics only to overthrow the government and create a different régime, whether inspired by high command or by soviets of soldiers. The Putsch and its failure on the one side and the October Rising on the other indicated as much.

The Kerensky government, the last variant of the dual-power system, could only survive if it revived a world in which the army could play its twofold role of patriotism and repression, and politics could again be a matter for the 'republic of parties'. After the Putsch, as the Bolsheviks made progress, the 'political nation' was less and less identified with the people as a whole; however, since representation hardly changed between February and the second congress of soviets, Kerensky still stood at the centre in the role of mediator. As head of the government and victor over Kornilov, he was able to impose the rules of the political game, and in doing so he had the support of the men of February, the populists,

Socialist Revolutionaries and Mensheviks who, even if personally not very favourable to him, were still solid with the régime they had established together.[12] They were the more hostile to soviet power, as they now began to lose control of it; and Kadet participation in government was their eternal subject of debate.[13] In September and October they tried a new pseudo-representative experiment together. Kerensky, as head of the government, tried to repeat his exploits of the spring, visiting the army to restore discipline; his political allies had the idea that, to achieve this and forestall a Bolshevik rising, some change of policy could be made. By the time they had debated over this, and split over the possibility, shattering the already worm-eaten base of the dual-power system, the republic of orators had itself collapsed.

A   Compared to the social upheavals, the political stage, with its gestures and speech-making, seems in retrospect a kind of shadow-play where the same actors trotted yet again through their roles, before an audience less and less attentive, and increasingly occupied elsewhere. However, the first act had some novelty. In the precincts of the Petrograd Soviet, the very heart of the Revolution, on 31 August 1917 – the height of popular mobilization against Kornilov – a Bolshevik resolution, presented by Kamenev, won the majority, the first time this had happened since February.[14] Like most socialists he reckoned that the resignation of the Kadet ministers in the middle of the crisis showed that they were in collusion with the Putschists, and the resolution once more condemned in principle any coalition government, sanctioned the changes that the Bolsheviks had made in their agrarian policy, and established its position regarding workers' control. Without explicitly mentioning soviet power, it called for a government in which the bourgeoisie did not figure.[15]

Tseretelli once again repeated the litany of advocates of coalition:

> total transfer of power to the working classes does not suit the needs of the hour and is not based on reality. The reforms demanded by the Bolsheviks are at the present time unrealistic: either they will deceive the masses, or they will provoke anarchy. Transfer of power to revolutionary democracy without the support of other social groups will be the defeat of democracy; a soviet take-over of power is ardently awaited by the enemies of the Revolution.[16]

B   The response was a *prikaz* to the army and navy which, blaming the Putsch for the disorganization of these armed forces, 'forbids all political struggle within the army, to enable it to concentrate on the defence of the country'. Kerensky ordered arrests of officers to stop, and also ordered special units to be set up, under the pretext of combating counter-revolution. The soldiers' organizations were told not to block the communications network. These moves were really aimed against the soldiers, not the officers, and affected the defenders of the February régime rather than the men who wanted to overthrow it. Besides, far from carrying out the expected punishments, he allowed ordinary military justice to go ahead, and limited himself to asking the soviet to delegate two of its members to sit on the extraordinary commission set up to investigate the affair. Even though some of the Cossacks stated that they had been deceived, had not really taken part in the plot, and, like the soldiers, wanted the guilty to be punished, Kerensky himself would accuse, but would not strike at the guilty men. It was a triumph for the Bolsheviks, who could claim that it was all 'proof that there was collusion between Kerensky and Kornilov'.[17]

C   The proclamation of the Republic on 1 September 1917 by Kerensky was saluted by the *TsIK*, and appeared to be a declaration of war on the right; but it was an empty gesture, at most designed to mark a change.[18] Kerensky himself saw it otherwise, and felt, as a lawyer, that since he had broken the February agreement on 'non-determination of the future form of state before the decision of the constituent assembly', he had effectively crossed the Rubicon. The decision signalled the end of some monarchical institutions, such as the Council of State and the Duma; at the political level, it also marked a final breach between the February régime and the right, the 'Kadet Bolsheviks' of Milyukov – a divorce which, in its way, was equivalent to the breach on the left between the social democrats and Lenin's men.

D   The 'leftward shift' of Kerensky was simply a return to the situation before February when, belonging neither to existing institutions nor to the illegal opposition, the radical bourgeois representatives and the moderate socialist petty-bourgeois were squeezed between forces much stronger than themselves. In September they had broken their bridges with representatives of these crushingly strong opposing forces, the Bolsheviks on the left, and the monarchists or right-wing Kadets on the right, so that the 'men of February' – the Kadet left, Mensheviks, Socialist Revolutionaries, etc. – could have an opportunity to make themselves heard only in institutions where they were over-represented, so as to perpetuate the illusion that their mediation was legitimate and necessary. Such were the assemblies created after the Kornilov Putsch, on the initiative of the *TsIK* and the government (democratic conference, council of the republic). Kerensky, taking part in these debates, kept a promise he had made to the socialist parties when they offered him help against Kornilov – to let 'organized democracy' define the bases of the new power and its policies, or, in effect, let them have the power. He also, implicitly, accepted that he was responsible to a 'pre-parliament'.[19]

The democratic conference, convoked and organized by the executive council of the soviets, reflected, in its composition, the great variety of institutions that the Revolution had thrown up rather than their numerical strength or real power. Over thirty types of organization were represented, from the league of clergy and laymen to the soviets, although the nationalities, for one, had only 43 places out of 1,250. The Socialist Revolutionary and Menshevik organizations, which had lost influence more outside the soviets than inside them, and still had a majority on the administrative council, flouted democracy and distributed seats as suited them. Workers' and soldiers' soviets were allotted 230 places, as were the peasant soviets, whereas the municipal councils took 300, the *zemstva* 200 and the co-operative movement 161. Despite this 'electoral geometry', the voting, when it came, was full of surprises.[20]

The principle of bourgeois participation in government was approved, but only after confused, debated and contradictory voting and amendments.[21] Kerensky said, 'I can't understand it', and he was not alone. The debates that followed were ridiculed by the right and the Bolsheviks: delegates were unable to lay down a clear political line, and could not even make themselves heard above the banging of desk-lids and a tumult of yelling and whistling that made the proceedings an absurdity.[22] The democratic conference's second task was to establish the 'pre-parliament's' nature, the body to which the government was to be responsible. Kerensky and Tseretelli wanted the government to decide the composition and conditions of assembly of this 'pre-parliament', rather than the conference, though at least the conference could set some conditions. It decided, by 744 votes to 383, that the bourgeois could be represented. Kerensky set the number of bourgeois representatives at 250, that of 'democratic' ones at 402, chosen proportionately among the 1,300 members of the conference, with 38 seats for the soviets, 24 for the co-operatives and so on.[23]

The Bolsheviks, when this was given out, left the meeting. Bukharin announced that 'The *TsIK*, in convening this conference, has shown how little it really understands the problems of today.' The conciliators were quite content, including even Chernov although he was on their left wing: 'We have accepted a programme [that of 14 August] and also, in principle, we have made the government responsible in a way it has refused to accept since February; we have also got, in principle, an agency for democratic control [in the 'pre-parliament'] and those who reject such principles will have democracy against them.'[24] Chernov had always been a dreamer, and could not see that the programme was empty, for there was no real power behind it, while the agency of control, in view of the way it was to be recruited, would have few lessons to give in democracy. Still, the politicians thought that they were once more in charge of affairs.

Kerensky opened the session of the 'pre-parliament', or council of the republic on 7 October. It was chaired by Yekaterina Breshko-Breshkov-skaya – a woman, 'a unique spectacle'. Kerensky, who was heartily applauded, defined for the first institutions of the Republic the tasks of the new government: defence of the country, restoration of its military strength, and the establishment, in agreement with the Allies, of con-ditions for a lasting peace. Then Trotsky spoke, in the name of the Bolshevik group:

'The official aim of the democratic conference assembled by the soviets' executive committee was to replace an irresponsible per-sonal régime that had led to the Kornilov affair by a responsible government, able to end the war and guarantee that the constituent assembly would meet. But, behind the conference and in the wings, Kerensky, the Socialist Revolutionaries and the Mensheviks have arrived at a result that is the complete contrary of what they were supposed to achieve: they have set up a power in which clandestine Kornilovites play the leading part. The totally irresponsible character of this government has even been openly announced. The council of the republic is a deliberative body, a replica of the Bulygin Duma; the number of bourgeois representatives in it bears no relation to what is right, as the elections have shown. Even so, the Kadets who wanted a government dependent on the Duma now refuse, eight months after the Revolution, to have a new cabinet dependent on this council. . . . In industry, agriculture, food supply, the policy of the government and the propertied classes intensifies the disruption caused by war. The bourgeoisie, provok-ing peasant uprisings [tumult, protests, cries of 'rubbish'], civil war, are now trying to halt it – openly fomenting famine, so as to strangle the Revolution and the constituent assembly. The foreign policy of the government and the bourgeoisie is quite as criminal. After forty months of war, capitalism faces a deadly threat: the idea of sur-rendering the capital causes not the slightest indignation among the bourgeoisie [noise, protests] – on the contrary, it is accepted as an essential part of a policy to facilitate the counter-revolution. To meet the threat, there is a plan to shift the government to Moscow. Instead of seeing that the salvation of the country requires peace, instead of suggesting an immediate peace to all of the war-torn peoples, over the heads of the imperialist governments and the diplomatic corps, so as to make it impossible for the war to go on, the Provisional Government accepts the orders of Kadet counter-revolutionaries and allied imperialists to prolong this devastating war needlessly. It is ready to give up Petrograd and destroy the Revolution while Bolshevik sailors and soldiers die at the side of other sailors and soldiers as the price of their errors and crimes [strong protests from centre and right]. The supreme command, so-called, attacks the Bolshevik newspaper presses . . . and so we, the Bolshevik section of social democracy, declare we have nothing in common with a government that betrays the people [noise from centre and right: 'scum'], with the complicity of the council of the Counter-Revolution [noise, shouting]; and in leaving it, we call on workers, peasants and soldiers to watch out and show their courage.'

This philippic over, to general stupefaction, all the Bolsheviks rose and left – the first act of the October Insurrection.[25]

The Bolsheviks' spectacular walk-out was indeed seen as the prelude to a new uprising; and, given the government's weakness and the army authorities' inability to act with force, the government wondered what might be done about it. In the next two weeks, once the new Kerensky government had been set up,[26] the only question under discussion was what the Bolsheviks would do, in view of the second congress of soviets, which was forthcoming, and where, with a certain majority, they would announce that all power should go to the soviets. Every day, the extreme left-wing press discussed the possibility of a Bolshevik coup. Kerensky and Tereshchenko reported to the British ambassador, Buchanan, what they had already told the other ministers, that strong disciplinary measures would be taken and that any Bolshevik uprising would be immediately put down. Tereshchenko added, 'We must go into battle, and even start one, for the only hope of saving the country is a counter-revolution, though not necessarily a monarchist one.'[27]

On 17 October, in the council of ministers, Kishkin declared that the government could deal with disorders, but not with an insurrection. At the time there had as yet been no measures against the Bolsheviks, and no one knew who was responsible for them – General Polkovnikov, commanding the garrison, or the minister of the interior, or Kerensky himself. 'We cannot just sit about like dummies,' said Tretyakov. That day, Kerensky came back from a tour of the armies, and he wanted to go back, but was dissuaded by Konovalov. The situation in Petrograd was too serious, he said. Nikitin and Verkhovsky, however, were quite confident, and Kerensky even said he wanted the Bolsheviks to rise 'so that we can deal with them'. But when the minister of justice renewed the order to arrest Lenin, Polkovnikov answered that 'I have no way of carrying this out'. Whether this was illogicality on the part of the government, or over-confidence, it released other Bolsheviks. Dybenko told Raskol'nikov, leaving prison, 'They are crazy to let us go.'[28]

The imminence of a rising, which was shown in the radicalization of attitudes, led part of the 'conciliatory' majority to think up a complete turn-about in the policies hitherto advocated.[29] Since pursuit of the war had not had the intended effect of putting a brake on social and political disintegration, peace would be tried instead. Announcement of this decision would, it was expected, paralyse the Bolsheviks and 'cut the ground from under their feet' to assure the future of democracy. Moreover the army, once freed, by demobilization, of its most volatile elements, and once it had been purged, would again be able to carry out its repressive function in the interior. There would not be a separate peace, only a proposal of peace to all the warring states which would at least clearly document that the government was effectively putting pressure on the Allies: as Stankevich wrote to Kerensky, 'Given the general desire for peace, it would be right for the government to present things in such a way that the responsibility for refusing peace should lie with the enemy, not with Russia and the Allies; I implore you to do something about this essential matter.'[30] As on the eve of the abdication of the Tsar, in the period of palace plots, traces of such plans turn up in several political circles – all with the same aim, though not necessarily in league with each other. The Kadet Baron Nolde launched a trial balloon in *Rech*, to the effect that not all the enemy's peace proposals should automatically be regarded as tricks.[31] The *TsIK*'s own peace plan for Stockholm became *prikaz* no.1 for Russian diplomacy, permitting the return to Germany of her colonies, and scouting the possibility of self-determination for the Poles of the Russian empire, though for no one else.[32] There was also a public proposal from general Verkhovsky, 'for an immediate peace, and the establishment of a "rump" army that would restore order'. Verkhovsky, the war minister, was at once dismissed.[33] Kerensky planned to announce grandiosely the opening of peace negotiations, with a Decree on Land. Issued just as the October rising began, it was intended to allow this movement to be crushed as a preventive measure.[34]

For by now the rising was under way. The members of the Provisional Government deliberated, assembling in the Winter Palace.[35] Kerensky wanted to arrest the members of the *PVRK*, the revolutionary committee set up in October. As he said, 'I did not want to begin the test of strength with the Bolsheviks before I had obtained the explicit agreement of the nation's representatives', and he went to the Mariynsky Palace, where the 'pre-parliament' met. The minister, Nikitin, was in mid-speech, and he gave way to Kerensky who, 'pale and agitated, his eyes red with tiredness, but still with an air of triumph, said that the government had instructed him to report on the situation'. This speech, his last, was also one of the best-applauded. He attacked the advocates of dictatorship, whether of left or right, read out the documents of the week that showed Lenin's appeal for a rising, and said that this rising was happening just at the very moment the procedure was being worked out for committees temporarily to settle the agrarian question until the constituent assembly could deliberate on it, as the sovereign decision-maker. 'Our government may certainly be blamed for . . .' 'Stupidity', interrupted Martov . . . 'of weakness, of extreme toleration', Kerensky went on, 'but at least no one can say that we have acted against liberty as long as there was no danger to the state. But today, the state is in danger.'

Kerensky's speech was several times broken by applause. His per-oration was greeted by a standing ovation from almost the whole of the provisional council of the Republic. Only a small group of left Socialist Revolutionaries with Kamkov and the Menshevik Internationalists around Martov remained seated. Kerensky pointed a finger at them: 'You have now to make up your minds if you are for or against liberty. . . . If you believe that right is on the other side, behave like men and take your places there.' Once more the assembly rose, noisily applauding Kerensky, to general emotion. 'On leaving the platform', Sukhanov wrote, 'Kerensky collided with me. He had seen that I had kept my seat; he looked me in the eye and then gave me his hand.'[36] Kerensky, who was sure of obtaining a vote of confidence, left the Mariynsky Palace. After this interruption of their session, the groups once more acted in concert: the emotion over, the republic of orators could resume its ways. In the Mensheviks' name, Dan attacked the Bolsheviks for their policy of the greater evil: 'We must not defeat them by force of arms, but rather by measures to satisfy public opinion, especially peace. . . . There must be immediate negotiations.' Martov in his turn said that 'if the action under way [the Bolshevik rising] leads to civil war and counter-revolution, the responsibility is this government's.' The Socialist Revolutionaries, Kadets and Kuskova's co-operative movement proposed a vote of confidence, a kind of blank cheque to Kerensky, but the Socialist Revolutionary apparatus, at Gots's suggestion, associated itself with Dan's proposal for immediate issue of the Decree on Land, and the estab-lishment of a committee of public safety acting in collaboration with the government. The conclave went on interminably. Some of the council's members had left when news came in that the guard on the bridges had changed, and that the Petrograd telegraph was in Bolshevik hands. There was, finally, a vote: by 122 votes to 102, Dan's motion prevailed, Martov's group having supported it. Announcement of the result struck those present 'like a thunderclap': Kerensky thought, 'They can't surely have meant this, it's not a vote of confidence.'

He at once handed his resignation to Avksentiev, the president of the council of the Republic. Gots and Dan spoke up, for they too had not meant this. Avksentiev, who had been against the motion, agreed to join them in asking Kerensky to stay on. Kerensky met them haughtily. 'We insisted', Dan said, 'on the government announcing that very evening that it would take important steps regarding peace, land and the constituent assembly. Kerensky answered that he did not need our advice. The time was for action, not talk, he said. Then he consulted the members of his cabinet and drily declared that he would register our refusal to give him unconditional support; the die had been cast.'[37]

The members of the government, now alone, once more looked into the steps that might be taken to stop the insurrection. Kartashev was the most outspoken, and Kerensky flung at him, 'How blood-thirsty is the minister of God.' He left the caretaker arrangements to Konovalov, and went off to the head of the troops who were supposed to march on the Smolny Institute, the headquarters of the Bolsheviks and the second congress of soviets. Not finding a car, he borrowed one from the American embassy. It was early in the morning, and as he went by, the soldiers and civilians acclaimed him as they had always done, right up to the end, even when they meant to overthrow him. Kerensky himself recorded that the greetings were friendly; he laughed, and remembered that 'as I turned the palace corner, I saw that during the night someone had painted in enormous letters, "Down with the Jew Kerensky, Long Live Trotsky".'[38] There were Red Guard patrols everywhere, and he at once understood that he no longer controlled the city. Trying to avoid recognition, he went very fast through the city, to which he never returned. It was a crossing of the ways, for, some hours earlier, Lenin had emerged from hiding. Not understanding how far the situation had changed, he too wanted to escape the patrols and to avoid recognition. He succeeded, and arrived, though not without some alarm, at the Smolny Institute. He took charge of the leadership in this second Revolution, for which, since July, he had continually prepared.[39]

Lenin: the strategist of October[40]

For Lenin, the need for a second Revolution had been obvious since the end of the July Days, which had had the result of 'handing power over to the Kaledins'. Kaledin, the Cossack general, had said himself at the Moscow conference that this had happened; the conciliators pretended not to hear him when he said, 'It is you, the socialist ministers, who called us in to help you on 3 July.' No one could deny this . . . the

Cossack general spat in the faces of the Mensheviks and Socialist Revolutionaries, and they cried, 'It's manna from heaven', wiping it from their faces. The Mensheviks and Socialist Revolutionaries would not see the truth for what it was, even if 'the Kaledins did not immediately seize their chance to set up a complete military dictatorship'. Lenin, in his journalism, added that,

A power has to be judged by what it does, not what it says. Since 5 July the acts of the government showed that the Kaledins had come to power, slowly but surely, each day gaining both large and small 'concessions' – one day immunity to the officer cadets who pillaged *Pravda* and carried out arbitrary arrests, next day a law prohibiting certain newspapers, after that the law against meetings and congresses, or that on exile without trial, or imprisonment for offences against Allied embassies, or forced labour for offences against the authority of the government, or on restoration of the death penalty at the front. The Kaledins are not fools. Why should they rush in, head down, and risk failure, when every day they obtained, piece by piece, what they want? These deluded dimwits, the Skobelevs, Tseretellis, Chernovs, Avksentievs, Dans and Liebers can go on crying 'victory, a victory for democracy' at every step the Kaledins take, and seeing a victory in the fact that the Kaledins, Kornilovs and Kerenskys don't simply swallow them down at one gulp;

and Lenin concluded that

Obviously, a decisive change, at the present time, not only is not easy, but has become quite impossible without a second Revolution. . . . Power is already in other hands, has left revolutionary democracy, and others have taken it and strengthened it.[41]

Lenin thought that the constitutional way could lead to nothing in these circumstances, with 'signs of impending social change' that had not yet been resolved into conditions for a second victory. But he was wrong: for the Kaledins were indeed fools. They did rush, headlong, into their Putsch and its failure; and this altered the respective strengths completely, such that Lenin could at once propose a new tactic of seizing power. The 'soviets' unity' again existed. The vote of 31 August displayed the infinite possibilities that had opened up, and in his article 'On Compromise' Lenin explained that co-operation with the other parties of the soviets was now a possibility for the Bolsheviks, who could therefore return to their old pre-July watchword of 'All power to the soviets', implying that the Revolution could continue pacifically. 'The Bolsheviks, for their part, will meanwhile refrain from giving priority to their demand for transference of power to the proletariat and the poor peasantry, and they will also not give priority to their demand for a revolutionary way of action to achieve this programme.' Two days later he added a postscript to this article: since the Mensheviks and Socialist Revolutionaries would not oppose Kerensky absolutely there was no sense in a pacific revolution. He went back on this again some days later, for, as the Moscow Soviet aligned itself with the Petrograd, Lenin thought 'pacific revolution remains possible, for all power is shifting towards the soviets'.

The Bolshevik leaders were lulled by these remarks, and they rejected a scheme for boycott of the democratic conference that Kerensky was assembling. Since the failure of the July Days, the Petrograd committee and the military organization no longer dared to adopt extreme attitudes, and they associated themselves with the advocates of participation. They had been hard hit by the 'July complex', and opposed adventurism, a term they applied to any method that was not representational in orientation. They forgot their own mentor, Marx, who had warned against the illusions of representation and its essentially conservative virtues. Lenin, by contrast, reckoning that the political situation had wholly altered since the failure of the Kornilov Putsch, sent letter after letter to the centre committee, explaining that the Bolsheviks must take power. Even on 30 August, in the thick of the fight against Kornilov, he wrote, 'Only the extension of this fight can carry us to power, but, while we agitate, we must not expressly talk of this, though we know that even tomorrow events alone will carry us to power; and once we have it, we will never let go.'[42] A few days later, he entrusted Smilga, as member of the Petersburg committee, to carry to the central committee and to the Petrograd and Moscow committees a letter entitled, 'The Bolsheviks must seize power'. He showed that, the Bolsheviks having won a majority in the Petrograd and Moscow Soviets, they must take the power now within their grasp:

> They can take it, because the active majority of the revolutionary elements of the masses of the two capitals is enough to pull the rest of the people along, to conquer the enemy's resistance and to destroy him, to seize power and retain it. The Bolsheviks, proposing a democratic peace and immediately giving land to the peasants, will restore the institutions and liberties that Kerensky has 'democratically' dragged through the mire, and set up a government that no one can overthrow. [They] must do this, because the Provisional Government is incapable of stopping the surrender of Petrograd to the Kaiser's army. . . . Our party must be clear as to what it must do: to put on the agenda an armed insurrection in Petrograd, Moscow, and the surrounding areas, for conquest of power and overthrow of the

government. The party must think up how to propagandize this, without revealing it in the newspapers; it must remember the words of Marx on insurrection — insurrection is an art.[43]

Lenin sent another document with this letter, showing that from the Marxist viewpoint that July revolt had been 'Blanquism', but that, after the Kornilov affair, insurrection was legitimate. He wanted a general staff to be set up to organize it, and he thought out the first operations, explaining what Marx had called the art of insurrection. He ended his letter to the central committee with a pressing summons:

to wait for a formal majority in the soviets would be naïve for us: no Revolution can wait on that, and Kerensky & Co. won't wait either. They are preparing to give up Petrograd. It is these very pitiable hesitations by the democratic conference that will and must cause the workers of Petrograd and Moscow to lose patience. If we do not seize power now, history will never forgive us.[44]

The Bolsheviks regarded such talk as inopportune and impetuous: to them, Lenin was obsessed with power. They had decided to take part in the democratic conference, and Lenin told them, 'You will be traitors and scoundrels if you do not send the Bolshevik group instead into the factories, to encircle the democratic conference and imprison the whole lot.' This stupefied the members of the central committee, who did not know what to do next. They decided to burn Lenin's letter. However, they also rejected a motion of Kamenev's which stated that it was 'impossible, in present circumstances, to organize a street demonstration'. They took part in the democratic conference, but on 21 September, encouraged by a session in the soviet the day before, where the conference had been pronounced unrepresentative, the central committee again discussed whether it should participate or not. Trotsky, supported by Stalin, argued for a boycott of the 'pre-parliament' with Kamenev and Rykov against them. The boycotters won, narrowly, with 9 votes to 8, but the majority was held to be insufficient, and a decision was made to consult the provincial delegates. Boycott was rejected by 77 votes to 50, one of the delegates saying, 'We mustn't get involved again in the stupidities of July.' Lenin was enraged. He stated his disillusionment from Vyborg, where he was now in hiding: 'There is too much vacillation at the head of the party. . . . Trotsky was for the boycott, good for him.'[45]

Every day Lenin bombarded the central committee and the Petrograd committee with letters, but the parliamentarists would not listen. They had been strengthened by the adhesion of Zinoviev, who had been traumatized by the July failure and feared that if the party began a rising it would be finished just when it was constantly winning ground in the soviets. The fact that Trotsky, a recent convert to the party and one not much caring for the destiny of the party as such, supported a rising strengthened the position of the parliamentarists. Kamenev, Rykov and their allies regarded the Bolsheviks' victory in the second congress of soviets as a guarantee that there would be a constituent assembly where the Bolsheviks, with a third of the seats, could put through various structural changes. The question of elections – to the constituent assembly, the soviets, and the rest – was on the agenda, and Zinoviev, with the approval of the central committee, appealed to the workers on 20 September not to act in isolation, and proposed an alliance with the left wing of the Mensheviks and the left Socialist Revolutionaries. Lenin answered with a furious article, 'The Crisis is Ripe', saying that 'The Bolsheviks would be miserable traitors to the proletarian cause if they let themselves be deceived by constitutional illusions.' The central committee held up publication of this article for over a week.[46]

The same day, in an amendment to the party, Lenin wrote that 'There is a tendency within the party to wait for the congress of the soviets. This tendency works against an armed rising. We must overcome it. Otherwise the Bolsheviks would be covered in shame for ever: if we fail for one moment, and wait for the congress, it is either stupidity or treason.' Elsewhere he gave details as to how the revolt could be effected: 'We have thousands of armed soldiers to take the Winter Palace at a stroke, as well as the headquarters and telephone buildings . . . the troops will not march against a government that makes peace . . . Kerensky will have to give in.' But the central committee did not heed Lenin's letters, so that on 29 September, the founder of Bolshevism offered his resignation from the central committee, 'seeing that the central committee has ignored, and left unanswered, my most importunate letters . . . that the central committee has suppressed from my articles any reference even to errors as obvious as the shameful decision to take part in the "pre-parliament", and the offer that was made to the Mensheviks of a seat on the presidium of the soviets, then I can only conclude that the central committee wants me to resign. I am forced to offer my resignation, . . . reserving the liberty to carry out propaganda at the party base and in the congress.[47]

The Bolsheviks' constant progress, the adhesion of the Moscow committee to Lenin's theses, and the sympathy that they also evoked in the capital, in the Petersburg committee, all acted to make the party's policy change. Battle was joined over a proposal by Trotsky to stage a spectacular walk-out from the 'pre-parliament', after the Bolsheviks had read out their declaration demanding all power for the soviets. As Kamenev said, this decision predetermined the party's tactics for the immediate future. When Lenin, returning to Petrograd, succeeded in putting the problem of insurrection on the agenda, three questions faced the members of the central committee:

1 If the Bolsheviks take power, will they be able to keep it?
2 Why substitute an insurrection for a seizure of power through decision by the soviets, when it is clear that the Bolsheviks will have a majority there?
3 Why fix the date of the uprising before the congress of soviets meets?

Among opponents of the rising, a final question underlay the others: did not the example of July count against such new 'adventures'?

The Bolsheviks' seizure of power was no longer an academic question, and, since the failure of Kornilov, many commentators and politicians, among them Martov, the editorialist of *Delo Naroda*, and the newspaper *Rech* as well, saw it as a possible solution to the crisis of the Kerensky régime. The Bolshevik alternative was treated more seriously than elsewhere by Bazarov, in *Novaya Zhizn'*, who argued that, if the Bolsheviks took power, they would not retain it for long.[48] Lenin answered these arguments: contrary to Bazarov's assertion, 'the proletariat is not isolated from other classes in the country' – already in the democratic conference, the majority of soviet representatives were against coalition with the bourgeoisie, even the peasant representatives agreeing; the proletariat was also no longer isolated from other 'vital forces' of democracy, given that the left Socialist Revolutionaries and the provincial Menshevik Internationalists would support a purely Bolshevik government. In particular, Lenin showed that it was quite wrong to suggest that 'the proletariat is incapable of learning the technique of statecraft' because the task was not to learn it, but, as Marx had said, to destroy it and find another technique, much as had been attempted by the Paris Commune.

In the Russia of 1917, the new machinery is called soviets of workers' soldiers' and peasants' deputies. The working of the new state apparatus is guaranteed. Since the Revolution of 1905, Russia was governed by 130,000 landowners who did violence to 150 million people, and imposed limitless repression on them . . . and now we are told that the 240,000 members of the Bolshevik party will not be able to lead and govern Russia, in the interest of the poor rather than the rich. . . . Besides, we have a wonderful way of beginning our apparatus of state, right away. . . . We will bring in the poorer classes to the daily toil of state management. . . . We are not utopians, and we know that not just any navvy or cook will be able to run the state at once. What sets us apart from the Breshkovakayas, Tseretellis and the Kadets is that we demand an immediate breach with the prejudice according to which only rich functionaries of state, or civil servants from rich families, can administer the state and carry out the ordinary work of government.[49]

On this, Lenin had no opposition from within his own party. But there were many who felt, quite apart from the question of the uprising's chance of succeeding, that Lenin was wrong in automatically associating a seizure of power with an armed uprising. Lenin had already said that the government would obviously not allow the congress of soviets to take power without acting one way or another: it would block the very first moves of the congress, which, he thought, had to be forestalled by preparation for an armed rising to guarantee the soviets' victory. However, the Bolsheviks had at most a defensive vision of it all. As Latsis said, 'Few of us imagined the rising as an armed seizure of all governmental institutions at the same time. . . . We foresaw the insurrection as a simple seizure of power by the Petrograd Soviet, which would cease obeying orders from the Provisional Government, would declare itself the supreme authority and replace those in its way.'[50] Others supposed that the government would take steps to prevent such developments, so that men would have to be ready to defend the soviets' congress against any possible armed threat to it. Insurrection might be inevitable, but it was not, they thought, necessary: they had to behave as if it had to be started; it must be prepared, and the insurgents must act as though they were convinced, and could convince others, that they were legitimacy, defending itself. Such was Trotsky's view. Both such views could be squared with Lenin's own, so that the rising could be put on the agenda even without a universal offensive interpretation of it. This was why, at the central committee meeting that discussed the rising, it was agreed to by ten votes to two. The two against were Zinoviev's and Kamenev's.[51]

They had an altogether different position. They refused to link seizure of power with insurrection, and also refused to put the whole question of power in such out-and-out terms of now or never. They rejected insurrection only in so far as it was associated with a problem of power: they felt that, since the way they proposed, of constituent assembly plus soviets, did not depend only on the Bolsheviks, then enemies could force the party to engage in a decisive struggle before the constituent assembly elections.

We will join in [the vote for rising] in that event, for it would be the only possible solution. But then, we should have the help of a substantial part of the petty-bourgeois camp. However, since the government is often unable to exert its counter-revolutionary designs, and since we have some choice, we ought for the moment to be content with a defensive move.

'For the moment', in Kamenev's and Zinoviev's view, meant that the ratio of strength was unfavourable: if it proclaimed an insurrection at once, the party would at a stroke stake its future, that of the Revolution and the International Revolution as well. Kamenev and Zinoviev did not rule out an insurrection completely, if it was meant to defend the Revolution; but they would include it in their plans only if it involved questions of power-seizure. Kamenev and Lenin had opposing concepts of power, and they had already clashed for some time. This time Lenin had an easy victory, because there was a threat of repression and the need to organize the defence of the Revolution put other considerations on ways of taking power in a secondary category. There was question only of a new *Kornilovshchina*, in the form of a voluntary withdrawal of the front line. The Petrograd Bolsheviks had had wind of it, for, at the Vyborg district committee, Orlov, returning from the front, announced that 'commissioner Voytinsky has threatened undisciplined units with a breach of the front.'[52] In the Petrograd Soviet, where there had also been similar reports, a 'conciliatory' proposal was for the establishment of a committee for defence of the Revolution in the capital (*PVRK*). The Bolsheviks agreed to join it, which was no sooner said than done, for on 9 October a commission was established to set up the *PVRK*. Trotsky left the chairmanship to a young left Socialist Revolutionary, Lazimir, and Sverdlov reported to the central committee on this question on 10 October, just before Lenin asked for the insurrection to be tabled: 'something very odd is happening on the northern front, with the withdrawal of troops to the interior, and from Minsk we have heard that a new Kornilov rising is in preparation. The place has been surrounded by Cossacks, and there are negotiations of a suspicious character between the staff and GHQ.' This alarming report impressed the central committee. By ten votes to two the final resolution tabled the armed insurrection, declaring it 'inevitable', associating its necessity with the 'obvious preparations for a new Kornilovite rising'.[53] There was no mention either of congress of soviets or of seizure of power.

Lenin had won a first great success. But it was not complete, for the question of taking power was not directly associated with that of the armed rising, and Kamenev and Zinoviev, in any case, did not believe they had been hopelessly beaten. They did not resign from the central committee, and were even elected to the seven-member political committee that was set up at the end of this meeting, with Trotsky, Stalin, Sokolnikov, Lenin and Bubnov. The decision that had been taken was in fact based on a misunderstanding, as the following days showed. There were in reality several tendencies among the leading Bolsheviks, and this emerged when the date for this uprising had to be fixed.

Associated with Kamenev were all who opposed the insurrection but would, despite themselves and because of solidarity with their colleagues, go along with it. Zinoviev agreed, here, with Kamenev and also with some members who had been absent from the meeting on 12 October, such as Rykov, Nogin and Ryazanov. Lenin, by contrast, wanted an armed insurrection before the congress of soviets had met, and he wanted a date to be fixed. For him, time pressed: there must be action, not talk, and besides, as soon as it was known that the Bolsheviks were planning a coup, any delay would be treason. Since everyone, particularly the government, supposed that the rising would occur when the congress assembled – up to 17 October, the 20th was the date foreseen – Lenin wanted to stage it before the assembly, without any connection with the meeting but in accord with the soviets. It was also clear that if initiative for the rising came from the Bolsheviks, they would the more easily take power if they won in association with the soviets, even if these were Bolshevized.

Trotsky had a different view. He hardly bothered to state a position in the party bodies, but in the soviets he invoked the need to take power and act without delay. In the council of soviets of the northern front, on 12 October, he said, 'In this mortal struggle with the counter-revolution, we must take power ourselves, even if we have to pay for it with our lives.' He linked the uprising to the defence of Petrograd, and saw it as a response to government action against the soviets.[54] Although after 1924, in order to identify himself with Lenin's action against Stalin, he recorded that he had 'linked the insurrection and the taking of power', the fact was that seizure of power by the soviets was his first aim, and the only point of the rising was to guarantee things: to him, it was more inevitable than necessary. No date should therefore be fixed for it, he thought, and perhaps it could even be dispensed with, although preparations ought to be made. Lenin meant to treat insurrection as an art; in Geyer's well-turned phrase, 'Trotsky treated soviet legality, rather than armed insurrection, as an art.' If he succeeded, uprising or not, he would end the split in the party; if he failed to reconcile Bolshevik and Menshevik, he could at least reconcile Bolshevik and Bolshevik.[55] The armed rising as such did not enter his plans.

Opposition to the uprising did not give way, among the Bolsheviks, until the last moment. At the meeting of 16 October, Kamenev and Zinoviev were still against it, and as the central committee went ahead, and appointed a five-man revolutionary committee to act with the *PVRK*, they offered their resignations. As Lenin had proposed doing some days before, they fought at the base of the party, sending a circular letter against the principle of insurrection. It fell into the hands of *Novaya Zhizn'*, which published it on 18 October and thus publicized the party's plans. Lenin angrily attacked the 'traitors and blacklegs' and a vote was taken in the central committee concerning their resignation.[56] Rumours of the uprising had in fact been going round political circles since 12 October, but the publication of this letter made it still more difficult to prepare and successfully launch the uprising. Trotsky was forced to disavow such intentions in haughty tones, which again weakened the already wavering morale of the troops, who did not understand why the uprising was necessary.

The Bolshevik military organization, like the Petrograd committee, had had its fingers burnt in July and was reserved as to the mood of soldiers and workers. G. I. Chudnovsky, an ally of Trotsky, spoke against any uprising before the congress had met, and was supported by Volodarsky, Larin and Ryazanov. Bubnov explained, 'We can't give a definite date, only it ought to be before the congress', but Kalinin thought it should happen 'maybe in a year's time'.[57] Sverdlov spoke up: 'The central committee's decision has been taken, and I can't allow it to be reconsidered.' Podvoysky wanted a delay of ten days to rally the units, but Lenin, annoyed, said it was too long. He was angry that no one had checked whether the heads of the Red Guard had any military competence: 'it was then', said Podvoysky, 'that I really understood what the point of the Red Guard was.'[58]

The radicalization of the masses had been transmitted by the Bolshevization of the revolutionary institutions. However, the party had not radicalized its own policies, and Lenin had once more to enforce this. At the grass-roots level, many committees and armed groups were ready, impatient for action; but, as in July, the greater the responsibility, the greater the pessimism and doubt, and the party's higher levels tried to hold the lower. However, unlike July, part of the central committee had been won over, though Daniels is right in saying that the Bolshevik leaders, Lenin and Sverdlov apart, had less confidence in the enterprise than their enemies supposed. Paradoxically, it may be added that whereas the armed rising was intended in principle to give power to the Bolshevik party and its central committee, that same central committee was the body least able to manage the uprising: hence the creation of the five-man committee. The party, at least its activist elements, could really only act through institutions that were already more Bolshevik then the central committee – the Petrograd Soviet, or the *PVRK*.[59]

The strategy and tactics of October: Lenin and Trotsky

The supreme command once more exploited the German menace by attempting to send part of the garrison to the front. No one believed it, and the Petrograd Soviet interpreted it as the start of a second *Kornilovshchina*. It was easy to see what the military were doing: either the troops would obey the order and the army could rid the city of revolutionary elements, or they would disobey, so that the supreme command could open the front and allow the enemy to occupy Petrograd – the country then putting the blame on cowards and traitors who had failed to defend the capital. The name of St Petersburg, like that of Lyons in the French Revolution, would then be razed from the pages of history.

To forestall this, to save the Revolution and, if the menace was real, the capital as well, Petrograd would have to undertake its own defence, creating a revolutionary supreme command. This was to double for the proper military authority, and stop any transfer of the city's defenders. Reality was different, for although the government did discuss the German threat, it was so as to exploit it in another way. It expected to send troops to the front, thereby clearing them from the city; it did not intend to open the way to the Germans. However, since the government would obviously act prudently in going to Moscow, the capital would then be included in the supreme command's zone of authority, and would be under martial law, with meetings and assemblies forbidden. It would mean the end of the Petrograd Soviet, and could easily turn into a second *Kornilovshchina*. On 6 October, in the Petrograd Soviet, Trotsky warned the government against using this manoeuvre: 'The Soviet protests against the plan to transfer the government to Moscow, for it means that the city will be handed over to the mercy of fate. If the Provisional Government cannot defend Petrograd, let it conclude peace or make way for another government. Going to Moscow is desertion of the front line.' Three days later, the order to transfer troops caused the military section of the soviet to envisage setting up a revolutionary high command. The Mensheviks and Socialist Revolutionaries were against, for 'it means dual command, which would weaken the defence'. But in the end a 'committee for co-operation with the Headquarters of the military district' was set up, or 'committee for defence of the Revolution', *PVRK*.

Its task was, in principle, to defend the capital. None the less, it was obvious that its objectives, now that the Bolsheviks had decided on a rising, would cease to be antagonistic to those of the Bolsheviks and would come closer to them. The rising was becoming a patriotic demonstration against incompetent leaders, whose only ability was to plot against the people. Kerensky denied that the government would go to Moscow, and rumours that the front would be purposely opened were shown to be, if not wholly incorrect, at least seriously misrepresented. The *PVRK* still existed as a military counter-balance to the supreme command,[60] and at the conference of soviets of the northern region, assembled on Trotsky's prompting to prepare for the second congress, the Bolsheviks reigned supreme. Antonov-Ovseyenko was in the chair, and he accused Kerensky of wishing to hand over the capital. The Bolshevik section publicized Lenin's letter of 8 October, and the decisions taken regarding the armed insurrection. Speakers and participants were very hostile towards the government, and the final resolution was for 'immediate action', adding that 'on the soviet side is not only Right, but Might; the time for phrases is past, and that for action, a rising (*vystupleniye*) has come'. Another resolution of solidarity with the Kresty prisoners, who had just started a hunger-strike, stated that 'We are on the eve of a mass rising'. The practical question was then raised of how, where and when a rising should be decided. Breslav said that 'We supposed the conference would be the centre of the rising and would start it without waiting for the congress.' However, no decision was made, except to make certain that this assembly would meet, and so a possible rising was put off until 20 October. According to Ilin-Zhenevsky, the idea was prevalent that action should be 'delicate, and not cause too much damage'. At the time, there was talk of establishing a centre for the rising in the northern front, but this was discarded as unsatisfactory.[61]

The executive committee of the soviets, the *TsIK*, held its last session before the second congress, and discussed the likelihood of a Bolshevik coup. But the Bolsheviks hardly bothered to attend bodies where they were in a minority, and they had sent only Ryazanov as observer. In any case, they no longer needed certificated Bolshevik orators to make their programme heard, for, one after another, the delegates of the various armies did this for them. They all, without exception, said that the war could not go on in these conditions. The front was obsessed with peace; many units demanded it, in whatever conditions, even on separate terms. One of the speakers said, 'If it had to be a shameful (*pokhabny*) peace, then let it be one'; and the soldiers declared categorically that they would not stand another winter of war at the front.

Thus struck the tone. Gots told the delegates that the soviet would do all it could to conclude peace, but added, 'I cannot believe that there are any soldiers in the Russian army who would accept a degrading or a separate peace, and I am sure the men will do their duty towards the country and the Revolution.' Dan spoke, and, since Tseretelli, who had fallen ill, had left for his native Caucasus, he was the recognized authority in the *TsIK*. His experience, his connections with Martov (his brother-in-law) and above all his strength of character made him the acknowledged head of the conciliators. He spoke of the need to defend Petrograd, the centre of the Revolution, but warned, 'there are some who are preparing for a new rising of the workers and soldiers, and we must ask our Bolshevik colleagues, "where will this lead you?"' Ryazanov, from his place, called out, 'We demand peace and land', Dan answered, 'Peace and land? This rising will get you neither of them, it will be the end of the Revolution.' He pointed a finger at Ryazanov, 'The Bolsheviks must say whether or not they are preparing a rising. I demand a yes or no. There can be no other answer.' Ryazanov was taken by surprise and found it difficult to answer – 'I regret that I cannot answer such a serious question before such a small gathering. . . . In July this room was full.' He launched into a long digression. The chairman asked him to come to the point, and he spoke out, 'So long as the Provisional Government and the Mensheviks have the task of defending this city, the situation will be serious. . . . It must be the Soviet that undertakes defence . . . the only way to save the country . . . the movement that is under way is caused by the policies of the last seven months. We cannot yet tell the date or the hour of the rising, but we are telling the masses to prepare for the decisive fight for peace, land, bread and liberty. If it has to be a working-class government, then we'll be in the front rank of the insurgents.'

Emotion ran high, for Ryazanov had faced up to the moment, and had confirmed that there were plans for a rising. He made no mention of the second congress in his purely Leninist address. Bogdanov thought that he had not really answered the question; and it was true that, to give a yes or no answer, the Bolsheviks themselves would have to have decided already, and they had not done so. He remarked ironically, 'To everyone's surprise, the Bolsheviks are now talking of the defence of the country, of the sacred and indispensable virtues of patriotic defence.' He said he would vote with Dan, 'that taking into account the military threat to Petrograd, and preparation for a counter-revolutionary pogrom such as is now being undertaken by the reactionaries . . . we call on the citizens of Petrograd to do their duty, and consider that in present conditions any kind of insurrection would be inopportune, would feed the counter-revolution and would lead to the ruining of the Revolution.'[62] The *TsIK* postponed the meeting of the second congress from 20 to 25 October, so as to make certain that there would be an over-representation of the front committees, which there had been some difficulty in convoking. The *TsIK* thought it was 'gaining five days', and did not appreciate that the *PVRK* needed this delay to complete preparations for the rising.[63]

While the Bolsheviks' central committee split, and the Petrograd Soviet's executive committee took fright, the *VRK* was going ahead. The

Socialist Revolutionaries in the Petrograd Soviet, on 15 October, tried
to have the problem of the *PVRK*'s composition and function taken off
the agenda, to postpone discussion – in effect, *sine die*. They failed,
refusing to enter debates if the sole debating parties were the left Socialist
Revolutionaries and the Bolsheviks, although they did figure through
their military and naval organizations, and the like, and they were also in
contact with the revolutionary five-man centre.

From 11 October, several units in the capital, recognizing the *PVRK*
as the body organizing the insurrection, sent resolutions to the Petrograd
Soviet to say that it alone 'can defend the city'. Sometimes these resolutions went through as a simple majority vote, as with the 1st reserve
automobile section (251 votes to 173, with 57 abstentions), and sometimes they were adopted unanimously, as with the Yeger reserve regiment, the 6th reserve sappers, the 180th reserve: 'If the Soviet appeals
for it, we should leave the city of the Revolution with valiant but serene
hearts, to die at the front for the sake of the country and of liberty'; 'But
to a government we do not trust, if it sent us such an order, without first
consulting the Soviet, we should have to refuse.' The Red Guard
declared around 15 October that it had between 10,000 and 12,000 men
in readiness; and the *PVRK* also knew, from its links with the district
committees, that almost 10,000 men could be mobilized, for instance,
in the Vyborg district, and that 'the enemy forces here count at most
2,300 men – a unit of the Battalions of Death has had to go away, and
there are 5,000 rifles at our disposition'. On 15 October eight of the
nineteen districts were ready, especially where there were Finns,
Estonians and Letts. To prevent the despatch of troops to the northern
front, on 18 October, the military section of the Petrograd Soviet
organized an assembly of the capital's regimental committees: a dozen
regiments spoke out against the government, and declared their readiness
to march at the appeal of soviet or congress, but two others disagreed, and
one or two others wavered. The next day the *TsIK*, the executive committee of the congress of soviets, in turn called together regimental
representatives, at Dan's suggestion. The representatives would not vote
a resolution prepared by the committee, but some of them were more
circumspect, and two others declared against the insurrection – the
soldiers of the Peter-Paul Fortress, and the armoured car division. Having
carried out this referendum, the executive committee named a commissioner to maintain links with GHQ and to supervise its activities.
Under his orders would be the commissioners of the various districts, a
bureaucratic way of controlling the military sections of the committees
in the capital – among them the *PVRK*. The Petrograd Soviet refused
to let this happen.

However, these enquiries did show that, as Trotsky later wrote of the capital's armed forces, 'the large garrison did not want to fight: the naval detachment was not numerous, and the Red Guard lacked technical capacity'. Not only was it difficult to mount an armed uprising, but also, though there was marked hostility and aggressiveness towards the authorities, and trust in the soviets, there was almost complete absence of any reference to the Bolshevik party. The fact that almost all the soviet leaders were Bolsheviks counted for little, except among militants of other parties: the leaders were followed not as Bolsheviks but as soviet leaders, even though they had become soviet leaders only because they had adopted Bolshevik platforms.

The trial of strength concerned control of the garrison, as the *PVRK* accused the supreme command of 'refusing to collaborate' with it. It declared invalid any order sent without its counter-signature to the garrison. Bowing to a government ultimatum, the *PVRK* agreed to negotiate, but by then government forces were already invading the premises of Bolshevik newspapers.[64] This began the conflict. R. V. Daniels has identified two successive phases in the insurgents' behaviour.

A   There was an initial defensive phase, in which the press was muzzled, and the government raised bridges over the Neva (see Eisenstein's *October*) while the Red Guard and other insurgents sought to forestall repression by seizing strategic places. The defensive plan's cohesion was such that, though Stalin and Trotsky tried to explain things otherwise, the democrats were sure that the Bolsheviks were quite determined on an uprising. On the evening of 24 October, in the soviets, the whole 'republic of militants' attacked Trotsky and Volodarsky, in a scene well-described by John Reed.[65]

B   There was then an offensive phase, closely associated with the direct engagement of Lenin himself, for he came out of hiding to guide operations against the government. This phase, technically, began with the seizure of the post office and telegraph; and politically, the arrival of Lenin had immediate impact. He had no sooner arrived at Smolny — after legendary vicissitudes — than he set clear aims, to be achieved at once: seizure of the Winter Palace, arrest and imprisonment of the ministers. According to Antonov-Ovseyenko, it was all an improvisation, and had to be carried out at night, accompanied by a salvo from the *Aurora*; its main aim was to hearten the masses.[66]

This first step was accompanied by others. Even before an ultimatum had been issued to the Provisional Government, Lenin issued an appeal from the *PVRK* declaring that the government was overthrown and that it had taken over. On 25 October, at 2.30 p.m., Trotsky repeated in the soviet session that the government no longer existed. Lenin, father of

Bolshevism, appeared in public for the first time since June, and said,

'Comrades, the Revolution of workers and peasants, the necessity of which the Bolsheviks have always stressed, is now a reality. What does the workers' and peasants' revolution mean? That we shall have a government of soviets, the power belonging to us all, and that there will be no bourgeois element. The oppressed will themselves create power. The old state apparatus will be destroyed utterly, and a new apparatus of government will be set up, with the soviets' own organization. It is a new stage in the history of Russia, and this third Russian Revolution must lead to the victory of socialism. One of our first tasks will be to stop the war at once. But the war is closely associated with capitalism, and to stop it, we have to defeat capitalism itself. We will get help in this from the world-wide working-class movement already breaking out in Italy, England and Germany. . . . We have the strength of a mass organization that can overthrow everything and lead the proletariat to world Revolution. We must devote ourselves in Russia to the construction of a working-class socialist state. Long Live the World Socialist Revolution.' [Lively applause.]

'You are anticipating the will of the soviets,' shouted someone. 'No,' answered Trotsky. 'It is the workers and soldiers who, by their uprising, have anticipated the will of the congress.' Antonov, Podvoysky and Sadovsky feverishly prepared the attack on the Winter Palace. They expected to take Kerensky alive, not knowing that he had left. In his absence the cabinet had entrusted the action against the insurrection to Kishkin, minister for social security. It thereby committed its final act of clumsiness, for Kishkin was a well-known conservative. When the commander of the northern front, in his GHQ in Pskov, received a telegram from him, he assumed that this Kadet minister had deposed Kerensky, and held up sending reinforcements to Petrograd. By the time the matter was cleared up, October was a fact.[67]

The palace guard had been entrusted to Palchinsky, who was energetic enough but who, up to that afternoon, had not known a rising was under way. To parry it, he had in all — the expected reinforcements not having arrived — two and a half classes of cadets, a battery, two armoured cars and a unit of the women's battalion. The government and the military district in the palace received the ultimatum of the *PVRK* towards 6.30 p.m. which read,

By order of the *PVRK*, the Provisional Government is overthrown, and all power is transferred to the Petrograd Soviet. The Winter

Palace is surrounded by revolutionary forces, the guns of the Peter-Paul Fortress and the cruisers *Aurora* and *Amur* are trained on the Winter Palace and GHQ, and members of the supreme command will be arrested. The junior officers, soldiers and clerks will be disarmed and, after examination, released. You have twenty minutes to reply. This ultimatum expires at 7.10 after which we shall open fire.

(signed) Antonov, president of the *PVRK*; commissioner of the Peter-Paul Fortress.[68]

The ministers decided unanimously not to reply to the ultimatum, but the command of the military district, which met in the palace, were not aware of this by 7.10 p.m. when the Red Guards, not having received an answer, occupied the palace, arresting generals Paradelov and Bagration.

There was also considerable disorder among the attackers. At 7.10 the searchlight of the Peter-Paul Fortress, which should have given the *Aurora* the signal to open fire, failed to work. Antonov and Blagondarov went off towards the Peter-Paul Fortress to find out what was happening there. There was thick fog over the bridges, the Neva and the fortress. Antonov, who was short-sighted, stumbled around in his wanderings, and then Blagondarov got lost. The nervousness was extreme, and time went by with neither a signal nor the *Aurora*'s guns showing themselves. Finally, at 9.35, the signal beam was repaired, and at 9.40 the salvo from the *Aurora* rent the night. It was blank shot, 'so as to avoid damage to an historical monument', but the noise was vast, and was remembered by several eye-witnesses. A little later, machine-gunnery and rifle-fire crackled around the palace. The government members were terrified, though, not knowing the full extent of their disaster, they did not give in like the cadets, who did. The women's volunteer unit refused to follow, and even wished to attack, for honour's sake. Around 10.00 p.m. the attackers had re-formed, and all was ready for a final assault, if need be, in an hour's time. At Smolny, Podvoysky said, 'Lenin was like a caged beast: he had to preside at the second congress and so had to have the Winter Palace, at whatever cost. The palace was the last barrier on the soviet's road to power, and Vladimir Ilich screamed and yelled, ready to have us all shot.'[69]

The second congress opened on 25 October at 10.40 p.m.[70] The assault on the Winter Palace had not yet been sounded, though by then the significance of what was happening was plain. Emotions ran high, and Dan, on behalf of the old *TsIK*, opened the session: 'Comrades, this congress of soviets is meeting in exceptional circumstances . . . and I think it is pointless to begin matters with a political speech. You will understand when I say that I am a member of the presidium of the congress of soviets, and cannot say nothing while my party comrades are being shot up in the Winter Palace, where they have been carrying out their functions as ministers responsible to the soviets.' Then the presidium was set up. Following the rules of proportional representation, there were 14 Bolsheviks, 7 Socialist Revolutionaries, 3 Mensheviks and 1 Internationalist. The Mensheviks and Socialist Revolutionaries refused to take their seats. Among the Bolsheviks there were only the 'democrats' who attended – Zinoviev, Rykov, Ryazanov, Nogin and their group leader, Kamenev, who had by now replaced Dan as president. The walls were shaken by a new cannon-shot, and a renewed cannonade – the assault on the Winter Palace.

Martov decided to speak. He was in a rage, and said, 'What is all this? Civil war has begun, and our comrades are being killed in the streets. We must find a peaceful solution, for the question of power is being settled by a military conspiracy mounted by one of the revolutionary parties. There is a possible solution to the conflict, the constitution of a power based on democracy.' In the unitarists' name Lunacharsky supported this, and so did Kamkov, for the left Socialist Revolutionaries. The Mensheviks protested, and Khinchuk, president of the Moscow Soviet, read out their declaration condemning 'the military conspiracy that had been organized behind the backs of the soviets'. They walked out of the congress, followed by the Socialist Revolutionaries and the *Bund* who supported them. Delegates from the front spoke in the same way, though other such delegates disapproved, and were manifestly in a majority. They attacked Martov, who again tried to prevent rupture and find a compromise. He was interrupted by Trotsky who, in John Reed's words,

> stood up with a pale, cruel face, letting out his rich voice in cool contempt, called out to him: 'No! A compromise is no good here. To those who have walked out and to those who come with suchlike proposals, we must say, "you are – pitiful isolated individuals, you are – bankrupts; your role is played out. Go where you belong from now on – into the dustbin of history."'

'We'll go', said Martov, in rage. Trotsky at once took his place on the platform and read out an improvised resolution: 'The second congress sees that the departure of the Mensheviks is a criminal and hopeless attempt to destroy the representativity of this assembly at a time when the masses are defending the Revolution against onslaught by counter-revolutionaries.'

Just as this was being voted upon, Antonov-Ovseyenko penetrated the palace. No reinforcements had arrived, and the cadets' moral was too low for them to resist attack. Apart from a charge on a wing of the palace, the attackers won by pressure of numbers rather than by fighting in the true sense, and there was no real battle. Defenders and attackers were inextricably intermingled, and everywhere discussions and negotiations were interrupted by pressure from the attackers. In an indescribable tumult, Red Guards and soldiers, firing into the air so as not to hit each other, reached the palace, with more of a fright than anything else, for the assault cost not one casualty among the attackers, although Antonov said there were six on the defenders' side.

He and Chudnovsky, now masters of the palace, promised Palchinsky to spare the lives of the defenders, and went off to find the ministers. Palchinsky easily got them lost in the labyrinth of rooms, and he discreetly had the ministers informed that the palace had been taken, and that they must flee. Tereshchenko thought 'Better die here than flee', and a cadet in charge of the council guard said that all was ready for their defence. The overwhelmed ministers said, 'It's pointless, we don't want bloodshed', and 'We'll surrender'. Having found the right route, the little force under Antonov rushed into the council chamber. Malianovich has left a picture of the scene: 'A little man, with half-opened coat, a hat on the back of his head, long red hair, a little moustache and spectacles, the upper lip reaching his nose when he spoke, eyes colourless and face tired, collar very high, hiding the neck, but revealing a very dirty man in his shirt sleeves.' Konovalov, deputizing for the prime minister, spoke to him: 'We are the Provisional Government. What do you want.' Antonov came up, short-sightedly peering at the ministers, and shouted out, 'In the name of the military revolution committee, I arrest you.'

Two hours later the second congress voted a resolution drawn up by Lenin and giving 'all power to the soviets'. Then came readings and adoptions of the Decrees on Land, Peace, and soon also on people's rights of self-determination (see chapters 4 and 5). For the Russians, the most important thing was that the armistice negotiations should be effective and the war ended. 'Faces were radiant, the *International* was sung, and then the Farewell to the Dead' which sounded poignant, as the crowd sang it with a sob in their voices. October was over.[71]

3 October: the Bolsheviks and the people

Since October, supporters and enemies of the Bolshevik coup have discussed the nature of the event – *coup d'état*, insurrection, or Revolution. Supporters insisted on the mass character of the affair and the general support for it, whereas enemies have seen in it the plot of a single party, which went on to keep power for itself, for ever, with the subsequent institution of the Terror.

Lenin's coup

In the *PVRK*, the offensive tactics against the Provisional Government were adopted during 25 October and not before. The choice had not been explicit, in the same way as the overall strategy for the insurrection had been defined, over the previous weeks, in the Bolshevik central committee: the passage from defensive to offensive was marked by spontaneous actions in the capital, though also in decisions of the *PVRK* prompted by Lenin. The offensive tactics were not limited to operations, for a corollary was the establishment of a political centre and the creation of a new political power. This power, proclaiming itself sovereign, was of the *PVRK* rather than the congress of soviets – for at 10.00 a.m. on that day it declared 'that the Provisional Government is overthrown, and we are taking power'.

This proclamation of the *PVRK* before the soviets had taken power was, given the views taken in the Bolshevik central committee, the Petrograd Soviet and the various other revolutionary bodies, a true *coup d'état*. The coup bore Lenin's signature. The original function of the *PVRK* had been to prevent a new *Kornilovshchina*, to protect Petrograd from the consequences of a withdrawal of the front line, and also to make safe the congress in which the soviets would take power It was not meant to take power itself. Lenin had, in an initial version of the proclamation, written 'The *PVRK* convokes the Petrograd Soviet today at noon, and immediate measures will be taken to establish soviet power' – but then he scratched out the words. It was a significant act of omission. Despite the success of the insurrection, with an offensive character marked by the storming of the Winter Palace that enabled men to present the seizure of power that evening as a *fait accompli*, Lenin took out a further guarantee. He mistrusted the 'revolutionary legalism' of the Petrograd Soviet – i.e. Trotsky – and the conciliatory spirit of his Bolshevik colleagues in the central committee, for both might weaken the victory. They could fail to take power, or negotiate over its definition with other socialist parties and social institutions. To prevent this, to avoid any ambiguity, to mark a breach with the past and to prevent power from going to Trotsky, its president, Lenin did not deal through the Petrograd Soviet. He withdrew his own phrase, and substituted one that gave power to the *PVRK*. The new power thus emanated from an institution that had been created in the process of insurrection; it affirmed its own authority, and imposed itself without depending on any institution, even the congress of soviets.[72] Lenin's gesture was one of mistrust, but it was also an act of authoritarianism, with incalculable consequences. For the immediate future, he wanted a breach between Bolsheviks and other revolutionary organizations, including even the Internationalists. This had the effect of aligning the party with the most progressive section of the popular movement, but this time, through Lenin, the Bolshevik party could claim that it was filling the historic mission it had assigned to itself since 1903 – that of occupying the very front line. This accounts for its behaviour in the face of the first acts of the new popular authority.[73]

For and against October

The tactics of Lenin, the aggressive behaviour of Trotsky at the second congress, and the first acts of the *PVRK* insurgents before the new authority of the people's commissars had been set up, all contributed to determine, in advance, the relationship that the new leaders would have with other social or political groups. On 26 October, when the first soviet of people's commissars was set up, it included only Bolsheviks, and had the support of no other group. The chairman of the new *TsIK*, Leonid Kamenev, who had now rallied to the movement, was better placed than any other leader to see the full extent of the Bolsheviks' political isolation among the other parties. However, there were limits to the isolation. It existed in terms of relations with other parties, but not as far as the masses were concerned. Kamenev assured the other members of the *TsIK* that 'the soviet of people's commissars is unquestionably an emanation of the workers and soldiers, and the proof is that the commissars for labour, posts and telegraphs, and transport have already entered communication with the trade unions to cope with their problems, while a liaison committee has been set up to govern relations with the peasant soviets.' Volodarsky said that, in these conditions, soviet power could work as it was, through a council in which there were 62 Bolsheviks, 29 left Socialist Revolutionaries, 1 Maximalist and 6 Internationalists, but he was told by Krushinsky, of the railwaymen's union, in agreement with the left Socialist Revolutionary Kamkov, the Internationalists Bazarov and Karelin that it was vital to set up an all-socialist government with a wider power-base. The conditions posed for this – dismissal of Trotsky and Lenin – were such that the cabinet remained as before. What was the force behind it, and which forces could it oppose to Kerensky's efforts to re-take the capital or, after his failure which the White generals were glad to see, to their raising the standard of Civil War?[74]

The participants of October

By all accounts, the number of active participants in October was very small. This is shown in cinema films, where a handful of men are seen to be guarding Smolny, and the documents confirm it, for the roll of sentries in the night of 23–24 October contains only thirty names. There were also twenty-seven liaison officials who went into the city and stayed there. Another film of relevance is the reconstruction that was made, a year later, for the anniversary of October. It included former participants who responded to the appeal of S. M. Eisenstein, published in *Pravda*, and this astonishing document has survived in the Stockholm archives: its author was inspired by it, eight years later, to make *October*, in which two or three hundred participants were employed in the breaking-down of the grills.[75]

Other data bear these figures out. One of the most certain is an *anketa* discovered by Starchev, covering a quarter of the strength of the Red Guard. Of the 3,663 Guards who answered the enquiry (about a quarter of the total) those who took part in the Kornilov action numbered 241, while on 24 and 25 October there were respectively 126 and 413 involved in taking the Winter Palace. These figures should be multiplied by four.[76] The army was also there, and an indication of its numerical representation may, indirectly, be the analysis of 104 orders found in the archives of the *PVRK*. The distribution of recipients was:[77]

to Red Guard	3 orders
to factory committees	12 orders
to district committees	5 orders
to military units	47 orders
to naval units	3 orders
to others	20 orders

The *PVRK* clearly relied, in its operations, more on the army's regulars than on the Red Guards, who were composed of very young workers, 'inexperienced lads' who were undisciplined and were inclined to act quite independently. The *PVRK* used the Red Guards only for their proper function, the securing of factories, bridges and working-class districts; they were involved in the city only for the attack on the Winter Palace. There are other statistics: for instance, the arrival of 706 sailors from Kronstadt, the sending of 200 soldiers to Smolny, the participation of two regiments (the Kexholm and Pavlovsky) in the assault on the Winter Palace, though with all of their companies. These figures do not allow a rigorous evaluation, but such seems hardly necessary.

A closer approximation to reality may be gained from the fact that, out of about 180 military units in the capital, 36 signed a refusal to go to the

front in July, while 51 signed the *PVRK*'s appeal in October for the overthrow of the Provisional Government. During the uprising the *PVRK*
maintained liaison with 27 of these units on 23 October, and with 41 on
25 October – a quarter of the capital's effective military forces. These
proportions can be compared with those of the industrial works controlled by the Red Guard. Of the 670 working for defence, 236 were
represented at the factory-committee conference in June, and 180 had a
Red Guard in October.[78]

The number of guards and soldiers involved in the uprising has to be
given a correct interpretation. It was small enough, but it represented a
quarter of the workers and soldiers, and that quarter cannot be described
as a 'minority' because it met no opposition, at least at the time, from
any military unit or factory. The active participants were therefore not
really activists, in the sense of a militant group fighting in the name, and
instead of, a larger group: they were a fraction from within that group.
The small numbers sufficed because there was nothing against them, and
the men could be infinitely replaced according to the requirements of the
embryonic institutions that the masses had set up for themselves – as
leaders of the Red Guard, *PVRK* commissioners or leaders of the district
committees. The fraction continually grew. A week after the uprising, the
number of Red Guards who took part in fighting General Krasnov at
Gatchina, the soviet 'Valmy', was almost 3,000, while at the time the
PVRK had links with 113 units in the capital, 44 provincial towns
(though only 6 villages, 4 of which were near the city).[79] Support flowed
in over the next few days – central committee of the Baltic Fleet, naval
revolutionary committee, committees of the II, III, V, X and XII Armies,
while the workers' organizations were represented by the soviet of
Petrograd trade unions and the all-Russian soviet of factory committees.
To this support, which was predictable in view of the Bolshevization that
some time before had affected these bodies, came others – anarchists,
union of industrial and commercial clerks, conference of workers of
Kronstadt, Petrograd and Sestroretsk, with the printers (though not the
master ones), tramway, hotel, nutritional workers. It was 'a dizzying
rush of supporters', said a contemporary, who ascribed it to 'the illusion
that the soviets will do what the masses want'.[80]

The opposition

A diagram of the opponents of October in Petrograd would reveal that
they were the exact contrary of the supporters: there was a great number
of political parties and organizations, but few military units, factories or
workers' organizations other than the co-operative movement. The first

group to launch an appeal was the central committee of the peasant soviets, which the Socialist Revolutionaries controlled: 'The Petrograd Soviet promises peace, bread and land, but it is a lie, for it will only bring civil war, monarchy and poverty.' The Mensheviks of the Petrograd Soviet followed, stating that the Bolsheviks had acted behind the workers' backs; and the Menshevik-Defensists and Menshevik-Internationalists also talked of 'a military conspiracy' while the socialist-populists, the Socialist Revolutionaries and Mensheviks of Petrograd issued a joint appeal, followed by the Unitarists (350 supporters). The council of the Republic in turn appealed to the population to rally round the Committee for the Salvation of the Nation and the Revolution which, housed in the city *duma*, promised to govern until the constituent assembly had met. It would, it said, have representatives of the congress of soviets, the *duma*, the council of the Republic, the peasant soviets, the Socialist Revolutionary, Social Democrat (Menshevik) and socialist-populist parties, the *Yedinstvo* group, etc., and it issued an appeal to soviets, workers and citizens calling on the population not to serve the new government. The co-operative movement alone responded.

The Kadet party refused to. It believed that, in condemning the Bolshevik coup, the committee for salvation was not being wholehearted, and failed to rule out compromise with the victors of the day. Shingarev said, 'There can be no question of compromise with the Bolsheviks,' when he was summoned by *Vikzhel*, the railwaymen's union, to enter upon negotiations, and he also refused to join in formation of a Democratic Centre such as Tseretelli proposed. The Kadets, having broken with the coalition, and having become the first victims of repression, transferred their activities to the south of the country, meeting there generals Alexeyev, Kornilov and Kaledin who were raising a volunteer army against the Bolsheviks.

Resolutions of hostility to the coup were rare from workers and soldiers – only from the state paper-works, the urban electricity stations who had split at the assembly of civil servants, with the cardboard and printing workers following, and then the typographers, who rallied all defenders of the liberty of the press. By contrast, the typically petty-bourgeois organizations were solid in condemning the coup – the clerks, civil servants, administrative assistants on the Murmansk–Nikolayevsky railways, bank-clerks, municipal employees, land committees, union of town councils, employees of the naval construction and military department offices, the Deka factory, the association of engineers, the judges, the journalists' union, clergy, teachers, professors, 'student youth', engineers of the Nikolayevsky engineering school, students of the civil service school, the girls' schools, the school for NCOs and the united

student association of Petrograd, with eleven of the great institutions of
the city.[81]

The misunderstanding of October

The absolutists of October represented a large part of the army and the
Petrograd workers. Few social organizations supported the revolt, and
only one political party approved it. Conversely, there were no military
units in the opposition to October, and only those trades associated with
the press (paper, cardboard) as well as the majority of petty-bourgeois
institutions and all other political groups except the anarchists. This
demarcation was in fact a misunderstanding of the issue. In its first acts,
the new government displayed that it was more an emanation of the
Bolshevik party than of the soviets, and when it also appeared to be
delivering the streets over to popular institutions and terror, the reversal
of some previous supporters of the régime was immediate. By 26 October
they were declaring themselves 'against the fratricidal strife among
revolutionaries' and wanted 'an end to the terror; the government must
include all tendencies of socialism'. Menshevik-Internationalists,
Unitarists, some of the Socialist Revolutionaries associated with Gorky
in *Novaya Zhizn'* were the standard-bearers for this 'conciliatory' option
which involved the overthrow of the Kerensky government and the
establishment of an authority that was socialist, not merely Bolshevik.
This proposal was supported by the Polish socialist party, the Jewish
social-democratic party (*Bund*), the left Socialist Revolutionaries and it
won 150 votes in the soviet congress, which meant that a substantial
number of the Bolshevik delegates had supported it.

This 'pacific' opposition chose *Znamya Truda*, the anarcho-syndicalist
newspaper, as its mouthpiece, and there were soon several adhesions —
political committees of the armies of the western front, the inter-army
committee, the bureau of the military organizations' soviet attached to the
war ministry, and the association of war-wounded. The workers' organizations that condemned the taking of power by a single party and the
terror were still more numerous: at their head was the soviet of the union
of unions (which was the first to reverse its stance in view of the October
'misunderstanding'), with the soviet of factory committees of the Nevsky
district and the soviet of leather-workers. The working-class districts
and the large factories, which were supposed to be unconditionally
Bolshevik, expressed solidarity with this semi-opposition, and even the
Vyborg district soviet, in the great centre of Bolshevism, sent out a
unitarist appeal expressly signed by Bolsheviks, Socialist Revolutionaries
and Menshevik Social Democrats. It was similar at a meeting of the

workers of the munitions factories, Arsenal, Putilov, Reikhel, Atlas and Vurgunin works, the port of Petrograd, the all-Russian union of clerks and workers on the waterways, which blamed the Bolshevik chiefs in Petrograd for 'irresponsibility'.[82]

Leadership of this pacific opposition then passed from political to labour organizations, especially the railwaymen's union, *Vikzhel*. It 'refuses to join a fratricidal combat' and demanded a conference of all socialists. The great success of *Vikzhel* was to rally support both from Mensheviks and the new Bolshevik *TsIK*. The latter insisted, as a pre-condition, that Lenin and Trotsky should remain in the government, at its head, and in exchange the Mensheviks wanted dissolution of the *PVRK*, on which they blamed the terror, and transfer of the public order service to the municipal *duma*. The *PVRK* was the real power, and this demand caused a rupture, followed immediately by the resignation of eleven members of the new government, all of them Bolshevik, as well as five members of the party's central committee – Kamenev, Rykov, Zinoviev, Ryazanov and Nogin. Once more, in October as in July, both before and after the seizure of power, there were two antagonistic concepts of Bolshevism within the party, and party discipline appeared to be mythical. For the first time, it seemed too that soviet power, even if the soviets were Bolshevik, was mythical. The Revolution in future knew only the authority of leaders – Lenin, Sverdlov, Trotsky, Stalin. This was based directly on popular terror.[83]

4 The Bolsheviks and terror

The initial gestures of the new régime had symbolic importance, for sometimes they dictated future decisions and attitudes, and opted in an irreversible way. In this respect, the first acts of the October victors are the more significant because, for a few days, they stemmed not from Bolshevik leadership, which was occupied in having congress vote for the seizure of power and the appointment of people's commissars, but rather from members of the *PVRK* who were, except in Antonov-Ovseyenko's and Podvoysky's cases, humble militants, the NCOs of the revolutionary army. These men were a part of the insurgent masses as much as of the Bolshevik party, and their acts revealed the masses' will rather than decisions of the central committee or party bodies.

On the evening of 26 October, before Lenin had been made president of the soviet of people's commissars, and before he had adopted his Decrees on Peace and Land, the members of the *PVRK* closed down seven bourgeois newspapers, confiscated socialist pamphlets condemning the rising, established their own control of the wireless and telegraphs, made a plan to requisition empty offices and dwellings, effected their right to requisition cars and ordered shops to open. Armed groups independent of the *PVRK* also occupied the city *duma*, all of these measures, as well as operational orders, being taken in the few hours that followed the legitimation of the seizure of power, the vote of the second congress – i.e. during the day of 26 October, after 3.00 a.m.[84]

Contrary to legend, the suppression of the bourgeois press and the Socialist Revolutionary news-sheets came not from Lenin or the Bolshevik leadership; like pogroms, these acts were prompted by the public, in this case rebellious popular elements, and their rising bureaucrats, whether Bolshevik or not. They acted spontaneously in the sense of the wishes they had expressed just after the Kornilov Putsch.[85] Of course, neither Lenin nor the Bolshevik party made a single gesture to restore the liberty of the press. The decree that was signed a few days later even left the possibility of all kinds of interpretations, and not one of the Bolshevik leaders, as such, was really responsible for these acts. It was the same with violence, and with the requisitioning undertaken against private individuals. The district committees simply responded to the impatient badly-housed, and acted in quite imaginative ways, as in the division of houses.[86] It is significant that both the first Bolshevik film and the first anti-Bolshevik one made in 1918 should have chosen not the Decree on Peace or Land as their theme but rather the requisitioning of dwellings. It was traumatic for the bourgeoisie, large or small, for they identified Bolshevism with rapine and theft. Bolshevism, before being blamed for dissolution of morality and perversion of youth, was accused of breaking up the home. This it owed to measures which had come not from the leadership but from the populace of the districts.[87]

The fact is that the Bolshevik leaders did no more to stop such acts than they had done to save the liberty of the opposition press. In Russia, society both at the top and the bottom had never known tolerance or practised liberty, and, as in the France of 1789–93, the rapid political and cultural upheaval allowed men to wrap a cloak of theory around the violence, and to identify or suppress as enemies of the people who opposed the new leaders, i.e. the Bolsheviks, as they were collectively known. But the true Bolsheviks, the militants and the party leaders, in their anxiety to identify with the people, were different from other revolutionaries in that they abandoned the traditional role of politicians, that of arbitrating and interceding for the popular will, and thus neutralizing it irreversibly. To retain power alone they identified with that will, and separated from the 'republic of party militants'.[88]

In such circumstances there was no stopping the rise of terror except, for a brief space, when tactical necessity supervened for the top or the base of the apparatus of state, 'to avoid frightening people, and to get support'. The Civil War was an occasion for particularly feverish terror, but terror went on both before and after foreign intervention, both when there was Civil War and when there was not. It was a permanent feature, and, in Soviet Russia as elsewhere, it defined the 'state of emergency'. The *Cheka* in its early days illustrated the link between the terror and the new régime.[89] Its establishment, as early as 10 December 1917, was an act from above, a decree: the régime was setting up its police. The task of organizing it, however, went to the local soviets, the local bodies alone had rights of policing. In the preceding chapter it has been shown how such bodies were set up, who sat on them, and what the structure of power was: the local bodies acted more as a popular authority than as an expression of Bolshevik power. However, the Bolsheviks did not act against their abuses, rather the reverse, for Lenin protested to Zinoviev on hearing that 'the Petrograd *Cheka* has restrained the workers' when, after the assassination of Volodarsky, they wanted to start a mass terror; he said, 'I firmly protest — we are compromising ourselves, for though we do not hesitate, in our resolutions, to threaten mass terror to the soviets of deputies, when we actually have to do it, we restrain the revolutionary initiative of the masses, even though it is quite justified. It must not be — the terrorists will regård us as sob-sisters. We must encourage the energy and the popular nature of terror, especially in Petrograd, where the example has to be decisive' (26 June 1918).[90] Terror, with such encouragement from the leadership, could be unleashed to give free range to pent-up resentment and energy. Since the Revolution was threatened, the leaders could have a clean conscience, and, like leaders elsewhere, they themselves kept clean hands, and so could feel that the masses' doings had a legitimacy deriving from the historical process.

None the less, contrary to legend, the terror was clearly no deviation, a decline of standards relative to some idyllic policy or era. From the start, it struck at bourgeois, socialist militants, anarchists, non-party people, peasants and workers alike. The terror was not merely a 'necessity' prompted by circumstances, i.e. the anti-Bolshevik movement, because it emerged in October, and executions began before the Civil War. The terror was not solely the doing of the Bolshevik leaders, however, and it came up from the depths; only, at the same time, and in a way that their political rivals had foreseen, the Bolshevik leaders showed their predisposition to take it over and encourage it, since it reinforced their control of the state. By early 1918, persecution of anarchists came from Bolshevik circles, and them alone. Soon it was the same with non-Bolshevik militants, who were regarded as accomplices of the soviets' enemies. Terror struck also at non-militants, officers and peasants. When the anti-Bolshevik movement began, i.e. opposition to the form of popular power instituted in October, repression fell with a fury that only increased year in, year out. All opposition was destroyed. Melgunov, analysing the reports of Latsis, an early *Cheka* leader, has composed an impressive picture of the executions in 1918–23 – a forgotten document, reproduced in *Terror under Lenin*.

The régime's practice of terror was not of course its only definition: the positive side has been shown in chapters 6 and 7. Besides, terror modified as the years passed. By the later 1920s the power-structure had become plebeian enough for the leaders to be able to take less account of pressure from below, and the emerging elements allowed the disposing of incompetents, *spetsy*, and the institution of purges, deportations of large numbers of people, a circulation of the ruling elements, all of which, in Stalin's time, became Bolshevik, while at the top Stalin eliminated his rivals. The start of the war in 1941 apparently marks the end of this twin-centred terror, for from then on it was a matter for the top of the state administration alone; and this too was softened by the Twentieth Congress.

Appendix: October in the provincial towns and the army

If we examine the reactions of the provinces to the insurrection in Petrograd, several models of response can, as John Keep has shown, be constructed.[91]

1   Towns and regions with an ancient working-class tradition, and a militant one, with a working class that was relatively homogeneous (mining, metallurgy, textiles) such as Inanovo-Voznesensk, or Kostroma, or the Urals mining towns Chelyabinsk, Perm and Ufa, gave the Bolsheviks considerable preponderance; in the Urals alone, they had the majority in 88 out of the 145 soviets. Where they lacked a majority, the factory committees were more active, and more radical, than the soviets. In these areas, the October Revolution was translated into a simple change of majority in the democratic tradition. When the new revolutionary bodies were set up – committees of popular authority, equivalent to the *PVRK*, the Mensheviks, Socialist Revolutionaries and Maximalists were included, and even Menshevik Defensists. This situation did not last, for the non-Bolshevik elements soon became decorations, with no more real usefulness once it seemed clear that the opposition was offering no more resistance, either in Petrograd or Moscow, and they were rapidly expelled from the committees. The

October victory had been that of advanced democracy, and once it had been achieved, the Revolution again became a matter for the Bolsheviks.

2   In the great commercial and industrial centres such as Kazan, Samara, Saratov, Nizhny Novgorod and the like, which were socially less homogeneous and had been swollen with refugees, workers established professional categories that were clearly distinguishable – factory workers, small-workshop workers, railwaymen, etc. – and these were not uniformly radicalized. The soviets were not as greatly Bolshevized, and retained their Menshevik-Socialist Revolutionary majority, as at Nizhny Novgorod. A pro-Bolshevik counter-balancing power would then be established, frequently on the basis of factory committees or (as in Kazan) the garrison. After the October events, there would sometimes be a fight, which the counter-balancing power would win. A place was left for the losers on the revolutionary committees, since the local powers remained faithful to the socialist tradition of unity and usually the Bolsheviks supervised the running of the town, without taking all power for themselves even if they had a majority. It was only much later that the minorities were expelled.

3   In medium-sized towns, which were industrially less developed than the preceding ones, and were agricultural centres as much as commercial ones, with a strongly-felt rural presence all around – such as Kursk, Voronezh, Oryol, Tambov, the Siberian towns – the initiative was often taken by the non-Bolshevik radicals, usually left Socialist Revolutionaries. The Bolsheviks would play a part that bore no relation to their numerical strength in representative bodies. In the Voronezh Soviet, for instance, they had 24 out of between 120 and 140 members, 4 out of 45 members of the soviet's executive committee, but 2 out of 6 in the presidium. When the assembly of the soviet decided to set up an anti-Bolshevik committee of public safety, soldiers stepped in and the executive committee was changed. When the committee of public safety resisted, as in Kaluga, the Bolsheviks would summon elements from outside to 'normalize' the situation.

Conclusion

There have been, in the historiography of October, two opposing sides. To some, such as Fainsod, the October Revolution was a *coup d'état* that succeeded because of the Bolshevik party's discipline: in the void that was created when the Provisional Government degenerated, in which, as Schapiro says, any organized group could have seized power, that which was best-constituted, Lenin's, was able, as Ulam writes, to seize power 'on the wing'. Moreover, through its apparatus, the party was then able to keep power to itself for ever.

Thus, the Revolution is presented as a kind of historical accident: as Robert Daniels has remarked, the point was and is made that the Bolsheviks had against them the peasants, the front soldiers, the civil servants, and lacked all popular support in the towns. In so far as they had any such support, W. H. Chamberlin said, they obtained it not because of their ideas and programme but because the country was in 'abnormal circumstances' created by war and defeat.[1] According to these writers, therefore, the October Revolution could not be explained by 'the logic of history' or the will of Russia; it was a consequence of the Bolshevik leaders' abilities, and the incompetence or frivolity of their opponents – a tragic twist of fate.

Soviet historians who have tried, on the contrary, to show that Bolshevism had legitimacy behind its seizure of power, have demonstrated the reverse. They state that at every stage of its development, Russian society was corresponding to the Marxist model, and that the development of capitalism led naturally to the failure of all the régimes and inevitably produced the victory of the proletariat, through the activities of its vanguard, the Bolshevik party. Thus the Bolshevik victory in October was logical, scientifically predictable, and an historical necessity; it occurred at the time it did because the party was true to the arguments and the interpretations of its founder. Quite consequentially, it became an

268

essential task of Soviet historiography to demonstrate that Lenin had been right: in its latest official version, Mints's, a straight line is established for the Revolution from February to October, studded with the activities of the Bolshevik party, which guided the masses, who finally adhered to it because of the deeds of its heroic militants.[2]

My own work is not determined by questions of historical legitimacy; but the interpretations that I have suggested make considerable corrections to the arguments of both sides, especially as far as the conditions for the change of régime are concerned. What I found here confirmed the relationship between war and Revolution that I identified in the first volume, and also demonstrates the failure of the February régime. I hope to have clarified the problems posed in the introduction – the nature of the events of October, the causes of the Stalin terror, and the contrast between the centralized organization of present-day Soviet society and the extraordinary upheavals of Russia in 1917.

1 The significance of the October Rising

Before October 1917 the discipline of the Bolshevik party was an act of faith, not a palpable reality. Rabinovitch has shown this for the July Days, and Robert Daniels for the October Days. There was a clear contest in the party's leadership, between Kamenev's line and Lenin's; the lengthy conflict between Trotskyists and Stalinists over the ultimate destiny of the Revolution concealed this other conflict which was just as important, and concerned the relationship between the Communist party and society. During the Revolution, there was no other protagonist, except perhaps the Menshevik Tseretelli, who exercised as much influence in matters of theory as the leaders of these two tendencies – not Stalin, not Sverdlov, and not Trotsky. The first divergence between Kamenev and Lenin started over tactics to be used as regards the dual-power system, and the divergences carried on over the role of the soviets. Kamenev tended to regard the soviets of workers', soldiers' and peasants' deputies as the parliament of democracy, and he was convinced that the Bolsheviks would inevitably win a majority in them; he therefore wished the principle of majority rule to be scrupulously respected within the soviets. Lenin disliked this 'revolutionary legalism'. An appeal to violence, through pacific demonstrations – and later, after June, armed ones – against the representative majority seemed to him quite legitimate inasmuch as the representatives, once they had been elected, no longer expressed the grass-roots will. In any case, it would strengthen the party's position if their hand were forced. Lenin took the same attitude towards the first congress of soviets, where he claimed power for the Bolsheviks, although at the time they had only a small minority. It is notable that his position did not change even when the Bolsheviks won a majority in the soviets, feeling that violence against his own majority could only strengthen the party's power, since it ruled out any of the parliamentary compromising that could have discredited it.

Kamenev not only judged that violence and insurrection were risky; his democratic susceptibilities were shocked by Lenin's ideas. At bottom, he was against any single-party dictatorship, and from this point of view he was closer to the Menshevik Martov than to Lenin. Lenin did not even pose as a democrat: he was of 'the old party' and even proposed to give up the label and call it communist rather than social-democrat. Before October, he remained democratic, but in a rather different way, for his actions were inspired by a wish to identify a majority of sailors, soldiers, and committees against a majority representation that might even be soviet or Bolshevik but would also be inclined to compromises. Here, Sverdlov and Bukharin were closer to Lenin, while Trotsky and Zinoviev tended towards Kamenev. When, at the centre of the party, the problem came up in these terms, it was Stalin who proposed a vote.

The divergence between Kamenev and Lenin also stemmed from theoretical considerations that went back some way. To Kamenev, the preconditions of socialism had not been fulfilled in Russia, and a seizure of power by the Bolsheviks seemed to him inopportune, since the party would be unable to construct real socialism and would therefore be discredited. This reasoning, which the Mensheviks and Socialist Revolutionaries had suggested in February 1917, struck Lenin as absurd and anachronistic. He mocked Kamenev and his allies as 'Old Bolsheviks': at any time, he said, there could be revolution in Germany, and the Russian experiment could be based on that. This act of faith, to Lenin a certainty, explains something of the scarcely democratic declaration he made in September 1917, that 'If the party takes power, no one will ever be able to depose it'. The seizure of power and the establishment of truly revolutionary action seemed to him to be so imminent, and so exalting, that some effort ought to be made to adapt ideas and principles.

After October, with Lenin having been proved right twice already – in taking power for his party, and it alone – the Bolsheviks forgot their democratic scruples and, within the party, Lenin was able to act still more independently. The coup by the *PVRK* had been his work alone, and there is no indication that he consulted anyone else in modifying the agrarian programme that had been worked out by the Bolsheviks who had been given that responsibility, for the Decree on Land. There is also no sign that he was ever elected or appointed president of the *PVRK*, although this did not stop him from signing an order without a co-signatory, which was not the usual way. These relatively significant actions in the first hour of the Revolution prefigured the start of a dictatorship of opinion within the party; an inevitable consequence of this was that there was greater discipline in the working of the party – which helped it retain and strengthen its power later on, but before October had been too illusory to be counted as a serious explanation of the success of the rising. These explanations must be sought elsewhere.

Since 1917 the revolutionary movement had been judged, in political and historical tradition, in terms of the strength of the Bolshevik party as shown by the number of its delegates and militants. This argument puts both the supporters and the enemies of October in an iron ring: supporters had to justify the seizure of power 'by a small number of people' and therefore had to show that town and country, *muzhiks* and Kirghiz, any radical at all, were Bolshevik. Conversely, enemies of October insisted on the 'passivity' of most people, which had been offered as an explanation for the seizure of power by a small number. But in 1917 there was almost perpetual movement – hardly 'passivity'.

It is true that, viewed from within the political parties and in the militants' writings and speeches, the numerical relationship is very important. Political parties were always counting their troops, feeling their pulse and gauging their mood. To them, this was a matter of fact, and the rise in the Bolsheviks' effective strength was unquestionably seen as an indication of the strength of the revolutionary movement. But to us, with the advantage of hindsight, the indication may well appear less reliable. It does not, for instance, reveal the degree of revolutionary change in the countryside. In June, again, when Lenin's party was still very small, the mobs none the less carried Bolshevik slogans; and in October, debates within the party reveal that, in some cases, 'the spirit was Bolshevik where the party did not exist, and . . . where the party does exist, its spirit is sometimes not combative'. These were sincere enough remarks: what is their weight? The Bolsheviks, themselves constantly dealing in figures, in fact contributed to the legend of their own weakness, which they regarded as a reflection of the revolutionary movement's own weakness: hence the credit they gave to the putschist thesis and the insurrection. 'The Russians are said to be surrendering in droves, and the soldiers to be running away in confusion; it is all said to be the outcome of Bolshevik-inspired disorganization at the front, but that is to do us too much honour' – Stalin's judgment and commentary, to which he added an explanation: 'No single political party could obtain such results. We are 200,000, and 200,000 people could not destroy an army of 20,000,000 by its influence alone.'[3] How then are we to relate the destruction of the army, the movement in town and country, the explosion of the nationality question and, at the same time, the installation of the Bolsheviks, alone, in power some weeks later?

In my first volume, when dealing with the relationship of society's aspirations and the policies of the Provisional Government, I suggested that divorce was necessary and the bankruptcy of the February government inevitable. In this volume, the failure of the government can clearly be shown not to have been caused by mistakes of analysis made by the Mensheviks and Socialist Revolutionaries, which in any case were shared with minor differences by most of the Bolshevik leaders, Lenin always apart. The failure stemmed more from general failure: a failure on the part of all who, in normal times, traditionally maintain social relationships, the continuity of authority, the domination of a small number. The failure of such leaders, judges, officers, priests, bureaucrats, came together with a challenging of institutions and a radicalization of opinion and behaviour, largely associated with Bolshevik or anarchist notions; this altered the attitude of the citizenry towards law and of the soldiers towards their commanders. It also produced an institutional vacuum that committees, soviets, trade unions, *rada* and the like filled at once, taking over some of the activities of the state.

In all this the role of political parties, including the Bolsheviks, was not necessarily decisive. They might found the new institutions, and encourage the movement, but they could not stop it. The district committees, for instance, were a creation of the Petrograd Soviet and hence of the parties leading it, but the soviet of district committees was set up at the districts' own initiative, and in the same way many of the factory committees emerged spontaneously. If the Bolsheviks were responsible for co-ordinating this movement by convoking the Petrograd conference of factory committees and also for setting up the soviet it elected, the party then had to apply brakes to this soviet's actions when they began competing with the trade unions.

These institutions, whether or not created by their own people, and whether or not patronized by the parties, always fought for extensions of their own fields and for predominance, regardless of origin and any ideology or party-political affiliation. Like the political parties, the factory committees, the unions and the co-operatives each created an individual theory of state to legitimize their own right to prevail. They fought before October, playing the parties off against each other, while after October the Bolsheviks played one institution off against another. The struggle for control of the apparatus, or bureaucratization, was, before October, the chief form of this fighting.

Before October, these institutions formed a relatively organized whole, a true embryo of the proletarian state, which was politically anonymous and which the parties all tried to dominate through methods of election and bureaucratization. There was, however, not so much conflict as alliance between these two movements, a symbiosis of parties and revolutionary institutions. This benefited the Bolsheviks who, because of the radicalization of opinion, democratically controlled the apparatus of an increasing number of institutions, and could also offer to mediate in cases of conflict. Moreover, the institutions' own ambitions coincided in at least one essential with the Bolsheviks' aims: to survive, they had to break with the Provisional Government, to destroy the old state and replace it. When, after October, the real power passed not to the soviets but to a political party, the Bolsheviks, there was more real opposition among the political parties than in the institutions, even *Vikzhel*, the railwaymen's union, which was strongly Menshevik. The institutions remained united with the new authorities for obvious reasons – they were its constituent elements.

The October rising was thus not solely the act of a political party acting under cover of an institution: 'the soviets acted as a fig-leaf for the Bolshevik party', as has been said. It was a test of strength between a government without a state, and a state without a government.

The victors were also not representatives of a minority, as has been suggested, made up of the big towns and the soldiers of the reserve. In the army the front line showed itself, in the end, as revolutionary as the reserves, and if there was resistance to the tide it came from well-defined military units alone. The relationship of the peasants to October was more complicated. There was no uniform movement, and each part of the countryside responded autonomously, without necessarily an association with the party conflicts or the rise of the revolutionary tide. It was neither coherent nor homogeneous. However it did activate the process of revolution, for the ruin of the rural economy had a direct impact on the soldiers' and workers' attitudes. Among the nationalities, the various movements of 1917, which were at least in appearance more explosive and more varied still than the countryside's, did have a stronger connection with the proletarian movement because the centres of decision involved were constantly concerned with what happened in Petrograd. Depending on distance, relative strength, class-relations, these movements absorbed some of the repressive force of the state, whatever their orientation, whether separatist, social-revolutionary or both at once. Even if these movements tended towards proletarian revolution, as in Latvia, they still were not united with the Russians or integrated into a Bolshevik strategy that was conceived as centralized. The radicalization and Bolshevization of Latvia preceded similar events in Russia, and were stopped only by

German occupation. Then the Lettish riflemen helped the Russian Bolsheviks to seize power, and acted in the spirit of proletarian internationalism even before the *Komintern* had been created.

In the movement which led up to the October victory, with the embryo proletarian state staking its all for survival, the personnel and the participants were thus not necessarily Bolsheviks, or even Russians; the Russian Bolshevik party, being present in all the institutions – sometimes even in non-Russian ones – was the only one able to guarantee both co-ordination and an interim representativity. It gave an overall direction to a movement that was both incoherent and convergent – the will to overthrow the régime. The victory and permanence of October followed from the prior existence of this embryo state, which was not quite separately constituted, but was still already living, together with the existence of centrifugal forces that acted independently of the embryo state and permitted destruction of the old order.

This dispels an apparent contradiction: the October Rising can be seen as a mass movement although only a small number took part in it, for the Bolsheviks were able, later, to remain the only masters of the state. Lenin's gambles and miniature coups in taking the institutions into the charge of a single party made this seem correct and obvious, but the phenomenon was happening independently of deliberate action by the party, and was the doing of a state apparatus that was more zealous still than the Bolsheviks. The process of institutional bureaucratization then went ahead towards Bolshevism, and added its effects, to cement the radicalization (see chapter 7).

Since before October, activists of all leanings had been preparing to suspend democratic freedoms: indeed, from suspension to final abolition, they needed only follow the example of the 'democratic' socialists who suppressed the Bolshevik press after the July Days. Within the Bolshevik party, the victors had never claimed to be particularly democratic, but in any event, for the apparatus of state, which was not necessarily Bolshevik, there could be no question of 'democratic liberties' being used as a pretext to weaken or shake the state, or have it change hands. For this apparatus of state the matter was one not of morality, or even of politics, but of simple survival. It therefore kept up its guard. In Russia, it was not even necessary to have Bolshevism in October to lose a certain concept of democracy.

2 October and the origins of Stalinism

An irreversible result of October was that the leaders' world changed. But this change did not simply mean, as has been suggested, that power was transferred to Bolshevik hands and to the Bolsheviks' 'historic leaders', for, together with them, other new holders of powers formed a heterogeneous social grouping. These new elements were of popular origin, emerging essentially from the factory or the army; some of them were quite urbanized, but others were young people, born in the countryside. The cultural difference and the age-gap between these militants or militiamen and their superiors in the various bodies of the Soviet state (soviets, party committees, etc.) for the moment gave the leading Bolsheviks an unquestioned ascendancy. It is the ambiguity of status of the members of the new state apparatus that accounts for the variation in figures given for Bolshevik strength. It appears to have been 24,000 in February 1917, while Sverdlov talked of 400,000 a week before October, and then of 300,000 at the seventh congress four months later. Another calculation showed 115,000.

More significant is comparison of the number of Bolsheviks of 1917 who remained in the party after the Revolution. There had been 24,000, and the figure went to 12,000 in 1922 and 8,000 in 1927; whereas there were already 600,000 party members in 1920. Clearly, there was a rapid evaporation of the early Bolsheviks, who were submerged by new members, exerting pressure from bottom to top, aiming at posts occupied by the old Bolsheviks on the one side, and the *spetsy* on the other, whom the leadership had had to call in to train the new communists. Gradually the new officials took over from the *spetsy* and traditional Bolsheviks, the aristocracy and Old Guard of politics, who fell and soon struck the rising classes, impatient for promotion, as just as feeble as the old intelligentsia from whom they had themselves separated early in the century. The political impact on the purges is obvious: and their social function was to assist the promotion of neo-Bolsheviks of popular origin in great numbers. First these new men were from the towns; later the majority were of rural origin.

This dual transfer of power, in and after 1917, had repercussions on a much wider movement that had begun at the end of the nineteenth century and grown with the war and the Civil War: the mass migration that industrialization and the opening of hostilities had brought, and that ended in a great increase of the urban population in a short space. The Russian village was shifted to army and town, submerging the old urbanized elements, the older practitioners of ancient social conflicts. They brought to political and social relations a violence that hitherto had existed only in the countryside. It expressed a difference that in Russia was greater than elsewhere, between the immense backwardness of the poor and the refined civilization of the minority. Violence in 1917 successively struck at officers, large landowners, *kulaks*, urban authorities, political opponents at grass-roots level, and then those at the top. To begin with the violence was individual, started by men of rural origin, but in the 1920s they acted in the name of the state. The Bolshevik leaders, in order to 'be close to the masses' and to keep power, did not condemn this: the October Rising institutionalized and legitimized it. In the so-called Stalin era, the advent of which was obvious even in 1917, the reversal occurred as it did elsewhere in Europe, with violence being a sign of legitimate power. In Russia, however, the social significance of the violence was different.

The dual transfer of power was also shown in what happened as regards the measures affecting women and the family. To begin with, the Bolshevik intelligentsia's authority was unchallenged, and the ideas of Alexandra Kollontai, who was of upper middle-class origin, prevailed. Measures were taken that frequently went further than the new leaders imagined or desired. The people had never spontaneously emancipated women in the Revolution, though they had spontaneously seized land or factory. The double social and sexual emancipation of women was carried out by the Bolsheviks alone. There was a reaction when popular elements intervened massively at the head of the state: the men did not mean to forfeit, in their homes, the power that they had just acquired in the towns, and equally, women of the people rejected a liberty which, at their stage of cultural development, meant insecurity rather than emancipation. The considerable number of non-Russians at the base of the leading institutions sealed the fate of the 'objective alliance of kaftan and blouse'. Exceptional, and unique, measures of social equality were taken, and gave the leaders a clean conscience even when some of them felt that the order of family life was the surest guarantee of a solid state.

The proletarianization of the apparatus, the slow subversion of socialist and libertarian ideas by traditionalism acted against women's emancipation, which had been prompted by the avant-garde or the intelligentsia. It was the same in art and culture: academicism triumphed in the 1920s[4] and later traditionalism also accounted for a revival of anti-semitism. The problem of liberty and its suppression thus resulted from a convergence of two movements.

A   First was a movement from above, associated with the identification of a political party with a class, which in turn had been defined as the historically emergent one. When this party made centralism and organization its reason for existence, any minority that would not join with it was automatically anti-historical, counter-revolutionary, and the control that was the obverse of all organization necessarily made for the destruction of any spontaneity in social life.

B Second was a movement from below which, changing the social structure of the new authority, also caused a subversion of fundamental principles of the revolutionary ideology. The peasant, traditionalist mentality slowly succeeded the bourgeois cast of mind, of which the Bolsheviks were an expression, and rejected any difference and cultural gap as inequality and abnormality. Educated people were the last possessors of a visible capital, their culture, and they lost the opportunity of exploiting it very far. Liberty of thought counted as oppression if it was not available to others, the poor. The same ostracism soon affected the avant-garde, whether in art or in social matters.

This dual movement, though feeble and scarcely detectable to start with, proceeded by fits and starts. In 1917 and just after it, the suppression of liberty came more from below than above, while revolutionary creation came more from above than below. Then the two came together. Their association marked the shift of the Revolution to its second, so-called Stalinist, phase, in so far as the personality of Lenin's successor aptly symbolized it all — plebeian, rough, anonymous. The transformation of Soviet society could be explained less in terms of 'Bolshevik absolutism' than by the evolution of the social structure of power. (This dual movement, the vicissitudes in the rise of Stalin to the top of the party structure, took on an almost epic quality, as is well-displayed in the works of Deutscher, Souvarine and others.)

3 The new society

The Revolution of October proclaimed Soviet power, workers' control, land to the peasants, the right of self-determination for peoples. In fact, the old state had declined before the insurrection happened, and October made for the triumph of a popular state that already had most of the attributes of a state — armed forces, administrative personnel, regulations and methods. The state lacked the sanction that seizure of power and the violent occupation of strategic places could give, and Lenin succeeded in imposing this on colleagues who had entertained a parliamentary vision of the conquest of power.[5]

The decrees also merely registered in part a reality that had already happened. However, they did create a new situation, in that they legalized measures taken by workers and peasants and extended their application all over the country.[6] They represented a second aspect of the transfer of authority rather than a true change in the method of production, for, in the countryside, even though the landowner had disappeared and the committee had taken his place, life was still much the same. Town and state were still suspect, and there was latent or open hostility to them. The year 1917 was not a great turning-point as Stalin's collectivization was. In the factories the bosses had disappeared as the landowner had done, and again a committee took over, but by December 1917 the state started to supervise its composition, activities, and the factory's output. For anyone not involved in such bodies, the change was in the relationship to the new authority, and in the régime's social measures, which in spirit met the aspirations of the workers for social insurance, insurance against accident, protection for working women and for children, unemployment pay, etc. But the economic crisis and the sabotage of industry by the great capitalists, with the horrors of Civil War, prevented workers from truly benefiting from the change, even partial, that had come with the alteration of their status. They left the factories. Of course, they might also, now, enter the structure of the new authority, but in essence, for those who remained, factories remained factories and workers remained workers. Efforts at self-management went on and on.

Paradoxically, before forced collectivization and industrialization in the Stalin era, it was relations between Russians and non-Russians that, in a gigantic shift of social power, most durably marked the country's future. The nationalities that sought independence got it only against the régime's will. The Finnish case was a good example of this: it was enough for a small nucleus of Finns talking 'in the name of the Finnish working class' to declare for 'proletarian unity of the Russian and Finnish peoples' for the independence of Finland, which the Lenin government had recognized a few weeks earlier, to be equated with the bourgeois counter-revolution and combated as such. The Finns won, partly because of foreign intervention, but neither the Ukrainians nor the Georgians nor any other people that had imagined it would benefit from the decree on self-determination benefited in reality. Although this decree was not even once applied, relations between the nationalities and the Russians or the new Soviet state did change. The change affected equally the individual status of a minority and the collective status of a nationality.

The practices of the Bolshevik party before 1917 (as with the Mensheviks and Socialist Revolutionaries) had shown that, within a revolutionary organization, a Jew was not simply a Jew nor a Georgian a Georgian. It was also clear that, in these organizations, there could equally well be a social-democratic party for Jews — the *Bund* — or a Ukrainian Social Revolutionary party. A member of a minority could operate in a socialist organization of the minority, or, as an individual, in any organization he liked. This continued as a model. After 1917 the harmonization of the nationalities with the Soviet system caused many people from them to be brought into the structure of the state. Thereafter they figured, no longer as individual militants in the Bolshevik party, as Stalin and Trotsky had done, but increasingly as communists representing their own nationality within the Soviet state.

It seemed in 1917 that the state apparatus had passed from Russian to non-Russian hands, but though this was partly the case at the top, it was not at all the case at the base, for the proletarianization of the apparatus counted, at first, in the Russians' favour. Latterly, given that there was a decline in the number of people of minority origin in the Russian Communist party, the supply of non-Russians to the top of the apparatus began to dry up, and the pressures of medium-level officials towards the top came, almost completely, to favour the Russian element. This explains why, in the Presidium and the Politbureau, from 1917 to 1919, Russians and non-Russians were equal in number, while later, gradually, the proportion of non-Russians went down. By the later 1920s they were only half of the Russians' members, and they are still less numerous, in proportion, today.

For the minorities, these developments were compensated by the influx of delegates from the Republics who were simultaneously elected to the federal bodies of the Soviet state and to the government of their own nationalities. Only the Jews felt these changes negatively and unilaterally because their participation in government dried up both at the top of the communist apparatus, as happened with other minorities, and at the base, since they did not have their own territory; and even the ephemeral creation of Birobidzhan did not solve this. The Jews were gradually eliminated from the bodies of the state, and this was assisted, where required, by the latent anti-semitism of new leading groups that came from barely urbanized elements, and by the ambiguity of the Leninist and Stalinist view of the 'Jewish nation'. Minorities of other nationalities could, by contrast, have a feeling of true promotion, for such integration enabled many individuals to set off to conquer the state and its honours. For nationalities that were conscious of a collective identity, such as Georgians, Baltic peoples, Ukrainians, there was still frustration, and a feeling of collective alienation, even though it was limited by the participation of an increasing number of individuals of the nationality in the management of the state, and by the policy of reviving languages and cultures.

Does all this mean that, with these nationalities, co-habitation in the same state will, in the long run, alter their natures, and allow a supranational Soviet consciousness to emerge? Will it be possible to create a single Soviet people in a Union where mixed marriages are rare, racialist reactions barely controlled and the advance of minorities is reviving Great-Russian chauvinism?[7] The Soviet leaders believe so, and stress that, in the USSR, the question of nationalities is 'a family affair'. This expression having been also applied to the People's Democracies, we may say that, after regenerating, creating, suppressing and re-creating the nationalities, the Soviet leadership have an interest, from now on, in returning, at least in this matter, to the Marxist sources.[8]

4 The USSR and Europe: similarities and differences

After 1917, the USSR showed at once an original situation, which accounts for certain individual choices and attitudes (in family policy, or as regards the nationalities) and also a situation that had factors similar to those in Europe as a whole, for instance, the political leaders' mission to popularize their programme rather than to apply a programme already popular. To account for the blackest aspects of the Stalin era, and to advance beyond the criticism involving 'cult of personality', there are various interpretations – those that stress the specificity (Elleinstein's) and others that insist on the 'deviations' in choice – i.e., as Bettelheim would have it, from the ideal line of Lenin, or from an imaginary ideal line, as Althusser argues.[9]

These in some ways mutually contradictory explanations have the common feature (which is paradoxical, given that they are all Marxist) that they ignore the class structure of the apparatus of state that was set up in 1917, and the evolution of it – for it never allows the workers themselves to speak, only those who do so on their behalf. These explanations do not, in other words, examine the problem of power, its foundations and its legitimacy. This work has been intended to meet this question; and it has been designed to provoke reflection on the features of our own times, for the history of the USSR is not a unique, and now ended, past, but is a variable in a model of development that is common to all countries which, in a revolution, change their system of government.

Documents

Translator's note: The French original (pp. 449–69) contains several documents printed as appendices. Only those that are directly referred to in the text have been translated into English, below.

1 Peasants answer an inquiry (Province of Ryazan) (*Ek. Pol.* (601) III, pp. 386–7)

We, undersigned, peasants of the Knyazhevskaya *volost*, having been summoned by the chairman of the *volost* land committee to a general assembly where the answers to be made to the questionnaire presented by the Great Agrarian Committee were to be discussed, have unanimously replied as follows:

1 Which procedure is more suitable in partition of the land: by individuals or by households?

Resolution: By household, among all inhabitants.

2 Are women to be excluded from distribution, or should land be partitioned among men and women alike?

Resolution: Distribution for all, without exception – men, women and children.

3 Should land be distributed to all who are registered in the *obshchestvo* or only to those who, at the moment, work in it?

Resolution: Distribution among all *obshchestvo* members, except temporary residents.

4 How is it more just to distribute the land – should only peasants have some, or should any inhabitant prepared to work it?

Resolution: All inhabitants anxious to work it should have it.

5 Should a reserve of land be kept for the coming generation, or should all land be given out?

Resolution: No land reserve should be set up, but there should be a revision of distribution every twelve years.

6 Is it desirable to divide up the land in lots of ten *desyatins* or more?

Resolution: Seize it and divide it up equally among all.

7 Should land go to the workers with or without indemnity?

Resolution: no indemnity.

8 If without indemnity, who should pay the debts of the land banks, whose bonds are mainly in foreign hands?

Resolution: The government should find the means to pay them off.

9 What should be done in the case of those who bought their land in the last few years, often at very high prices?

Resolution: It should be seized without indemnity.

10 What is the most desirable form of soil-utilization, by household or by commune?

Resolution: Household.

11 What should be done about enclaves outside the commune?

Resolution: Have the residents transfer if they want to, with considerable help from the government.

12 In what order and to whom should the land thus divided by distributed?

Resolution: To all who need it.

13 As in the *volost* there is too little land, what should be done for those who will not have enough?

Resolution: Have them transfer to non-occupied land.

14 If there is to be a transfer of population, in what order should it occur?

Resolution: For a proper transfer to be manageable, there must be considerable government assistance.

15 Once the working people have been given the land, all kinds of enterprises that supply seed, potato flour and bulls will disappear. How should these be acquired in the future?

Resolution: In every district there should be a kind of centre where the peasants can acquire what they need.

2 Resolution of the Commission of the All-Russian Conference of Factory Committees on relations between factory committees and trade unions, 20 October 1917 (*Okt. Rev. i. Fabzavkomy*, 2. *Nakanune Okt.* (Moscow, 1927), p. 193).

1 The existence of factory and works committees is essential (a) for control of the bases of labour and the organization of an internal order in the factory, and (b) for control of production (unanimously adopted).

2 Each council (soviet) of factory committees will be divided into sections according to branch of production (unanimous).

3 The control of working conditions must be carried on under the direction of the trade unions (majority, one vote against).

4 Each section, with its agreement, may be validated by the corresponding section of the trade union. It will become the factory-committee section of this (adopted by six votes to three).

5 The conference will elect a centre of factory committees that will be the recognized department for regulation of production and workers' control with the all-Russian soviet of trade unions and the council of trade unions (five votes for,

three against, one abstention).

6 Similar arrangements will be made as regards relations between the local councils of factory committees and the local councils of trade unions (six for, three against). The overall resolution received seven votes, with two against: commission members Amosov, Deryshev, Ukhta, Vorobieva, Buryshkin, Levin, Petrovsky, Linkov and Yuriev.

3 Plan for the extension of the Red Guard, adopted at a session of the general staff of the Red Guard by the representatives of the Petrograd districts (GAORSS, Lo., 4592, 1, 2, 11 (unpublished))

1 Service in the Red Guard is a compulsory revolutionary service for the workers of Petrograd.

2 Formation of the Red Guard depends on works and factories. It is a matter for the factory committees.

3 All workers recognized to be fit for service may be called up by the factory committee for service with the Red Guard. (Note: this means men who are physically and morally healthy, physically able to bear arms and who may be absolutely trusted.)

4 The formation of armed groups by factory, shop, etc., depends on vigilant and constant control by the factory committee.

5 The number of Red Guards called up by the factory committee in each enterprise will be 20 per cent of the total number of workers there.

6 The Petrograd proletariat consisting of 400,000 men approximately, the Red Guard should contain 800,000 [*recte* 80,000], or 2 corps, 256 detachments of machine-guns, 16 field batteries, and 42 liaison groups.

7 Of this, 12.5 per cent or 10,000 men must be on active service for a whole week, after which they will return to the factory as a reserve. In this way, in two months, the 80,000 men will have carried out their service.

8 The 10,000 Red Guards on active service will be split into two parts: one half (5,000) for defence of the town, which will pay the Guards; the other will be factory reserve, the Red Guards receiving their pay from factory managements or the government.

9 Recruiting of the Red Guard will be undertaken by a committee including three persons elected by the general assembly of the workers, and three members of the factory committee.

10 It is essential that in each factory the list of members of the Red Guard should be well kept up to date, in case it should be necessary to set up a contingent urgently.

4 Discussion with Kerensky (Oxford, 1963) (see *La Quinzaine littéraire*, 15/30 November 1966) by Marc Ferro

The first time he received me, it was with some roughness. 'What do you want to know? I've written it all down.' I insisted, and reminded him of his unhappy fate – once adulated, but now alone, exposed to attacks by enemies who, for fifty years, had used their propaganda apparatus to attack him, on the left for betraying the ideals of the Revolution and, among the *émigrés*, for having acted as a sheath for the Bolshevik sword. He had listened to me standing like a great oak, barring the entrance to his house, but finally his face softened, and he said, 'Well come and sit there.' He took my hand for me to lead him, for, at eighty-six, Kerensky could not see well.

I then told him the marvellous story of his revolutionary youth and his hopes; I reminded him of his Duma speeches. He often interrupted, adding a detail or making a correction, so that soon he was launching off: yes, it was he who had called on the soldiers to demonstrate before the Duma on 27 February 1917, the day of the Petrograd rising. But instead of joining in with the movement, the deputies vacillated, and he and Chkeidze, the Menshevik leader, had had to go out to the demonstrators to greet them in the Duma's name. . . . He was silent as he remembered the scenes I depicted. Suddenly, be brightened when I asked him why the government had not passed more reforms. 'Reforms? In two months we passed more than any other régime. . . . Besides, many of the supposedly Bolshevik reforms were worked out by the Provisional Government.' He enumerated them. 'The bosses wouldn't see how things were, and every time we went ahead, the Bolsheviks accused us of not going far enough, every party tried to outbid us, and no one was happy. Everyone wanted to give orders.'

I asked him, 'Do you think it was a mistake to go on with the war, and not having Lenin arrested, as you were reproached for doing?' He replied, 'I did not want to, and could not have him arrested because we had not set up liberty to knock it down again . . . as to the war, we had to go on with it because the country was against a separate peace.' 'In reality', he went on, 'I made a mistake in accepting the ministry of war. Had I stayed in Petrograd I could have stimulated the other ministers, just as before April I had influenced the government's foreign policy, and got an agreement with the soviet as to war aims . . . but what would have happened to the army?' As he took me round the Oxford lawns which reminded him of the Field of Mars (in Petrograd), he repeated to me what he had told the soldiers to convince them to fight. This fervour, this authority in the tone, and the charm of his voice had conquered all Russia. 'Fifty years later, it is me that Kerensky wishes to conquer,' I thought. 'Let us do as Cachet and Moutet did, and sing together . . . what tune was it . . . the *Chant du Départ* [of the French Revolutionary armies]', and as he struck up the first bars with vigour. I remembered Lenin's jibe – 'the balalaika of the régime'.

'Did you think in April 1917 that Lenin would one day be master of Russia?' 'Certainly not. When the disaster came, the Bolsheviks weren't very popular.' 'The disaster – you mean October?' 'No,' he answered, 'when Nicholas abdicated.' 'Ah,' I said. He went on, 'And Lenin's words made people laugh, in any case. He said that the biggest capitalists should be arrested, and that is not Marxism.' 'How do you account for his success?' I went on. 'Demagogy, the Bolsheviks promised the moon: peace, but they got a civil war; land to the peasants, but the food was taken away; workers' self-management, which didn't last six months; more liberties still, and Lenin abolished them one after the other. Then there was the military plot – Kornilov's rising weakened the government's authority so that the Bolsheviks could strike.' 'The Bolsheviks accuse you of conniving with Kornilov,' I said, and he answered, 'That's quite wrong, the fact is that Kornilov had the right with him, with the generals and the Allies. I could only neutralize him by calling for collaboration. Then he prepared the Putsch . . . I declared I completely trusted him, and waited too long to disengage – maybe from fear of looking ridiculous. In France you had an identical situation [with Salan] but de Gaulle managed to avoid civil war where I didn't.' 'But when Kornilov was beaten, you could no longer rely on the right against the Bolsheviks?' I asked. 'Yes, that's right,' he answered, 'but that is enough.'

The former prime minister does not like to remember the last hours of the *Kerenshchina* – the rising, flight, exile. Up to the last moment he was cheered because he had never had shed blood. 'When I left the Winter Palace, I saw, in large letters, "Down with the Jew Kerensky, Long Live Trotsky",' he chuckled. The time had come for me to go, as it was getting late and I had to take the old man back to his house. He wouldn't go back – 'This way, this way', he said, dragging me towards the lawns that fascinated him, and, as if in a prayer, he said these final words, 'Let us sing the *Chant du Départ* again.'

5 Volin on 'Bolsheviks and Anarchists' (*Golos Truda*, 20–21 October 1917)

The Bolsheviks and the Anarchists are by and large agreed in believing that the Revolution has a considerable chance of changing into a social revolution. They also agree in saying that it is right and necessary for all revolutionary forces to work for this change. They agree in presenting the peasant question, the labour question and all of the great political questions in much the same terms.

But the Bolsheviks and Anarchists disagree broadly speaking on the definition of ways and means towards this social revolution; they are also in disagreement when they define the nature of this revolution, when they consider the future methods of organizing the masses or when they describe the ways and approaches by which the masses will create a new society. . . . Let us briefly look at where this watershed goes.

The Bolsheviks want nationalization of the land – obviously, in other words, that the state (i.e. the government) will take the decisions affecting the countryside. They admit the principle of elections to different political and governmental assemblies with a drawing-up of lists containing their own candidates. They also accept that a constituent assembly should again be elected, with a list to be drawn up for candidates, including those of their own party. Thereby they are presupposing that, parallel to organizations of the non-party masses, there should be, to carry out the Revolution, an organization of those masses who do adhere to a political party. They allow that a political party's taking power will be the first phase of the social revolution – the seizure of power, formally by soviets, but in reality the party. They favour governmental centralization and a social change that would be carried out by a political authority. They wish for central control and decision.

The Anarchists do not want land-nationalization because they are against state intervention, of whatever kind, because in its name there would in effect be a government to act and sort out the agrarian question. They are against any election with 'lists of candidates', for whatever political or governmental institution. They are against constituent assemblies. They are against political parties and organization of the masses in a party. They are against the seizure of power as a specific act sufficient in itself as 'first step' towards the social revolution. They believe that such power, seized by a party, would not in any way be sufficient in itself – as if you only need to touch the feather of a phoenix to accomplish miracles.

The Anarchist idea of power is quite different, and so is the Anarchist view of the start and continuation of social revolution. Anarchists do not see centralization as at all needed for social revolution to be accomplished; even, they think centralization makes it impossible. They are against any leadership from a centre. . . .

In the place of power-taking and central creation, the Anarchists believe that 'the seizure of power' will be carried out without violence, by the simple fact of social revolution; therefore they have a wholly different concept of the making of this revolution.

The organization of workers must, beforehand, be set up everywhere locally, by firms – mines, factories, workshops, railways, post offices, etc. There have to be committees and other institutions set up and freely led by the masses themselves. These bodies will be able to unite quite freely (by towns, districts, provinces) and can join together in soviets set up by the workers themselves. . . . It is the same for organization of the rural masses in hamlets, villages, cantons and then in regional or provincial soviets. The soldiers' network of organization will be the same and they will come together in soviets of soldiers.

The work of these local bodies will be effective, creative and concerted. Its essential goal will be the very task that is these bodies' main reason for existing in the first place – transfer of the country's economic life into the working people's own hands, such that economic life will depend on these local institutions. In a word, there is to be organized expropriation of the means of production, their distribution and reorganization whether with land, coal, minerals, workshops, factories, shops, housing, communications and other elements of economic life.

The great creative work will be the establishment of proper relations between town and country, the organization of output of consumer-goods in harmony with needs.

The concerted intervention of all these non-party workers' organizations, free from affiliation with any specific political group, will be directed towards the transfer of economic activity into their own hands. The process of expropriation will present no problem for bodies that are more or less ready for it, though in some cases it may be carried through with the help of the military elements associated with these bodies.

Such, in brief, is the pattern for preparation and execution of the social revolution. It is that way, and that way alone, that will bring about what can truly be called the dictatorship of the workers. We believe that power is in fact . . . the organized transfer of land and factories and military strength into the hands of workers' organizations, and that this transfer deserves the name of seizure of power. We give to that expression a meaning wholly different from that given it by the political party organizations. Therefore we are against any 'political' seizure of power, as if that power existed on its own purely 'political' terms.

It is only if some obstacle occurred on the road leading to spontaneous workers' organization that the workers' own bodies (and not just a political party) would have to shift it . . . not for the particular ends of a political party or by specifically political methods but for the specific occupation of political power.

Notes

Introduction: the illusions and delusions of revolution

1 Y. Plekhanov, *God na Rodine*, I, p. 26.
2 Quoted in Astrakhan (531), p. 218. On the penetration into and use by the Russian bourgeoisie of Marxism, K. Korsch wrote (1932), 'On the new soil of Russia, bourgeois principles could not be dressed up in their now . . . tattered illusions. . . . To penetrate the east, the rising class needed new ideological trappings, and . . . it was Marxist doctrine that seemed most suitable to give this remarkable service' (K. Korsch, *Marxisme et contre-révolution*, documents chosen and edited by S. Bricianer, Paris, Le Seuil, 1975, pp. 143–4). On Struve's evolution, see R. Pipes, *Struve, Liberal on the Left* (Harvard, 1971).
3 See vol. I, especially chapters 4 and 5.
4 Appeal of the soviet, published in *Izvestiya*, 28 February 1917.
5 Review of the debates in *Arkhiv Oktyabrskoy Revolyutsii* (30), I, p. 67.
6 See chapter 7.
7 On the hopes, the faith, and the Revolution understood as a dynamic transformation of reality, see Erich Fromm, *Hope and Revolution* (New York, 1968).
8 Marc Ferro, 'Les débuts du soviet de Petrograd', *Revue Historique*, April–June 1960, pp. 353–80.
9 Alexandre Skirda, *Kronstadt 1921* (Paris, 1971), *passim*.
10 Archives Pathé, Paris.
11 On Lenin's attitude at the start of the Revolution of 1917, see vol. I, pp. 198–211.

Chapter 1 The political crisis

Note A The Bolsheviks and German Gold

Like most of the clandestine revolutionary groups, the Bolshevik party received money from 'generous' – sometimes interested, and usually anonymous – donors. Proof has never been established, but it seems likely that the Bolsheviks, through the German social democrat Parvus (formerly an Internationalist, who had then joined the Majority), received 'help' from the German government – though very little before October and apparently without their knowing the source of the gift. Once the German archives became open in 1945, Zeman, Katkov and Hahlweg have sought 'proofs of Bolshevik guilt', but in vain. Katkov, properly, admits in his latest work that the German government tried to help Lenin, with or without his knowledge, but appearances certainly counted against the Bolsheviks as they remitted funds, whether commercially or disguised as such, through Sweden. The accusations made by Alexinsky, a French spy, were in part slanderous, but the whole matter is so complex that neither Kerensky nor Perevertsev can, in view of the documents collected in July, be accused of bad faith when they said the Bolsheviks were 'guilty'. The political exploitation of the question is another matter altogether. The baroque narrative of Solzhenitsyn's *Lenin in Zürich* troubles waters that are already muddy enough concerning the Bolsheviks' funds; but he adds nothing to the documents collected by Hahlweg. Overall the question may be best examined in the critical study of G. Bonin in the *Revue Historique*, i, 1965, which contains a list of works on the subject, summarized in my own *La Révolution russe de 1917* (Flammarion, Questions d'Histoire), pp. 126–9.

1 Except for Kerensky, whose career is examined below.
2 *Org. Sov.* (325), p. 54.
3 Voytinsky, in his memoirs (273), p. 312, states that Prince L'vov had said that 'for two months the soviet has failed to send representatives to the commission preparing for the constituent assembly's meeting'.
4 It is also significant that in four provinces (*gubernii*) I have considered – Saratov, Oryol, Crimea and Yekaterinoslav – the municipal councils, which were dominated by the bourgeoisie, never demanded the convocation of a constituent assembly in their addresses to the Duma. CGIAL, 1278, 5, 1264, 33ff.
5 See vol. I, pp. 60–4 and 219ff.
6 In fact the Petrograd Soviet received, on this occasion, only about a hundred *privety* of congratulation – not much (GAORSS, Lo., 7384, 9, 170).
7 See L. Shapiro, 'The Political Thought of the First Provisional Government', *Revolutionary Russia, a Symposium* (517), pp. 123–45.
8 See chapter 8.
9 *Rech*, 29 March 1917.
10 'There will be no order so long as these conciliationist policies go on,' said representatives of fifty factories to the *TsIK* during the July Days (*Dok. J.* (23), p. 22).
11 *Spartak*, 20 May 1917, p. ii.
12 On the methods of this policy, see vol. I, pp. 234ff.
13 The Internationalist Laribe declared to the Menshevik conference of Petrograd that 'If Germany promised to give up Serbia, Belgium and Romania, and if France and Great Britain continued holding on to Mesopotamia, their colonies and Alsace-Lorraine, we should be *forced* to make a separate peace' (NJ despatch of 18 July 1917).

14 See vol. I, pp. 239ff on Kerensky's vain efforts to get some diplomatic advantage out of the offensive; cf. Ignatiev (570), pp. 290–8.

15 When the conciliatory soviet took stock, the day of 18 June clearly showed that the Bolsheviks were masters of the streets (vol. I, chapter 6).

16 Znamensky (564), pp. 15–17.

17 Ibid., p. 18.

18 *Rayonniye soviety* (334), *passim*.

19 CGIAL, 1278, 1, 1363, 530; also in Znamensky.

20 On the April fraternizations, see vol. I, pp. 211–12.

21 On this analysis of film, see my article in *Annales ESC*, 1973/I, 'Le film, une contre-analyse de la société'.

22 This account owes much to Alexander Rabinowitch, *Prelude to Revolution. The Petrograd Bolsheviks and the July 1917 Uprising* (563).

23 These soldiers belonged to the Pavlovsky, Izmailovsky and 1st reserve regiments, see *Rev. mae i iyune*, pp. 483–5; in July, they were of the 1st machine-gun regiment.

24 After this turn-about, Smilga and Stalin objected and wanted to resign; Volodarsky and Trotsky also protested, while Tomsky and Rakhia feared that 'the party will cut itself off from the masses when it cuts itself off from the anarchists'. On 12 June the anarchists had managed to assemble the delegates of 150 factories. Rakhia prophesied, 'This is dangerous because they might take to the streets two or three thousand strong and provoke a confrontation that will weaken the Revolution and lead to counter-revolution.' The fact was that the party did not want to act before the offensive had failed, so that public opinion would not accuse it of causing the defeat. On the internal crisis of the party around 18 June see Rabinowitch (563), pp. 86–102.

25 On this see I. Tobolin, 'Iyul'skiye dni v Petrograde', KA (26) XIII, pp. 13–20 and 58–63, and also XIV, pp. 63–4 with Rabinowitch.

26 Rabinowitch (563), pp. 116–36. In June the Bolshevik military organization had about 2,600 members, representing sixty units (in all Russia): see Rabinowitch, pp. 116–24.

27 Rabinowitch (563), pp. 140–8; on the slogans, there are many instances in *Dok. Jt.* (23), pp. 22ff.

28 Archives of KPSS, Leningrad F. 4000, 547, 5, 547, 2045. This (unpublished) document displays the grass-roots unity of anarchists and Bolsheviks.

29 GAORSS, Lo., 101, 1, 8, 3–5: complete text in *Annales* 1971/I, p. 39.

30 *Dok. Jt.* (23), p. 16. The Putilov workers also marched, but, it seems, on their own, and elsewhere (GAORSS, Lo., 131, 1, 166, 47).

31 Archives of KPSS, Leningrad, F. 4000, 5, 526, 1618. This (unpublished) document demonstrates that by 2 July the Bolsheviks considered Trotsky to be of their number.

32 Raskol'nikov's memoirs, translated by J. J. Marie (537), pp. 74–5.

33 This was Rakhia's formula (Rabinowitch (563), p. 159).

34 Ibid., p. 162.

35 Raskol'nikov (561), pp. 74–5.

36 BV despatch of 3 July 1917.

37 Rabinowitch (563), p. 152.

38 *Dok. Jt.* (23). There were many more workers than previously. *Izvestiya* of 5 and 17 July named eighteen factories alleged to have demonstrated or struck, which was not, in fact, a large number. The Tulmantsi, who had been forced by the Putilov workers to join the demonstration the day before, refused to march on 4 July. *Dok. Jt.*, p. 513. On the workers' behaviour in general see chapter 6.

39 *Dok. Jt.* (23), p. 17 for the text. According to the authors of this collection, it was published only on 5 July.

40 On this, see Rabinowitch (563), pp. 175ff. Trotsky's 'Interdistricts' (unitarist) also issued an appeal to demonstrate; cf. a remark by Uritsky to Sukhanov in Sukhanov (120), p. 439.

41 Podvoysky's account, quoted in Rabinowitch (563), pp. 183–4.

42 On the government action, see the paragraph below; on the grounds for these accusations, see below.

43 A further proof of the spontaneous character of the demonstration of 3 July is that there were no demonstrations on that day in other Russian towns. By contrast, on 4 July and later there were almost 400,000 demonstrators, between 4 and 14 July in thirty-four towns, especially the industrial ones (see Znamensky (564), pp. 202ff).

On 4 July the Bolsheviks, reflecting the indecision of their leaders in the capital, came out with contradictory watchwords. Sometimes they recommended a demonstration with loaded rifles – e.g. at Ivanovo-Voznesensk – and sometimes without arms at all; sometimes they left it open. Only the slogan 'All Power to the Soviets' was everywhere in evidence. But it was obvious that the demonstrations were not intended to overthrow the government (*Dok. Jt.* (23), pp. 102ff).

44 On the recrimination between the Bolsheviks and Mensheviks, see vol. I, pp. 230ff.

45 *Spartak*, June 1917.

46 At the time, the implicit meaning of this change was not noted.

47 On the periphery, these negotiations between Mensheviks and Bolsheviks continued until October, for instance on the Romanian Front (see *Procès-verbaux* (335), p. 136). Unlike the militants, the workers and soldiers could not easily distinguish between the groups: Astrakhan, in his work of 1973 (531), pp. 73ff, quotes accounts that show this and confirm the viewpoint taken in my vol. I. *A fortiori*, the workers and soldiers were ignorant as to the Menshevik schism (Sukhanov (120), p. 490).

48 This official reason appeared in *Rech*, 5 July, p. 2.

49 Even Zinoviev said this, in the evening of 3 July, at the soviet meeting (*Izvestiya*, 4 and 6 July 1917). He did of course have a great deal to say at the time; see his account in the appendix.

50 On this, see the accounts of Tseretelli, Sukhanov, Trotsky and Voytinsky.

51 The confusion was total. Even at the allegedly Bolshevik Vyborg, the workers would not 'go against the Soviet': CGAORSSSR, 1244, 1, 15, 3 and cf. the document by the 2nd crew of the Baltic Fleet: 'We will not demonstrate in arms to impose a political decision on the soviets elected by the people' (CGAORSSSR, 1244, 1, 15, 251, and 252).

52 Text of a telegram from Kerensky encouraging Perevertsev to 'hasten' the spread of this news: Mints (512), II, p. 606. On the basis of these accusations, see Note A.

53 Sukhanov (120), pp. 445–7.

54 Tseretelli (127), II, pp. 249–357. The Girondin precedent was in everyone's mind: 'Petrograd should be declared non-Russian' said *Utro Rossii*, of Moscow, on 5 July. Sukhanov (120), p. 455.

55 Like many others, they thought '(i) that the Kadets' resignation is a sign of the bourgeoisie's intransigence; it is desertion; (ii) that the demonstration was a stab-in-the-back to the Revolution.' This verdict by the Tammerfors garrison (CGAORSSSR, 1244, 1, 15, 269) was repeated in many 'conciliatory' soviets – Zhitomir, Voronezh (which also attacked the anarchists) – and several military committees: see *fondy* 1244, 1, 15, 189–212 and Voytinsky (273), pp. 309ff.

56 Rabinowitch (563), pp. 211–13, Znamensky (564), pp. 110–15 and *Dok. Jt.* (23), pp. 38ff.

57 Ibid.

58 On Eisenstein's *October* the now leading work is P. Sorlin and M. C. Ropars, *Octobre, écriture et idéologie* (Paris, Albatros, 1976).

59 The decree for arrests of 10 July did not bear Trotsky's name, and he protested 'out of solidarity with Lenin, Kamenev and Zinoviev'. In his letter to the minister, published on 15 July, he insisted that he had summoned the demonstrators on 3 July to go home peacefully. He did not call himself a Bolshevik and explained his relations with them by reference to his leading role in the 'Interdistrict', 'which has no disagreement with the Bolsheviks'.

60 *Doc. Ker.* (35), III, pp. 1386–9. A press campaign in favour of restoration of the death penalty followed, and four of the newspapers mentioned general Kornilov in this connection – *Birzheviye Vedomosti, Vecherneye Vremya, Novoye Vremya* and *Narodnaya Gazeta*.

61 Lenin (129), vol. XXV, pp. 181–7. During the discussions at the Third Conference of Towns, at which Lenin, in hiding, could not be present, Ivanov set the slogan 'Dictatorship of the Proletariat' against 'All Power to the Soviets'. He added that 'the class-content of this watchword must change'. Stalin answered that the expression, 'All power to the soviets' was meant to convey that power should be given to the masses, not institutions; on this transition from singular to plural, see chapter 7.

62 *Sotsial-Demokrat*, 4 August 1917.

63 'The left-Socialist Revolutionary group states that hitherto it has accepted the decisions of the party majority. . . . But in view of the fact that it has had to abandon the principles of class struggle and Internationalism, it reserves full liberty of action' (Communiqué of 12 July). The irreversible break occurred during the October Days; the left Socialist Revolutionaries, once expelled, set up their own party.

64 Plekhanov's text appeared in *Yedinstvo*, 8 July; on Lebedev and Chernov, see Radkey (297), p. 285; on the victims, CGAORSSSR, 3, 1, 302, 128; on the anti-semitic pamphlets, see BV despatch of 14 July.

65 For instance, he had Zlotnikov, a notorious monarchist and anti-semite,

arrested on 18 July. At the request of the Mogiliev Soviet, he had the diffusion of the *Gazette of the Central Committee of the League* forbidden by the army and navy, because it was too counter-revolutionary. The conference organized by this League was also forbidden (BPP (43), number 104).

66 'What is to the credit of revolutionary democracy occurs as a debit to the Kadets', said *Birzheviye Vedomosti*, the business newspaper, on 7 July. On Lieber and Berg, *Birzheviye Vedomosti* 8 August 1917; on *Zemlya i Volya*, despatch of 12 July in BPP (43).

Chapter 2 The failure of counter-revolution

1 Session of 18 July. According to Maslennikov, about fifty or sixty deputies were present; the press reviewed this debate. There were protests, demanding dissolution of the Duma. GAORSS, Lo., 4605, 1, 8.
2 Znamensky (564), p. 222.
3 Radkey (532), pp. 289–93.
4 Ivanov (565).
5 Ibid., *passim* and Laverychev.
6 The representatives of these Leagues met at Grand Duchess Olga's house and drew up an anti-semitic manifesto (RV despatch of 31 July and 6 August). The articles on the 'Bolshevik rabble and the reigning bunch of scoundrels' appeared in *Rus*, which replaced the *Malen'kaya Gazeta* forbidden by Kerensky, *Groza* and *Veche*. At Kiev there was an assembly of sixty officers from 10 to 12 July and it sent a delegation to Grand Duke Michael: see Kapustin (566), p. 125.
7 Astrakhan (531), pp. 180–7.
8 Ibid., pp. 187–212 and 310–50.
9 According to the memoirs of Generals Denikin, Gurko and others.
10 Kapustin (566).
11 Denikin (191), *passim*.
12 Kapustin (566), pp. 79–95 and *Dok. Mai.* (22), p. 381.
13 On this conference, *Doc. Ker.* (35), II, pp. 989–1010 and Znamensky (564), pp. 233–7.
14 Discussion with Kerensky, 1967.
15 The title is borrowed from a work by Vasyukov (569).
16 On this, see vol. I, pp. 195ff; Kozlowski in *Trybuna*, the Polish Bolsheviks' newspaper, 30 July 1917.
17 Telegram from Janin, of the French military mission in Petrograd, which read that the Americans should be approached for locomotive supply to be used as a way of exerting pressure (T. 1861–4); telegram from Albert Thomas, in the contrary sense, urging delivery of aircraft to the Provisional Government (T. 91 of 8 May), Vincennes, Na. 6, 4 and discussion in Na. 6, 5.
18 On Stockholm, see vol. I, pp. 242ff. The verdict on the causes of failure is Axelrod's, in a letter to Olberg on 9 June 1917: Axelrod archive, Amsterdam, 18, 8; protests against Allied 'sabotage' from, for instance, the Caucasus army, in CGAORSSSR, 6978, 1, 316.

19 On American sympathy, Kennan, *Russia leaves the war* (1956), pp. 8–27. Statistics on troop movements: Marc Ferro, *La Grande Guerre* (English ed., London, 1972).
20 Ignat'ev, pp. 317–19.
21 Ibid., pp. 324–9.
22 Ibid., pp. 330–49.
23 Ibid.
24 Ibid., pp. 318–20.
25 Censorship archives, Nanterre, BDIC.
26 Buchanan, pp. 159–63 and Knox, pp. 670–8. After the July Days the British suggested the following measures: restoration of the death penalty, disarmament of the workers, general military censorship, ex-servicemen's or war-wounded men's militias.
27 Censorship archives, Nanterre, BDIC.
28 This was told by Somerset Maugham in *Izvestiya*, 4 November 1962. The two Russian terms mean respectively 'reign of Kerensky' and 'reign of Kornilov'; they are used because in Russia the suffix 'shchina' is added to a name to give it a slightly pejorative effect.
29 See the appendix on my discussions with Kerensky.
30 CGAORSSSR, 3, 1, 251, 40.
31 Lukomsky, vol. I, pp. 251 and 225 and Denikin, quoted in Ivanov, p. 21 and Knox, p. 679.
32 On this ministerial crisis see Radkey, pp. 289–313 and *Doc. Ker.* (35), vol. III, pp. 1402ff.
33 Savinkov, a former Socialist Revolutionary and 'terrorist', had become violently anti-Bolshevik. He happily praised the 'virility of the fighting men', contrasting it with 'the cowardice of the men in the rear'. This talk had a ring of the Italian Fascism of the same period.
34 Discussion with Kerensky, 1967. Kerensky had the same viewpoint as regards the soviets as did the Kadets: see the extract from *Vestnik Par. Narod. Svob.* in Morokhovets (347), p. 132.
35 CGAORSSSR, 6978, 1, 356 and 366, 1, 234ff. Protests like this came from soviets such as Samara, Omsk, Kiev; about forty such texts have been collected in *Dok. Avg.*, pp. 378–415. A peasant assembly in Voronezh also sent a protest.
36 *Dok. Sent.*
37 Many provincial soviets approved this, for instance Pskov: CGAORSSSR, 1, 356, 19.
38 The Menshevik Garvi wrote in *Rabochaya Gazeta* 9 August 1917 that it was 'a new blow in the back of democracy when it is just about to fight reaction'.
39 Documents and speeches in *Doc. Ker.* (35), III; Trotsky, *History*, II, 16 and 162.
40 *Proletarii*, IV of 16 August 1917, Moscow. Many soldiers' protests against the speeches of Kornilov and Kaledin in CGVIA, 2031, 1, 1585; see chapter 3.
41 The best overall discussion is in Ivanov (565) using the main accounts and unpublished archives.
42 Telegram to Kerensky 7 August in CGAORSSSR, 3, 1, 251, 8, 84.

43 N. G. Dumova, 'Maloizvestniye materialy po istorii Kornilovshchiny', *Voprosy Istorii* (1968), 11, no. 82.

44 Ivanov (565), *passim* and CGAORSSSR, 1, 3, 1, 362, 450−3. Lenin, unaware as to Kerensky's real intentions, wrote 'Kerensky is the most dangerous of the Kornilovites'.

45 The false news of a Bolshevik demonstration for 27 August was put about on 22 August by *Russkiye Vedomosti*.

46 Some generals, such as May-Mayevsky, resisted these orders; Kornilov and Markov wanted them to be transferred. CGVIA, 2067, 1, 60, 195. On this, see Lukomsky's memoirs, pp. 94−113.

47 Ivanov (565), *passim* and *Doc. Ker.* (35), vol. III, p. 1557.

48 An overall collection of documents has been published in *Doc. Ker.*, vol. III; see also Kerensky, *Prelude to Bolshevism*, pp. 131−8.

49 Immediately, telegrams supporting Kerensky came in from all corners: workers' and soldiers' soviets of obscure places, Murmansk, the towns of Chernigov, Vologda, Ufa, and the Ural Kirghiz. See *fondy* in CGAORSS, Mo., 3, 1, 164 nos 233−95 and CGVIA, 2067, 1, 3821; many regiments joined in, such as the Valvinski Battalion of Death, the Kexholm Life Guards: CGAORSSSR, 1244, 1, 15. The soviet of mobilized peasants in Helsinki greeted 'Kerensky, head of the Revolution' and wanted 'the return of Chernov, our defender': CGAORSSSR, 3, 1, 362, 263. The same message came from the land committee of the Moscow *uezd* (CGAORSSSR, 3, 1, 361, 190). See also CGVIA, 2067, 1, 3815, 37.

50 On the behaviour of the Kadets, who later said they had known nothing of the 'plot', *Doc. Ker.* III, documents N. 1542−3 and Astrakhan; see also the 'defeatist' report of the Kadet Prince Trubetskoy in *Doc. Ker.*, III, pp. 1573−4, which is corroborated by messages that Kerensky received from bourgeois circles, for instance the engineer Ketler, of Rostov on the Don: 'I recommend compromise because here much of the country is behind Kornilov. . . . There is a rumour you are a Jew' (CGAORSSSR, 3, 1, 362, 374−7).

51 Colonel Orlov of the 'Union of Officers' sent a telegram at 10.45 a.m. on 28 August to all army corps and institutions: 'L'vov, Procurator of the Holy Synod, and Savinkov have suggested sharing power with general Kornilov. . . . The General accepted, after some hesitation . . . and generals Klembovsky, Valuyev, Denikin and Shcherbachev have been associated with him' (CGVIA, 2067, 1, 3815, 100−2, 193, 349).

52 The overestimation of the chance of success was partly explained by the mass of reports stressing the 'satisfactory situation' on the military railways, the posts, the supply centres and even the army workshops. Alarmist reports concerned only the soldiers' mentality. The staff expected the structure to hold (CGVIA, 2067, 1, 60). However, by 24 August the Mogiliev printers refused to set up the *Gazette of the Central Committee of the Officers' league* (ATV Despatch).

53 Co-ordination worked between the district committees, the Red Guard, and the factory committees supplying arms: see chapter 8.

54 Lenin's words appeared in *Rabochy Put*, 28 August. This line had been upheld by Kossior and Bubnov even on 27 August, at seven o'clock in the

evening. See Ivanov, p. 139. Lenin adopted it on 30 August: see Lenin, *Works*, vol. 25, pp. 311–16; 500 copies of Lenin's letter were distributed: Ivanov, p. 129).

55 See Lenin, vol. 25, pp. 333–7.

56 The reference is to the massacre of the Charonne *métro*: Kerensky, conversation with the author, 1967.

57 Until then the working-class militia had been deprived of arms. On 3 July the Kronstadt sailors had gone to Petrograd with 2,920 rifles and 25,460 cartridges, and they went back to Kronstadt with 2,077 and 8,580 respectively. Thus 843 rifles were left in the city; and the sailors had certainly not fired 16,880 rounds, so that the rest of the cartridges remained in the workers' hands (calculated according to the report of 25 July 1917 published in *Baltiyskiye Moryaki*, pp. 154–5). In all this was little enough. At the Dynamo factory, 1,000 workers had 11 rifles between them; at the Phoenix, 2,000 had 20: see Ivanov, p. 148. The factories changed this themselves, Putilov delivering from 28 August to 31 August about 100 guns and machine-guns for the fight against Kornilov. They were useful in October.

58 Cf. Startsev, p. 130, Ivanov, pp. 150–6 and chapter 7 below.

59 'The Bolsheviks will have to see that they are alone', the Menshevik Gorev wrote in *Rabochaya Gazeta* of 1 September; Lenin, vol. 25, pp. 266–74.

60 See the congratulatory messages to the Soviet 'for adopting the Bolshevik viewpoint', CGAORSSSR, 1, 1244, 1, 15, 5.

61 Except for Volodarsky, who said, 'The leaders are going right, the masses left. . . . If you say counter-revolution is winning, you mean the leaders, not the masses, because today's caliphs, the Tseretellis, Kerenskys, Avksentievs cannot do anything without the masses', *Third Conference*, pp. 70–4.

62 Ibid., p. 113.

63 See newspapers of 3 August, 22 August and 30 September; also *Procès-Verbal*, p. 330 and Popov (541), p. 72.

Chapter 3   The failure of the traditional institutions and authorities

1 The police department and the gendarmerie had been abolished by the government in March, and also the *volost* courts.

2 'Uman Agricultural Society', in CGAORSSSR, 3, 1, 314, 305; it was also said that 'the laws of Tseretelli and Peshekhonov are not known', *Ek. Pol.* (601), p. 307.

3 CGAORSSSR, 3, 1, 314, 257–9.

4 Ibid., 3, 1, 362, 230–1.

5 *Kommunistichesky Put* (Kazan, 1922), pp. 47–9 and *Den*, 29 September 1917.

6 CGAORSSSR, 398, 2, 123.

7 W. Rosenberg in *Cahiers du monde Russe et Soviétique*, 1968, pp. 52ff.

8 'Mart-Mai 1917 goda' in K.A. (26), XV (1926), pp. 40–1.

9 *Doc. Ker.* (35), vol. I, pp. 250–4 and 312–16; see also chapter 7 below.

10 Emelyakh (668), p. 65.

11 Alain Besançon, *Le Tsarevitch immolé* (Paris, 1967), p. 126.

12 'This development was not reflected in any way by a movement in the heart of the church', says Jutta Scherrer in an excellent article on the religious 'quest' of the intelligentsia (CMRS, 1974, 3/4, pp. 297–314; Seton Watson, *The Russian Empire* (1967), pp. 640–5 and Emelyakh (668), p. 74.

13 There was the same contentment in the bishops of Smolensk and Perm: see Emelyakh, p. 74.

14 S. Fedorchenko, *Narod na voyne* (Kiev, 1917); N. P. Kranshikov, *Po etapam* (668), p. 9; on the attitude of the church to the February events, see Curtiss (360), pp. 26–43 and my volume I, pp. 302–3.

15 Klibanov (673), pp. 2–15 and BPP (43) of 1/14 August.

16 Klibanov, pp. 277–85.

17 Curtiss (360), pp. 14–15 and 26–43; on the council, my vol. I, pp. 302–3.

18 Emelyakh (668), p. 68. Another instance from the minutes of a regimental committee on 19 September is that 'After the Kornilov affair . . . there was an examination of the activities of officers who helped in it: there are the following suspects – general Goncharenko who, since 9 August has not allowed the committee to meet without officers present; the chaplain, who has always tried to arrange meetings at the same time as the regimental committee's ones', CGVIA, 2067, 1, 3821, 93.

19 The queues at Moscow are shown by Kushova in *Doc. Ker.* (35), vol. III, p. 1732. Peasant activities: CGAORSSSR, 3, 1, 363, 229 and Emelyakh (668), p. 67, Curtiss (360), p. 20, *Ek. Pol.* (601), vol. III. p. 367, etc. The request of the bishop of Moscow is a public manuscript in the 'Museum of Religion and Atheism'.

20 Emelyakh (668), p. 91.

21 *Sotsial-Demokrat*, December 1917.

22 Pierre Pascal, *Avvakum*, pp. 573–4.

23 Borisov, Kolarz, Curtiss, *passim*.

24 Bishop Tikhon issued this anthema: 'I conjure you, blessed children of the church, to have nothing to do with that human scum, in any way.' On persecutions of individuals and institutions, see the documents collected by B. Szczesniak, Kolarz and N. Struve (671).

25 On the church, the family and the changes of the state, see chapter 7 and the Conclusion.

26 There were similar events at the university of Moscow (see Fitzgerald (685)); for Odessa, the minutes of which I have used, see *Odessky universitet* (678), pp. 1–45.

27 Ibid. At the Petrograd polytechnic there were 999 sons of better-off peasants out of 6,077 registered students: see Potekhin and T. Ilyuchenko, *Trudy LPI*, No. 190/1 (1957), p. 78. In the first year of medicine at Moscow they made up 20 out of 138 (Tsiklik, *Sovetskoye Zdravookhraneniye* (1964), vol. I, p. 33).

28 *Odessky universitet, passim*.

29 Ibid., p. 122.

30 Ibid., p. 132.

31 Ibid., p. 136.

32 Ibid.

33 McClelland (684).

34 D. Konchalovsky (680).
35 Cf. A. Lunacharsky's *Uplotneniye* of 1918 and A. Zarkhi's *Baltic Deputy* (1937).
36 N. I. Podvoysky (558), vol. VI, p. 65.
37 This legend, that German troops were being transferred to the west, started in July 1917: see O. A. Dobyansh-Rozhdetstvenskaya, *Chto takoye Frantsiya v proshlom i nastoyashchem i za chto ona boyuyetsya* ('France, her Past and Present, and Why She is Fighting') (Petrograd, July 1917, Publications of the Party of the People's Liberty (Kadets)). In fact the number of German divisions remained stationary in the east in April 1917, rose from 72 to 75 in May and 78 in June: see Marc Ferro, *The Great War*, p. 193. Also, at the last battle on the Russian front, at Moonsund from 3 to 6 October, the Germans broke off the action because 20 per cent of their ships had been damaged (Mints (512), vol. II, pp. 811–12).
38 According to statistics on the first hundred motions of the soldiers, published in *Izvestiya*, the soldiers expressed their confidence in the government only in three cases, and in the soviet in eight (*Annales ESC*, 1971/I, p. 38).
39 On *Prikaz* No. I, see vol. I, pp. 94, 196–200; statements as to liberalization of regulations made up 25 per cent of the cases, those on improvement of conditions 8 per cent; on land questions only 7 per cent.
40 Before the soviet's appeal for a peace without annexations, the soldiers, in twenty of the hundred cases said that they would do their patriotic duty, and only in three did they speak of peace.
41 G. Wettig (583), p. 186.
42 Verkhovsky confided to the head of the French military mission that 'Our officers lack political education and can only react to what is said. . . . They do not even try to win their men's trust' (Vincennes, Bulletin 12 of the 2nd Bureau, p. 19).
43 Commissioner Filenko, who was thought to be quite open-minded as to current problems, could only suggest, as a reform, that 'from now on before addresses are made to the troops, they should be told beforehand that they should be "at ease"', BV Despatch of 12 August 1917.
44 CGAORSSSR, 3, 1, 362, 369ff. Another wrote, 'The bad thing is that the soldiers, having hardly had any training, do not know how to obey.' CGVIA, 2148, 1, 813, 305. On relations between officers and men, there is another instance, on Czech troops: 'The soldiers of the 2 regiment terrified their commander, Kotkevich, by answering his morning salute with the words "thank you, sir". The old colonel hastily left his headquarters to confer with his aide de camp, under the impression that there had been a mutiny. He was told that the title of "Excellency" had been abolished on higher orders' (Bradley (596), p. 52).
45 On the desire for peace before the February Revolution, see Sidorov's collection of documents (584), pp. 146–313. In March, twenty out of a hundred soviet motions followed the soviet's appeal for a peace without annexations.
46 The complete text sent by a group of soldiers in the 202 regiment appears in the appendix to vol. I; see CGIAL, 1278, 5, 1329, 1–4 and GAORSS, Lo.,

7384, 9, 244, 63a and b, 64.

47 Ibid., 7384, 9, 244, 33.

48 Ibid., 7384, 9, 259 for the soldiers and CGAORSSSR, 1244, 1, 15, 118 for the sailors.

49 This is frequently attested in Shlyapnikov (125), vol. II, pp. 136ff and Sukhanov (120), vol. II, pp. 307ff; see also Freydlin (627), pp. 69–94. It was partly this that convinced the workers they should organize a guard – see Startsev (363) and chapter 7 below.

50 The contradiction lasted for a long time, at least until the Kornilov Putsch. 'There are symptoms of their favouring a military reaction', telegraphed Paléologue, the French ambassador, to his ministry late in March. 'The soldiers attack workers' despotism, arrogance and excessively high wages, hence the demonstrations of patriotic character' (Vincennes, NA 6–4, telegram no. 424). Even late in June, workers' demonstrations at Perm, Samara and elsewhere were broken up by troops: Znamensky (564), p. 21. Another complaint appears in *Spartak* of 6 June, p. 29, from the 302 regiment (reserve): 'We who only eat cabbage and kasha', cf. CGAORSSSR, 6978, 1, 356, 40. The idea of sending to the front those men who cried 'War to the bitter end' was expressed by March. It was not unique to Russia: see the French trench-newspapers, and in the case of Italy the collection of accounts in Mario Isnenghi's *Caporetto*.

51 On the very first fraternizations, see vol. I, pp. 209–12.

52 Wettig (583), pp. 192ff and 264ff.

53 *Rev. Dvizh.* (584), *passim*, Volfovich and Medvedev (589), pp. 87–91.

54 Wettig is incorrect in stating that 'the soviets at first agreed with the fraternization . . . they did not collaborate as the Duma accused them of doing, but they did not disapprove of the movement and tried to cover it'. In fact the soviet leaders were at first taken by surprise by the whole phenomenon, and condemned it unambiguously – see *Izvestiya* of 30 April 1917 and the documents on Frunze's tour quoted in vol. I, pp. 211–12. There was a second fraternization in October, see Mints (512), vol. II, pp. 857–62.

55 There were many resolutions among Russian units for a resumption of 'active operations': e.g. the 1st light battery of 66 artillery regiment (CGAORSSSR, 1244, 1–15, 246), 1 Siberian rifle division, artillery park of 17 infantry division, 718 infantry regiment, 14 Don Cossack division, 15 cavalry division, 2 Siberian corps, 70 infantry division and 6 cavalry *sotnya* CGVIA, 2031, 1, 1585); 38 division of III Army and the hospital ship *Ariadne* deserve mention, all of these resolutions affecting the northern front. Some non-Russian units should be added, for they volunteered.

56 For instance, 669 infantry regiment, 2 battery of 12 heavy artillery division in CGAORSSSR, 1244, 1, 15, 241 and 242; 2 battery of 24 Siberian division stated in point 3 that 'measures should be taken not only against deserters but also against shirking workers', and in point 7 'that the Battalions of Death should go into the trenches instead of parading' in GAORSS, Lo., 7384, 9, 234, 3.

57 See in the appendix the resolution of twenty-six military units in Petrograd that refused to go to the front (GAORSS, Lo., 101, 1, 8, 3–5 (unpublished)

and note 60).

58 With a different route, I have come to much the same conclusions as Rabino-witch in connection with the July Days' causes – see Rabinowitch (563) and chapter 1 above.

59 CGVIA, 2148, 1, 813, pp. 3–23. Gaponenko (585) reproduces this docu-ment, pp. 234–62. In the original, each assertion was based on one or more statements by witnesses, the names of which I have omitted.

60 Forty-eight battalions refused to fight (Kapustin (566), pp. 34–54); 185, 5, and 20 Siberian refused to obey an order to regroup. General Trikovsky was subjected to humiliation and was deprived of his motor-car; he had to go back to his headquarters on foot. He was much shaken, and got leave for a nervous breakdown (*Dok. Jt.* (23), p. 399).

61 This debate was reported in *Spartak*.

62 On the French army mutinies, see G. Pedroncini, *Les Mutineries de 1917* (Paris, 1967). The mutinies had no link with the pacifist movement, just as the revolt of the Russian soldiers in France had no connection with the French munities – see Marc Ferro, *The Great War*.

63 CGVIA, 2067, 1, 60, 33 (XI Army).

64 CGVIA, 2067, 1, 60, 32 (XI Army). The soldiers of the Luga garrison sent a petition asking for general disarmament of officers, who were declared to be 'all traitors to the Revolution', *Dok. Avg.* (538), p. 263. The *Voice of III Army* wanted general Lukomsky to be tried because he had wanted to confiscate the newspaper's printing press (*Izvestiya*, 12 August).

65 In a soldier's letter of 9 August this anger was vividly expressed: 'In the trenches I read your newspaper, and hear the soldiers talking . . . they discuss war, discipline, punishments, occupations for soldiers etc. . . . all that is good for the bourgeois . . . but why should the others talk about "fatherland in danger", all those Kerenskys, Skobelevs and Chernovs. . . . Nicholas II could talk that way, but not you. . . . Be warned that if peace hasn't come by the winter, you can pack your bags. . . . You have betrayed Russia, sold her to England and France' CGAORSSSR, 6978, 1, 531, 4–5, quoted in *Dok. Avg.* (538), p. 41.

66 Not all commissioners and generals reacted like this: for instance the com-missioner V. A. Zhdanov, a Menshevik, talked of the 'catastrophic character' of the restoration of the death penalty (Kapustin (566), p. 41).

67 CGVIA, 2067, 1, 60, 52; 1, 60, 229; 2067, 1, 3829, 52–3 (quoted in Gaponenko) and 2067, 1, 60, 61.

68 Gaponenko (585), pp. 278–9.

69 CGVIA, 2067, 1, 3821, 29–30.

70 See below, chapter 8 and cf. CGAORSSSR, 1244, 1, 15, 1–14; 1236, 1, 12; 1235, 53, 9; and 6978, 1, 580. See also the very pessimistic report of generals Markov and Denikin in CGVIA, 2067, 1, 60, 279.

71 *Soldatskiye pisma* (588), p. 110 of 9 August 1917.

72 From mid-July and especially in August, petitions and messages to the Petrograd and Moscow Soviets used watchwords from the Bolshevik press; cf. the series of documents published in the USSR (585 and 586).

73 Countless telegrams supporting Kerensky before and during the Putsch, for

instance in the Moscow region CGAORSS, Mo., 3, 1, 164, 233–95; CGAORSSSR, 6978, 1, 359; CGVIA, 2067, 1, 3821, 94 and CGAORSSSR, 1244, 1, 15. Many reports to the Supreme Command left an impression that 'order has been restored'. Kornilov must have misunderstood how representative they were, because documents stressing the soldiers' fury were not addressed to him (CGVIA, 2067, 1, 60). Moreover, the often spontaneous conflicts between the Battalions of Death and the Lettish Rifles or others show that at least part of the army could be regained by commanders: on this, see below.

74 CGVIA, 2067, 1, 3815 and 2067, 1, 3821 for XI Army.

75 The 507 regiment in the Caucasus Army (CGVIA, 2031, 1, 1585).

76 CGAORSSSR, 1244, 1, 15, 4 and 6978, 1, 248, 1.

77 Used as regards Kerensky, the expression 'he is tricking us' appears on 9 July. It recurred after the failure of the Putsch when he took no measures against Kornilov and opposed dismissing the bourgeois ministers from government (CGAORSSSR, 6978, 1, 248 and below, chapter 8). On the Bolshevization of the Petrograd garrison, see Rabinowitch (593), p. 180. That Bolshevik influence increased after July and especially after the Kornilov affair in regiments where up till then there had been no Bolsheviks.

78 Tkachuk (594).

79 CGAORSS, Lo., 7384, 7, 36–48. In the context of the Caucasus army, point 5 concerned the Moslem population; point 6 was 'whether the existence of a committee puts a brake on the process of disintegration often'; the response to point 9 can be explained by popular pressure, see above; on the south-western front general Janin reported that soldiers accused of 'cowardice' were often acquitted and 'borne off in triumph' by those present (Vincennes, Source A, bulletin 15, p. 8. Details reported on 30 October from the Tarnopol region).

80 CGVIA, 2148, 1, 813, 471–9: 'It's different in the artillery', the report says.

81 On 13 August, 'desertion has stopped in VIII Army' (CGAORSSSR, 3, 1, 362); on 19 August, 'There have been 350 desertions and 103 returns to service in II Army' (CGVIA, 2067, 1, 60, 229); on 4 September, 'Still no deserters' was stated in an investigation of fifteen regiments in the Caucasus Army (CGVIA, 2100, 1, 276); on 24 October in an investigation of eight regiments in 7 divisions 'few deserters' (CGVIA, 2148, 1, 813, 471–9), etc.

82 CGVIA, 2067, 1, 60 and *Helsinki* Fb, 1270–5, 2, 49. On Kiev, Vincennes, *Renseignements généraux*, bulletin 5.

83 Trotsky (121), vol. II, p. 287.

84 On the exact figure for units present in line at the armistice, see L. M. Gavrilov in *Istoriya* SSSR, 1967, 5. In September there were 100 refusals to go into line, in October 300 (Mints (512), pp. 857–62). Soldiers' resolutions on desertion went through three phases: in March, they condemned men who took advantage of circumstances to go home; in May and June they attacked desertion, threatening men who did not rejoin their units with exclusion from the benefits of agrarian reform. Such deserters were equated with shirking workers. After July, the soldiers began to defend deserters, stating that the counter-revolutionary generals deserved court-martialling as much as they.

85 In the Moonsund, particularly naval officers were affected (see Mints (512), pp. 813–14).

86 For officers who joined the Reds, the 'specialists', see J. Erickson (598), pp. 25–84. There was no lack of such men in other bodies, and later they were a large part of the *trudyashchiyesya*, 'the working intelligentsia', see R. Pipes (ed.), *The Russian Intelligentsia*, 'The Soviet Intelligentsia' (Columbia University Press, 1961), pp. 63–80; their integration into the Soviet system is considered below, chapter 7.

87 In the cavalry losses were four-fifths killed and one-sixth prisoner, whereas in the infantry the respective figures were two-thirds and one-quarter. These figures were worked out by general Andolenko (592). Cavalry was therefore the 'arm of sacrifice'.

88 On the Cossacks' first reactions to the reformers' plans, see vol. I, pp. 447–8; on land-seizures CGAORSSSR, 3, 1, 302, 135. The Cossacks had 1 wounded man on 3 July, 35, with 6 dead, on 4 July (CGAORSSSR, 336, 1, 22).

89 CGAORSSSR, 336, 1, 222, 95–100 and Vincennes, Source A, bulletin 1, 13, p. 14.

90 *Volnaya Kuban* of 26 September 1917 and CGAORSSSR, 336, 1, 22, 134 and 213 and also *Borba* (591), *passim*.

91 CGAORSSSR, 3, 1, 362, 405.

92 See above, chapter 2. In May general Gurko, brother of the army commander, told general Janin that 'to carry out repression, we would use a Lettish militia, six regiments of Circassian mercenaries, two Polish divisions and perhaps two divisions of Old Believers from Orenburg and Kazan' (Vincennes Na 6–4, telegram 1572–4).

93 Cf. *CMRS* (370), pp. 147–8.

94 This has been properly analysed by Kapustin (566).

95 See Bradley (596).

Chapter 4   The nationalities: disintegration, reunion and fusion

1 This had been clear at the conference of nationalities in Lausanne in 1916, where a large number of the empire's nationalities were represented, though not their socialist organizations. On this, and the overall position of the nationalities as regards the war, see my article of 1961 in *Cahiers du Monde Russe et Soviétique* (370), pp. 131–9.

2 Among recent literature on the emigration after 1917, that by Hans-Erich Volkmann, *Die russische Emigration in Deutschland 1919–1929* (Würzburg, 1966) deserves mention (here esp. p. 154); on relations between the first and second emigrations in the USA, the Baltic states and eastern Europe before 1939, see *Lloyd-Journal*, livre 2 (Paris, 1931), p. 144 (in Russian).

3 On the aspirations of the nationalities in February, see vol. I, pp. 102ff and 137ff.

4 Ibid. and von Tatarow, 'Der Zusammenschluss der russischen Muhammeda-ner', *Neues Orient* (June 1917), p. 268.

5 See vol. I, pp. 137ff.

6 Ibid. and Dimanshteyn (364), p. xxxix.

7 Hayit, *Turkestan im XX. Jahrhundert* (Darmstadt, 1956), *passim*.

8 The formula of extra-territorial autonomy suits, of course, peoples without a territorial base, such as Jews, Armenians of Georgia, Crimean Greeks, etc.: a sovereign body would legislate, from Petrograd, for all citizens belonging to this nationality.

9 See vol. I, pp. 137ff.

10 Ibid. and B. Gurevitz, 'Un cas de communisme national en URSS, le Poale-Zion 1928–1928', *CMRS* (1974), 3/4, pp. 333–63.

11 Ibid. and Tokarev (356), pp. 87–9.

12 On the problems of Russian Islam, the works of Bennigsen and Quelquejay (400) and H. Carrère d'Encausse (402) are important; on Moslem feminist movements, see vol. I, pp. 106ff and pp. 286–7 and the works quoted as (663) to (666).

13 There was a similar alliance between the Bolsheviks and the Turkestan *jadid*: see Carrère d'Encausse (402), pp. 225ff.

14 Dimanshteyn (364), pp. 443–57.

15 On the attitude of the congress of soviets, see vol. I, pp. 295–6.

16 Dimanshteyn (364), p. 634 and for an overall view Pipes (365), pp. 53–75.

17 *Neues Orient*, 15 September 1917, pp. 516ff.

18 Reshetar (387) and newspapers cited in the bibliography.

19 The problem as a whole is covered in the works cited in note 12, and by Zenkovsky and Park (404 and 405). On the Bolsheviks' attitude at Kazan, see Mukharyamov, *Oktyabr i natsionalny vopros v Tatarii* (Kazan, 1958), pp. 40ff.

20 Zenkovsky, p. 144 and BV despatch.

21 Ibid.

22 *U.S. Foreign Relations: Russia*, II.

23 The text is in *Neues Orient* of 5 October 1917. Memories of the great revolt of 1916 were green (see vol. I, pp. 107–8).

24 Carrère d'Encausse (402), pp. 190–239.

25 Dimanshteyn (364), p. 56.

26 Session of the Council of the Republic in *Vestnik* (51), 14–23 October 1917.

27 The significance of the Decree on Peace is well explained in Arthur Ransome's *Six Weeks in the Soviets' Russia* (London, 1919); overall, see the classic by E. H. Carr (276), III, chapters 1 and 2, Deutscher (281), chapters 10 and 11; and A. O. Chubaryan, *Brestsky Mir* (Moscow, 1964).

28 Gankin and Fisher (37), pp. 691–3.

29 Carr, III, p. 16 and Deutscher, *passim*.

30 Gankin and Fisher, pp. 683ff and Carr, III, pp. 116–17.

31 On the emergence of the *Komintern* see, apart from the works indicated in vol. I, p. 462, Pierre Broué (ed.), *Premier Congrès de l'Internationale communiste* (complete documents) (Paris, 1974).

32 On the general theory on nationality of Marxists before 1914, see G. Haupt (707), pp. 9–63 and, for Lenin, pp. 52–61; also Carrère d'Encausse (706). My volume I, pp. 84ff and for February–October pp. 297ff covers the history of the development of Russian parties', especially Bolsheviks', attitudes to the matter.

33 Carrère d'Encausse (706), p. 230.

34 See vol. I, pp. 153 and 290.

35 On Latvia, 'Bolshevized' before Russia but soon occupied by Germany, see Ezergailis (710).

36 Delavoix (380), p. 80 and BPP (43) of 5/18 July 1917.

37 Ibid. and Dimanshteyn (364), pp. 68–9.

38 Ibid., p. 47; Bazarov's editorial in *Novaya Zhizn'*, 20 July, and for the Bolsheviks, *Rabochy i soldat* of 5 August.

39 Dimanshteyn, pp. 55, 70. On the food crisis, see a declaration by Peshe-khonov according to which 'out of 4,000 waggons of grain meant for Finland, 348 have been loaded, and only one has reached its destination by 22 August', BPP of 22 August.

40 The social democrats won 92 seats, a loss of 11, and the bourgeois parties 108 or 109 depending on calculations (an increase of 11 or 12). Among these, the Swedish party won 21 seats. The voting was 30,106 for the social democrats against 41,222 for the anti-socialist coalition. ATP despatch on 21 September, and 2 October 1917.

41 On the exchanges with Sweden, see Helsinki archives 1270/1275: 2, 1, 23, 37, 40 and 44, and the remarks by (naval) captain Dumesnil who telegraphed to the Naval Staff in Paris on 22 August 1917, 'I venture to hope that the attitude of the Finns and their feelings towards the Entente powers will be diffused through the Allied press and that we shall cease to regard as an oppressed race people so deliberately hostile to us whereas they have greatly profited from the war without having to shed blood for it', Vincennes, bulletin 11, p. 7 and bulletin 10, p. 6.

42 The incidents were near Vyborg and Raibol (Helsinki 1, 8 and 10).

43 Tokoi declaration, in Soderhelm (381), p. 30.

44 Ibid., pp. 25–6.

45 The Tampere group also controlled Tornea, Byeloostrov, had stationery printed, said it would keep order, fight delinquency, see that the laws were observed and fight the counter-revolution (Helsinki 2, 460).

46 Sokolov, in his report to the *TsIK* said that non-recognition of the Provisional Government by the *seim* was 'an act of mistrust towards the coalition, but not really an appeal to consider its orders invalid'. He also advised the government to satisfy its demand for withdrawal of Russian troops (on 27 September) CGAORSSSR, 6978, 1, 190.

47 *Izvestiya Peterburgskogo kommissariata po delam Natsionalnostyey*, pp. 9–21.

48 Stalin (257), IV, pp. 1–5 and 22–4.

49 Lenin stated on 22 November, 'Today we are "conquering" Finland – I am using that horrible word – not as the capitalists and international sharks do, but by offering her complete liberty to unite with us or with other peoples. We guarantee total support to the workers of any land against the bourgeoisie of whatever country', Lenin (129), XXVI, p. 360.

50 There are said to have been 20,000 dead and 70,000 prisoners – at least according to U. Sirola in *Izv. Peter. Kom po del. nats.* (1920), *passim* and Carr (276), I, pp. 294–5. On the Civil War in Finland see C. Jay Smith's study in T. T. Hammond, *The Anatomy of Communist Take-overs* (Yale University

Press, 1975), pp. 71–94. This carefully analyses the German role; see also Fol (712), which I have not been able to use.

51 On the pro-Finnish and pro-Russian movements in Karelia, see von Heden-strom, *Geschichte Russlands 1879–1918* (Berlin, 1922), p. 317 and *Izv. P.K.* (see note 47), pp. 21–7. On the Karelian Republic, K. Arkhipov, *Sovietskiye avtonomniye oblasty i republiki* (Moscow, 1925), pp. 58–9.

52 K. Devlin, 'Finland in 1948: the lesson of a crisis' in Hammond (see note 50), pp. 433–48, which has a good bibliography.

53 Ibid.

54 Ibid.

55 On the second modification, see Carrère d'Encausse, *L'Union Soviétique de Lénine à Staline* (Paris, 1972), pp. 111–27. The instances quoted in this model are taken from Carr, Pipes and Carrère d'Encausse (see above). Apart from the works by Branko-Lazitch and Drachkovitch, quoted in vol. I, I have also used the *Biographical Dictionary of the Comintern* (Hoover Institution Press, 1973).

56 On the question of the frontiers of the USSR, see J. B. Duroselle (ed.), *Les frontières européennes de l'URSS 1917–1941* (Paris, 1957).

57 This passage should be compared with T. T. Hammond 'The Communist Take-over of Outer Mongolia: Model for Eastern Europe?' in Hammond, pp. 107–45.

58 Carrère d'Encausse (quoted in note 55).

59 The anti-Stalinist Communist tradition owes much to Stalin: on Rakovsky and the national problem, see F. Conte, 'La polémique Racovski-Staline (1921–1923)', *CMRS*, XVI/1 (1975), pp. 111–17. See chapter 7 for the problem of the allegedly Stalinist bureaucracy.

60 Carr, I, chapter 10 on the apparatus. The same 'impossible cases' appeared when the sectional creation of the *Komintern* began; its history is full of anecdotes on this problem.

61 See the excellent analysis of the Kalmuks by Paula G. Rubel in *Soviet Nationality Problems* (Columbia University Press, 1971), pp. 211–41. On the contradiction between Marxist theories and Lenino-Stalinist practice con-cerning the nations and races, see Carrère d'Encausse (708).

62 George Ginsburgs, *Soviet Citizenship Law* (Leyden, 1968).

63 It is a development all the more remarkable for overcoming the handicap of a unfavourable demographic evolution, the non-Slav population growing faster than the Slav one, the Tatars faster than the Russians or the Balts. A good test is the number of women who have had secondary education. By 1959, the ratio was two to one between the most advanced Republic, Latvia, and the most backward, Uzbekistan; in 1917 there could have been no comparison at all. On these problems, see M. Suzikov and G. Demakov (717).

64 See *Ferment in the Ukraine* (720).

Chapter 5 The Revolution in the countryside

1 *Dok. Okt.* (540), pp. 436–59.

2 On the isolation of the Russian village, see S. P. Dunn and E. Dunn in *Ethnology* (603), pp. 320ff. On relations between peasants and merchants, Kauffmann-Richard, *Origines d'une bourgeoisie russe*, pp. 218–19.

3 E. Wolf (621), pp. 60–9, and on the weakness of the distributional network, Basile Kerblay, *Les marchés paysans en URSS*, pp. 75–9.

4 Wolf, *passim.*

5 Ibid.

6 This shook it more than war, the effects of which were added to those of capitalism: see the stimulating discussion by Roman Sporzluk in *Slavic Review*, XXVI, March 1967, pp. 70–84.

7 There was only one working link between the peasant and the rest of society, the co-operative movement: in 1917 it included 5,500 agricultural societies, but for 1,600,000 members in the countryside, it had only 1,454 selling-points and 1,223 places for exchange (Kabanov (640), pp. 55–6).

8 Dunn (603 and 604).

9 S. Harcave, *First Blood. The Revolution of 1905, passim.*

10 CGAORSSSR, 398, 2, 123.

11 See vol. I, pp. 122ff and the questionnaire and answers in the appendix, reproduced in *Ek. Pol.* (601), III, pp. 386–7.

12 Ibid. and vol. I, pp. 122ff.

13 *Ek. Pol.* (601), III, p. 67.

14 Ibid., p. 400

15 Ibid., 220, 237, 241 and 401.

16 CGAORSSSR, 398, 2, 123, 1–6.

17 Ibid., 22–98, and see Moisseva (606), pp. 46–7 for a general view of the composition of the agrarian committees; for the later period, see note 45.

18 Ibid.

19 *Ek. Pol.* (601), III, pp. 402–4. Of 1,189 'legal violations' noted for June and July, 258 affected occupation of land, 332 on use of meadows and pasture, 130 seizure of draft or other animals, and the rest were over timber. The provinces mainly concerned were those of Penza, Kazan, Mogilev and Saratov.

20 *Trudy vtoroy sessii glavnogo zemelnogo komiteta. Zasedaniya 1–2 iyulya 1917 g.,* pp. 35–9, partly reproduced in *Ek. Pol.* (601), III, pp. 284–9.

21 Chernov never managed to get the other members of the government to grant complete legitimization of the land committees. But people did see that he was 'on the peasants' side'. During the autumn, in the Kozlovka region of Tambov, peasants who seized lands or implements said that they were 'in possession of a paper from Chernov': BV despatch in *BPP* (43) of 20 October.

22 *Protokoly zasedaniy 3go gubernskogo krestyanskogo syezda 20–28 avg. 1917 g.* in CGAORSSSR, 6978, 1, 423 and D. S. Tocheniy, 'Bankrotstvo politiki S-Rov v Privolzhya v agrarnom voprose', *Istoriya SSSR*, IV, p. 196.

23 Ibid.

24 Later on, Axel learned the lesson of these events, and, in the province of Simbirsk, put his own land and stocks of material at the land committees' disposal (CGAORSSSR, 3, 1, 314, 264–6).

25 Tocheniy (607).

26 CGAORSSSR, 6978, 1, 423.

27 Ibid.

28 This escape is explained by the answer that Chernov had given Klimuchkin: 'You cannot make a law out of a locally-taken decision', CGAORSSSR, 1, 423, 91.

29 CGAORSSSR, 6978, 1, 423 and Tocheniy (607), p. 117.

30 Ibid.

31 Report of the Buguruslansky committee (Samara province) in *Ek. Pol.* (601), III, pp. 290–1 and CGAORSSSR, 398, 2, 139, 1. The peasants often reversed the terms of the relationship between their and the constituent assembly's decisions: instead of waiting for its convocation to take their measures, they said they were taking measures 'valid until the constituent assembly meets': for Penza province, CGAORSSSR, 406, 2, 212 and Smirnov (608), p. 25; also Pershin (605), I, p. 373.

32 Figures in *Ek. Pol.* (601), III, p. 502 (note).

33 This did not, however, rule out occupations of land, which would then be rented out to the workers: for the Poltava area CGAORSSSR, 3, 1, 2, 251, 40.

34 On Makhno see below, and J. Pluet, *Autogestion*, nos. 18–19, p. 310.

35 On Siberia, Razgon (610) and on Byelorussia, Fikh (613).

36 See Bobrinsky's report to the council of ministers of the Tsar on 10 October 1916. Dependence on abroad was particularly felt in the field of agricultural machinery from Austria-Hungary and Sweden, and fertilizer from Germany. *Ek. Pol.* (601), III, pp. 16–32 and 457.

37 S. Grosskopf, 'Expropriation, utilisation et partage des terres à l'époque de la NEP', *CMRS*, XIV, pp. 513–35.

38 Ibid. and *Ek. Pol.* (601), III, pp. 74–121. Here was the great difference with 1905, when the peasants had not seized implements or animals. See Pershin (605), I, pp. 413ff. In the province of Ryazan, these were seized even in March 1917 (CGAORSSSR, 7384, 9, 147, 6).

39 On average, 11.2 per cent of the population was mobilized, or 22.6 per cent of the male population and 47 per cent of the working males. The figure was above 50 per cent in the frontier provinces (*Rossiya v mirovoy voyne 1914–1918 gg. v. tsifrakh*, Moscow, 1925, p. 21), and by July 1916 Sturmer was asking generals Brusilov and Kuropatkin to free labour for the needs of the rear. Norman Stone (592b) shows that the figures are too high.

40 *Ek. Pol.* (601), III, pp. 37, 53, 63.

41 There were about 130,000 prisoners of war in the countryside: ibid., p. 64.

42 Complaint of peasants against prisoners, CGAORSSSR, 406, 2, 544, 23–8 and 69–71.

43 Ibid., 3, 1, 302, 186–7.

44 Ibid., 3, 1, 361, 32–4; protests by 1,200 landowners of the Poltava region in ibid., 3, 1, 314, 25–79 and Pershin (605), I, p. 379.

45 In the provinces of Tambov and Ryazan the *volost* committee were wholly made up of peasants: neither large landowners nor doctors and teachers were in them, whether because they refused or because they were not allowed. Pershin (605), I, p. 353 and KA (26), XV, 1926, pp. 41–5.

46 In the Poltava area: CGAORSSSR, 3, 1, 302, 174.

47 *Dok. Jt.* (23), pp. 327–8. The *prikaz* particularly forbade the resistance to harvesting carried on by machine, or seizure of tools, prisoners of war, etc.

48 Chernov, Tseretelli and Peshekhonov documents in *Ek. Pol.* (601), III, pp. 237–43.

49 The transactions had been forbidden, then forbidden unless they were actually being carried out. The peasants were hard put to know what was forbidden and what was not. Pershin (605), I, pp. 390–6.

50 Moisseva counts seventeen uprisings put down by force between March and June, and 105 in September/October: (606), p. 142.

51 See Pershin's analysis of the total number of risings (605), pp. 407–18. Judging from the central archives, there seem to have been between 5,782 and 6,103 risings and various violations between February and October. But not all complaints were registered there, and the evidence given by local archives which are more complete would show a total, depending on the province, three to eight times greater. Moreover, not all seizures and violations were necessarily the subject of a complaint that was registered. According to Pershin the number of risings as such was 2,818. The central zone is thought to have accounted for half, at least in the summer; then came the Ukraine and the Baltic provinces.

52 Ibid., pp. 420ff.

53 BV despatch of 5 September 1917 in *BPP*.

54 Before July of 1,426 identified conflicts, 1,318 were between peasants and estate-owners, 72 peasants and *otrubniki* or *kulaks*, 36 peasants and clergy or entrepreneurs (*Ek. Pol.* (601), III, 52). In Tambov province, 30 of the 81 actions against *kulaks* occurred in September, and there were equivalent proportions in Penza and Voronezh (Pershin (605), p. 417).

55 Chamberlin (275), p. 265 and Grosskopf as in note 37.

56 Melgunov (577), appendix and p. 204.

57 On the Bolsheviks' and Socialist Revolutionaries' agrarian programme, see vol. I, pp. 97–9, and on Lenin's variations between February and October, P. Sorlin (349); on the drawing-up of the Decree on Land see Lutsky (615). There is an overall view of the Decree in Carr (276), II, pp. 34–40 and E. Kingston-Mann (616).

58 A week before October S. Maslov, minister of agriculture, signed a law on relations between the state and the local land committees: see *Doc. Ker.* (35), II, pp. 577–80 – as Lenin's saying ran, 'a betrayal of the peasantry'.

59 Chamberlin (275), p. 326 and Lenin (129), XXVI, pp. 268–9.

60 See Jan Meijer's excellent article in Pipes, *Revolutionary Russia* (517), pp. 331–61.

61 *Sovety v oktyabrye* (544), pp. 314–79. In the Tver region, all land had been put at the disposal of the local committees by July 1917 (*Ek. Pol.* (601), III, pp. 292 and 365).

62 *Sovety* (544), pp. 314–79.

63 Ibid.: cf. the text on p. 172 and questionnaire pp. 374–5.

64 CGAORSSSR, 405, 6, 249, 1–5.

65 The incidents were followed by a flaring-up of anti-semitism. By March the peasants were demanding fixed prices for industrial goods: cf., for Samara

province, CGAORSSSR, 3, 1, 314, 26.

66 CGVIA, 560, 43, 206 and CGAORSSSR, 3, 1, 251, 23.

67 CGAORSSSR, 3, 1, 363, 96.

68 NV despatch 26 August. The incident was said to have occurred in the Lipetsk district of Tambov province.

69 Many beatings-up of members of supply committees recorded in Moisseva (606), p. 144. Requisitions of foodstuffs (*prodrazverstka*) caused many battles before October. The committees' way of setting about things counted more than their actual doings. It showed townsmen's feelings towards peasants.

70 See the pamphlet of early 1918 giving advice to a militant going to the country-side, in Burov (617), pp. 6–9.

71 CGAORSSSR, 3, 1, 361, 62/64; and 363, 129; *Dok. Sent.* (539), p. 266 and *Fab. zav. komy* (625), II, p. 194; Moisseva (606), p. 145.

72 As peasants concealed what they fed themselves with, requisition affected sowing-grain, hence the need to reduce sown areas and even the density of sowing. The yield per *desyatin* went down by about half in a few years, while the total of requisitions trebled between 1917 and 1922 (Grosskopf (622b)).

73 The Bolsheviks did try to exert their influence, especially near the cities. They organized recruiting of soldiers and workers who came from the nearby villages; they would go off to spread the doctrine. After the seizure of power, a pamphlet was printed to help in this (Burov (617)). As well as advice, it supplied the names of leaders of soviets or local committees. However, before October this propaganda effort remained very modest and it is difficult to imagine that it contributed very much to the radicalization of the rural move-ment in the way historians have assured us. For the six or seven provinces in the capital's orbit (Pskov, Vitebsk, Kaluga, etc.) the Bolshevik party was able to mobilize ten men from the Skorokhod factory, eight from the Cable factory, etc. At Minsk the party was able to use about 100 workers and soldiers. But these figures are, relatively, derisory. They were found by T. Tregonova, quoted in Pershin (605), I, pp. 398–9.

74 By 1923 productivity of labour had gone down by 55 per cent per labourer and 44 per cent per agricultural implement. But from 1895 to 1912 the average fluctuation of harvests had been only between 18 and 21 per cent: see Mints, report of 1923, translated in (621c) and Grosskopf (622b).

75 Before the enforced collectivization of the 1930s, Russia experienced a form of spontaneous collectivization, the rural communes. Originally these emerged at the initiative of Socialist Revolutionary or anarchist militants, Christian sects, especially Baptists and Mennonites. The spirit was somewhat similar to that of today's communes, and had more a moral than an economic purpose: 'Our village will become a family, we shall live as children of the same father, our soviet.' The members of rural communes shared out the work according to the principle, 'from everyone according to their abilities, and to everyone according to their needs'. According to R. G. Wesson, *Soviet Communes* (Rutgers University Press, 1963): I am grateful to Basile Kerblay for bringing this work to my notice; cf. for the first regulations for the rural communes in the north in *Pervy Syezd komitetov derevenskoy bednoty Soyuza severnoy oblasti* (Petrograd, 1918) about 3,000 were created, one of the largest near Tsaritsyn,

with nearly 8,000 members.

Many of them were created by peasants, but after 1919 the tendency went the other way, because of the difficulties of life in the towns, and it was townsmen who set them up.

To begin with, the popular régime, even where Marxist or Bolshevik, was not at all against them. The commissariat of agriculture supported the movement, wishing to regulate the communes to make them productive, though of course at this stage of the Bolshevization of institutions, the commissariat was still largely made up of left Socialist Revolutionaries. But the Bolsheviks encouraged the creation of communes in so far as they were models in the organization of communal living. The favourable connotation appears in the fact that legislation associated them with the poor peasants. However, by the end of 1919, the Bolshevik leaders asserted their 'economist' conception and government help went to the state farms. With the proclamation of NEP, Lenin took a position against the communes and they, stifled by the state, finished towards the end of the 1920s.

Chapter 6   Labour against capital

1 S. S. Ostroumov (641), pp. 209–10.
2 Ibid., pp. 202–18.
3 See my analysis in *Mélanges Braudel* (Toulouse, 1975), vol. II, pp. 221–7.
4 On this division of the working class, see vol. I, chapter 1 and P. B. Volobuyev (355), pp. 15–41 and particularly O. O. Shkataran (628), pp. 192–307.
5 See vol. I, pp. 112ff and, more recently, Astrakhan (531) who confirms this view.
6 See my analysis already quoted (note 3) in *Mélanges Braudel*, and the *Cahiers du Cinéma* on Eisenstein, nos 226 and 227, especially Pascal Bonitzer's article. On the working-class claims in February, see vol. I, pp. 112–20.
7 See Pankratova (626), pp. 35–45 and especially F. I. Kaplan (629), pp. 43–142. Pankratova is a good source for study of the struggle between committees and employers. However, her analysis is ambiguous in dealing with relations between the factory committees and the Bolshevik party. For instance, on p. 36, she writes that 'the working class understood the need to become boss', and 'working class' has sometimes been taken as meaning factory committee, and at other times the bodies that spoke in the name of the working class, such as soviet of factory committees or Bolshevik party; while boss, in the author's view, appears sometimes to be factory committee, and sometimes the Bolshevik party identifying itself with the workers.
8 Kaplan (629).
9 See Auerbach (27), XIV and my vol. I, pp. 202. There is an instance of stock-taking in the offices of the higher administration at Kharkov on 23 August 1917 in CGAORSSSR, 3, 1, 251, 23. According to Yegorova (634), p. 92 there were 90 arbitration tribunals in Petrograd in spring 1917. In the Konsin Company in Moscow, they allowed 47 complaints by workers, 2 more were reckoned illegitimate, and 19 others were not followed up. Ibid.

10 *3 konf.* (624), p. 253: protests by manufacturers against price-stops in CGAORSSSR, 3, 1, 314, 234ff.

11 Freydlin (627), p. 129. There were not only situations of conflict: at the Nevsky factory there was an agreement between factory committees and management. CGAORSSSR, 472, 1, 18, 109.

12 Freydlin (627), p. 93.

13 Yegorova (634), p. 94.

14 CGAORSSSR, 472, 1, 18, 14–16.

15 Generally, sequestration happened after an employer had refused to take account of the proposals of an arbitration tribunal or when he wished to shut down. Mints (512), vol. II, p. 823 supplies a table of sequestrations.

16 Table in Yegorova (634), p. 83, following Andreyev.

17 This famous phrase was used at the second all-Russian congress of commerce and industry held in Moscow from 3 to 5 August 1917: see *Vtoroy vserossiysky syezd v Moskve 3–5 avg. 1917 g.* (Moscow, 1917), pp. 7, 8. It was a current idea there, Shingarev telling the *Manchester Guardian* correspondent that 'we have to look at the facts as they are . . . the spectre of famine is already here' (*Forward*, 4 August 1917, New Style).

18 Analysis of an experiment in self-management was possible only if I had access to archives or information on the different people and institutions with whom the factory committee had relations (see Figure 1). Only in the case of the Brenner factory was this so.

19 *Okt. i fab. zav. kom.* (625), vol. I, p. 147.

20 Ibid. and CGAORSSSR, 472, 1, 18, 7.

21 *Rayonniye K.* (334), vol. II, p. 184.

22 Ibid., pp. 187, 195.

23 CGAORSSSR, 472, 1, 18, 1.

24 Ibid., 18, 2.

25 *Dok. Jt.* (23), pp. 342–3 and CGAORSSSR, 472, 1, 18, 8.

26 *Dok. Jt.* (23), p. 566.

27 CGAORSSSR, 472, 1, 18, 3.

28 *Rayonniye K.* (334), vol. II, p. 251.

29 CGAORSSSR, 472, 1, 18, 52.

30 *Rayonniye K.* (334), vol. II, p. 259.

31 Ibid., p. 263.

32 See vol. I, p. 262.

33 These matters are discussed below, in this chapter.

34 Figures in the works quoted in note 7.

35 Ibid.

36 At Skobelev in Turkestan the trade union of employees and workers in the mine was formed only on 6 September, with 1,800 members. At Kherson the first conference of metal-workers was on 21 September and demanded the eight-hour day. *Dok. Sent.* (539), p. 320.

37 The socialist right wing favoured sequestration, e.g. *Den* on 7 July 1917: 'The government has been able to defeat one of the chiefs of industrial feudalism [the boss of the Goujon factory] for refusing arbitration.' The Menshevik left also continued to sing the praises of sequestration, for instance Varsky in

Novaya Zhizn' of 19 August 'because since then output has risen'.

38 On the bourgeoisie's programme, see vol. I, pp. 84ff and Voloboyev (354).

39 Quoted in *Spartak*, 19 August 1917, signed 'N.B.' (Bukharin) referring to *Promyshlennost i Torgovlya* 26/27, p. 34.

40 On *Mednoprokatny*, CGAORSSSR, 472, 1, 18, 203.

41 *Novoye Vremya*, 22 August 1917. For the overall measures against factory committees *Okt. i fab. zav. kom.* (625), vol. II, pp. 8–15.

42 In the engineering works of Petrograd, for instance, the reaction was more subtle, and the management compromised; but as soon as Skobelev's words were known, it refused to pay the 5,800 roubles meant as wages for the members of the factory committee, and would pay only 3,000 (CGAORSSSR, 472, 1, 18, 24–8).

43 Volobuyev (355), pp. 246–62 and *Ek. Pol.* (24), vol, I, pp. 230–2.

44 See an article by Serinov, basing his views on France and Italy, 'and even England, where there is none the less a strong democratic tradition', in *Birzheviye Vedomosti* of 30 July.

45 For instance, the French consul in Kharkov had complained of the situation at Makeyevka. The government answered that it would act energetically to protect foreign interests. *Ek. Pol.* (24), II, pp. 470–1.

46 CGAORSSSR, 6978, 1, 195, 3 and 427, 1, 18, 166.

47 *Rannyeye Utro* (Moscow), 5 October in BPP (43), 148.

48 Volobuyev (355), p. 303.

49 The arrest of French citizens by a popular committee at the Shcherlinov mines near Yekaterinoslav was linked with this (BPP (43), no. 131, 21 September 1917).

50 Volobuyev (355), pp. 302–21 and *Ek. Pol.* (24), I, docs 316–18.

51 Chernov (123), p. 228.

52 For a general picture of economic factors, see vol. I, pp. 19ff and for more detailed analysis, the best study is, I think, E. E. Kruse in Freyman (513), pp. 398ff.

53 Kruse and Freyman (513), with CGAORSSSR, 3, 1, 314, 118 (Tashkent).

54 N. Stone has demonstrated that inflation also played a part, causing dealers to stock their grain: trains would arrive at certains stations and leave empty, because the suppliers had not parted with their stocks. Use of rolling stock was thus indirectly linked with price inflation (592b).

55 Tsukublin's report in *Ek. Pol.* (24), II, pp. 56–60.

56 In the Moscow area it was more constant. From August 1916 to August 1917 production grew from 3,042,000 *poods* to 4,018,000 but the number of workers grew more still, from 6,950 to 10,485 (CGAORSSSR, 3, 1, 362, 339). For the Donbass, the decline came faster (CGAORSSSR, 3, 1, 362, 340–1).

57 Bolov's report in *Ek. Pol.* (24), II, pp. 48–9 and 53–4.

58 Ibid., pp. 47–94.

59 *Russkiye Vedomosti*, 8 September 1917.

60 Ibid.

61 Kruse and Freyman (513), *passim.*

62 Ibid.

63 Ibid. The price-index (1913 = 100) reached 740 in October 1917 and 1,020

in November; the wage-index reached 600 in the second half of 1917: see Volobuyev (355), pp. 219–22, following Strumilin.

64 On the food crisis see R. Pethybridge, *Essays* (639).

65 For the Donbass and the Volga area, CGAORSSSR, 3, 1, 314, 308 and 3, 1, 361, 62–4; for Stavropol and Astrakhan, RV despatch of 25 August in BPP; for Tashkent, Popov (541), p. 103; for Chelyabinsk *Ek. Pol.*, II, p. 272; for Berzhansk GAORSS, Lo., 7384, 9, 147, 46 and Volobuyev, pp. 226–7.

66 Cf. Rodzyanko's report in January 1917, *Ek. Pol.* (24), I doc. 1 with the Prokopovich report in *Doc. Ker.* (35), III, p. 1, 463.

67 Lenin (129), vol. XXV, pp. 347ff.

68 *3 konf.* (624), pp. 125–6.

69 Interjection by T. Osipov and T. Tseytlin in *Okt. i fab. zav. kom.* (625), I, p. 122—3.

70 The Bolsheviks thereby brought some confusion into vocabulary in describing as 'control' what was in fact a beginning of management. In August, to defend the committees from the 'accusation' of 'factory patriotism', Levin slid still further in this direction, for he said, 'Some people, consciously or not, confuse control and occupation.' In fact, control, as the Bolsheviks, who wanted nationalization, understood it, was the opposite of management, as it was worked out by the workforce of small and middle-sized businesses; and the 'occupation' undertaken by the workers was only one aspect of their factory's change of status. Nationalization also implied occupation, though by the state rather than by the workers. See *3 konf.*, pp. 50–9 and 100, *Okt. i fab. zav. kom.*, I, p. 171 and Kaplan (629), pp. 43–118.

71 *Okt. i fab. zav. kom.*, I, pp. 230–3.

72 The problem of rivalry between various labour organizations is examined in the next chapter. Here it is examined from the viewpoint of the workers within a factory. Rivalry between factory committees and trade unions had the result that in August there were few unions (leather, cloth, etc., i.e. the older industries) that protested against Skobelev's circular limiting the activity of factory committees (see report in *4th Union conf.*, 13 March 1918, p. 25).

73 On the traditional hostility of the Bolsheviks towards the unions, see Schwarz and Hammond (317) and (318). On the *volte-face* of 1917, A. G. Yegorova, pp. 41–61. By March the Bolsheviks called on party members, for instance at Ivanovo, to set up unions and keep to them. On the attitude of the party in relying on factory committees rather than unions in the period March–July, see vol. I, pp. 271ff.

74 *3 konf.*, pp. 59–95.

75 Ibid., pp. 95–7.

76 Ibid., pp. 452–3.

77 Ibid., pp. 315–19.

78 Ibid., pp. 125–6.

79 *Okt. i fab. zav. kom.*, I, pp. 227–33.

80 In July Lenin had even supposed that the factory committees could become the basis of a revolt, and is said to have told Ordzhonikidze, 'We must alter our slogan, and instead of "All power to the soviets" we should say "All power

to the factory committees"' (Chamberlin (275), I, p. 184).

81 At the all-Russian conference of factory committees, the distribution of delegates was: Bolsheviks 86 (62 per cent); Mensheviks 8; Socialist Revolutionaries 22; maximalists 6; anarcho-syndicalists 11 and unattached 4 (*Okt. i fab. zav. kom.*, II, p. 114).

82 There is a useful assessment in M. L. Itkin (632).

83 *Okt. i fab. zav. kom.*, II, pp. 130–7.

84 Ibid., pp. 167–74.

85 Ibid., pp. 188–93: the text of the suicide resolution in appendix 6.

86 Bunyan (635), pp. 5–7 for the Lenin-Shlyapnikov decree. It had in fact two stages, the first version not creating such a clearly hierarchical system reducing the committees to a minimal role: M. Brinton (630), pp. 16–19 discusses this.

87 On ways of applying this, Carr (276), II, pp. 104ff.

88 The movement of co-ordination of committees grew stronger and more rapid in October: Itkin (632).

89 Shlyapnikov's report, in Bunyan (635), p. 20 (20 March 1918).

90 Ibid., pp. 21–2 and Pethybridge (726), p. 171.

91 D. A. Bayevsky (637), ch. 1.

92 *Rukovodstvo po rabochemu kontrolyu* (Moscow, 1918), p. 6; there is a good discussion in Brinton (630), pp. 25–8 and D. Limon, *Autogestion* (1967).

93 This was a symbolic date. The nationalization of factories occurred in waves, the date of nationalization marking the turning-point. The history of the (Bolshevik) trade unions and their struggle to remove from the (also Bolshevik) ministry the management of factories is another matter, in which Mensheviks and anarchists, and occasionally the workers as well, were involved. The story is excellently told in Carr, Kaplan, Brinton and elsewhere.

94 On the workers' claims in October see chapter 8.

95 Cf. the council of elders from which the factory committees derived, and was a transposition from village customs (Kaplan (629), p. 404).

96 *Okt. i fab. zav. kom.*, I, p. 190.

97 N. Bukharin, *Programma komunistov (Bolshevikov)*, 1918: Kaplan (629), pp. 142ff.

98 Including the 'Workers' Opposition' led by A. Kollontai: see the Gelinet edition. trans. P. Pascal (Paris, 1974).

Chapter 7   The state – from soviets to bureaucracy

* To my knowledge, there has been no study of the problem discussed in this chapter, a summary of which was delivered as a paper to the Banff conference in September 1974. On all matters concerning the history of the soviets of deputies, see Anweiler's classic account (320), which has been translated ably into French by S. Bricianer, with a preface by P. Broué (Paris, 1971). Study of the bureaucratic phenomenon in the USSR is often linked with Trotskyist criticism, but has not gone into the origins. Earlier, there were several pioneer studies in *Socialisme ou Barbarie* (1949–60), reprinted by C. Castoriadis, *La Société*

bureaucratique (collection 10/18) and by Claude Lefort, *Eléments d'une critique de la bureaucratie* (1971); in this work there is also an article, 'Qu'est-ce que la Bureaucratie?', published in *Arguments*, where different theories of bureaucracy are analysed (Weber, Burnham, Crozier, Touraine). This work, though it is superior, is ignored in John Markoff, 'Government bureaucratization: general process and an anomaly case' in *Comparative Studies in Society and History* (October 1975), pp. 479–503. Pierre Naville, *Le Nouveau Leviathan, V, La Bureaucratie et la Révolution* (Paris, 1972) should also be read. Its historical analysis begins from the moment the Soviet system was set up. Here, it is the formation and emergence of the system that are discussed.

1 CGAORSSSR, 3, 1, 263, 217.
2 Anweiler (329), pp. 119ff.
3 From the start the Bolsheviks challenged these principles and this definition of function, but the institutions still emerged with this orientation: see for the Moscow region, the statutes of the Sushchevo-Mariynsky Soviet, published in the Moscow *Izvestiya* and used as a model for many local institutions, Tokarev (356), p. 102.
4 *Spartak*, June 1917.
5 Trotsky (121) *passim*.
6 *Org. Sov.* (325), pp. 196 and 216–17 (report on the provinces of Kherson, Bessarabia and Tauride).
7 Lenin, *The State and Revolution, Works* (129), vol. XXV, pp. 457–8.
8 Freydlin (627), pp. 69–73.
9 Relations with the workers continually worsened. On 20 March the soviet appointed a commission 'to find out what the factories are really saying'; it asked workers to wait calmly for the calculation of a vital minimum. 'Things are not such that your claims can be met', said Grinevich (Freydlin (627), pp. 69–93 and 101–11).
10 Tokarev (356), pp. 87–9.
11 'The smaller the soviet, and the more distant from central power, the less they used Menshevik watchwords, even if they were themselves Menshevik' (Freydlin (627), pp. 110–11).
12 *Org. Sov.* (325), pp. 58–9 and 216–17.
13 *Pervy* (30), p. xxvii. On Reval, Tokarev (356), p. 28 and the table appended.
14 See vol. I, pp. 297ff and *Pervy* where these interjections are all printed. It was the same with delegates of all socialist parties. For instance, at the presidium of the Socialist Revolutionary party, the 'peasants' party', there were nineteen intellectuals, a worker and no agriculturalist (Radkey (532), p. 224). For the Bolshevik case, see below in this chapter.
15 Often the factory committee appeared as rival of the trade union even before a body was created to unite the committees at town level. By mid-April such conflicts occurred at Moscow, Nizhny-Novgorod, Voronezh and Ryazan (*Org. Sov.* (325), pp. 99–101).
16 *Fab. zav. kom.* (625), I, pp. 142–3.
17 On the politico-cultural role of committees and unions, see Yegorova (634).
18 *Rayonniye soviety* (324), vol. I, pp. 3–20.
19 Ibid. all three vols and thematic index, III, pp. 400–3.

20 Ibid., III, pp. 248–331.

21 Ibid.

22 Ibid. and Ivanov (565), pp. 135–42.

23 *Ray. Sov.*, III, pp. 248–331.

24 Ibid.

25 Startsev (363), pp. 41–98.

26 Ibid., pp. 147–88.

27 Startsev, pp. 249–88 and Mints (512), II, pp. 1127–35, with a complete list of estimated numbers in the provinces. Mints counts 150 towns and centres with a total of 47,670 men, with 96 identified Red Guard corps. Fifty-two other smaller centres, for which no figures exist, should be included, not counting Moscow and Petrograd.

28 Ibid., pp. 98–146.

29 The term 'bureaucracy' is understood here in its political sense – control, by the administrative council of an organization, of the institution's working.

30 On anterior events, see vol. I. There is a list of soviet constitutions in Tokarev (356), p. 28 (table appended).

31 *Novaya Zhizn'*, 29 July 1917. In the same way the *TsIK* decided to take part in the Moscow Conference without consulting the Petrograd Soviet (see *Proletarii*, 22 August 1917).

32 Pershin (605), vol. I, pp. 348–64.

33 CGAORSSSR, 6978.

34 *Ray. Sov.* (334), III, pp. 248–31 and 347–86.

35 Calculated from the lists published in *Fab. zav. kom.* (625), II, pp. 217–64. Among the members bureaucratically appointed by the party to the 4th conference was, curiously enough, Trotsky.

36 M. Ziv and Kulikov, *Rozhdeniye Komsomola* (Leningrad, 1933). At a factory in Vyborg, the workers' soviet had also refused to accept a representative of organizations of youth. Krupskaya protested (*2 i 3 konf.* (534), p. 37 and *Ray. Sov.* (334), III, p. 328, note 137; see also E. Kherr, *Na Puti v Revolyutsiyu* (1925), I).

37 See the photographs of I. Evsenin, *Ot fabrikanta k Krasnomu Oktyabryu* (Leningrad, 1927); other photographs are mentioned in *Kino i fotodokumenty* (504); status of the committees in Tokarev (356), pp. 48–58.

38 GAORSS, I., *Fond* 101 and *Ray. Sov.*, II, pp. 91–326.

39 *Ray. Sov.*, III, pp. 248–331.

40 Ibid., III, pp. 347–404.

41 GAORSS, Lo., *Fond* 101 and *Ray. Sov.*, *passim*.

42 *Uplotneniye* ('Cohabitation'), script by A. Lunacharsky and A. Panteleyev, screenplay by E. Panteleyev (Brussels *cinémathèque*, 1,560 m).

43 About 1,000 names can be identified in 12 of the 14 district soviets of the Petrograd area: *Ray. Sov.*, I, p. 7 and III, pp. 347–65.

44 Startsev (363), pp. 249–88.

45 Calculated from minutes of the *PVRK* (*PVRK* (542), pp. 17–162).

46 Startsev (363), pp. 249–88. The Red Guards expected to survive. They had drawn up draft statutes that were rejected, see below (Document 3).

47 I suggested this in *The Great War* (1970). In the Russian case it has been corroborated by the remarkable work of F. X. Coquin, *La Sibérie: Peuplement et immigration paysanne au XIXe siècle* (Paris, 1969). It has also been corroborated for the USA by Stanley Cohan, 'A Study in Nativism: the American Red Scare of 1919–20', *Political Science Quarterly*, 79, 68 (March 1964) which shows that the most revolutionary elements in the USA came from the Ukraine, southern Italy and Catalonia.

48 G. Haupt and J. J. Marie, *Les Bolcheviks* (528), *passim*, and W. Mosse, 'Makers of the Soviet Union', *Slavonic and East European Review*, 1968/ XLVI, pp. 141ff. A nationalist, anti-semitic pamphlet, *Kto pravit Rossiyeyu* (New York, 1920) listed the main leaders by ministries and branches of the civil service in 1918: of 545 names, there were 447 people of Jewish origin, 34 Letts, 30 Russians, etc. Although wilful errors are numerous, especially as regards omission of non-Jewish Russian leaders, the list does give an indication. From 1918 to 1924 the proportion of non-Russians is said to have gone from three-quarters to three-sevenths, and of Jews from 70 to 25 per cent.

49 L. S. Feuer (681b), p. 54.

50 See Z. L. Serebryakova (518b), pp. 3–29.

51 'We call for the election of new delegates for a soviet power' ran a resolution by 5,000 workers of the Bryansky factory at Yekaterinoslav: see CGAORSSSR, 1244, 1, 15, 294. The Bolsheviks' request dated from early March; for Petrograd the commission appointed to examine the question met only on 25 May 1917 (Serebryakova (518b), p. 15).

52 Popov (541), p. 90.

53 On 25 September the assembly included 200 Bolsheviks, 102 Socialist Revolutionaries, 54 Mensheviks and 10 Menshevik-Internationalists; 13 Bolsheviks, 6 Socialist Revolutionaries and 3 Mensheviks were elected to the executive committee, and in the administrative council, with Trotsky as president, there were 3 Bolsheviks (Kamenev, Fedorov and Rykov), 2 Socialist Revolutionaries (Chernov and Kaplan) and the Menshevik, Breydo.

54 Popov (541), p. 105. At a meeting of the soviets of the Volga region early in October the Mensheviks and Socialist Revolutionaries, in a minority, left the assembly. At once the assembly passed a motion 'attacking the departure at a time when counter-revolution threatened . . . the signatories hope that this cowardly and treacherous policy would be properly judged, for these deserters are now not to be linked with those who fight in the workers' cause' (Popov (541), p. 111). These are gestures and attitudes that prefigure October.

55 Popov (541), p. 104 and p. 107.

56 Ibid.

57 Between mid-September and mid-October, the Bolshevization of factory resolutions was amazingly fast: on 25 September the Nevsky factory, on the 26th the Izhorsky and Vulkan, on the 27th the Sestroretsky, on the 28th the Russo-Baltic, etc., with the texts in *Dok. Sent.* (539), *passim* and Popov (541), pp. 98–103.

58 Trotsky (121), II, pp. 393–8. Bolshevization had repercussions in the non-

proletarian assemblies, such as the municipal councils of Kostroma, Tsaritsyn and Kronstadt, where the Bolsheviks had majorities, and of Tomsk and Samara, where they were the largest party. In Moscow they had 52 per cent of the votes but only 30 per cent of the registered electors took part in the vote. To disaffection as regards elections was added a process of splitting in the electoral body – the masses did not bother to vote for municipal councils and the middle classes refrained from taking part in district committees.

59 Boky's report in *3 konf.* (534), pp. 1–21.

60 *Protokoly* (535b).

61 Daniels (576), pp. 109 and 116–19, and Khesim (582b), pp. 39–53.

62 On Reisner, see Carr (276), I, pp. 131–2; on the co-operative movement, latterly V. V. Kabanov (640).

63 Sukhanov (120), p. 552: 'Long live the Constituent', headline of the editorial in *Delo Naroda* (Socialist Revolutionary newspaper) on 5 September; again in the 30th, 'A New Revolution or the Constituent Assembly?' According to Radkey (532), pp. 7–15, the Socialist Revolutionaries devoted themselves wholly to preparations for the elections to the assembly, in the meeting of their central committee on 21 October. Six days later the problem of a Bolshevik rising had been raised, because the whole press talked of it; the decision was 'to study the matter'. On the social populists, see *Volya Naroda*, 3/4 October 1917; for Kerensky, my discussion with him in 1966.

64 By a significant act of omission, in defining, for early August, the 'respective functions of the four great workers' institutions, the factory committees, trade unions, soviets and parties', Lozovsky 'forgot' to define the function of soviets: *Okt. i Fab. zav. kom.* (625), p. 228.

65 *Anarkhiya* of 11 September remarked that, unlike the Bolsheviks, the anarchists arrested in July had still not been set free. On the Kharkov congress see *Anarkhiya* of 17 September. In *Golos Truda* of 18 August, Rayevsky remarked that Lenin's change of attitude towards the soviets and his use of the expression 'dictatorship of the proletariat' could only mean that Lenin intended to centralize power in the event of his party's winning. For studies of the anarchists, see P. Avrich (533).

66 L. Schapiro (284), pp. 73–88.

67 Carr (276), I, pp. 187–27.

68 Feuer (681b), p. 58. The constitution gave the president of the *TsIK* the function of head of state. The *TsIK* appointed members of the council of people's commissars (Sovnarkom). On the evolution of the constitution, see Michael Lesage, *Les Régimes politiques de l'URSS et des pays de l'Est* (Paris, 1971), and also his *Les Institutions soviétiques* (Paris, 1975), pp. 9–15.

69 On Lenin's views, see Geiger (643) and on Kollontai's, Stora-Sandor (650). On the overall question of relations between family and state as seen by German and western Marxists, see Gertruda Alexander, pref. Klara Zetkin (645).

70 Klara Zetkin (652), *passim* and Geiger (643).

71 Krupskaya criticized these ideas: 'The bourgeoisie are trying to split off the young from the workers, by encouraging them to set up their own move-

ments', she said in 1917, 'and we must not play their game.' As a factory committee refused to accept a representative of the young in its sessions, she remarked that 'to reject the young is bad tactics: if you have ever heard boys of thirteen or fourteen you can see how far they have a proletarian instinct. You ask that they should be in the party, but you ought to accept their being non-party' (*2 i 3 konf.* (534), p. 37 and *Ray. Sov.* (334), III, p. 328, note 137). As adults did not see things in this way, the young set up their own groups, sympathizing with all of the extremist groups. In *Trud i Svet* they adopted the anarchist watchword, 'Tremble, tyrants, for the young are on the watch'. They demanded 'the vote at eighteen, the six-hour day, equal wages, universal right to study, and the right to learn boxing so that the older ones will listen to us', E. Kherr, cited in note 36, p. 32.

72 F. Venturi (295), II, pp. 869–72.

73 Amfiteatrov (647), pp. 30–40, and on the image of man in Russia, V. S. Dunham (725), pp. 459–83.

74 A. B. Sebelev in *Nauchniye*, p. 50. In Petrograd in 1917 there were ten establishments for women's higher education, i.e. more than there were girls' secondary schools in Paris. The Women's School of Architecture had 160 students, the Women's Medical Institute 2,065, the Women's Institute of Agricultural Economics 1,600, the University (Faculties of Letters and Science) 6,074, etc. See *Nauka v Rossii* (Petrograd, 1920), pp. 22–5, 47, 52, 64. On women's social activity see Elnett (644), a careful study of Tsarist policy towards the emancipation of society women, pp. 46–89.

75 On the role of women in February, see vol. I, pp. 40ff and Barulina (655), N. A. Veletskaya (656). For the role of soldiers' wives, see for Ivanovo, Masinistova, 'Rabota organizatsii soyuza soldatskikh zhen v 1917–1918 gg.', *Na Leninskom Puti*, 1926/5, pp. 43–9.

76 Pathé-Paris cinema archive. On the feminist movement, Kollontai (648), pp. 1–33 and Barulina (655), pp. 190ff. For provinces, see at Penza CGAORSSSR, 398, 2, 123, 8 and CGIAL, 1249; below for the countryside and nationalities.

77 Eisenstein made fun of women's battalions in *October* – was it because they supported Kerensky or because he at the time was anti-feminist? These battalions were patriotic and revolutionary rather than feminist, and had the task of 'defending the Revolution against internal and external enemies'. At the end of June 1917, 700 women from Yekaterinburg went to Moscow, and 300 volunteered in Tashkent (GAORSS, Lo., 7384, 9, 139, 2). Three battalions were set up (see Kapustin (566), p. 90). One unit fought at Malodetsano, another was entrusted with defending the Winter Palace. Among them B. Beatty (*The Red Heart of Russia*, New York, 1919, pp. 90–115) has counted domestic servants, typists and peasant women.

78 Barulina (655), pp. 190ff.

79 Ibid.

80 Ibid., p. 194. There was a similar split among the Yaku women, whose 'Union for the Rights of Women' was Kerenskyite. On 16 April, under Bolshevik influence, the dailies and female servants formed a separate 'Workers' Union' (Ivanovo (667b), pp. 103–13).

81 A. G. Yegorova (634); on Lunacharsky see my analysis of his first film, *Uplotneniye* in *Annales ESC*, 1973/1.

82 K. Samoylova, *Chto dala rabotnitsam Okt. rev. i sov. vlast*, pp. 1–8 and Kollontai (648).

83 Geiger (643), ch. 3 and Halle (654), pp. 93–109.

84 Geiger (643), *passim*.

85 Geiger (643), p. 352 and Trotsky, 'From the old family to the new' in Caroline Lund (653).

86 Geiger (643), ch. 3 and *passim*; Trotsky in *Pravda*, 13 July 1923. 'Is it true that Bolshevism teaches people not to respect their parents?' asked the American newspaper, *Liberty*; 'No,' said Trotsky (*Liberty*, 14 January 1933) quoted in Lund (ed.), L. Trotsky, *Women and the Family* (New York, 1970).

87 Halle (654), pp. 109–67 and the various works of Lenin and Kollontai quoted in the bibliography. On the urban utopias, see F. Starr's article in *Annales ESC*, 1977 and L. M. Samsonovich, *Sots. Goroda* (Moscow, 1930), and works by A. Kopp. On the films of the 1920s and women's emancipation, see M. N. Féart's article in *CMRS* 1977.

88 Pethybridge (726), pp. 46–57.

89 M. N. Féart (660). On the past of the Russian peasant woman, see Elnett (644).

90 Ibid.; on the status of Tatar women, vol. I, pp. 356–7 and Nalivkin (664).

91 Elnett (644), pp. 90–134.

92 Barulina (655), pp. 204–6; *Org. sov.* (325), pp. 124, 215; *Okt. i fab. zav. kom.*, II, pp. 217–31. The calculations are mine.

93 A. G. Khartsev, *Brak i semya v SSSR* (657), p. 148 and Pethybridge (726), pp. 46–57.

94 Khartsev, p. 144.

95 T. H. Rigby (530), pp. 360–1.

96 Halle (654), pp. 117–37.

97 The fate of psychoanalysis, as described by Jean Marti, was a corollary of this fleeting modernism. It was women such as Tatiana Rosenthal and Sarah Neidich who played a pioneering role in it, but the practical experiments of the Revolution's first years, for instance the establishment of a Children's Home in Moscow, followed the same path as the emancipatory measures that Kollontai wanted for women. As Marxist theories on the family crossed with psychoanalysts' suggestions, such experiments could be tried out by the intelligentsia, Bolshevik or not, and then they were stopped in their tracks by the reaction of popular feeling. To explain their failure, Jean Marti (who seems unaware of my work) offers the traditional explanation: repression from above, associated with the party struggle and the elimination of Trotsky. But he does say (confirming my hypothesis) that 'the fate of the Children's Home was illustrative. Hardly had it been founded, in August 1921, than the authorities sent . . . a commission of enquiry on the basis of popular rumours . . . and its subsidy was stopped.' See Jean Marti, 'La psychanalyse en Russie' in *Critique*, March 1976, p. 226. On the educational experiments, see the documents collected by F. Champarnaud (686b), pp. 119ff.

98 On the successive retreats just after 1918, Geiger (643), pp. 50ff.

99 *Documentation Française* (Paris): dossier on women in Soviet Russia (662).

100 Rigby (530), p. 361 and 'Zhenshchiny v SSSR' in *Vestnik Statistiki*, I, 1970, p. 7, which shows that 62 per cent of the medical corps consisted of women even by 1940. For the promotion of women of the nationalities, see the final paragraph of chapter 4.

Chapter 8 The October Rising

1 Rosa Luxemburg, quoted in Daniel Guérin, *Rosa Luxemburg et la spontanéité révolutionnaire* (Paris, 1971). On his side, Trotsky wrote in July, 'Why harm your own cause by violence towards individuals: individuals are not worth your attention.'

2 See Table 18 in this chapter.

3 Sukhanov (123), preface.

4 The first wave of anti-semitism, in June, came from the Monarchist intelligentsia; in September it was popular in origin. It is evidenced in the provinces and the towns of Kherson, Bender, Tambov and Ostrog (CGAORSSSR, 3, 1, 362, 229 and GAORSS, Lo., 7384, 7, 36–7). Abramovich reported to the *TsIK* on this recrudescence of pogroms, and the Jewish soldiers appealed to the soviet and the government 'in the name of the half-million Jews under arms': see *Birzheviye Vedomosti*, 3 October 1917 and CGAORSSSR, 6978, 1, 129, 3.

5 Mints (512), vol. II, pp. 857–62.

6 The press: on the rise of terror see the editorial of *Zemlya i Volya*, 5 October.

7 The only attested instance was at Yakutsk: 'armed left-wing social democrats invaded the session of the committee of public safety. Trade union members left the session in protest' (CGAORSSSR, 3, 1, 251, 12–14).

8 Lenin wrote on 27 September: 'The soviets, in taking all power, can even now, though it is probably their last chance, make certain of the pacific development of the revolution' (*Protokoly* (535b), pp. 103–4).

9 D. Geyer (580), pp. 210–16.

10 For the Urals, Mints counts as follows:

	Economic strikes	Political strikes	Mixed strikes
March–June	41	1	?
July–October	60	71	78

There was a similar phenomenon in the Ukraine, where more than half the strikes after July were political in origin: Mints (512), vol. II, pp. 823–7. The railwaymen, who were not threatened by lock-outs, did not take part in October: see Augustine (636b).

11 Conversation with Kerensky, 1967.

12 Their animosity towards Kerensky was less. A motion by Kamenev making the government out to be a 'personal dictatorship' was rejected; Tseretelli defended Kerensky, stressing that the *TsIK* had given him *carte blanche* (CGAORSSSR, 6978, 1, 122, 1–3).

13 On this point, the bloc of conciliators began to dissolve. At the *TsIK* session of 1 September, Bogdanov reckoned that in view of their attitude during the Putsch, 'we can no longer collaborate with the Kadets'. In the name of the Trudoviks and populist socialists, Znamensky thought the same. Chernov also opposed it. But Skobelev and Tseretelli felt that the constitution of a coalition government was still necessary (CGAORSSSR, 6978, 1, 122, 1–3).

14 In fact the Bolsheviks had once achieved a majority, but only in the workers' section of the soviet: Freydlin (627), p. 98.

15 *Protok.* (535b), p. 84.

16 The press, and *Doc. Ker.* (35), pp. 1, 671ff.

17 *Rabochy Put* on 7 September wrote 'Kerensky = Kornilov'.

18 'Proclamation of the Republic is intended to give a moral satisfaction to opinion,' confided Tereshchenko to Eugène Petit (private papers).

19 CGAORSSSR, 6978, 1, 185, 1 and 2.

20 With 161 representatives, the co-operative movement was the great bene-ficiary of this 'manipulation'. Its leaders were friends of Kerensky's – E. D. Kuskova, N. V. Chaikovsky (ex-Trudovik). These delegates attempted to create a central bloc – the democrat right and the bourgeois left – but when the co-operative movement entered representative political life in force, representationalism had lost all its strength.

21 *Volya Naroda*, 19 September 1917. The campaign for coalition was waged particularly by the Socialist Revolutionary right (*Den* and *Volya Naroda*), by Plekhanov in *Yedinstvo* and by the labour socialist-populists, Peshekhonov and Myakotin in *Narodnaya Slovo*.

22 See the press of the next day for the cacophony of 25 September.

23 Gordin in *Anarkhiya* on 2 October wrote, 'The Pre-parliament's father? Tseretelli. Its mother? Conciliation, pusillanimity, wheeling-and-dealing, opportunism. Tseretelli is worse than Kornilov.' Sukhanov in *Novaya Zhizn'* called it 'the pitiful fruit of cowardice and opportunism'.

24 *Delo Naroda*, 22 September.

25 *Doc. Ker.* (35), III, pp. 728ff; Trotsky (121), II, p. 389.

26 It was more independent of 'soviet democracy', further to the right than its predecessor, and included neither Tseretelli nor Chernov, but rather Kadets and progressives, including Konovalov, right Socialist Revolutionaries such as Maslov and Avksentiev, and non-party Mensheviks such as Skobelev and Prokopovich.

27 Buchanan (175), pp. 187, 191.

28 *Istorichesky arkhiv*, 1960/5 and Rayman (514), p. 312. On the 24th, it seems, officers came to arrest Lenin at his residence. They mistook the building, the alarm was given and they were arrested by Red Guards (Daniels (576), p. 149).

29 The best overall view of this is Melgunov (577).

30 CGAORSSSR, 3, 1, 251, 85–7.

31 According to Nabokov (237), p. 48, Tretyakov, Struve, Rodzyanko, Neratov and Nabokov himself had agreed; the text is in *Rech*, 17 October by Boris Nolde.

32 Returning from western Europe, one of these 'peace pilgrims', Erlikh (see

vol. I), had reported to the *TsIK* in tones of pessimism on the attitude of western leaders towards the Russian Revolution. He was particularly perturbed at a project for Franco-German peace at Russia's expense (i.e. the Briand-Lancken discussions) (CGAORSSSR, 1, 126, 1) – 12 September. On these discussions, see G. Pedroncini, *Les Négotiations secrètes pendant la Grande Guerre* (Paris, 1969), pp. 68–73. On 29 September *Rabochaya Gazeta* wrote, 'Only the Stockholm conference can dispel the danger of a peace at Russia's expense.' (CGOARSSSR, 6978, 1, 129, 1–3; cf. Sorokin's protests in *Volya Naroda*, 7 October. The expression 'Prikaz I' is A. Pilenko's in *Novoye Vremya*, 8 October.)

33 Melgunov (577), ch. I. Verkhovsky had confided this to the French embassy: 'The demagogic attitudes he is reproached with are only adaptations to circumstances', telegraphed the ambassador on 18 October (Vincennes, bulletin 14, p. 11).

34 In September 1966, Kerensky told me that he had hoped 'for a great coup with a peace with Austria' and that 'this was on the point of success when the October rising occurred'. I have found nothing that confirms this assertion. It is true that in the soviet's peace conditions Austria was spared, but there is no evidence that people close to Kerensky, except perhaps Gots, were involved. Besides, the members of the Soviet commission were at odds with Tereshchenko, who did not recognize them as proper partners (CGAORSSSR, 6978, 1, 129, 1 and despatch R in BPP, 6 October 1917). Daniels (576), p. 115, mentions Kerensky's allusion to this Austrian offer, but without details.

35 The best source is Dan (186) and see the account of Kerensky in *Catastrophe* (124), pp. 326–31.

36 Sukhanov (123) and overall view in Melgunov.

37 Ibid.

38 Conversation with Kerensky.

39 On Kerensky's efforts after leaving Petrograd the only reference is in Melgunov (577b) and pp. 97–198 of the English-language edition.

40 For this and the next paragraph I have relied largely on the work of my predecessors, especially Daniels (576), Geyer (580), M. Rayman (514) and the proceedings of the Leningrad colloquium (581). I should like to thank the authors concerned, particularly Daniels, who sent me his manuscript before publication. I have used it more than I have the other works.

41 Lenin, *Pages* (129), XXV, p. 317, published in *Rabochy*, 1 September 1917.

42 Written on 30 August 1917, published 7 November 1920: Lenin (129), XXV, pp. 311–16.

43 Written on 12–14 September, published in 1921; Lenin (129), XXVI, pp. 6–12.

44 Ibid.

45 Written on 23 September 1917, published in 1924, ibid., pp. 50–1.

46 Written on 30 September 1917, published on 7 October (delayed), ibid., pp. 68ff. 'They would betray internationalism', he writes here, which is an allusion to events in Germany where two sailors had been shot at Kiel and where Admiral von Capelle had said that 'the Russian Revolution has turned

the heads of some of the sailors'. Lenin was not alone in having illusions as to events in Germany: see the editorial of *Golos Truda*, 1 September. Another anarchist newspaper, *Anarkhiya*, also had illusions on revolutionary happenings in the Argentine and Turkey (25 September).

47 'The Crisis is Ripe', Lenin (129), XXVI, p. 79.

48 *Novaya Zhizn'*, 23 September 1917.

49 Lenin, XXVI, pp. 83–134, finished and dated 1 October 1917, preface of 9 November, published in 1918.

50 Quoted in Daniels (576), p. 82.

51 Ibid., pp. 82ff.

52 From now on roles were reversed, and alarmist news was spread abroad by the Bolsheviks (CGAORSSSR, 6978, 1, 195, 3). A *VRK* was set up in nearly eighty different places: see Kheshin, pp. 38–53.

53 Daniels (576), pp. 73–4.

54 Rayman (514), pp. 298–9.

55 Trotsky succeeded in this on 18 October when he declared to the soviet that, 'The Petrograd Soviet is the parliament of the workers and soldiers. Its sessions are public, its decisions printed in the newspapers. The soviet has taken no decision as to an armed rising, but if events force it upon the soviet, workers and soldiers will rise as one man at the soviets' appeal.' Kamenev, Lenin and Zinoviev supported this (Rayman (514), p. 310 and Trotsky (121), II, p. 417). The slipping from singular to plural is noteworthy: an order by the Petrograd Soviet (Bolshevik) will bring about a rising by 'the soviets', not all Bolshevik. On the point that armed insurrection did not enter as such into Trotsky's plans, see the remarks of the time (and not in later accounts) in Chamberlin (275), p. 303 that, 'The *PVRK* plan is to mount a gigantic procession, without clash or use of arms, even without showing arms. The masses must see that they are numerous and have the force and the will. . . . The very memory of the July Days has to be expunged from the minds of workers and soldiers, and arrange things such that the masses can say, "no one and nothing can get in our way".'

56 Lenin had asked for them to be expelled from the party; Sverdlov proposed resignation from the central committee, which was decided by five votes to three. Trotsky had stated his agreement, but not Stalin who wanted the vote. When the result was known, Stalin offered his resignation from *Pravda* but it was rejected. Daniels (576), pp. 116–17.

57 Ibid., pp. 81–107.

58 Ibid.

59 Trotsky in his *History* did not fail to say that during the preparation for the rising, neither Lenin (who was absent until 8 October) nor Zinoviev (under censure) nor Kamenev, who opposed it, nor Sverdlov took part in the preparatory meetings. They were arranged by Volodarsky, Chudnovsky, Kollontai, Trotsky and Lashevich (Trotsky (121), II, p. 390); Daniels (576), p. 89.

60 See note 40. These well-known events, here summarized, have been powerfully described by Reed (560); see Daniels (576) and Rabinowitch (563) for critical analysis.

61 On this, the most complete account is Trotsky's (121), II, pp. 397ff and Rayman's critical analysis (514), p. 300 and *Vosstaniye* (513), pp. 233ff. The Lettish delegate Peterson promised 4,000 workers to defend the congress.

62 For the whole debate, CGAORSSSR, 6978, 1, 131, 1–13.

63 Ibid.

64 See the *PVRK* minutes (542), vol. I, pp. 17–127; Daniels (576), pp. 132–65.

65 Reed (560), pp. 152ff.

66 Lenin (129), XXVI, pp. 240–1; Daniels (576), pp. 149–62.

67 Kerensky's statement.

68 Daniels (576), p. 180.

69 Ibid., pp. 180–200.

70 When it opened, there were 562 delegates – 382 Bolsheviks, 31 unaffiliated but attached to the Bolsheviks, 70 left Socialist Revolutionaries, 5 anarchists, 15 unitarist Social Democrats, 30 Menshevik-Internationalists, 21 Menshevik-Defensists, 7 nationality Social Democrats, 36 centre Socialist Revolutionaries, 16 right Socialist Revolutionaries, 3 nationality Socialist Revolutionaries. Not much meaning can be attached to these figures: see my conclusion. Cf. *Vtoroy* (543), and other figures in Radkey (532), p. 104.

71 Reed (560) and Daniels (576), *passim*.

72 Photocopy of the manuscript in V. V. Anikeyev, *Deyatelnost* (536), p. 441. Antonov thought that power would pass to the Petrograd Soviet: see text below.

73 In another miniature *coup d'état*, Lenin signed a mission order of the *PVRK* as 'president' and as sole signatory, whereas other orders of the *PVRK* were always signed by two people. Moreover, there is no sign that Lenin was ever even elected president of the *PVRK*. The manuscript has been reproduced photographically in *Istorichesky Archiv*, 5, p. 4.

74 On this see L. Schapiro (284), pp. 73–88.

75 *Lénine par Lénine* (522).

76 Startsev (363), pp. 249–88.

77 Calculated according to *PVRK* (542), I, pp. 53–162.

78 See above, chapter 1 and vol. I, chapter 8.

79 *PVRK* (542), I, pp. 452ff.

80 Popov (541). On the anarchists, see the first page of *Anarkhiya*, 26 October, which is an appeal to action: 'Be careful of the sabotage of our Revolution by the bourgeois', warned the clerks and workers of the port of Petrograd. 'The bourgeois shirt is sticking to its body. Let us gather our strength, show the bourgeoisie what we can do, and how we too can show leadership' (GAORSS, Lo., 4605, 1–8, 5 and 6).

81 Popov (541).

82 The *TsIK* of the first conference of soviets, which was still meeting, reckoned that schism within the Bolshevik party leadership would be unavoidable. It expected 'help from the factories so as to be able to hold a new session' (CGAORSSSR, 6978, 1, 133, 1).

83 The history of Bolshevik power has been recounted several times, as has also the story of the putting-down of various oppositions – political parties, whether bourgeois or socialist, trade unions, anarchist groups, etc. The best

overall analysis is Schapiro's (284).

84 *PVRK* (542), pp. 53–162.

85 The Petrograd press of less than a year later shows that the measures demanded by the masses and not in the Bolshevik programme (see Table 18 early in this chapter) were certainly endorsed by the party leaders in so far as they were not against the party's own programme. This was the case with compulsory labour for the bourgeois, meaning manual labour. The régime went further because it reserved the most painful jobs for the bourgeoisie – cleaning the streets, repairing the road at Oryol, unloading coal at Petrograd, digging trenches, etc., as Zinoviev himself announced. (*Izvestiya* of 19 October 1918, *Pravda* of 6 October, *Krasnaya Gazeta* of 16 October and Zinoviev in *Pravda* of 11 October (all 1918).)

86 Politically, this measure corresponded more to anarchist practice: see in Kronstadt, Yarchuk (Skirda edition) (533c).

87 *Uplotneniye* by Panteleyev and Lunacharsky, 1918; see also *Die Bolschewisten-greuel vom 21 August 1919 oder Kiews Schreckenstage*, 1750 feet, 1919. Both films have been analysed by me in *Annales* 1973/1, 'Le film, une contre-analyse de la société'.

88 Representatively, they were separated after the 'walk-out' of 8 October in the 'Pre-parliament'.

89 Documents on Cheka and terror under Lenin in J. Baynac's collection (732b).

90 This document, quoted by Baynac (732b) from vol. XXXV (Russian) of Lenin's *Works*, does not figure in the fourth edition of the works translated under the direction of R. Garaudy, but allusion is made to it in the table of events at the end of the work, under 26 June 1918 (vol. XXVII, p. 650).

91 Keep (578).

Conclusion

1 M. Fainsod, *Smolensk under Soviet Rule*, Schapiro (284, 306), Ulam (303, 519), Daniels, quoted in G. D. Jackson (579 and 576), Chamberlin (275).

2 Mints (512).

3 *3 Konferentsiya* (534), p. 66.

4 I have not considered this phenomenon here. On cultural policy early in the régime's years, see J. N. Palmier's works in the bibliography.

5 Yves Sturdze has ably shown the problem of symbolic places in *Organisation, Anti-organisation* (Paris, 1974).

6 Though very stimulating, the analysis by A. Inkeles (724) is excessive in its belittling of the achievements of October.

7 Memory of the period when a majority of Jews dominated the state apparatus has left a trace that can be added to the other elements making up the soviet anti-semitism that is officially denied and condemned. I might suggest that anti-semitism explains something of the conflicts of political tendency and then the purges of the Stalin era: see in this context the anti-semitic connotation of caricatures of 'the Left Opposition' in Carrère d'Encausse (733), p. 177.

8 In the Stalin era, seven nationalities were collectively deported – Crimean Tatars, Chechens, Ingush, etc. – for 'treason' during the Second World War. Those which constituted republics ceased to exist officially, and their names disappeared from the Soviet Encyclopaedia. Some were later restored. In parallel, both before and after the war, purges and deportations affected the intelligentsia of the Ukraine, and the Baltic states where armed action went on until 1950, followed by massive deportation into Soviet Asia: see Carrère d'Encausse (733). Conquest (710) and *Ferment* (720).

9 Elleinstein (732), Bettelheim (731), Louis Althusser, *Réponse à John Lewis* (Paris, 1973). On this last, and Althusser's work overall, see Jacques Rancière, *La Leçon d'Althusser* (Paris, 1974).

Bibliography

To the documents and the works cited in volume I of this history (*The Russian Revolution of February 1917*) (numbered 1 to 426) the following should be added. Either they bear particularly on the problems considered in this volume, or, having appeared since 1966, they should be added to the earlier bibliography.

1 Aids to research
2 Archives
3 History of the Revolution and of Bolshevism
4 Documents and works (memoirs, research, etc.) on the period July to October 1917
5 Books and articles on various aspects of the Revolution:
   (a) the army;
   (b) the agrarian question;
   (c) the workers' struggle and the workers' organizations;
   (d) problems of the family, women and children;
   (e) the church and religion;
   (f) the intelligentsia, education and teaching;
   (g) the Revolution in the theatre and the cinema;
   (h) the nationalities.
6 Interpretations of the October Revolution

These various works are cited from no. 501 onward.

1 Aids to research

To items (1) and (10) of vol. I should be added:

501 P. K. Grimstead, *Archives and Manuscript Repositories in the USSR, Moscow and Leningrad* (Princeton University Press, 1972).
502 *Narodnoye Khozyaystvo SSSR v 1917–1920 gg.* (Moscow, 1967). Bibliographical guide to books and journals in Russian 1917–63.
503 *K letiyu sovietskoy vlasti. Sbornik bibliograficheskikh i metodicheskikh materialov* (Moscow, 1967).
504 *Kino i Fotodokumenty po istorii velikogo Oktyabrya* (Moscow, 1958). The only

list of photographs and cinematic documentation. A guide to fictional films
and other cinematic documentation is currently in preparation.
See also the bibliographies of items 563, 577b, 583, 598, 622b, 629, 705 and 733.

2 Archives

The archives consulted for both volumes of this work are:
505 CGAORSSSR (Central Archives of the October Revolution)
Fondy 3 (Chancellery of the minister-president of the Provisional Government)
       336 (Commission attached to the Petrograd Soviet)
       398 (Ministry of the Interior)
       406 (Chief Security Office)
       472 (Soviet of Petrograd Factory Committees)
       1235 (All-Russian central executive committee of the soviets (*VTsIK*)
       1236 (Revolutionary committee of the Petrograd Soviet)
       1244 (Editorial board of *Izvestiya*)
       6978 (Executive committee of the first all-Russian congress of soviets)
       also nos 66, 133, 393, 410, 683, 1978, 5498.
506 KPSS Leningrad (Communist Party archives), *Fond* 4000 (Anarchism)
507 GAORSS, Mo. (Regional archive of Moscow), *Fond* 66 (Moscow soviet of
    deputies)
508 GAORSS, Lo. (Leningrad regional archive)
Fondy 55 (Soviet of deputies of the Kolomensky district)
       101 (Political committee of the Peterhof District Soviet)
       151 (Political committee of the Petrogradsky District Soviet)
       4598 (Factory committee of the Baltiysky works)
       4602 (Factory committee of the Petrograd Munitions Works)
       8878 (Political committee of the Komolmensky District Soviet)
also *fondy* 4754, 1000, 4592, 4601, 7384, 7389.
509 CGIAL (Leningrad historical archives)
Fondy 23 (Ministry of Trade and Industry)
       1247 (Institutes of education)
       1249 (Women's societies)
       1250 (Daghestan, Caspian Sea)
       1251 (Railwaymen)
       1259 (Learned societies)
       1264 (Ryazan and Penza)
       1266 (Red Cross)
       1267 (Yekaterinoslav, Ukraine)
       1275 (Teaching)
       1293 (Crimean and Black Sea area)
       1231 (Artisans)
       1338 (Moslems)
       1405 (Ministry of Justice)
       1276 (Council of Ministers)
       1278 (State Duma)

510 CGVIA (Central military archives)
Fondy 2031 (Northern front)
    2067 (South-western front)
    2148 (X Army)
also *fond* 2100.
511 Helsinki, *l. otdeleniye kantselyarii Finlyandskogo General-Gubernatora* 1917–2. *Fondy* FB. 1270–1276 series 1, 25, 26, 30, 47, 290, 291, 2, 10, 13.
Outside Finland and the USSR I have used archives in Paris, Vincennes, Amsterdam, London (as cited in vol. I).

3 History of the Revolution and of Bolshevism

To the classic works by Chamberlin, Carr and Deutscher, and the studies of the Bolshevik Party already quoted in vol. I, nos 275–322 (particularly B. Souvarine, L. Schapiro, P. Broué, R. Daniels and D. Shub), should be added, for the Revolution of 1917:

512 I. U. Mints, *Istoriya velikogo Oktyabrya* (Moscow, 1967–70, 3 vols). This sums up all Soviet work and acts as an authorized version of the events of 1917.
513 *Oktyabrskoye vooruzhennoye vosstaniye* ('The armed rising of October'), ed. A. L. Freyman, V. I. Startsev, Y. S. Tokarev and others (Leningrad, 1967, 2 vols). Though limited to the capital, this is the most detailed analysis of economic factors and of the preparation for the armed rising.
514 Mikhail Rayman, *Russkaya Revolyutsiya* (Prague, 1968, 2 vols). A good political history, translated from Czech, of which there is now an Italian version (Bari, 1969).
515 Marcel Liebman, *Le Léninisme sous Lénine*, I. *La Conquête du pouvoir* (Paris, Le Seuil, 1973). A good Leninist interpretation of Lenin's policy.
516 Jean Elleinstein, *Histoire de l'URSS*, vol. I (1970). A revision of the Stalinist account of the history of the Revolution, by a Communist historian.
Some volumes of essays should be added to the above, particularly:
517 *Revolutionary Russia* (ed. Richard Pipes), based on the Harvard Colloquium of 1967 (Harvard University Press, 1967, 2nd ed. 1968). I have relied considerably on the essays by J. A. Mayer, J. Keep, L. Schapiro, D. Geyer and O. Anweiler.
518 *Oktyabr i grazhdanskaya voyna v SSSR* ('October and the Russian Civil War') (Moscow, 1966). A collection of articles in honour of Mints's 70th birthday.
There are many outstanding contributions, and see also the *Record of the Leningrad Colloquium* of 1962 bearing more precisely on Lenin's activity and the preparations for the October Rising; see also works (576ff) on the rising itself, especially S. P. Melgunov and R. V. Daniels.
518b *Borba za pobyedu i ukprepleniye sovietskoy vlasti 1917–1918* ('Struggle for the Victory and Consolidation of Soviet Power 1917–19'), ed. Z. L. Serebryakova, K. M. Pervukhina, A. I. Razgon and others (Moscow, 1968). A collection of articles.

Also for interpretation, see nos 721ff.

On the Bolshevik party and its protagonists, there should be added to the works of pre-1967 quoted in vol. I:

519 Adam Ulam, *Lenin and the Bolsheviks* (1968). The most thorough and detailed account.

520 J. Laloy, *Le Socialisme de Lénine* (Paris, de Brouwer, 1967). A sharp critical analysis.

520b *Lenin, The Man, The Theorist, The Leader*, eds L. Schapiro and P. Reddaway (London, 1967). A set of monographs on Lenin as economist, Lenin and the problem of art, etc.

Lenin's letters have also been published in

521 *The Letters of Lenin*, trans. E. Hill and D. Mudie (Hyperion Press, Connecticut, 1973, a re-issue of the 1937 edition). The work is important for understanding of Lenin's character and especially his relations with his mother.

The iconography of Lenin emerges in a film assembled by myself with P. Samson:

522 *Lénine par Lénine* (59 minutes, Pathé 1970).

On other Bolshevik leaders there are several monographs, very useful in themselves but adding little to the history of the Revolution of 1917:

523 Stephen F. Cohen, *Bukharin and the Bolshevik Revolution* (New York, 1973).

524 Warren Lerner, *Karl Radek, the Last Internationalist* (Stanford, 1970). This contains a useful list of Radek's writings.

To these should be added two biographies of Stalin:

525 Robert C. Tucker, *Stalin* (1974).

526 Adam Ulam, *Stalin* (1974).

There is also a biography of the Menshevik, Martov:

527 Israel Getzler, *Martov, a Political Biography of a Russian Social-Democrat* (Melbourne and Cambridge, 1967).

On the overall history of the party and its members:

528 Georges Haupt and J. J. Marie, *Les Bolcheviks par eux-mêmes* (Paris, Maspero, 1967). Each autobiography is followed by a critical analysis.

529 W. M. Mosse, 'Makers of the Soviet Union', *Slavonic and East European Review*, 1968, vol. XLVI, pp. 141ff.

530 T. H. Rigby, *Communist Party Membership in the USSR 1917–67* (Princeton, 1968). A valuable sociological and quantitative study, with numbers of members in each period, by age, sex, nationality etc.

On relations between the Bolshevik and other parties

531 K. Markovich Astrakhan, *Bolsheviki i ikh politicheskiye protivniki v 1917 g.* ('The Bolsheviks and their political enemies in 1917') (Moscow, 1973).

On the Socialist Revolutionaries, to Radkey's first volume (vol. I, no. 297) should be added:

532 O. H. Radkey, *The Sickle under the Hammer* (Columbia University Press, 1963). Especially for the period after October.

On other political groups:

532b W. S. Rosenberg, *The Russian Liberals. Liberalism in the Russian Revolution* (1974).

Anarchism: to nos 319ff cited in vol. I should be added:

533a Paul Avrich, *The Russian Anarchists* (Princeton, 1967).

533b Paul Avrich, *Kronstadt 1921* (Princeton, 1970).

Two essential works:

533c A. Skirda, *Kronstadt 1921. Prolétariat contre bolchévisme* (Paris, ed. de la Téte de Feuilles, 1971). A translation of the chief writings of the Kronstadt leaders, Yarchuk, Petrichenko, with an introduction by Skirda.

These three works give a very full bibliography of Russian anarchism, to which should be added that of Jacqueline Pluet in *Autogestion* 18/19 (1972).

4 Documents on the period from July to October 1917

To the documentary collections nos 20−39 of vol. I should be added:

534 *Vtoraya i tretya petrogradskiye obshchegorodskiye konferentsii Bolshevikob v iyule i oktyabrye 1917 g. Protokoly i materialy* (Moscow, 1927).

535 *Protokoly tsentralnogo komiteta RSDRP(b) avg. 1917−fevr. 1918 g.* (Moscow, 1958).

535b *Les Bolcheviks et la révolution d'Octobre* (Paris, Maspero, 1964).

536 V. V. Anikeyev, *Deyatelnost TsKRSDRP(b) v 1917 g. Khronika sobitiy* ('Activities of the central committee of the CP(b) in 1917') (Moscow, 1971). A useful chronology of the central committee's doings.

For the period there are some essential documents collected in:

537 J. J. Marie, *Ces Paroles qui ébranlèrent le monde 1917−1924* (Paris, 1967).

The series of documents on the revolutionary movement in general (nos 20−24 of vol. I) has been continued, for this period, wth the following:

538 *Revolyutsionnoye dvizheniye v Rossii v avguste 1917 g. Razgrom Kornilovskogo myatezha. Dokumenty i materialy* (Moscow, 1959).

539 *Revolyutsionnoye dvizheniye v Rossii v sentyabre 1917 g. Dok. i mat.* (Moscow, 1960).

540 *Oktyabrskoye vooruzhennoye vosstaniye v Petrograde, Dok. i mat.* (Moscow, 1957).

A particularly valuable Menshevik publication of 1918 is:

541 A. L. Popov, *Oktyabrsky Perevorot. Fakty i dokumenty* (Petrograd, 1918, prefaced by N. Rozkov).

There should be added:

542 *Petrogradsky voyenno-revolyutsionny komitet: dok. i mat.* ('The Petrograd Military-Revolutionary Committee') (3 vols, Moscow, 1966).

On the soviets, to documents indicated in vol. I should be added:

543 *Vtoroy vserossiysky s'yezd sovietov R. i D. deputatov* (Moscow, 1928).

544 *Soviety v Oktyabrye. Sbornik dokumentov pod red. S. A. Piontkovskogo* (Moscow, 1928).

545 *Soviety krestyanskikh deputatov i drugiye krestyanskikh organizatsiy pod red. A. V. Shchestakova* (Leningrad, 2 vols. 1929).

Political events from July to October:

Eye-witness accounts and memoirs shown in vol. I bearing on the Revolution overall (especially Lenin, Sukhanov, Trotsky, Volin, Tseretelli, Kerensky, etc.) should be supplemented by works more particularly concerned with the July

Days, the Kornilov Putsch and the October Days:

546 V. A. Antonov-Ovseyenko, *V semnadtsatom godu* ('In 1917') (Moscow, 1933).

547 V. D. Bonch-Bruyevich, 'Ot iyulya do oktyabrya' ('July to October'), *Proletarsk. Rev.*, 1922/10.

548 F. Dan, 'K istorii poslednikh dney Vremennogo Pravitelstva' ('The last days of the Provisional Government'), *Letopis Revolyutsii*, 1923/1.

549 O. Dzenis, 'Kak mi brali 25. oktyabrya Zimny Dvorets; ('How we took the Winter Palace on 25 October'), *Pravda*, 6–7 November 1921.

550 I. P. Flerovsky, 'Iyulsky politichesky urok' ('The political lesson of July'), *Prolet. Rev.*, 1926/7.

551 A. F. Kerensky, *Iz daleka* ('From afar') (Paris, 1922).

552 I. P. Flerovsky, 'Kronstadt v oktyabrskoy revolyutsii' ('Kronstadt in the October Revolution'), *Prolet. Rev.*, 1922/1.

553 M. I. Latsis, 'Iyulskiye dni v Petrograde' (The July Days in Petrograd'), *Prolet. Rev.*, 1923/5.

554 M. I. Latsis, 'Nakanune oktyabrskikh dney' ('On the eve of the October Days'), *Izvestiya*, 6 November 1918.

555 P. N. Malianovich, 'V zimnem dvortse 25–26 okt. 1917 g.' ('In the Winter Palace 25–26 Oct. 1917'), *Biloye*, 1918/12.

556 V. I. Nevsky, 'Istoricheskoye zasedaniye Petrogradskogo komiteta RSDPR(b) nakanune Okt. vosstaniya' ('An historic session of the Petrograd Committee of the Bolsheviks on the eve of the October rising'), *Krasnaya Letopis*, 1923/2, 3.

557 B. V. Nikitine, *The Fatal Years* (London, 1938).

558 N. I. Podvoysky, 'Voyennaya organizatsiya TsK. RSDRP(b) i voyenno-revolyutsionny komitet 1917 g.' ('The military organization of the central committee of the Bolshevik Party and the military-revolutionary committee of 1917', *Krasnaya Letopis*, 1923/6, 8.

559 N. I. Podvoysky, 'Kak proizoshla okt. rev.' ('How the Oct. Rev. happened'), *Izvestiya*, 6 November 1918.

560 John Reed, *Ten Days that shook the World* (New York, 1919).

561 F. Raskol'nikov, 'Iyulskiye dni' ('In the July Days'), *Prol. Rev.*, 1923/5.

562 G. Zinoviev, *Sochineniya* ('Works') (Leningrad 1923–9, 7 vols).

On the July Days:

563 Alexander Rabinowitch, *Prelude to Revolution. The Petrograd Bolsheviks and the July 1917 Uprising* (Indiana University Press, 1968). Has an exhaustive bibliography. It completely revises the history of the July Days and makes obsolete all previous accounts except

564 O. N. Znamensky, *Iyulsky krizis 1917 goda* ('The crisis of July 1917') (Moscow, 1962). This is still useful for the political consequences of July in the provinces.

On the Kornilov Putsch:

565 N. Ya. Ivanov, *Kornilovshchina i eye razgrom* ('The Kornilovshchina and its defeat') (Leningrad, 1965). Very well-researched and well-written.

566 M. I. Kapustin, *Zagovor generalov* ('The Generals' Plot') (Moscow, 1968). This supplies some new information as to the military organization of the

counter-revolution.

567 N. G. Dumova, 'Maloizvestniye materialy po istorii Kornilovshchiny', *Voprosy Istorii* (1968), II.

On foreign affairs and the beginnings of intervention, see the works cited in vol. I, nos 407–18, the following to be added:

568 M. Futrell, *Northern Underground* (New York, 1963). On the clandestine activities of the revolutionaries, the Allies and the Germans in Scandinavia.

And the second work of

569 V. S. Vasyukov, *Preistoriya inverventsii* (Moscow, 1970) on the prehistory of foreign intervention.

570 A. V. Ignatiev, *Vneshnyaya politkia Vremennogo Pravitelstva* (Moscow, 1974). Contrary to custom, this author uses the same title as Vasyukov's work, quoted as no. 408 in vol. I. Ignatiev's book contains some important documents.

571 Rex Wade, *The Foreign Policy of the Provisional Government* (1968). A useful survey.

On intervention:

572 G. F. Kennan, *Russia leaves the War* (Princeton University Press, 1956). For the USA.

573 G. F. Kennan, *The Decision to Intervene* (Princeton University Press, 1958).

574 R. H. Ullman, *Intervention and the War* (Princeton University Press, 1961). For Great Britain.

575 J. Delmas, *L'Etat-Major français et le front oriental (novembre 1917–novembre 1918)* (3e cycle, Sorbonne, Paris, 1965). For France.

On the October Days: the best study overall is

576 Robert V. Daniels, *Red October. The Bolshevik Revolution of 1917* (New York, 1967), which should be complemented by

577 S. P. Melgunov, *Kak Bolsheviki zakhvatili vlast* ('How the Bolsheviks took Power') (Paris, 1953). For the days following October and Kerensky's last efforts; also for October in Moscow.

577b There is an English-language edition of this work, but without the section covering October in Moscow, though containing a usefully-revised bibliography, notes and an index by S. G. Puskarev (Santa Barbara, ABC, 1972).

On the provinces and the October Days in Moscow:

578 John Keep, 'October in the provinces', *Rev. Russia* (517), pp. 229–75.

579 G. D. Jackson, 'The Moscow Insurrection as a case study', delivered to the Banff colloquium, to be published.

There is a penetrating study of Lenin's strategy in October in

580 D. Geyer, 'The Bolshevik Insurrection in Petrograd', *Rev. Russia* (517), pp. 209ff.

On Lenin's role and the preparations for the Days, there is a huge literature. The most stimulating collection reproduces the discussions at the Leningrad colloquium of 13–16 November 1962:

581 *Lenin i oktyabrskoye vooruzhennoye vosstaniye v Petrograde* (Moscow, 1964). This includes contributions from the main historians of the Revolution. The role of other protagonists is examined in Daniels (576) and the earlier works of Deutscher, Souvarine, etc. On Zinoviev there is a balanced view in

582 Myron W. Heldin, 'Zinoviev's revolutionary tactics in 1917', *Slavic Review* (1975), pp. 19–44.

5 Aspects of the Revolution

The army

The most complete bibliography of this can be found in

583 G. Wettig, 'Die Rolle der russischen Armee im revolutionären Machtkampf 1917', *Forschungen zur osteuropäischen Geschichte*, 1967, pp. 46–389. This examines revolutionary events until July. There are some very useful collections of documents:

584 *Revolyutsionnoye dvizheniye v armii i na flote v gody pervoy mirovoy voyny*, ed. A. L. Sidorov (Moscow, 1967).

585 *Rev. dvizh, v russkoy armii v 1917 g.*, ed. L. S. Gaponenko (Moscow, 1968). This publishes the documents showing the radicalization and Bolshevization of the army, but not other documents. At least the former are published in full.

586 *Bolshevizatsiya petrogradskogo garnizona*, ed. A. N. Drezen (Leningrad, 1932).

587 *Oktyabrskaya revolyutsiya i armiya 25 okt.–mart 1918 g.*, ed. Gaponenko, (Moscow, 1973).

588 *Soldatskiye pisma 1917 g.* (Moscow, 1927) with preface by Pokrovksy.

589 *Tsarskaya armiya v period mirovoy voyny i fevr. rev.*, ed. M. Volfovich and E. Medvedev (Kazan, 1932) with

[590 missing in the French original]

591 *Borba s Bolshevizmom na yuge Rossii. Uchastiye v borbe Donskogo Kazachestva* (Fevr. 1917–mart 1920 gg.) (Prague, 1921).

592 G. Andolenko, *Histoire de l'armée russe* (Paris, 1967) and the memoirs of military attachés (Knox, Sadoul, etc.) in vol. I, 129b, 200, 215, etc.

Among works on the army, the following are important (other than Wettig, who takes the officers' viewpoint):

592b N. Stone, *The Eastern Front 1914–1917* (London, 1975). On the relationship between the war, the army and the disintegration of the economy.

593 A. Rabinowitch, no. 563 and also his 'The Petrograd Garrison and the Bolshevik Seizure of Power' in A. and J. Rabinowitch, *Revolution and Politics in Russia* (723). Some individual, and highly useful studies, are:

594 A. G. Tkachuk, *Rev. dvizh. v armiyakh yugozapadnogo i ruminskogo frontov nakanune i v period velikogo Oktyabrya* (Lvov, 1968).

595 F. A. Surygin, *Rev. dvizh. soldatskikh mass severnogo fronta v 1917 g.* (1958).

596 J. F. N. Bradley, *La Légion tchécoslovaque en Russie 1914–1920* (Paris, 1965).

On the beginnings of the Red Army and the Civil War:

597 John Erickson, 'The Beginnings of the Red Army', *Rev. Russia* (517).

598 John Erickson, *The Soviet High Command* (London, 1962). Both works are vital, with a very complete bibliography. Latterly there have appeared:

599 G. A. Brinkley, *The Volunteer Army and Allied Intervention in South Russia 1917–21* (North Dakota University Press, 1966).

600 Richard Luckett, *The White Generals* (London, 1971).

On the beginnings of foreign intervention, Ullman, Kennan, Delmas (above), etc., should be used; for the Soviet 'reconquista':

600b T. T. Hammond, *The Anatomy of Communist Take-Overs* (Yale, 1975).

The agrarian question

To the works quoted in vol. I (342–351) and Carr, vol. 2 and no. 545, add:

601 *Ekonomicheskoye polozheniye Rossii nakanune vel. Okt. sots. rev.*, vol. 3 (Moscow, 1969). An essential collection for documents of the rural revolution.

For an overall view of the peasantry as a long-term question:

602 P. I. Kusner, *Selo Viritiano v proshlom i nastoyashchem. Opit etnograficheskogo izucheniya russkoy kolkhoznoy derevni* (Moscow, 1958).

603 S. P. and E. Dunn, 'The Great-Russian Peasant: cultural change or cultural development?' *Ethnology*, vol. 11, no. 3, July 1963.

604 S. P. and E. Dunn, *The Peasants of Central Russia* (New York, 1967).

The most complete survey of the agrarian revolution 1905–28 is:

605 P. N. Pershin, *Agrarnaya revolyutsiya v Rossii* (1922, 2 vols, translated from the Ukrainian).

The political aspect of the agrarian movement is studied in:

606 O. N. Moisseva, *Soviety krestyanskikh deputatov v 1917 g.* (Moscow, 1967; cf. 545).

Among regional studies, I have particularly used Ushatova (350).

607 D. S. Tocheniy, 'Bankrotstvo politiki S-Rov Privolzhya', *Ist. SSSR*, 1964/4.

608 A. S. Smirnov, 'Krestyanskiye s'yezdy Penzenskoy Gubernii v 1917 g.', *Ist. SSSR*, 1967/3.

609 V. Andreyuk, 'Borba za zemlyu v Penzenskoy Gubernii v 1917', *Uch. Zap. Penzneskogo Pedagog. Instituta*, vyp. 16, 1966.

610 I. M. Razgon, 'Politicheskiye nastroyeniya sibirskogo krestyanstva', *Okt. i grazh. voyna* (518), pp. 211–33.

On division of the land in the provinces of Novgorod and Vladimir:

611 E. V. Ostrovsky, 'Raspredeleniye zemel v Novgorodskoy gub. v 1918 g.' and

612 A. Malyavsky, 'Raspredeleniye zemel v Vladimirskoy gub. v 1918 g.' *Okt. i grazh. voyna* (518), pp. 249–70 and 270–80.

613 B. M. Fikh, *Agrarnaya Revolyutsiya v Byelorossii* (Minsk, 1966).

On the movement of agricultural labourers, especially in the Ukraine:

614 A. M. Lichetsky, 'Iz istorii zabastovochnoy borby selskokhozyaystvennogo proletariata Ukrainy (mart–okt. 1917 g)', *Trudy kafedry ist. KPSS Kharkovskogo gosudarstvennogo universiteta*, VIII/1960.

On the Decree on Land, apart from Sorlin's article and Trapeznikov's work (348 and 349), the following should be consulted:

615 E. A. Lutsky, 'Podgotovka proyekta dekreta o zemle', *Okt. i grazh. voyna* (518), pp. 233–49.

616 Esther Kingston-Mann, 'Lenin and the beginnings of Marxist revolution.

The burden of political opportunity', *Slav. and E. European Review*, October 1972, pp. 570–88.

On the countryside after October, and for knowledge that every revolutionary was expected to know, there is a *vade mecum* in:

617 Ya. Burov, *Organiziruyte derevnyu* (Petrograd, 1918).

There is a general view of the period 1905–21, without hindsight, in:

618 S. M. Dubrovsky, *Ocherky russkoy revolyutsii. I. Selskoye khozyaystvo* (Moscow, 1923).

The place of 1917 in rural history is studied in:

619 *Istoriya sovietskogo krestyanstva i kolkhoznogo stroitelsvta v SSSR*, proceedings of a Moscow colloquium in 1961 (Moscow, 1963).

There are two especially penetrating studies, from the viewpoint of history overall:

620 Jan M. Maier, 'Town and Country in the Civil War', *Rev. Russia* (517), pp. 331–61.

621 Eric Wolf, *Agrarian Revolts* (London, 1966). Chapter on Russia.

621b O. Chaadaeva, 'Soyuz pomeshchikov v 1917 g.', *KA*, XXI (1927), pp. 97–121. On landlords' resistance.

For long-term comparison:

621c 'L'évolution agraire de l'Empire tsariste à la collectivisation', a collection of Soviet articles edited by A. Casanova in *Recherches internationales à la lumière du marxisme*, 85, 1975.

622 Sylvia Bensidoum, *L'agitation paysanne en Russie de 1881 à 1902* (Paris, 1975).

622b Sigrid Grosskopf, *L'alliance ouvrière et paysanne en URSS 1921–1928: Le problème du blé* (Paris, 1976). Contains a very valuable bibliography.

622c Teodor Shanin, *The Awkward Class. Political Sociology of Peasantry in a Developing Society, Russia 1910–25* (Oxford University Press, 1972). A profound statistical study. On the birth, life and death of rural communes before forced collectivization, see R. G. Wesson, *Soviet Communes* (Rutgers University Press, 1963).

The workers' struggle and the workers' organizations

The main sources are:

623 *Professionalny Vestnik, organ vserossiyskogo sovieta professionalnikh soyuzov okt. 1917–okt. 1918 gg.*

624 *Tretya vserossiyskaya konferentsiya professionalnikh soyuzov*: see the critical analysis by Kaplan (629).

625 *Oktyabrskaya Revolyutsiya i Fabzavkom* (2 vols, 1927).

626 A. M. Pankratova, *Fabzavkomy Rossii v borbe za zots. fabriku* (Moscow, 1923). (French translation in *Autogestion*, 1967.)

To works cited in vol. I, especially Carr, vol. II, pp. 55–146, Volobuyev (355) and Tokarev (358) add:

627 B. M. Freydlin, *Ocherki istorii rabochego dvizheniya v 1917 g.* (Moscow, 1967). A panorama of the subject, and

628 O. I. Shkataran, *Problemy sotsialnoy struktury raboch. klassa SSSR* (Moscow, 1970), a pioneering sociological study.

On the Bolshevik party's policy towards working class and institutions, the best overall work is:

629 F. I. Kaplan, *Bolshevik Ideology and the Ethics of Soviet Labour 1917–20, the Formative Years* (New York, 1968), with a good bibliography; see also:

630 Maurice Brinton, *Bolsheviks and Workers' Control 1917–1921. The State and Counter-Revolution* (London, 1970), and also a special number of *Autogestion* quoted above, with nos 18–19 on anarchism, and self-management.

On the problem of self-management and factory committees, there are two useful articles:

631 P. Avrich, 'The Bolshevik Revolution and Workers' Control in Russian Industry', *Slavic Review*, XXII, i (1963), pp. 47–63 and

632 M. L. Itkin, 'Tsentry fab. zav. komitetov Rossii v 1917 g., *Vop. Ist.*, 1974/2, pp. 21–36, which has a good bibliography. On these matters, the official view appears in:

633 A. G. Yegorova, *Profsoyuzy i Fabzavkom v borbe za pobedu Okt.* (Moscow, 1960).

634 A. G. Yegorova, *Partiya i profsoyuzy v okt. rev.* (Moscow, 1970).

On the beginnings of the Bolshevik régime, other than Kaplan (quoted above), see:

635 James Bunyan, *The Origin of Forced Labour in the Soviet State 1917–1921: Documents and Materials* (Baltimore, 1967).

636 A. F. Rastrigin, 'Rev. komitety v borbe s ekonomicheskoy kontr-rev.', *Voprosy Istorii*, KPSS, L967/5.

636b W. R. Augustine, 'Russia's Railwaymen July–Oct. 1917', *Slavic Review*, 1965.

637 D. A. Bayevsky, *Rabochy klass v perviye gody sov. vlasti 1917–1921* (Moscow, 1974).

637b M. Lorenz, *Les débuts de la politique industrielle de Lénine* (Berlin, 1974).

There are few good monographs on single factories, other than:

638 L. L. Evsenin, *Ot Fabrikanta k Krasnomu Oktyabryu* (Moscow, 1927).

The best picture of economic life in Russia during the Revolution is given by E. E. Kruse, O. N. Znamensky, A. L. Freyman in *Okt. Vooruzh. Vosstaniye 1917 goda v Petrograde* (513), vol. 1, ch. 7 and vol. 2, chs 8, 14. The picture being apparently limited to Petrograd, it should be complemented by other works on the economy, quoted in vol. 1 and especially N. Stone (592b).

638b The discussion started by Gerschenkron (340) on Russia's economic development and 'take-off' in 1914 can be usefully reconsidered with an article by M. E. Falkus, 'Russia's National Income, 1913, a Re-evaluation', *Economica* 137 (February, 1968), pp. 52–74. There is a good analysis of some economic and social aspects in:

639 Roger Pethybridge, *The Spread of the Russian Revolution 1917* (London, 1972) where problems of railways, post and supply are particularly studied.

On the development of trade unionism, to Chamberlin, Gelard and Schwarz add:

639b Thomas Lowit, *Le syndicalisme de type soviétique* (Paris, 1971).

The co-operative movement has found its historian in:

640 V. V. Kabanov, *Okt. Rev. i kooperatsiya 1917 g.–mart 1919 g.* (Moscow, 1973).

On Russian society on the eve of the Revolution and after, some cultural studies can be added to the works of Dunn and Shkaratan cited elsewhere:

641 S. S. Ostroumov, *Prestupnost i eye prichiny v dorevolyutsionnoy Rossii* (Izd. Mosk. Univ., 1960). This uses the investigations and analyses the statistics worked out by E. Tarkovsky in *Zhurnal Ministerstva* 1899/3 and 1913/10: very important.

642 G. Guroff and S. F. Starr, 'A note on urban literacy in Russia 1890–1914', *Jahrbücher f. d. Geschichte Osteuropas 1917*, pp. 520–31. See also Pethybridge, *The Social Prelude to Stalinism* (quoted below).

Problems of the family, women and children

643 H. Kent Geiger, *The Family in Soviet Russia* (Harvard University Press, 1968). Essential for the Soviet period. Other than the analyses by Marx and Engels, there is no analysis of the family before 1917, but Geiger has a good bibliography.

644 E. Elnett, *Historic Origin and Social Development of Family Life in Russia* (Columbia University Press, 1926, reprint 1973). A fine analysis, with a valuable selection of proverbs added.

645 Gertruda Alexander, *Istoricheskoye razvitiye zhenskogo burzhuaznogo dvizheniya vo Frantsii, Amerike, Anglii i Germanii*, pref. K. Zetkin (Moscow, 1920). The only systematic study from a Marxist viewpoint; it does not include Russia.

646 Milovidova i. K. Zetkin, *Zhensky vopros i Zhensk. dvizh.* (Moscow and Leningrad, 1929). This complements the preceding work.

There should be added the following memoirs and studies appearing before and during the Revolution:

647 A. Amfiteatrov, *Zhenshchiny v obshchestvennikh dvizheniyakh Rossii* (Geneva, 1905). A pioneering study.

648 A. Kollontai, *Rabotnitsa za god Rev.* (Petrograd, 1918).

649 *Chto dali rabotnitsam Okt. rev. i sov. Vlast* (Petrograd, 1920).

On the ideas of Lenin, Kollontai and Trotsky the best work is

650 J. Stora-Sandor, *Alexandra Kollontai. Marxisme et révolution sexuelle* (Paris, 1973) and also on Kollontai:

650a H. Lenczyc, 'Alexandra Kollontai, essai bibliographique', *Cahiers du Monde Russe et Soviétique*, XIV, 1973, pp. 205–42; over 210 titles.

650b Farnworth, 'Bolshevism, the Woman Question and A. Kollontai', *The American Review*, 1976/2, pp. 292–317; see also

651 Klara Zetkin, *Reminiscences of Lenin* (London, 1929).

652 Klara Zetkin, *Lenin and the Woman Question* (New York, 1934).

653 L. Trotsky, *Woman and the Family* (New York, 1970), documents collected by C. Lund and particularly including 'From the old family to the new' which appeared in *Pravda*, 13 July 1923.

There is a survey of the 1930s in:

654 F. Halle, *Women in Soviet Russia* (London, 1933), the only overall historical

and sociological survey.

Among recent works, for Bolshevik activity:

655 A. T. Barulina, 'Rabota Petrogradskoy i moskovskoy part-organizatsiy sredi zhenshchin-rabotnits (1917)', *Borba za pobedu Okt.* (Moscow, 1974).

656 N. A. Veletskaya, 'Partiya v borbe za zhenskiye proletarskiye massy', *Borba bolshev. partii za sozdaniye politich. armii sots. rev.* (Moscow, 1967), pp. 296–341.

For some sociological and statistical aspects: women, marriage, family, etc.

657 A. G. Khartsev, *Brak i semya v SSSR* (Moscow, 1964). Cursory but useful.

658 N. T. Dodge, *Women in the Soviet Economy* (Baltimore, 1966). Statistical studies on demography and the role of women.

For the transformation of the family from the revolutionary era to the Stalin period, the accounts in novels and firms are irreplaceable:

659 V. S. Dunham, 'From Free Love to Puritanism', *Soviet Society* (725), pp. 540–6, based on literature, particularly Katayev, Malyshkin, Zochchenko.

660 M. N. Féart, 'L'évolution de la famille en URSS au travers du cinéma' (MA dissertation, Paris I 1973).

661 Marc Ferro, 'Tchapaev, une étude de l'idéologie stalinienne au travers du cinéma', *L'Art et sa vocation interdisciplinaire, Francastel et après* (coll. Médiations, Gonthier 1975).

662 For developments up to 1970, *Documentation française* 31 July–2 August 1970.

On the emancipation of women among Russian Moslems, there is a good collection:

663 *Veliky Oktyabr i raskreposhcheniye zhenshchin sredney Azii i Kazakhstana (1917–1936)* (Moscow, 1971).

For women and the family before the Revolution:

664 V. Nalivkin and V. Nalivkina, *Ocherk bita zhenshchiny osedlogo Tusemnogo naseleniya Fergana* (Kazan, 1886).

Assessment up to 1927 appears in:

665 *Kommissii po ulucheniyu truda i bita zhenshchin vostoka 17 okt. 1927 g.* (Moscow, 1927); see also:

666 *Raskreposhcheniye zhenshchin sred. Azii i Kazakhs.* (Ashkhabad, 1972); proceedings of the conference held in October 1970.

667 F. W. Halle, *Women in the Soviet East* (New York, 1938), which is much less good than the same author's work on women in Soviet Russia. There is a good set of photographs (77) on the 1920s.

The church and religion

No work deals in detail with the attitude of the populace during the Revolution except for:

668 A. I. Emelyakh, 'Ateizm i antiklerikalizm narodnikh mass v 1917 g.', *Po etapam razvitiya ateizma v SSSR* (Leningrad, 1967).

By contrast there are many works on the church and religious life since October: the three most useful, in order of publication, are:

669 J. S. Curtiss, *The Russian Church and the Soviet State 1917–50*

(Boston, 1953).

670 W. Kolarz, *Religion in the Soviet Union* (New York, 1961).

671 Nikita Struve, *Les Chrétiens en URSS* (Paris, 1963), new and revised edition *Christians in Contemporary Russia* (1966).

There should be added a documentary collection with a good bibliography:

672 Borellaw Szczesniak, *The Russian Revolution and Religion, a Collection of Documents* (Indiana, 1959).

On the role of Lenin, Bonch-Bruyevich and their ideas on religion, the role of sects and the class struggle in the countryside, there is an excellent work in:

673 A. I. Klibanov, *Istoriya religioznogo sektantstva v Rossii* (Moscow, 1965).

The main Marxist-Leninist documents on religion are collected in:

674 *Kommunisticheskaya partiya i sovietskoye pravitelstvo o religii i tserkvi* (Moscow, 1961).

On anti-clericalism the best work is:

675 A. Ziegler, *Die russische Gottlosen-Bewegung* (Munich, 1932), which should be complemented, for the period just after 1917, by:

676 N. S. Timascheff, *Religion in Soviet Russia 1917−42* (London, 1943).

On the attitude of Communism towards Islam, see chapter 9 of

677 A. Bennigsen and C. Lemercier-Quelquejay, *L'Islam en Union soviétique* (Paris, 1968).

The intelligentsia, teaching and education

On the Revolution in one university, there is a unique source with the minutes of the university council from February to October:

678 A. I. Gladkovskaya, 'Odessky universitet v 1917−1940 gg.', *Odessky Universitet za 75 let (1865−1940)* (Odessa, 1940).

On the attitude of the intelligentsia, especially the universities:

679 Dimitri Konchalovsky, 'L'intelligentsia avant la révolution', *Revue des Etudes Slaves*, 1960.

680 Dimitri Konchalovsky, 'L'intelligentsia et la réforme de l'enseignement', *CMRS* 1964.

681 R. Pipes (ed.), *The Russian Intelligentsia* (Columbia University Press, 1961) especially the articles by Boris Elkin and L. Labedz.

681b L. S. Feuer, *Marx and the Intellectuals* (New York, 1969).

On changes made by the Soviet régime, the basic work is:

682 Oskar Anweiler, *Geschichte der Schule und der Pädagogik in Russland vom Ende des Zarenreichs bis zum Beginn der Stalin-Aera* (Berlin, 1964).

683 Ruth Widmayer, 'An historical survey of soviet education', reprint in *Soviet Society* (725), pp. 428−39. A very suggestive sketch.

For the early years of the régime, I am grateful to J. C. McClelland for letting me see his excellent manuscript:

684 J. C. McClelland, 'Bolsheviks, Professors and the Reform of Higher Education in Soviet Russia 1917−21' (Dissertation for Princeton Department of History, 1970).

On Lunacharsky, there is:

685 Sheila Fitzpatrick, *The Commissariat of Enlightenment. Soviet Organization of*

Education and the Arts under Lunacharsky (Cambridge University Press, 1970).

On the scientists' attitudes:

686 A. Vucinich, *Science in Russian Culture* (Stanford, 1970), conclusion.

On problems of education, culture and the transfer from revolution to the traditionalist spirit, see other than C. Frioux, J. M. Palmier and Anatole Kopp:

686b François Champarnaud, *Révolution et contre-révolution culturelle en URSS de Lénine à Jdanov* (Paris, 1975). A judicious and well-edited choice of documents.

The Revolution in the theatre and the cinema

On the Revolution in the theatre, a collection of documents and an analysis are fundamental:

687 *Sovietsky teatr. Dokumenty i Materially 1917–1967*, vol. I (1917–21), ed. A. Z. Yufit (Moscow, 1968) is the best theatre-by-theatre collection of sources.

688 *Istoriya sovietskogo teatra* I, ed. V. Rafalovich (1933): see the articles by S. Mokulsky, A. A. Gvozdev and A. Piontrovsky.

The proceedings of the session on the theatre organized by the *Agitprop* of the central committee of the Bolshevik Party in May 1927 are worth reading:

689 *Puti razvitiya teatra*, ed. S. M. Krylov (Moscow, 1927), as also:

690 A. Lunacharsky, *Théâtre et Révolution*, pref. and notes by E. Copfermans (Paris, 1971) and the various works on Lunacharsky quoted elsewhere, especially Claude Frioux and Sheila Fitzpatrick.

The first pieces of reporting on the new theatre have important information, especially:

691 O. Sayler, *The Russian Theater under the Revolution* (Boston, 1920).

Among more recent works, notable are:

692 H. Carter, *The New Spirit in the Russian Theatre 1917–28* (London, 1929).

693 Nina Garfunkel, *Théâtre russe contemporain* (Paris, 1931).

694 P. A. Markov, *The Soviet Theatre* (New York, 1935, repr. 1972).

695 N. A. Gorchakov, *The Theatre in Soviet Russia* (Columbia University Press, 1957).

696 In anticipation of G. Abensour's work on Meyerhold, see his article in *CMRS* 1963.

697 F. de Liencourt, 'Le public soviétique et son théâtre', *CMRS* 1961/2, 3. These present his first sociological work on Soviet theatre and are most stimulating.

On theatrical life among the nationalities, a first collection of reports and documents was published in 1972:

698 *Teatr narodov SSSR 1917–1921*, ed. A. Z. Yufit (Leningrad, 1972) in the series *Sovietsky Teatr*.

On Soviet cinema, the most usable work remains:

699 Jay Leyda, *Kino, a History of Russian and Soviet Film* (London, 1960).

For the silent-film period, the collection published by the Brussels *Cinémathèque* is particularly valuable:

700 *Le film muet soviétique*, Musée du Cinéma, ed. Michelle Sterling, printed by C. Hannoset and generally edited by J. Ledoux (Brussels, 1965).

701 Paul Babitsky and J. Rimberg, *The Soviet Film Industry* (New York, 1955). This is particularly stimulating.

There are two useful Soviet works:

702 *Ocherky Istorii sovietskogo kino*, vol. I (1956), with article by S. I. Felix, 'Nachalo sovietskogo kino', pp. 27–67, and filmography pp. 427–91.

703 *Istoriya Sovietskogo Kino 1917–67*, 4 vols, vol. I (1969).

704 For the great era of Eisenstein, Podovkin, Kulechov, etc., see the special numbers of *Cahiers du Cinéma*, nos 226–7.

Many of my own studies on the cinema in the USSR are recollected in Marc Ferro, *Cinéma et Histoire* (Paris, 1976).

The nationalities

To the works indicated in vol. I (364–405), especially Dimanshteyn, Pipes, Boersner, Carrère d'Encausse, Bennigsen-Quelquejay, St Page and Carr (276), add:

705 Edward Allworth, 'Materials for Soviet Nationality Study, the problem of bibliography', *Soviet Nationality Problems*, ed. E. Allworth (Cambridge University Press, 1971), pp. 241–82. There is little to add to this, except, on Marxism and the national question:

706 H. Carrère d'Encausse, 'Lénine et le droit à l'autodétermination', *Revue française de sciences politiques*, 1971/XXI.

707 G. Haupt, C. Weill and M. Loewy, *Le Marxisme et la question nationale* (Paris, 1974).

On the practical aspect of nationality policy, other than T. Hammond (600b), see

708 H. Carrère d'Encausse, *La Politique nationale des bolcheviks 1917–1924* (Paris I, doctorate, 1976) which I was unable to use.

709 R. Conquest, *Soviet Nationalities Policy in Practice* (London, 1967).

710 R. Conquest, *The Nation-killers. Soviet Deportations of Nationalities* (London, 1970).

On some of the nationalities:

710b Andrew Ezergailis, *The 1917 Revolution in Latvia* (Columbia University Press, 1974).

711 Tuomo Polvinen, *Venajan Vallankomous ja Suomi* (Helsinki, 1967).

712 M. Fol, *L'accession de la Finlande à l'indépendance* (Paris I, thesis, 1976) which I have been unable to use.

713 Pasdermadjian, *La Révolution de 1917–1921 en Arménie* (Paris, 1973).

714 R. G. Suny, *The Baku Commune 1917–1918* (Princeton, 1972).

715 R. Vajdyanath, *The Formation of the Soviet Central-Asian Republics 1917–1936* (New Delhi, 1967).

716 David Lane, 'Ethnic and Class Stratification in Soviet Kazakhstan', *Comparative Studies in Society and History*, 1975, pp. 17ff.

717 M. Suzikov and G. Demakov, *Vliyaniye podvizhnosti naseleniya na sblizheniye natsiy* (Alma Ata, 1974). New and suggestive, based on comparison of the Kazakhs with other Soviet peoples.

718 R. Portal, *Russes et Ukrainiens* (Paris, 1970).

719 O. S. Fedyshyn, *Germany's Drive to the East and the Ukrainian Revolution* (Rutgers University Press, 1971).

720 M. Browne and M. Hayward (eds), *Ferment in the Ukraine* (New York, 1973). A collection of documents on the opposition, with an excellent bibliography.

720b B. Gurewitz, 'Un cas de communisme national en URSS, le Poale-Zion 1918–1928', *CMRS* 1974 3/4, pp. 333–63.

On the Jewish problem, the bibliography in vol. I should be completed with that of A. Kriegel in *Les Juifs en URSS*, bulletin no. 23, p. 27. For Islam, see Bennigsen-Quelquejay (677).

6 Interpretation of the October Revolution

There is a theoretical picture of the systems of interpretation of October in:

721 Daniel Bell, 'Ten theories in search of Soviet realities', *World Politics*, April 1958, pp. 325–65.

The purely historical interpretations are analysed by:

722 J. H. Billington, 'Six views on the Russian Revolution', *World Politics*, 1966, pp. 452–73.

Soviet post-war historiography is studied by: R. Dewhirst, 'Historiographie soviétique sur la révolution d'Octobre', *CMRS* 1964 quoted above; a more general view, better linked with Soviet policy is suggested by John Keep, 'The rehabilitation of M. N. Pokrovski' in

723 *Revolution and Politics in Russia: Essays in Memory of B. I. Nikolaevsky*, ed. A. and E. Rabinowitch (Indiana University Press, 1972), pp. 293–313.

The evolution and the outcome of the October Revolution are the subject of numerous works. I have found particularly stimulating the socio-historical analysis of

724 Alex Inkeles, *Social Change in Soviet Russia* (Harvard University Press, 1968).

Also the collection of reading which he has edited with Kent Geiger:

725 Alex Inkeles and Kent Geiger (eds), *Soviet Society, a Book of Readings* (Cambridge, Mass., 1961). A selection of texts and articles otherwise often difficult of access.

More historical is the following publication whose arguments are often unusual:

726 Roger Pethybridge, *The Social Prelude to Stalinism* (New York, 1974). A series of essays on several problems: the régime and conformity with Utopian ideas, the cultural level of the masses, etc.

The following should also be read:

727 The special issue of *Survey* devoted to an evaluation of the 1917 Revolution, particularly the articles by W. Laqueur, M. Philips Price, S. Bahne, L. Labedz, *Survey*, April 1962.

728 Walter Laqueur, *The Fate of the Revolution, Interpretations of Soviet History* (London, 1967).

729 *The Impact of the Russian Revolution 1917–1967*, with an introductory essay

by Arnold Toynbee (Oxford University Press, 1967), with articles by Neil McInnes, Hugh Seton-Watson, Peter Wiles, Richard Loewenthal.

730 Isaac Deutscher, *The Unfinished Revolution, Russia 1917–1967* (London, 1967).

731 Charles Bettelheim, *La Lutte des classes en URSS, 1re periode 1917–1923* (Paris, 1974). A re-reading of the leaders' discourses.

732 Jean Elleinstein, *Histoire du phénomène stalinien* (Paris, 1975), A communist historian gives an account of several salient points while insisting on the special nature of the conditions of the construction of socialism in the USSR.

732b Jacques Baynac, *La Terreur sous Lénine* (Paris, 1975). Translation and analysis of 'forgotten' texts on the terror before Stalin.

733 H. Carrère d'Encausse, *L'Union Soviétique de Lénine à Staline 1917–1953* (Paris, 1973). An excellent, precise account with a valuable bibliography.

7 Works appearing since publication of the original French edition

734 Basile Kerblay, *La Société soviétique* (Paris, Belin, 1977), possibly the best introduction to present-day Soviet society.

735 A. Rabinovitch, *The Bolsheviks come to Power* (Norton, 1976). Completes No. 563. I have reviewed them both in *Annales (ESC)* (1979), 4.

736 John L. H. Keep, *The Debate on Soviet Power* (Oxford, Clarendon Press, 1979). Translates and analyses the debates of the *TsIK* of the Second Congress, i.e. the very first deliberation of the new régime.

737 G. J. Gill. *Peasants and Government in the Russian Revolution* (London, Macmillan, 1979). A systematic study of rural discontent.

738 Richard K. Debo, *Revolution and Survival* (Liverpool University Press, 1979). A study of the birth of Soviet foreign policy.

739 Robert Service, *The Bolshevik Party in Revolution 1917–1923, a study of organisational change* (London, Macmillan, 1979).

Index